THE
EARLY YEARS
TEACHER'S
BOOK

⑤SAGE | 50 YEARS

SAGE was founded in 1965 by Sara Miller McCune to support the dissemination of usable knowledge by publishing innovative and high-quality research and teaching content. Today, we publish more than 750 journals, including those of more than 300 learned societies, more than 800 new books per year, and a growing range of library products including archives, data, case studies, reports, conference highlights, and video. SAGE remains majority-owned by our founder, and after Sara's lifetime will become owned by a charitable trust that secures our continued independence.

Los Angeles | London | Washington DC | New Delhi | Singapore

THE EARLY YEARS TEACHER'S BOOK

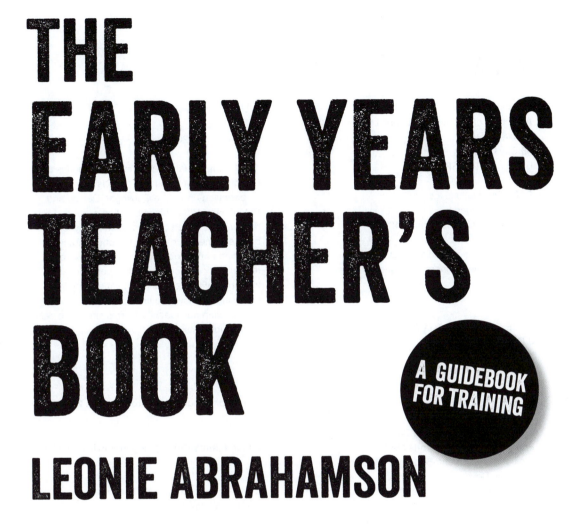

A GUIDEBOOK FOR TRAINING

LEONIE ABRAHAMSON

SAGE | LearningMatters

Los Angeles | London | New Delhi
Singapore | Washington DC | Boston

Learning Matters
An imprint of SAGE Publications Ltd
1 Oliver's Yard
55 City Road
London EC1Y 1SP

SAGE Publications Inc.
2455 Teller Road
Thousand Oaks, California 91320

SAGE Publications India Pvt Ltd
B 1/I 1 Mohan Cooperative Industrial Area
Mathura Road
New Delhi 110 044

SAGE Publications Asia-Pacific Pte Ltd
3 Church Street
#10–04 Samsung Hub
Singapore 049483

Editor: Amy Thornton
Development editor: Geoff Barker
Production controller: Chris Marke
Project management: Swales & Willis Ltd,
    Exeter, Devon
Marketing manager: Lorna Patkai
Cover design: Wendy Scott
Typeset by: C&M Digitals (P) Ltd, Chennai, India
Printed by: Henry Ling Limited at the Dorset Press,
    Dorchester, DT1 1HD

Library of Congress Control Number: 2014954890

British Library Cataloguing in Publication Data

A catalogue record for this book is available from
the British Library

ISBN 978-1-4739-1750-7
ISBN 978-1-4739-0572-6 (pbk)

MIX
Paper from
responsible sources
FSC
www.fsc.org   FSC™ C013985

At SAGE we take sustainability seriously. Most of our products are printed in the UK using FSC papers and boards.
When we print overseas we ensure sustainable papers are used as measured by the Egmont grading system.
We undertake an annual audit to monitor our sustainability.

To my parents, Cathy, Vanessa and Bobby

Contents

About the author

Leonie Abrahamson is an experienced educator and trainer who has worked in early years since 1990, initially as a crèche worker and nursery practitioner and then as a nursery teacher in East London and at the Anna Freud Centre. Leonie then delivered and managed family learning programmes for the Workers' Educational Association and childcare training at Coram Parents' Centre and was tutor and accreditation assessor for the Pre-school Learning Alliance.

Leonie has taught and assessed Early Years Professionals since their introduction in 2007. She currently delivers Early Years Teacher Initial Teacher Training (EYTS) alongside the Postgraduate Certificate in Education (PGCE) in Early Childhood at London Metropolitan University and her website at **www.earlyyearsteacher.info** provides information and resources for Early Years Teacher trainees.

Leonie also delivers teacher training and professional development events at adult education centres and further education colleges. Leonie designs bespoke programmes that include knowledge cafe forums, focus groups and peer visiting programmes and facilitated a tutor-led think tank programme at the Mary Ward Centre and the development of 'Gatekeepers, Midwives and Fellow Travellers: The craft and artistry of the adult educator' (2005). This publication was sponsored by the Department for Education and sent to all UK colleges to support innovative and creative approaches to staff development.

Leonie has a PGCE (Primary) and a Postgraduate Certificate in Child Development, Early Years and Introduction to Counselling from the Institute of Education and an MA from the Tavistock Centre in Emotional Factors in Teaching and Learning. Her MA dissertation was on the impact of trauma on thinking and learning and strategies to address individual and organisational barriers to learning.

Acknowledgements

With all my love and thanks to Cathy Cherry, for always being there, and to my parents who helped me through this process with meals, proof reading and dog walking. Thanks also to my sister Vanessa Abrahamson and my cousin Debbie Feld for their humour and advice, Emily Abrahamson and Lesley Hayoun for their encouragement and Max Abrahamson for his advice.

Thanks also to Bobby Hanlon, you taught me everything I ever needed to know about children, and to Felix von Reiswitz, especially for all your help with my website. To Wendy Caldon, Margaret Allen, Heather Tailby, Annie Myers, Jackie Stevens, Sue Hayward, Marion Rosenberg, Janice Emmott and Wendy Northway, thank you for all your years of friendship and support.

Thanks to Mercedes Menendez, my companion at our unforgettable writers' retreat and thank you to Ellie Fiori Bakari and Albie Battell, you are both brilliant. Many thanks to all my family and friends, you have been so encouraging and supportive and my apologies if I have not mentioned you by name.

Particular thanks to Kelly Cooper, Kathryn Falzon-Perera and Maria Dominguez, our Early Years Teacher assessors and the Early Childhood Studies team at London Metropolitan University. It has been such a pleasure to work with you all. Many thanks also to the students, mentors and settings who have so generously shared their practice with us.

Thank you also to the Early Years Teacher team at Tribal Education, especially Sally Newton, Elaine Voice and Cathie Clark, the assessor team and students. Many thanks to the Pre-school Learning Alliance, especially the Reflecting on Quality team and Wanda Allen and Bridget Allison for their support.

I would also like to thank Gerald Jones, Josie Turner, Sonia Spencer and Andry Anastasiou who I had the pleasure to work with at the Mary Ward Centre, for the opportunity to collaborate on *Gatekeepers, Midwives and Fellow Travellers: the craft and artistry of the adult educator*, and for encouraging me when I embarked on this book.

In memory of Susan Duke Cohan, Beth Eppel, Anna Craft and Rae Walker, with grateful thanks for making such a difference to the lives of many children and to Louie Fiori Bakari, the bravest of boys, remembered with love.

And finally a heartfelt thanks to my editors, Amy Thornton, Geoff Barker, Caroline Watson and Liz Williams, and the team at SAGE who have made all this possible.

1   Introduction to your Early Years Teacher Status

In 2013 Early Years Teacher Status was launched to build on the successes of the Early Years Professional Status which had been introduced in 2007 to increase the numbers of graduates leading practice within early years settings. In this chapter we will look at the role of the Early Years Teacher and how this relates to recent policy developments that promote the professionalisation of the early years workforce.

This process of professionalisation has led to the development of a generation of Early Years Professionals (EYPs) and Early Years Teachers and has been a stimulating, reflective and fruitful journey for all concerned. You can feel proud to become a part of this tradition.

The introduction of the Early Years Professional

The journey began in 1997, when the new Labour Government chose to prioritise the needs of the youngest children and their families. In the Ten-Year Strategy, *Choice for Parents, the Best Start for Children: A Ten Year Strategy for Childcare* (HM Treasury, Department for Education and Skills, DWP and DTI, 2004), the Government laid out a commitment to *reviewing the qualifications and career structure and investing in training and support in order to further develop a workforce fit to deliver the kinds of services children and parents expect in the 21st century*.

The intention was to establish a graduate in every full-time early years setting by 2015 in the belief that this would raise standards, and Early Years Professional Status was introduced alongside this national framework for change. This framework was underpinned by the Children Act 2004 and *Every Child Matters: Change for Children* (Department for Education and Skills, 2003) and designed to improve the experiences of the youngest and most vulnerable members of society. It can be helpful to see the role of the Early Years Professional and Early Years Teacher within this context.

The *Evaluation of the Graduate Leader Fund* report evaluates the impact of Government attempts to professionalise the early years workforce. It examines the use of the Graduate Leader Fund (replacing the Transformation Fund in 2007) providing funding for settings to employ a graduate or EYP by 2015 *to lead practice across the Early Years Foundation Stage (EYFS). It highlights the role of these graduate leaders in supporting and mentoring others, as well as modelling skills and good practice to secure high quality provision* (Mathers et al., 2011).

The Children's Workforce Development Council (CWDC) was tasked with introducing this first professional status for early years practitioners working with children from birth to age five. It was designed to be broadly equivalent to Qualified Teacher Status (ages 5–18) and to achieve this practitioners were required to hold a degree and successfully complete an assessment in an early years setting. By early 2009 there were more than 2,500 graduate-level EYPs and a further 2,400 in training and by August 2012 the number of EYPs reached the 10,000 milestone (The Guardian Teacher Network, 2012).

Why the emphasis on graduates?

The *Evaluation of the Graduate Leader Fund* identified a positive *relationship between qualifications and the quality of early years provision* (Mathers et al., 2011). The final report in 2011 identified the *increasing impact that graduates have on the delivery of quality early years education and the resulting improvements in outcomes for young children* (Department for Education, 2014).

In particular, it noted that:

> Settings which gained a graduate leader with EYPS [Early Years Professional Status] made significant improvements in quality for pre-school children (30 months to five years), as compared with settings which did not. The evidence also suggests that EYPS provided 'added value' over and above gaining a graduate ... Improvements related most strongly to direct work with children, such as support for learning, communication and individual needs, reflecting the role of EYPS as 'leaders of practice'.

(Mathers et al., 2011)

The role of the Early Years Professional

According to the Children's Workforce Development Council, which was responsible for the delivery of Early Years Professional Status, the EYP was *a catalyst for change* who would:

- *take responsibility for leading and managing play, care and learning;*
- *develop, introduce, lead and supervise development work;*
- *act as a team leader and inspire others;*
- *possess up-to-date knowledge and understanding of early years practices;*
- *help colleagues to develop and improve their practice.*

(Children's Workforce Development Council, 2009)

As many EYPs have formed local support networks, their work now has a positive impact beyond their own setting.

One of the most exciting aspects of Early Years Professional Status was that any graduate, whatever the individual background or role, could take on leadership responsibilities. The Graduate Employment Pathway, in particular, encouraged many graduates to consider a second career in early years and this had a positive impact on the diversity of the workforce. I had the pleasure of working with musicians, secondary school teachers, scientists, nurses, dancers, artists, accountants, managers and school governors, all of whom brought something unique with them into their setting.

Early Years Practitioners were encouraged to lead and support practice in ways that addressed the individual needs of their setting. As a result, the work of many Early Years Practitioners has been varied, creative and often unique to their setting. I have been able to observe at first hand the positive impact of these enthusiastic and committed professionals: baby room gardens transformed, toddlers designing role-play areas, young children growing fruit and vegetables, parents creating story sacks and rebuilding the garden and practitioners working with architects to design purpose-built units. Now that Early Years Teachers have taken on this mantle, they too are creating stimulating and inspiring environments for children and families.

The introduction of Early Years Teacher Status

In January 2011, the current Government announced its continued support for Early Years Professional Status and acknowledged the benefits of developing a highly skilled workforce. However, In January 2013 the Department for Education published *More Great Childcare* (Department for Education, 2013), which set out plans for improving quality in early education and childcare. Its aim was to raise the status and quality of the early years workforce and involved replacing Early Years Professional Status with Early Years Teacher Status, building on the strengths of the previous programme.

Early Years Teacher Status: the debate

There has been much debate about the introduction of Early Years Teacher Status. On the one hand, the National College for Teaching and Leadership has emphasised that practitioners will benefit from the respect in which the term 'teacher' is held and that parents find this term familiar. They state that this creates parity of esteem with teachers in primary and secondary schools and that Early Years Teacher Status and Qualified Teacher Status are parallel routes with equivalent value (Gov.uk, 2014). However, some existing EYPs have said that the term 'teacher' does not convey the complexity of their roles.

With the introduction of Early Years Teacher Status some changes were made to the Teachers' Standards (Early Years) to bring them further in line with the Standards for trainee teachers in primary and secondary school. This, and the introduction of the same entry requirements, creates further parity between the Qualified Teacher Status and Early Years Teacher Status routes. There is, however, concern that the changes to the Teachers' Standards (Early Years) has reduced the focus on the needs of the youngest children, even though trainees still need to demonstrate their practice with children from birth to age five.

Another concern is that, despite meeting the same entry requirements and a similar set of Standards, Early Years Teachers will not access benefits such as teachers' pay scales, terms and conditions and the Teachers' Pension. However, this position may be untenable in the long run and beneficial changes may be introduced, bringing Early Years Teacher Status further in line with Qualified Teacher Status.

Becoming an Early Years Teacher

Although there are still many unanswered questions about the place of the Early Years Teacher, there is no doubt that gaining your Early Years Teacher Status will involve you in an inspiring and invigorating journey that will have a significant, positive impact on your career. It will undoubtedly stretch and challenge you, extend your professionalism and expertise and develop your confidence as a leader. You will be responsible for raising expectations of and encouraging colleagues to move forwards in their careers and take on leadership roles themselves.

I hope that the process of working through your Early Years Initial Teacher Training provides you with time to take stock of what you already have achieved, and to appreciate the depth and breadth of your professionalism and the positive impact you have had on the children, families and colleagues you have supported.

Where next?

Becoming an Early Years Teacher can take you in many directions. Many Early Years Teachers have taken on positions as nursery or reception teachers in academies and free schools as these are free to appoint teachers without Qualified Teacher Status. Others have stayed within their settings but taken on extra responsibilities or promotion. Some Early Years Teachers have decided to embark on further studies and applied for a Masters. Others have enjoyed their school-based or age-related placements so much that they decided to specialise in this area. Whatever you decide, you can feel confident that the process of working through your Early Years Initial Teacher Training has developed your skills as a sensitive, reflective practitioner, your understanding of the needs of all children and families in your care and your ability to support the professionalism of those around you.

I wish you all the best for your future.

2 Early Years Teacher Status requirements

Introduction

This chapter is an overview of the requirements for your Early Years Initial Teacher Training programme. When you apply for the programme your provider will talk to you about the requirements you need to meet before you can enrol and those you will meet during the programme so that you can achieve your Early Years Teacher Status. Most of these pre-course requirements apply nationally as they have been set down by the National College for Teaching and Leadership (NCTL). The current requirements apply to the academic years 2014–15 and 2015–16; these may change slightly at some point in the future. There may also be some requirements that are particular to your provider.

In this chapter you will find information on the entry requirements, placement requirements, the routes or pathways you can take, the Teachers' Standards (Early Years), the requirement to work with children from birth to five and the assessment requirements. You may find it helpful to share this chapter with your mentor so that he or she understands what will be involved.

Getting to know the terminology

As you progress through your Early Years Initial Teacher Training you will come across a range of terminology. The status you will achieve is known as Early Years Teacher Status or EYTS and this is of equal value to Qualified Teacher Status (QTS). However, the course or programme that you follow is referred to as Early Years Initial Teacher Training, Early Years (ITT), or Initial Teacher Training (Early Years).

The university that provides your training is known as your provider, or ITT provider. In this text we will refer to both your Early Years Teacher Status and EYTS, Early Years Initial Teacher Training and Early Years (ITT), and provider and ITT provider so that you become familiar with the range of terms used. The Standards that you will evidence to achieve your Early Years Teacher Status are known as the Teachers' Standards (Early Years), but for the sake of simplicity we will refer to these as 'the Standards' throughout this text.

Early Years Teacher websites

You can find further information on the requirements on the Government websites. Information on how to become an early years teacher is available on the Get into Teaching website at **www.education.gov.uk/get-into-teaching/subjects-age-groups/early-years**. You can also access information through the NCTL at **www.gov.uk/government/organisations/national-college-for-teaching-and-leadership** and at **www.gov.uk/early-years-initial-teacher-training-a-guide-for-providers#training**. Your provider's website will also have information on the EYTS requirements.

Initial Teacher Training (Early Years), QTS or Early Years Teacher Status?

There are several decisions that you need to make when you apply for your Early Years Initial Teacher Training and the first of these is whether you wish to apply for QTS or EYTS. There are two possible routes for Early Years ITT: the primary or early years teaching route that grants QTS and the early years route that awards Early Years Teacher Status. The Government states that these two routes are equivalent and the entry and assessment requirements for them both are the same. As mentioned in Chapter 1, many professionals have questioned the lack of pay parity, status and terms and conditions between QTS and EYTS and if you are deciding which route to take then this might be a consideration for you. However, the question you need to ask yourself is, 'do I want to work with children from birth to three?' If you do, then Early Years Teacher Status is the appropriate route for you.

Initial Teacher Training with QTS and early years

This text focuses on the requirements for Early Years Teacher Status, but if you are an Initial Teacher Training trainee on the QTS route but working within early years, this text can help you. As long as are aware of the differences between the Teachers' Standards and Teachers' Standards (Early Years) you can use this guide to identify how you can interpret and evidence the Standards in a way that is appropriate for early years practice. When you are working with older children, for example, in Key Stage 1, then you will obviously need to follow the guidance from your provider.

What is an Early Years Teacher?

We now need to look at what an Early Years Teacher is. Early Years Teacher Status is now the only current professional status for practitioners working in early years settings that recognises their expertise as practitioners and professional leaders. It forms part of the Government's drive towards a more professional early years workforce and is of an equivalent postgraduate level to QTS. However, each status is based on a different set of skills and knowledge.

Early Years Teachers are specialists in early childhood development who are trained to work with babies, toddlers and young children up to the age of five. They are graduate leaders who are responsible for leading education and care and *support and lead staff* to promote high-quality provision (Gov.uk, 2013a).

As an Early Years Teacher you will support the needs of babies, toddlers and young children and provide a safe and stimulating environment which motivates and challenges all children. You will demonstrate vision and values, contribute to the ethos of your setting and raise the quality of your provision so as to improve outcomes for young children. You will support and motivate your colleagues so that they feel able to lead and develop practice themselves.

Entry requirements

To be accepted on the Early Years Initial Teacher Training programme you will need to meet the same entry requirements as a primary or secondary teacher trainee (Gov.uk, 2013a). This means that you will need to:

- have achieved a GCSE grade C (or equivalent) in English, mathematics and a science subject;

- hold a first degree from a UK higher education institution or equivalent qualification (in the case of graduate routes);

- have taken part in a rigorous selection process designed to assess your suitability to teach;

- have passed the professional skills tests (Gov.uk, 2014).

The skills tests

Your ITT provider will guide you on how to apply for the professional skills tests and will support you through this process. However, if you need any additional information you can look at **www.education.gov.uk/sta/professional** or find support and guidance in *Passing the Professional Skills Tests for Trainee Teachers and Getting into ITT* (Bond et al., 2013).

Training routes and funding

You and your ITT provider will need to decide which programme is best for you. This will be referred to as the 'route' or 'pathway'. There are four possible routes or pathways, and the route your provider will recommend will depend on your experience and personal circumstances.

The four main routes are the Graduate Entry Mainstream and Graduate employment-based, and the Undergraduate Entry and Assessment Only routes. The Graduate Entry Employment-based and Assessment Only routes are for experienced practitioners. The Graduate Entry Mainstream and Undergraduate Entry pathways are for those who would like to work with children and pursue a career in the early years. There is also a Schools Direct route available, but at present the numbers for this are small. Two routes are funded by NCTL and two are not.

Graduate Entry Mainstream (full-time)

This route is open to graduates who have little or no previous experience in the early years. This is a full-time academic route and you will work towards your Early Years Teacher Status and complete at least two placements. This route usually lasts a year and some funding will be available from NCTL.

Graduate Employment-based (part-time)

This route is for graduates who are employed in an early years setting and who require further training and/or experience before they can fully demonstrate the Teachers' Standards (Early Years). This route may suit you best if you have only worked in early years for a short time or need to extend your experience with babies, toddlers or young children. You can expect to spend up to a year on this route and some funding is available for employers to contribute to the cost of cover while you are attending training and other support costs such as salary enhancements.

Undergraduate Entry (full-time)

This route is for those who wish to undertake a level 6 degree in an early childhood-related subject and work towards their Early Years Teachers Status while completing at least two placements. This route is usually a full-time three- or four-year route for trainees who are entering the profession. Unfortunately there is no funding available, but you can apply for a student loan to help you with the course fees.

Assessment Only

This route is for graduates with recent experience of working with babies, toddlers and children up to five years old and who can demonstrate the Standards without any further training. This route consists of the assessment process, which usually lasts for three months, and you will have to fund this route yourself. Some overseas early years teachers choose this route.

Does the route I have chosen affect my study plans?
You may wonder whether the pathway you are on affects your study priorities. This is a good question and you will find that completing your action plan (see Chapter 8) will help you to organise your study timetable. However, there are some useful generalisations that can be made.If you are new to early years and are on the Graduate Entry Mainstream, Undergraduate Entry or Schools Direct routes, your priority will be to immerse yourself in learning as much as possible about the early years so that you have some context for your placement experiences. If, however, you are an experienced practitioner on the Graduate Entry Employment-based or Assessment Only routes, your priority will be to get to know the Standards as quickly as possible so that you can identify any gaps in your practice or evidence.

Placements

According to NCTL:

> Trainee teachers must be trained to teach across the Early Years Foundation Stage (from birth to 5 years old). They must also understand how early education links to education beyond age 5 and into key stages 1 and 2 in school.
>
> Your training programme will need to provide trainees with enough time in early years settings or schools to allow them to show they meet the standards ...
>
> Placements should take place in at least 2 schools or early years settings and include at least 2 weeks in a school in key stage 1.

> (Gov.uk, 2014)

This means that you will need to spend two weeks in Key Stages 1 and 2 classrooms and be able to evidence recent experience with babies, toddlers and young children. If you lack recent experience with any of these age groups you will need to complete an additional early years placement with this age group for a minimum of 20 days. However, if you are on the Graduate Employment-based route, your provider will decide how much time you will spend on each placement.

Age-related requirements

To achieve your Early Years Teacher Status you will need to be *judged to have met all of the Teacher' Standard (Early Years) in practice from birth to the end of the Early Years Foundation Stage (EYFS)* (National College for Teaching and Leadership, 2014). This means that you will need to evidence your practice with each age group and address the needs of each age group in your evidence for the Standards.

If you are not able to work with all three age groups where you are currently placed, then you will need to consider taking on a placement with this age group. There is information to help you make this decisions in Chapter 5.

Your provider may tell you how you to present the evidence from this placement, for example, by giving you a placement portfolio to complete for each of the three age ranges. Chapter 5 will help you organise your evidence and looks at how you can evidence your practice with each age group in your evidence for a Standard. For example, in your evidence for 2.2 which relates to child development you can highlight your understanding of the developmental needs of children in this age group.

The Teachers' Standards (Early Years)

> Training and assessment are designed around the Teachers' Standards (Early Years). These standards focus on the birth to 5 years old age range.

> (National College for Teaching and Leadership, 2014)

9

The Teachers' Standards (Early Years) operate in parallel with the current Teachers' Standards. They are not identical as they need to be appropriate for the role of the early years practitioner. They are referred to as the 'Teachers' Standards (Early Years)' or the 'teaching standards for early years', but we will refer to them here as the 'Standards'.

In order to be awarded your Early Years Teacher Status you will need to demonstrate that you have met each of these Standards so the assessment process evaluates your practice against each Standard in turn.

There are eight Standards that are divided into 38 supporting statements. These supporting statements are not separate Standards in their own right, but provide amplification for the main statement and help you to assess and track your progress against each Standard heading.

Each of the eight Standards has a Standard number ('Standard 1') and Standard Supporting Statement ('1.1') and a Supporting Statement Summary (*Establish and sustain a safe and stimulating environment where children feel confident and are able to learn and develop*).

These Standard Supporting Statements and Supporting Statement Summaries are also known as 'bullet points' or indicators' and for the sake of simplicity we will refer to them as 'indicators' throughout this text.

Getting to know the Standards

Chapter 3 on getting to know the Standards contains a series of activities that can help you get to know the Standards better. Once you are familiar with the Standards as a whole, you can start to read the eight Standards chapters to help you get to know each indicator in detail.

Assessment requirements

You will find detailed guidance on the assessment requirements in Chapter 4, so this section only provides a brief outline. As you need to '*be judged to have met all of the Teachers' Standard (Early Years) in practice from birth to the end of the Early Years Foundation Stage (EYFS)* (National College for Teaching and Leadership, 2014), you need evidence of your practice with babies, toddlers and young children and refer to your practice with these age groups in your evidence for the Standards.

Each ITT provider can decide how they wish to assess this evidence, and how much evidence you need to provide. Your provider can decide, for example, that you need to provide two pieces of evidence for each Standard or two pieces for each indicator, and can decide what form this evidence is to take.

All providers have to assess each Standard holistically, which means that your evidence needs to show breadth and depth in relation to most of the indicators for each Standard, but not necessarily for all of them. However, as you need to achieve a 'met' for each Standard to achieve your Early Years Teacher Status it is best to provide evidence for every indicator to avoid the risk of not meeting a Standard.

Presenting your evidence

You can present your evidence in various formats and your provider will give you guidance on what is required. You will probably be observed by your tutor, assessor or mentor while carrying out a range of routine tasks, such as leading a group activity with children, meeting with parents or mentoring a student. You may be asked to write a series of assignments which are designed to help you evidence each Standard. You will probably be asked to collate a range of work documents into a portfolio.

You may be able to take your assessor on a tour of your setting to show the impact you have had on the provision for each age group. You might be able to ask a practitioner or parent to complete a witness testimony that evidences your practice in relation to certain Standards. You may also have the opportunity to answer a series of questions that relate to the Standards, such as, 'can you describe how you acted to protect a child from harm?' to help you evidence 7.3 on child protection.

At the end of the chapters on each indicator you will find suggestions on how you can evidence that indicator. However, you do need to follow your provider's guidance and adapt the suggestions to fit the model you are working to. For example, if you are told that you cannot include photographs in your portfolio, you must not do this.

You will be told when you need to hand in all your evidence. It is very important your evidence is well prepared before this date and that you follow your provider's guidance and stick to the prescribed format, otherwise it can become difficult for your assessor to evaluate your work.

How recent is your evidence?

Although you need to demonstrate that you have worked with babies, toddlers and young children within the course of your pathway, you can provide some evidence from your work in previous years. This is particularly useful for Standards that relate to incidents that may not occur frequently, such as dealing with a safeguarding concern for 7.3. Your provider will tell you how recent this evidence needs to be and many providers allow you to evidence experience from up to five years ago, as long as you can evidence this in enough detail after all this time.

The assessment decision

You may not hear whether you have met all eight Standards and achieved your Early Years Teacher Status for some time. This does not mean that there were any problems with your work, but is because your provider will follow a rigorous process of internal and external moderation. During this process their initial judgement may be overturned, so most providers wait until the decision is finalised before they notify you.

Your assessor will look carefully at all the evidence you have presented and will decide whether you have enough adequate, relevant evidence and are a 'met', or whether there are significant gaps in your evidence and you are a 'not met'.

Although your provider may not grade your evidence, your assessor makes decisions about the strength of your evidence whilst evaluating it to help judge whether you have provided enough good-quality evidence for each Standard. You may find it helpful to look at the system your assessor will use to evaluate your evidence before you present it.

Table 2.1 Strong, satisfactory and weak evidence

Strong	• Evidence comprehensively addresses all aspects of the Standard
	• Evidence demonstrates that knowledge and understanding inform practice
	• Evidence is endorsed by an external source (e.g. local authority or Ofsted)
	• Evidence demonstrates a sustained commitment to developing expertise in this Standard
	• Good evidence of reflective practice
	• Evidence of actions is detailed and a comprehensive rationale is provided
	• Detailed and wide-ranging evidence of leadership
Satisfactory	• Evidence addresses most aspects of the Standard
	• Evidence relates to a factual occurrence rather than a generalised assertion
	• Evidence shows a clear, self-evident link between the narrative and a Standard
	• Some evidence of reflective practice
	• Some actions are recorded in detail and some rationale is provided
	• Some good evidence of leadership
Weak	• Evidence addresses only part of the Standard
	• Generalised assertions are made, lacking detail or practical examples
	• Evidence requires the assessor to infer a link between the narrative and a Standard since this is not self-evident
	• Little evidence of reflective practice
	• Actions are not described in detail and little rationale is provided
	• It is not clear that a document was written by the trainee
	• It is not clear how a document has been used by the trainee
	• The evidence is presented in an incorrect format
	• No evidence of leadership

3 Getting to know the Standards

Getting to know the Standards: your first task

You might, at this point, be asking yourself, why is getting to know the Standards such a priority? As you embark on Early Years Initial Teacher Training you are bound to feel overwhelmed by the amount of information you have to take in. However, the most helpful strategy at this stage is to focus on getting to know the Standards. For example, there is no point worrying about assessment methods until you understand what it is that you will be assessed on. It would be like writing an exam paper without reading the questions!

There are many other reasons why taking time to get to know the Standards is helpful. Once you form an overview of what it is that you need to evidence, the task will feel more manageable and this can help you feel less anxious.

When you are familiar with the Standards you can tune into their careful use of language. You will see how the wording of each indicator tells you exactly what it is that you need to evidence.

If you examine each Standard in detail you can make lists for yourself of what you need to evidence for each indicator. You will then be far less likely to miss out a key aspect of a Standard and become a 'not met.'

Once each aspect of each Standard becomes second nature to you:

- You will have enough time to address any gaps in your experience for a particular Standard.
- You are less likely to forget to evidence one part of a Standard.
- You will find it easier to organise your evidence later on.
- You will automatically identify how one good piece of evidence can provide evidence for other Standards.
- You will be able to look at a piece of evidence and be able to judge how strong it is by asking yourself questions, such as 'does this highlight my own actions?' and 'how does this evidence a specific phrase in a specific Standard?'

In this chapter you will be introduced to a range of methods to help you get to know individual Standards and form an overview of the Standards as a whole. You can choose whichever activities are most helpful for you, or work through them in the order that they are presented. This will help you to see how the Standards work together and why they are in the order that they are.

There are many ways to gain your own personal overview of the Standards and if you have your own methods, then use these. Activities 3.1 and 3.2 present two methods. The first is a written, linear approach, and the second provides a visual overview; you can choose whichever method suits your own learning style.

ACTIVITY **3.1**

Describe each Standard in your own words

Find three words to describe each Standard.

This will help you form a picture in your mind of what each Standard is 'about'. Make a list of the first three words you think of when you read through each Standard.

These three words will provide you with a mental short cut to help you remember the focus of each Standard. Gradually you will flesh this out with more information, but these key words will be your anchor.

The three words I first associated with Standard 1 were 'environment,' 'goals' and 'values.' For me, these three words represent the cornerstones of early years practice and help me appreciate how this Standard sets the scene for the others and provides the context in which the others are embedded. Now I will always remember why this Standard comes first. Here are some of my notes that will help you when thinking about the other Standards:

- Standard 2 looks at child development within the context of children's interactions with their parents/carers and practitioners.

- In Standard 3 you demonstrate the theoretical underpinnings of your practice. It is your chance to showcase your knowledge and understanding of child development and the Early Years Foundation Stage (EYFS) and how these inform your practice.

- Standard 4 is interesting as it looks at how your provision responds to the needs of the child. It is an opportunity to demonstrate that you are a reflective practitioner and that you review your provision to ensure that it takes account of the needs of all children.

- Standard 5 extends the themes in Standard 4 by looking at the needs of individual children, but in more detail. You can evidence how you plan for individual children, adapting education and care to take account of special needs, disabilities and the impact of transitions and other factors in a child's life.

- Standard 6 reminds you that you are working within a statutory framework. It extends your focus on EYFS in Standard 3 by looking at the statutory assessment requirements. You can evidence your role in carrying out progress checks at age two and completing an EYFS Profile, and the feedback you share with parents and carers.

- Standard 7 looks at how you keep children safe. You will evidence your role in promoting health and safety, children's well-being, safeguarding and child protection.

- Standard 8 contains the essence of your role as Early Years Teacher as it looks at the strategies you use to support your colleagues and improve practice within your setting.

The Standards in 2-D

Many people find that it helps to have a visual image of the Standards, so here are two images that you can use to inspire you to create your own representation (Figures 3.1 and 3.2).

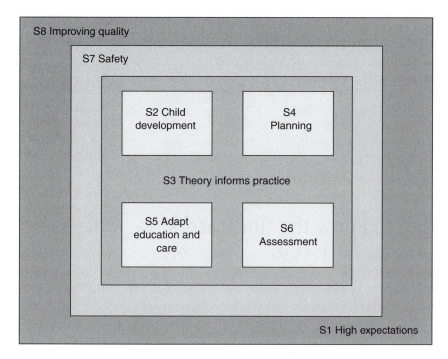

Figure 3.1 The Standards in 2-D

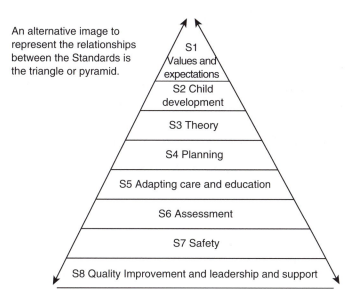

Figure 3.2 The Standards as a pyramid

15

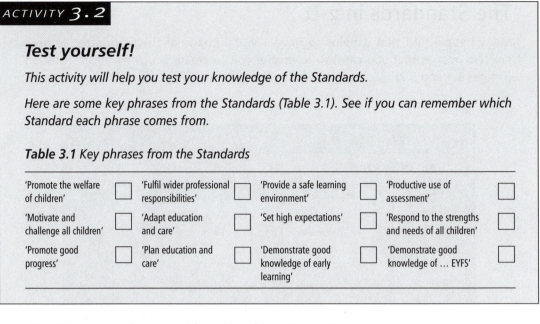

ACTIVITY 3.2

Test yourself!

This activity will help you test your knowledge of the Standards.

Here are some key phrases from the Standards (Table 3.1). See if you can remember which Standard each phrase comes from.

Table 3.1 *Key phrases from the Standards*

'Promote the welfare of children' ☐	'Fulfil wider professional responsibilities' ☐	'Provide a safe learning environment' ☐	'Productive use of assessment' ☐
'Motivate and challenge all children' ☐	'Adapt education and care' ☐	'Set high expectations' ☐	'Respond to the strengths and needs of all children' ☐
'Promote good progress' ☐	'Plan education and care' ☐	'Demonstrate good knowledge of early learning' ☐	'Demonstrate good knowledge of … EYFS' ☐

Getting to know the 'indicators'

So far we have looked at only the main statement for each Standard, but you will probably have noticed that each opening statement is followed by a series of bullet points, known as indicators. These are designed to clarify the meaning of each Standard and tell you what it is that you need to evidence.

Now we will look at these indicators in more detail in Activity 3.3.

ACTIVITY 3.3

Key points, topics or phrases

List the key points, topics and phrases that you think are most important in each Standard/indicator.

You can use your own shorthand so that you can easily find the information you need at a glance. Some suggestions have been added in Table 3.2 to help you start.

At the end of this process you should have a chart that records, in your own words, the key areas and phrases you need to remember for every indicator in each Standard.

Table 3.2 *Examples of important key points, topics and phrases in each Standard/indicator*

Standard 1	High expectations
	Inspire, motivate and challenge
1.1	Safe and stimulating environment
	Children are confident, learn and develop

1.2	Set goals
	Stretch and challenge …
	Children of *all* backgrounds, abilities and dispositions
1.3	Demonstrate and model
	Positive values, attitudes and behaviours
	(How do we adapt our expectations for children of different ages, and children with special educational needs?)

ACTIVITY **3.4**

Identify key verbs

Read through the Standards again and make a list of all the verbs you can find. The first one has been added for you.

Establish...

....

....

....

....

Now you have listed the verbs, what do they tell you?

Paying attention to the verbs will pay dividends when it comes to choosing what evidence you will include for each Standard. For example, if a Standard asks you to *know* something, it is asking for different evidence than when it asks you to *know and act upon*.

In 2.2 you are asked to *demonstrate knowledge and understanding of how babies and children learn and develop*. If you wished to evidence this through writing an assignment on attachment theory, you might evidence your knowledge. However, as you have been asked to *demonstrate* this knowledge, you might describe how you help a child to settle, as this *demonstrates* how you apply your knowledge of attachment theory.

Creating a Standards checklist for yourself

Now you have got to know the indicators for each Standard, you need a quick and convenient way to remind yourself of these. As you will be referring to these often it will really help you if you can make a reminder checklist that you can carry around with you.

Write out each Standard and indicator in full, to make sure that you pay attention to the detail. You can use this checklist in three ways: to check which topics you need to evidence for each Standard; to identify where you may have gaps in your experience; and to help you review an activity to see which Standards it can help you to evidence.

You can use the format suggested in Table 3.3 or design your own checklist.

Table 3.3 *Standards checklist*

Standard	Indicators	Links to other Standards
Standard 1 'Set high expectations which inspire, motivate and challenge all children'	1.1 Establish and sustain a safe and stimulating environment where children feel confident and are able to learn and develop	2.6 'confidence'
	1.2 Set goals that stretch and challenge children of all backgrounds, abilities and dispositions	
	1.3 Demonstrate and model the positive values, attitudes and behaviours expected of children	
Standard 2	2.1	
	2.2	
	2.3	
	2.4	
	2.5	
	2.6	
	2.7	

Practical activities to help you remember the Standards

Now you have your Standards checklist you can use it to help you get to know each Standard better and improve the quality of your evidence. The principle is that if you want to provide good evidence for something, you first need to know exactly what that 'something' is. Otherwise it's a bit like trying to get all the shopping you need without making a list first!

Here are some practical activities that Early Years Trainees Beth, Susan, Rae and Maurice said helped them the most:

- 'I keep my Standards checklist in my bag so when I am on the bus on my way home from work I read through one Standard and identify one activity I did that day that could evidence this.'

- 'I've written each Standard on a small piece of card with a hole punched in one corner. I've put the cards on my key ring so I can look at them whenever I have a moment.'

- 'I choose one activity a week to write about in my journal and then I map it to the Standards.'

- 'I link each Standard to a task I carry out at home. Standard 4.2 is my favourite as it is about providing *balanced and flexible activities*. When I let my child stay up late on a special occasion or when they are very involved in what they are doing, I call it 'a 4.2 moment'!'

ACTIVITY **3.5**

Finding similarities between the Standards

Find a large piece of paper or mind-mapping software on your computer. (Free mind-mapping software that is easy to download can be found on sites such as **www.top5freeware.com/mind-mapping-software-for-windows**.*)*

Make eight circles (or text boxes if that is easier), one for each Standard, and add a line coming out from each, one for each indicator that the Standard has.

See if you can find and draw any connections between different Standards. You can find one example in Figure 3.3 and in Table 3.3 (above).

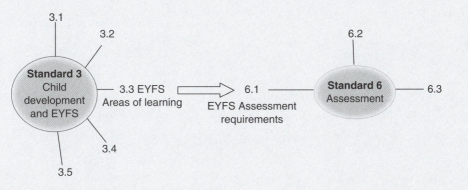

Figure 3.3 *Similarities between the Standards: example highlighting the similarities between Standard 3 and Standard 6*

If you are not a visual learner you might prefer to create a chart where you can list any overlaps between Standards.

4 Assessment methods

Introduction

In this chapter we will look at the forms of evidence you are allowed to submit and the methods that will be used to assess your evidence. From September 2014 each provider was able to choose the types of evidence they could submit and the methods used to assess the evidence against the Standards and Early Years Teacher requirements. This means that you need to pay close attention to the information you are given on both the format your evidence must take and the assessment methods your provider will use. If your provider suggests anything that contradicts the guidance in this book, you should always follow your provider's guidance.

We will look at the assessment methods and permitted forms of evidence that most providers will use. However, if your provider has different arrangements, you will need to adapt the information in this chapter and in the 'evidence' section in each chapter. Although the assessment methods may vary, the information here will still help you to identify how you can evidence your practice

To achieve your Early Years Teacher Status you will need to present your evidence for every Standard in a prescribed format that follows your provider's guidance, provide evidence of working with babies, toddlers and pre-school children and complete a two-week school-based placement. In this chapter we will look at the different ways that you can present your evidence and some of the assessment methods used to evaluate how well you have evidenced each Standard. We will also look at how you can evidence your work with each age group and use your experiences on your school placement to help you to evidence Standard 3.

'Met' or 'not met'

Your assessor will look at each piece of evidence to check whether you have provided adequate evidence for each Standard. If you have provided enough evidence that is detailed, demonstrates your practice, your leadership and/or your understanding and is relevant for that Standard, then this Standard will be described as 'met'. If you have not, then this Standard will be described as 'not met'.

If any of the Standards are 'not met' then you will not achieve your Early Years Teacher Status. Depending on your provider's arrangements, you may find that you cannot reapply later or if you can, you will have to pay. So, it is important that you provide as much evidence as possible for each Standard, and that this evidence is 'good'. There is no point including ten pieces of work that contain little evidence when you could carefully choose one piece that contains evidence that is 'good' or 'strong'.

Your assessor

As each provider can choose how to assess your evidence, the person who will complete the assessment may be your mentor, your tutor or an assessor you have not met beforehand. If the final assessment is completed by your tutor or mentor, then this may be the person who supported you right through your Early Years Teacher programme and you will need to appreciate that at this point that person's role changes to that of assessor. However, whatever their role, the process of evaluation and the decisions they have to make will be the same. For the sake of simplicity, we will refer to the person who makes the final decisions about your evidence as your 'assessor'.

Your assessor's judgements

Although you may not receive a final grade, your assessor will make judgements about the strength of each piece of evidence. This will help the assessor judge whether you have enough evidence for each Standard and that it is relevant and clearly evidences your own practice. All providers will use their own terms to grade your work while they make a decision as to whether a Standard is 'met' or 'not met'.

A detailed piece of evidence that clearly demonstrates your practice and/or your knowledge and understanding and that shows how you supported other practitioners and/or moved practice forwards in your setting may be graded 'strong', 'excellent' or 'very good'. A piece of evidence that is perhaps slightly less detailed or less relevant could be graded 'good', 'satisfactory' or 'adequate'. If it is not clear how a piece of work relates to a Standard or whether it is in fact evidence of your own work (for example, a planning sheet completed by a group of practitioners where you have not highlighted your own contributions), this may be graded 'weak evidence' or 'not met'.

Strengthening your evidence

You can strengthen your evidence in several ways. Your assessor cannot decide that a piece of evidence is strong if it is not clear whether a piece of evidence is your own work. If you are including a weekly plan, you will strengthen your evidence if you add a note to explain which activities you suggested and why.

You can also strengthen your evidence and make it easier for your assessor to find your evidence when you label it correctly. For example, if you include a copy of a lengthy policy you contributed to, you can highlight the sections you were responsible for and add a note in the margin to say which Standard and indicator this section evidences.

It is not a good idea to cross-reference one piece of evidence to too many Standards as checking each reference will take up too much of your assessor's time and the likelihood of one piece of work providing strong evidence for more than half a dozen indicators is low.

If you wish to strengthen your evidence for each Standard you also need to pay attention to the verbs within it. If you pay enough attention to them they will tell you what type of evidence you need. For example, if you are asked to 'model' something, your evidence will look very different from if you have been asked to 'reflect'.

You can make a list of all the verbs you can find in the Standards and ask yourself, 'what does each verb ask me to do?' Then, you can check that the evidence you have actually demonstrates this. For example, have you modelled how to use play dough or reflected on why play dough is important?

Holistic assessment

In each of the chapters on the Standards and their indicators you are encouraged to evidence every phrase within each indicator, even though your evidence for each Standard is assessed 'holistically'. When a Standard is assessed holistically your assessor will consider whether you have provided strong evidence for most of the Standard, even if you have little evidence for some of it. However, if you choose not to evidence part of a Standard, there is a risk that if your evidence for the rest of the Standard is not as strong as you think it is, you may not have enough evidence for the Standard as a whole. If you want to be as sure as you can be that you have good enough evidence for every Standard, you need to look at every indicator in detail, even though you know it will be assessed holistically.

How much evidence do I need?

Your provider will give you clear guidance as to how much evidence you need and in what format and there will be some variety between providers. You may be asked to provide two pieces of evidence for each Standard or for each indicator. You will probably also be told that each piece of evidence must come from a different 'source of evidence'. A 'source of evidence' refers to the format your evidence can take; for example, one source may be a written assignment and the other an observation or document.

What makes a good piece of evidence?

A good piece of evidence will clearly highlight:

- what you thought;
- what you did and why;
- how you communicated with children and their parents;
- how this had a positive impact on individual children's learning and development;
- how your actions supported children's parents and carers;
- how you supported your colleagues' professional development;
- why this helps to evidence a specific Standard.

Formative and summative assessment

During the course of your Early Years Teacher programme you will have been supported by your tutor and your mentor. They will have helped you to evaluate the evidence you have and identify and address any gaps in your practice. This process is called 'formative assessment'. It helps you to form a picture of where you are now and identify how you can get to where you need to be.

Summative assessment, on the other hand, is your final assessment which is conducted at a set point, and where the judgement is made as to whether you have enough 'good' evidence for each Standard. In this chapter we will look at the types of evidence you can provide for the summative assessment and the methods your assessor will use to make a judgement.

Summative assessment: top five tips

1. Your assessor needs to identify what you have achieved in relation to each Standard. You can make this easier for the assessor by clearly linking the evidence you present to specific Standards and indicators.

2. Your assessor will work hard on your behalf. You can make this easier for the assessor if you are organised so that your evidence that is well presented, easy to find and readable.

3. Your assessor is an early years professional. He or she will understand that situations change and that if s/he expected to observe you carrying out a certain activity, this may change at the last minute if there is an emergency or you need to adapt the activity so as to meet the children's needs at that time. It will not count against you if you have to change your plans as long as you explain the reasons for this clearly and behave in a professional manner.

4. Your assessor cannot tell you whether you have 'met' your Early Years Teacher Status, so please don't ask or try to interpret the assessor's body language.

5. You will have to wait for your final result as your evidence will be moderated and cross-moderated before you can be given your result. Please do not think that you have not achieved your Early Years Teacher Status just because you are waiting a long time to hear your result.

Sources of evidence

A 'source of evidence' is one of the permitted formats that you can use to present your evidence. You will be given clear instructions from your provider as to how much evidence you need to present and in what format. In this section we will look at each of the most commonly used formats and you will find reference to each of these in the 'evidence' section for each indicator in the main body of the text. These sources of evidence include written assignments, case studies, your reflective journal, a document portfolio, witness testimonies and observations. Your provider may have different names for each format, but in essence they will be similar.

Table 4.1 Sources of evidence

Indicator	Sources of evidence							
	Written assignment	Case study	Reflective journal	Document portfolio	Witness testimony	Observation	Other	Age range
Standard 1								
1.1 Establish and sustain a safe and stimulating environment where children feel confident and are able to learn and develop	Describe and reflect on the changes I introduced in baby room					Mentor observation in baby room		Babies
1.2 Set goals that stretch and challenge children of all backgrounds, abilities and dispositions		Support for child 'P' who has special needs		Individualised education plan for child 'P'	Parent of child 'P': witness testimony			Pre-school
1.3 Demonstrate and model the positive values, attitudes and behaviours expected of children						Mentor observations during circle time and planned activities		Pre-school

Choosing a 'source of evidence'

You will find that certain indicators are evidenced most effectively in a certain format, or 'source of evidence', and you can use your action plan to help you identify which indicator would be best evidenced in which format. For example, you may feel that you can best evidence that you provide a safe and stimulating environment for 1.1 through a series of observations, and that you can record examples of engaging in sustained shared thinking for 2.4 in your journal, where you can record and analyse a conversation in detail.

If you add this information to a chart, such as Table 4.1, you will be able to see at a glance whether your evidence is spread relatively evenly across the formats or 'sources of evidence', or whether you are relying too heavily on one format, such as the document portfolio. Beth, the Early Years Teacher trainee who you will meet in Standard 8, has added some examples to Table 4.1 to help you.

Tracking your evidence

Table 4.1 shows you how it is possible to track your evidence for each indicator. Once you can track your evidence you can make decisions as to whether you have too much evidence in one area and not enough in another. Tracking your evidence also enables you to see at a glance where there may be gaps in your evidence. You also need to track your evidence to make sure that you evidence your leadership role for Standard 8 as well as your personal practice and any leadership for Standards 1–7. You can also track your evidence of your work with babies, toddlers and pre-school children to check that you have enough evidence of each.

The best way to track your evidence is to create a tracking sheet for yourself. You can adapt the tracking sheet in Table 4.1, or design a system that suits you better.

Before you can track your evidence you must find out how much evidence you need and from how many sources. For example, you may be required to evidence each Standard or each indicator twice across all sources of evidence.

Beth was asked to evidence all 38 indicators across a series of five written assignments that addressed her work with babies, toddlers and pre-school children, and evidenced her work with parents and her role in a safeguarding scenario. She had to evidence each indicator at least once across all the assignments, and each indicator again in her document portfolio, her reflective journal, a witness testimony or an observation.

Beth decided to create a separate tracking form just for the written assignments, to help her decide which Standards she could include in each assignment.

In Table 4.2 you will find an example of a tracking sheet that looks at just one source of evidence. This can be useful if you want to look in detail at what you can include across a series of assignments or case studies, or to help you decide what to focus on in your reflective journal. You can adapt Table 4.2 to suit your own requirements and Beth has added some examples to show you how you can use this.

Table 4.2 Tracking one source of evidence

Standards	Assignment 1: babies	Assignment 2: toddlers	Assignment 3: pre-school children	Assignment 4	Assignment 5
1.1 Establish and sustain a safe and stimulating environment where children feel confident and are able to learn and develop	Setting up sensory room				
1.2 Set goals that stretch and challenge children of all backgrounds, abilities and dispositions		Training session on planning		Individualised education plan for child 'P' and cascading information to Key Person	

ACTIVITY 4.1

Which source of evidence is best for which Standard?

If you prefer an alternative approach to the chart in Table 4.1, this activity can help you decide which sources of evidence are most appropriate for each Standard.

Make a list of the Standards and their indicators, and note whether this is something you can evidence in an assignment, case study, reflective journal, document, witness testimony or observation. Ask yourself the questions shown in Table 4.3 and use the suggested coding to help you make a decision as you read through each indicator.

Table 4.3 Which source of evidence?

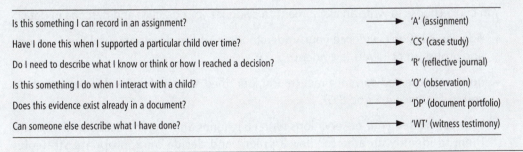

Is this something I can record in an assignment?	➤ 'A' (assignment)
Have I done this when I supported a particular child over time?	➤ 'CS' (case study)
Do I need to describe what I know or think or how I reached a decision?	➤ 'R' (reflective journal)
Is this something I do when I interact with a child?	➤ 'O' (observation)
Does this evidence exist already in a document?	➤ 'DP' (document portfolio)
Can someone else describe what I have done?	➤ 'WT' (witness testimony)

Written assignments

One of the most comprehensive methods for demonstrating that you are a reflective practitioner and your understanding informs your practice is the written assignment. Some providers will suggest that you produce a series of reflective written assignments to help you to evidence each indicator.

Assignments are a very useful source of evidence as they enable you to explain why you do what you do and how you do it. So, even if you are not required to write an assignment, you may consider doing so to evidence an aspect of your practice. You will be able to showcase your knowledge and understanding, your personal practice, your leadership role, your understanding of the needs of babies, toddlers and pre-school children or how children learn in school, and your ability to reflect on the positive impact of any changes you have introduced.

Many providers will not require evidence of academic writing with correct referencing and a bibliography, as the emphasis is on your reflective practice. However, you will need to demonstrate that you are working at a postgraduate level so your assignment will need to be written at level 6 (you might find it helpful to read about the requirements for writing at academic levels six and seven) and be reflective.

Your provider's handbook and your tutor will provide you with detailed information on what you need to include in each assignment. Different providers will have different requirements for assignment writing, so check this carefully. You may have to write each assignment following a prescribed format. If that is the case, you need to pay close attention to the wording on the pro forma you are to use as this will tell you what you need to cover in the assignment. Note any guidance you are given and use this as a checklist when you have completed this assignment so that you can check that you have addressed everything you are asked to include.

Beth's provider asked her to produce three age-related assignments to demonstrate her knowledge and understanding of children's development at each stage for babies, toddlers and pre-school children. She had to describe a 'change' she introduced with each age group that would address a gap in provision or practice that she had identified. Even if your provider does not ask you to write an age-related assignment, you might find that this helps you to evidence your work with each age group and meet the Standards that relate to your work with children in each age range.

You could choose to write an assignment to evidence your practice and describe in detail:

- how your actions evidence your understanding of the developmental needs of one age group (to help you to evidence 2.2);

- how you observed current practice and identified an area for development (to help you to evidence 4.5 and 8.6);

- how you shared your observations with colleagues and worked collaboratively with them to identify an area for development and decide on appropriate strategies to address this and introduce an appropriate change in practice or change to the environment (to help you evidence leadership for 8.6);

- the strategies you used to support the understanding and skills your colleagues need to enable them to introduce this change in practice (to help you evidence 8.4 and 8.5);

- how the change in practice that you have introduced relates to Early Years Foundation Stage (EYFS) requirements and promotes children's learning and development (to help you evidence 2.1, 3.2, 3.3, 4.2, 4.5 and 5.2);

- how you engaged with parents to involve them and inform them of the reasons for this change (to help you evidence 2.7);

- your observations of children before and after any changes you have introduced and how you use these to evaluate the impact of the change (to help you evidence 1.1, 4.5 and 8.6);

- verbatim records of your conversations with children in one age range (to help you to evidence 2.5);

- an example of engaging in sustained shared thinking with an individual child (to help you to evidence 2.4);

- an evaluation of the impact of the change, incorporating evaluations by staff, children and parents (this will evidence *a safe and stimulating environment where children feel confident and are able to learn and develop* for 1.1);

- next steps or adjustments that you have identified (to evidence 4.5 and 8.6).

You can use a short assignment to 'mop up' any Standards that you may not have evidenced in enough detail elsewhere. Often trainees use a short assignment to evidence their work with professionals from outside their setting, their support for a child during a transition to evidence 5.4 or to record their role in raising a safeguarding concern to evidence 7.3. You need to think carefully about which examples of your practice you want to showcase in an assignment.

You might find it helpful to consider using a short assignment to help you evidence a particular group of indicators that it might be difficult to evidence in other ways. For example, you could use a short assignment to evidence your work with:

- parents – to evidence 2.7, 4.3, 6.3 and 8.3;

- an individual child – to evidence 1.1, 1.2, 1.3, 2.1, 2.3, 2.4, 2.6, 3.2, 4.1, 4.3, 5.1, 5.2, 5.4 and 6.3;

- a child with special educational needs (SEN) – to evidence 1.2, 4.4, 5.1, 5.3, 5.5, 6.2, 8.3 and 8.7;

- other professionals – to evidence 5.5, 6.2, 8.3 and 8.7;

- your understanding of safeguarding legislation, policy and procedure and how you have acted to protect a child from harm – to evidence 7.1 and 7.3;

- leading and supporting your colleagues – to evidence Standard 8 and other relevant indicators.

Identifying your evidence in a written assignment

When you write an assignment you need to bear in mind that your assessor will be looking for specific pieces of evidence that meet a Standard statement and indicator. You can make this process easier if you phrase your sentences carefully so as to make it clear how your evidence relates to a specific Standard or indicator.

You also need to check that the information you provide addresses the requirements of that indicator. For example, if a Standard asks you to *demonstrate* something, make sure that you describe your actions. However, if a Standard asks you to *demonstrate your understanding*, then you need to describe how your understanding of theory informs your practice.

When you have completed each assignment state which Standard/indicator this evidences and whether it demonstrates your personal practice and/or leadership. Your provider will give you guidance on this, but most will ask you to record the Standard number in brackets at the end of the relevant sentence. There is more information on referencing personal practice and leadership in Chapter 10 on understanding 'personal practice' and 'leadership'.

What makes good evidence in a written assignment?

If you plan to evidence a particular Standard or indicator in a specific sentence or paragraph, you need to make sure that your description is detailed. Stating that 'I follow EYFS requirements when planning' tells us nothing about what you did or what you know. However, if you said 'two of my colleagues said they lacked confidence planning for toddlers so I led a staff development event on planning where I introduced the concept of … ' then we have a clearer picture of what you did and why.

You need to avoid evidencing too many indicators against each statement or paragraph in an assignment. This makes it difficult and time-consuming for your assessor and can lead to the assumption that you do not understand the wording of a Standard or indicator or do not have evidence of any depth to share. You need to aim to evidence roughly eight Standards or indicators per assignment and address each one in depth. Pay attention to the wording of each indicator and check that what you are saying matches what it is asking. Be as explicit as you can, and tell your assessor exactly what you did, step by step, and explain why you did it this way and how this supported your colleagues.

How much detail do I need in a written assignment?

You cannot be too detailed! Describe the thoughts that led you to make your decisions, the evidence you evaluated to reach a conclusion and the conclusions you drew. Describe in detail, for example, how your understanding of babies' developmental needs led you to introduce treasure baskets. If you are asked to demonstrate your communication with children, then record the conversation, sentence by sentence (or 'verbatim'), so that your assessor can judge its quality. If you want to demonstrate that the changes you introduced supported children's learning and development, provide an excerpt from an observation of the child before and after you introduced any changes, so that your assessor can see the impact that it had.

Assignments – top five tips

1. Ask a friend or colleague to proof-read each assignment. Your friend/colleague can look for any problems with spelling or grammar and check whether you have evidenced what you planned to evidence.

2. You can use three assignments to evidence your work with each of the three age groups and demonstrate the depth of your understanding of the developmental needs of babies, toddlers and pre-school children. This will also help you to evidence any indicators that relate to child development, such as 2.2, 3.1, 5.1, 5.2 and 5.3.

3. Read through the Standards and check which indicators require evidence of work with different age groups (see Activity 5.1 in Chapter 5 on age ranges). Then make sure that you evidence those Standards in an assignment that focuses on children in a particular age group. This is a particularly effective way to evidence 2.5.

4. Do not evidence too many Standards in each assignment. Your assessor will be looking for depth of evidence, not frequency. The assessor needs to read about what you thought, what you did, the conversations you had, the support you provided and the impact this had.

5. Do not quote from an indicator and record this as evidence. A statement only counts as 'evidence' if it describes your thoughts or your actions.

Case studies

A case study is a very effective way to evidence your support for a particular child. You can describe what you have learnt from your observations of the child, how you evaluated the child's progress against EYFS using development matters or the two-year-old progress check, the next steps you identify, how you plan activities based on their needs and interests and how you identify their needs. You will be able to evidence the indicators that relate to supporting a child's learning and development (such as 1.1, 1.2, 1.3, 2.1, 2.3, 2.4, 2.6, 3.2, 4.1, 4.3, 5.1, 5.2, 5.4 and 6.3) and supporting a child with special needs or a disability (such as 1.2, 4.4, 5.1, 5.3, 5.5, 6.2, 8.3 and 8.7).

If you are supporting a child with special needs, you can use a case study to record the stages in identifying the child's needs, your progress through the SEN assessment and your collaboration with the SEN co-ordinator (SENCO) or other professionals who work with this child. (The terms SEND (Special educational needs and disabilities) and SENDCO have recently been introduced in the new codes of practice. However, throughout this text we have used SEN and SENCO as these are still the most commonly used terms and are still used within the above documents where they refer to 'children with SEN or disabilities'.) You can also record the meetings you have with parents and how you share information with them and work together to support the learning and development of their child. You can use a case study to evidence the group of indicators that relate to working with parents (2.7, 4.3, 5.5, 6.3 and 8.3) and those that relate to working with other professionals (5.5, 6.2, 8.3 and 8.7). You may be able to describe how you attended a Team Around the Child meeting or worked with other professionals to complete a Common Assessment Framework form. You can also use a case study to record your role in identifying and acting upon a safeguarding concern.

You can also use a case study to catalogue the steps you have taken to support staff development within your team (for 8.4 and 8.5). You could record how you identified a need for professional development and then provided training and/or one-to-one support and mentoring to help colleagues develop their practice. You can then reflect on the impact this had on provision.

Your reflective journal

Your reflective journal is one of the most useful tools you have as it allows you to evidence your knowledge and understanding and the reasons for your actions and the decisions you take. Unless your provider states otherwise, your reflective journal can be written in any medium and any format. What is most important is that it is useful for you.

You can record your reflections in shorthand, in rough notes, as bullet points or in detail in longhand. What matters is that this provides a useful tool that helps you record and clarify your thoughts and provide a useful source of evidence. It is not there to create more work for you.

Unless you have been told otherwise, your journal can be written in any medium. It can be a small notebook that you slide into your pocket or carry about in your bag so you have it with you when you need it. It can also be a document on your computer, an app such as Event Note or even a specific program such as PebblePad that your provider sets up for you. You will need to think about issues of data protection and confidentiality and make sure all entries are carefully anonymised.

Your journal is not something you have to use every day, and should not become a chore. It is something you use only when it is helpful for you, whether to clarify your thinking, help you decide what to do next or to help you to evidence a specific Standard or indicator.

You can use your reflective journal to evidence indicators that can be difficult to evidence elsewhere or where you need to demonstrate your knowledge and understanding or the reasons for your actions. There are several indicators that you can evidence well through an entry in your journal.

You can use your journal to record your support for individual practitioners or groups of practitioners to evidence 8.4 and 8.5. The advantage of the journal format is that you can outline the reasons for your intervention, describe it step by step and then analyse how effective it was and what you might do differently next time.

You can also use your journal to record your thoughts over a period of time. If, for example, you have a concern about an area of provision you can use your journal to analyse your observations of practice in this area and weigh up alternative approaches to dealing with this before you take any action. You can then combine your early reflections with records of the actions you did take and your evaluations of the impact of your actions to help you evidence 1.1, 4.5 and 8.6.

Some Early Years Teacher trainees read through the Standards and make a list of the indicators that they think they could best evidence in their journal. They paste this list into the front of their journal as a reminder, and whenever an occasion that relates to an item on the list occurs, they record it in their journal.

What is most important when you use your journal is that you do not just record the facts of a situation, but that you analyse them and reflect on your actions. The idea is that you will analyse an event, such as a conversation with a child where you engage in sustained shared thinking (2.4) and analyse how well you supported the child's thinking, what this conversation tells you about the child, what you can do next to support that child and what you have learnt about your own practice. You can also reflect on how your actions relate to the specific wording of the indicator. In this situation you might use a reflection to identify how you both *lead* and *model* a range of *effective strategies to develop and extend children's learning and thinking* (2.4). You might also reflect on how you know that these strategies were effective.

You need to think about the style of your writing and identify the key components of reflective writing. You will need to think about both the reflective style of your writing and the stages of the reflective cycle that you will engage in. You can ask yourself, what is it that makes reflecting writing so different from other forms of writing, such as academic writing?

The texts listed below will help you to identify the key features of reflective writing. You might also find that reading about Kolb's learning cycle (Learning-Theories.com, 2014), with the stages of concrete experience, reflective observation, abstract conceptualisation and active experimentation, helps you to look at the stages within the cycle of reflective practice in more detail. The section on 'Suggested reading' in the chapter for 8.6 also has details of additional texts that can help you to develop your reflective practice and reflective writing.

Hallet, E (2013) *The Reflective Early Years Practitioner*. SAGE: London.

Lindon, J (2012) *Reflective Practice and Early Years Professionalism,* 2nd edn. *Linking Theory and Practice*. London: Hodder.

Paige-Smith, A and Craft, A (2011) *Developing Reflective Practice in the Early Years*. Berkshire: OUP McGraw-Hill Education.

Reed, M and Canning, N (eds) (2010) *Reflective Practice in the Early Years*. London: SAGE.

Reflective journal – top five tips

1. Unless you have specific guidance from your provider, you can choose a medium that suits you best for your journal: this could be a notebook, an app or a document on your computer.

2. Choose a style of writing and presentation that feels comfortable for you.

3. Consider issues of confidentiality and data protection and anonymise your entries.

4. Think about which Standards and indicators could be evidenced well in a journal entry.

5. Identify the key components of reflective writing.

Your document portfolio

Another effective source of evidence is your document portfolio. This may be a physical portfolio, where you place a series of documents in an A4-sized folder or ring binder. It can also be an e-portfolio where you scan and save a series of numbered documents. In both cases you will need to produce a contents list where you name and number each document and briefly explain how this evidences your practice and which Standard/s it evidences.

The pieces of evidence that you will include in your document portfolio are mainly work products; however, each provider will have their own guidance that you will need to follow.

It is good practice to include no more than 30 documents. Thirty documents may sound too few, but once you get to know the Standards you will realise that one document can evidence several indicators. For example, a detailed individualised education plan (IEP) can help you to evidence 1.2, 2.1, 2.2, 2.6, 2.7, 3.1-3.5, 4.1, 4.2, 5.1, 5.3, 5.5, 6.2 and 6.3.

There are a wide range of documents that you can include in your portfolio. They can evidence a range of Standards and help you to evidence key areas such as planning, working with other professionals, partnerships with parents, safeguarding, health and safety, promoting learning and development and leadership and support. You may want to think about which Standards and indicators can be met well through a document and make a list of these as a reminder. For example, some Early Years trainees include completed risk assessment forms and accident forms to evidence 7.2.

You can only include forms that you have completed yourself and signed – never a blank pro forma, even if it is one that you designed yourself. If you have designed a form, such as a new planning document, then it is a good idea to include this, but you will need to add a note explaining why you designed the form in this way.

Some of the documents that Early Years trainees include in their portfolios include:

- focus activity-planning sheets;
- weekly planning sheets you have contributed to and/or designed;
- child observations;
- entries in a profile book and next steps for your key child;
- an IEP you have contributed to;
- a completed two-year-old progress check or EYFS Profile;
- menus you have planned;
- a resources audit you designed and carried out;
- invoice for resources you ordered;
- a risk assessment form you have completed and signed;
- a copy of an entry in the accident book you wrote and signed;
- a completed medicine form you completed and signed;
- a policy you have contributed to;
- a parent newsletter you have written;
- leaflets you have produced for parents;
- training notes for a staff development event you led;
- information and handouts you produced for colleagues;
- guidance on EYFS that you have prepared for colleagues;

- a flow chart on reporting procedures when a safeguarding concern is raised;
- lists of contact numbers for other professionals;
- emails between yourself and other professionals;
- books you have made with children; for example, an 'all about me' book to help a child settle or a book about the new school to support a child in this transition;
- plans for any changes you introduce.

What is most important is that each document clearly demonstrates your actions and/ or your knowledge and understanding.

Ask someone else to read through each document; that person will be able to tell you what the document shows that you have done or thought. You also need to check that any documents that include sensitive and confidential information are carefully anonymised.

Your document portfolio – top five tips

1. Read through the Standards and decide which indicators you could evidence in a document and make a list of these as a reminder.

2. Once you know the Standards well you will realise that one good document can meet several Standards: each time you choose a document, ask yourself whether it can meet more than one Standard or indicator but avoid referencing too many indicators for each document.

3. Make sure that you follow your provider's guidance and that your document portfolio is well organised, correctly numbered and clearly labelled and make sure that all confidential information is anonymised.

4. Use sticky notes or a highlighter pen to record on each document what it is that you did and why, and where the evidence can be found if this is not clear within the document itself.

5. Draw a rough plan of your setting and walk round your setting with this plan. Make a mark on it at each point where you can see something you have introduced or used, for example, the profile book you completed. Then see if you have a document that can evidence this, such as your plans for a new book corner.

Witness testimonies

Your provider may or may not allow you to evidence your practice through witness testimonies. If these are allowed, there may be some limitations, for example, you are only allowed to include three witness testimonies, or that each witness testimony counts as one document in your portfolio.

If you are able to include witness testimonies they can be very valuable; however, you do need to choose your witnesses with care and clearly explain how they need to complete the testimony. You need to make sure that the witnesses you choose know your work well, and will feel confident writing about this.

If you are a manager you may find it more difficult to choose a witness. You can ask your deputy to provide a testimony and this can be a very positive and interesting experience for you both. You could also ask a local authority advisor for a testimony, if you feel s/he knows your work enough.

If you choose parent witnesses you need to be sure that they feel confident in their written skills and in writing in English and make sure that the process isn't intimidating for them. You need to make it clear that they do not need to write in an academic style or use any educational jargon. You can identify the particular indicators a parent may be able to evidence in advance, such as 2.7, and list these using 'layman's language' as a guide for them.

When you ask witnesses to write a testimony, you need to take time to prepare them well. You need to explain the requirements of Early Years Teacher Status and provide a summary of the Standards and indicators written in language that they will feel comfortable with. Your provider will have a standard pro forma that your witness will need to use and some providers have a separate form for parent witnesses. You may still need to summarise each Standard or explain the wording of a particular indicator.

You need to reassure witnesses that they are not being judged and that any issues with spelling and grammar will not matter. What is important, however, is that they provide detailed examples of your work to evidence each Standard. If possible, you need your witness to describe your practice in relation to the indicators rather than the Standard statements, as their evidence will then be more detailed and specific.

You need to encourage your witness to avoid general statements wherever possible as general statements do not always provide evidence that an assessor can rely on. A statement that you 'understand safeguarding procedures' is less helpful than one that states that you 'delivered training on the signs and symptoms of abuse and identified a safeguarding concern and followed the correct reporting and recording procedures in this instance'.

Witness testimonies – top five tips

1. Choose your witness with care: choose someone who knows your work well and can describe your actions and understanding in some detail.

2. Follow your provider's guidance and use their pro formas: there may be separate pro formas for parent witnesses.

3. Reassure witnesses that their spelling and grammar will not be judged.

4. Make sure that parent witnesses do not feel intimidated by this process and understand what they need to write about: you can summarise the indicators they may be able to evidence as a reminder for them.

5. Take time to prepare your witnesses: they will need to understand the requirements of Early Years Teacher Status and the Standards and that you need evidence that is relevant and specific.

Observations

When you read through the Standards you will see that there are several Standards and indicators that you can evidence during an observation. You need to read through the Standards and make a list of any you think you could evidence when you are observed and plan an activity where you can demonstrate this. You will find that some indicators are particularly well suited to being evidenced through an observation, especially those that ask you to demonstrate your practice, such as 1.3 where you *demonstrate and model the positive values, attitudes and behaviours expected of children*.

You can be observed in a range of situations, not just when you lead an activity with the children. You can be observed modelling an activity for a colleague, mentoring a student, leading a training event or in a meeting with parents or other professionals if they give their informed consent. You can also be observed carrying out a risk assessment and other health and safety procedures to help you to evidence 7.2, or a resources audit to evidence 8.1 or carrying out the two-year-old progress check for 6.1.

Each provider will have their own system for observing your practice. You may have an assessor who will observe you for a short time on one occasion or you may be observed by your tutor or mentor over several occasions. Your setting may encourage peer observations so a peer observation may be a possibility, too. Some of these observations will be formative and provide guidance on your next steps and other may be summative, recording your practice at the end of your Early Years Teacher programme. Any of these observations can contribute to your evidence.

Your provider will have their own observation forms that you will need to use and you will need to follow your provider's guidance carefully. Each provider will also have their own system for recording the observation and cross-referencing the observation to the Standards. Observers will probably highlight on the observation which indicators they think you have evidenced and any they consider that you are working towards. You can use this information to identify areas where you need to extend your practice and to help you plan your next observation.

You can provide observers with plans for the activity they will observe. This can help you evidence additional indicators. You can use an activity plan to *Demonstrate a critical understanding of the EYFS areas of learning and development* for 3.3 and demonstrate how you identify and *set goals that stretch and challenge children* for individual children for 1.2. Your plans can also demonstrate how you *Support children through a range of transitions* for 5.4, and that you *Have a secure understanding of how a range of factors can inhibit children's learning and development and how best to address these* for 5.4.

You may need to change your plans at the last moment, due to an emergency or because you need to adapt the activity so that it relates to the interests and needs of the children at that moment. If you explain the reasons for this change of plan clearly, your observer will appreciate that you are making an appropriate decision that demonstrates your professionalism.

Observations – top five tips

1. Read your provider's guidance carefully and make sure that you follow this.

2. Read through the Standards and pick out those you think you could evidence well in an observation.

3. Some observations will be formative, to evaluate your progress and help you identify areas for development and any gaps in your evidence: your final observation will be summative and identify which Standards you meet at that moment, as you complete your Early Years Teacher Status.

4. You can choose what you wish your assessor to observe, so think carefully about what skills or knowledge you want to demonstrate and choose an activity to showcase these.

5. You can use your activity plan to evidence several indicators. For example, an activity plan can evidence your understanding of EYFS (3.3) and how you set goals for children (1.2).

5 Age range requirements

Introduction

To achieve your Early Years Teacher Status you will need to demonstrate your practice across the full birth to five age range during the course of the programme and this is what we refer to as 'the age range requirements'.

The main age range requirements are that you:

- demonstrate your practice with babies, toddlers and young children;

- demonstrate your knowledge and understanding of the development of babies, toddlers and young children and can relate this to the Early Years Foundation Stage (EYFS);

- have some understanding of babies' and children's learning and development from the early years through to Key Stages 1 and 2;

- lead and support practice with babies, toddlers and young children;

- identify which Standards require evidence of your practice with each age group and provide this evidence;

- provide examples of your work with babies, toddlers and pre-school children across your evidence.

Unless your provider states otherwise, 'babies' applies to children from birth to 20 months, toddlers from 16 to 36 months and young children from 30 to 60 months.

ACTIVITY 5.1

Making an action plan to identify the age range requirements

You must demonstrate recent experience of working with babies, toddlers and young children. An action plan can help you identify whether you have sufficient recent experience with each age group and whether you have any gaps in your practice or leadership in relation to the Standards which have an age range component.

You can structure your action plan in whatever way is most helpful for you. Here is an example from Debbie, an Early Years Teacher trainee, who designed Table 5.1 to help her identify which Standards required evidence of her practice with each age group.

(Continued)

(Continued)

Table 5.1 *Action plan*

Standard/indicator with an age-related requirement	Gaps in practice	Action points	Dates for each action point	My evidence
2.5 'Communicate effectively with children from birth to age five'	Communication with babies	Arrange a baby placement at the children's centre	Arrange to meet the manager by end of October	

You can use the action points you identified in Table 5.1 to create a checklist that will:

- *remind you of any gaps in your practice and how you plan to address these;*
- *identify how you can evidence the age-related experience you do have;*
- *remind you of which indicators require evidence of working with children of different ages;*
- *identify which Standards would benefit from evidence of your practice with different age groups.*

ACTIVITY **5.2**

Using your journal to evidence age range requirements

Think about how you can use your journal to evidence the age-related requirements, especially those that relate to a specific Standard. Your journal can be a useful source of evidence as it enables you to record events as they happen.

You can use excerpts from your journal to evidence your practice with each age group and your understanding of the developmental needs of children at each stage. For example, Debbie used her journal to record an example of engaging in sustained shared thinking (2.4) with a toddler to demonstrate her listening skills with toddlers for 2.5.

ACTIVITY **5.3**

Identifying your evidence for each age group

In the previous activities you may have noted that, although some Standards require evidence of your practice with babies, toddlers and young children, you can strengthen your evidence for other Standards if you include examples of your practice with different age groups.

Create a table to help you to identify both where you are required to evidence your practice with each age group and where you can strengthen your evidence for a Standard by including examples that relate to different age groups. Debbie has added her thoughts to Table 5.2; she found that her list from Table 5.1 helped her to complete the first half of Table 5.2.

Table 5.2 *Identifying your evidence for each age group*

Standards require evidence relating to babies, toddlers, young children and children in Key Stages 1 and 2	Age range evidence required			
	Evidence of practice and knowledge and understanding/gaps in practice			Evidence of knowledge and understanding
	Babies	Toddlers	Young children	Key Stages 1 and 2
2.5 'Communicate effectively with children from birth to age five, listening and responding sensitively'	Observation which demonstrates how I follow babies' gaze	Gaps: read about communicating with toddlers	Assignment on introducing Every Child a Talker in pre-school room and witness testimony from when I modelled an activity to promote communication (L)	

Standards that would benefit from evidence relating to babies, toddlers, pre-school children and children in Key Stages 1 and 2	Age range evidence optional			
	Evidence of practice and knowledge and understanding/gaps in practice			Evidence of knowledge and understanding
	Babies	Toddlers	Young children	Key Stages 1 and 2
2.3 'Know and understand attachment theories, their significance and how effectively to promote secure attachments'	Evidence of supporting attachment with babies when I help them settle (P). Policy I introduced to promote key person relationships in baby room (L)			

See Chapter 10 for a full explanation of (L) (leadership) and (P) (personal practice).

Making the decision: an additional age-related placement

To achieve your Early Years Teacher Status you need recent experience with babies, toddlers and young children and Activities 5.1 and 5.3 will help you evaluate your experience. If you have identified that you lack adequate recent experience in one of the three age ranges you need to make a note of this and add this to your action plan. This will help you decide whether you need to extend your experience with any one age group by taking on a placement and whether it is possible to carry out this placement at your current workplace. Some trainees find that they need to extend their practice with two age groups, and if this is the case for you, you need to make sure you address this as soon as possible.

To decide whether you need to take on a placement with a specific age range to help you evidence specific Standards, you can also ask yourself the following questions:

- Do I have evidence that demonstrates my understanding of the development of babies, toddlers and young children for 2.2, 2.5, 3.1, 3.3, 4.2 and 5.3?

- Do I have evidence of planning and setting goals for individual babies, toddlers and young children for 1.2, 2.1, 2.4, 2.6, 4.1, 4.2, 4.4, 5.1, 5.2, 5.3, 5.5 and 6.1, as these indicators would benefit from evidence of my work across the age ranges?

- Have I had a positive impact on practice within my setting in the baby, toddler and pre-school rooms? Could I evidence how I have developed practice and led and supported colleagues in their work with babies, toddlers and young children?

- Can I evidence how I support colleagues in planning according to EYFS requirements for children at each stage of development for 3.3?

- Can I describe EYFS requirements for babies, toddlers and young children? Am I familiar enough with the areas of learning, development matters and early years outcomes (Gov.uk, 2013b) to assess the progress of a baby, toddler or young child or carry out a two-year-old progress check or EYFS Profile for 3.3 and 6.1?

You also need to think about how recent your experience is, your understanding of how children develop and learn in Key Stages 1 and 2 for 3.1 and 3.3, why you need to evidence your practice with toddlers and how much additional experience you need if you are a manager. The following sections will help you consider these issues.

Working with toddlers: the requirements

Although the Standards only refer to babies and young children, you need practical experience of working with toddlers so that you can evidence your understanding of how children's development progresses from birth to age five and how you meet their needs at each stage of development.

Working with children in Key Stages 1 and 2: the requirements

In Standard 3 you are asked to demonstrate some understanding of the continuity between how children learn and develop in the early years and Key Stages 1 and 2. You are required to carry out a two-week school-based placement and this is where you will gain the experience and understanding you need to evidence this Standard.

You will not need to evidence your work with children in Key Stages 1 and 2 in nearly as much depth as your work with babies, toddlers and young children and you are asked to evidence your understanding rather than your practice. You can find more information on meeting the requirements in relation to Key Stages 1 and 2 in Chapter 7 on the school-based placement.

Managers

If you are a manager or if your role in your setting means that you do not work regularly with specific children, you need to make sure that you have enough appropriate personal practice. You can ask yourself whether, for example, you *set goals that stretch and challenge children of all backgrounds, abilities and dispositions* (1.2), and *support children through a range of transitions* (5.4)? If you don't have this experience, you may need to arrange a placement with the required age group/s.

Recent experience

Although your experience with each age group needs to be recent (within the course of your EYTS), you can include some evidence from the last five years to evidence aspects of practice that do not occur regularly. For example, you can evidence an incident from two years ago when you last acted to protect a child from harm for 7.3. Your provider will have more information on this and may have their own guidelines.

However, if this experience was not recent, you do need to check whether you actually can evidence practice that occurred several years ago. Will you be able describe the changes you introduced or the conversations you had in enough detail?

You can find further information on preparing for this placement in Chapter 6 on preparing for placement. You can also find further guidance on how to evidence your practice with each age group in Chapter 6, Chapter 4 on assessment methods and in the chapters for each age-related indicator.

6   Preparing for placement

Introduction

There are two types of placement that can help you to achieve your Early Years Teacher Status. One placement is compulsory, and this is the school-based placement that we look at in Chapter 7. The other is a placement in an early years setting that enables you to extend your practice with one or more age group. This second placement is optional (unless you are on the Undergraduate or Graduate Entry Mainstream routes) and you can decide for yourself whether you need the experience this type of placement offers. Chapter 5 on age range requirements will help you to decide this.

If you are on the Assessment Only route you will already have decided that you do not need an additional early years placement. If are new to early years and are a trainee on the Undergraduate Entry or Graduate Entry Mainstream route, then all your experience will be on placement and your provider will organise a minimum of two early years placements for you as well as your school-based placement.

Graduate Entry Mainstream

If you are a trainee on the Graduate Entry Mainstream route you will carry out two early years placements and will be given detailed guidance on the tasks you need to carry out. The following sections will still be useful for you as they help you to prepare for each placement and appreciate how certain tasks help you to evidence the Standards.

Why you may need a placement

In this section we will look at why you might need a placement to extend your experience with a particular age group or, if you are a manager, to gain more hands-on experience with a group of children. You may need more experience of working with babies, toddlers and young children to address indicators requiring evidence of working with children at different stages of development, such as 4.2, which asks you to *Plan balanced and flexible activities and educational programmes that take into account the stage of development, circumstances and interests of children*.

If you are a manager or lead a drop-in session, you may need experience of planning for individual children to evidence indicators relating to setting goals, such as 1.2, which asks you to *Set goals that stretch and challenge children of all backgrounds, abilities and dispositions*.

You may need a placement where you can support a child with special needs to evidence how you *Demonstrate a clear understanding of the needs of all children, including those with special educational needs and disabilities, and be able to use and evaluate distinctive approaches to engage and support them* for 5.3. You may also need a placement where you have the opportunity to work with other professionals to support a child's development to evidence 5.5, 6.2, 8.3 and 8.7.

You may need a placement with babies or young children to demonstrate how you *Support children through a range of transitions* such as settling in and starting school for 5.4 or a baby placement to demonstrate how you support attachment relationships for 2.3.

You may also need a placement with a particular age range to evidence your leadership and reflective practice for Standard 8. Although Standard 8 does not explicitly require evidence of leading practitioners who work with each age group, your evidence would be incomplete without this. For example, you cannot evidence that you *model and implement effective education and care* for 8.4 unless you demonstrate this across the whole age range.

Activity 6.1 will help you identify whether you need an additional placement, and for more support on deciding whether you need an additional placement, see Chapter 5 on age range requirements.

ACTIVITY **6.1**

Do I need an early years placement?

To help you decide whether or not you need an additional placement, read through each Standard and indicator and make a list of any areas where you lack relevant experience with one or more age groups. The question you then need to ask yourself, is 'can I gain this experience through a placement in my own setting or do I need an additional placement elsewhere?' This will help you to identify whether an additional placement will help you gain the age-related experiences you need and whether you could carry out this placement within your own setting. Beth, an Early Years Teacher trainee, has added her comments to Table 6.1 to help you start.

Table 6.1 Reasons for an additional placement

Standards/indicators	Gaps in my practice	Can I address this in my own setting?	Do I need an additional placement?	Experiences I need	Evidence I need
1.1 Establish and sustain a safe and stimulating environment where children feel confident and are able to learn and develop	Developing environment in toddler room: I've developed areas in the baby and pre-school rooms, but not toddler room	Yes, my manager will allow me to change places with Shireen for three weeks	No	Introduce a change in toddler room so that it is more 'stimulating'	Observations

Journal entries

Plans for the change

Minutes of staff meeting where discuss implementing the change |

Standards/indicators	Gaps in my practice	Can I address this in my own setting?	Do I need an additional placement?	Experiences I need	Evidence I need
1.2 Set goals that stretch and challenge children of all backgrounds, abilities and dispositions	Set goals for toddlers	Yes, my manager will allow me to change places with Shireen for three weeks	No	Support key person and observe two toddlers to identify next steps and set goals	Observations and next steps Profile books
1.3 Demonstrate and model the positive values, attitudes and behaviours expected of children	Identify appropriate behaviour management strategies for toddlers	Yes	No	Read about managing toddlers' behaviour. Identify behaviours to model for toddlers. Be observed modelling positive behaviours with toddlers	Peer and mentor observations Journal entry
2.1 Be accountable for children's progress, attainment and outcomes	Observe, assess and plan appropriate activities for toddlers Carry out progress check at age two	Yes	No	Carry out progress check at age two	Two-year-old progress check Observations, next steps and entries in toddlers' profile books Focus activity plans
2.2 Demonstrate knowledge and understanding of how babies and children learn and develop	Understanding of toddlers' development	Yes	No	Plan activities to support toddlers' developmental needs	Journal entry reviewing reading on toddlers' developmental needs

Length of placement

If you have decided that you need a placement, your first question will probably be, 'how long does a placement last?' If you are on the Undergraduate or Graduate Entry Mainstream routes, your placement will last a fixed number of weeks and you will have a series of tasks to complete each week. However, if this is an additional placement you have taken on to gain specific experience, then this is a bit like asking, 'how long is a piece of string?' How long the placement needs to last will depend on what you need to achieve while you are there.

Every placement has to last a minimum of 20 full days, but it will be to your advantage to spend more time there if you can. You need to allow yourself enough time to address the gaps in your practice and generate the evidence you need.

For example, if you are planning a placement to evidence your practice and leadership and support with a specific age group, you need enough time to:

- extend your knowledge and understanding of children's learning and development at this age (2.2, 3.1, 5.2);

- find out what good practice with this age group looks like and consider Early Years Foundation Stage requirements and expectations for this age group (3.3);

- find out how the setting policies support the developmental needs of children in this age range (2.2);

- observe practice and review the environment to identify where there may be scope for development (4.5, 8.7);

- consider a range of leadership styles and methods to find an approach that is appropriate for your role in this situation: remember you are on placement to learn, so if you then plan to lead practice you need to earn the respect of your more experienced colleagues;

- gain the trust of your new colleagues and make sure they understand the Initial Teacher Training Early Years requirements that you must meet on placement;

- work co-operatively with colleagues to identify an appropriate area for development (8.4, 8.7);

- lead the introduction of this change or development, support colleagues in managing change and developing their skills (8.4, 8.5);

- observe and engage with children before and after you have introduced a change so you can evaluate whether the change was effective (1.1, 4.5, 8.7);

- involve parents, colleagues and children in evaluating the impact of a change you have introduced (1.1, 2.7, 4.5, 8.7);

- evidence how you have supported the learning and development of individual children: record examples of observation, planning and next steps and your contributions to an Individual Education Plan, Common Assessment Framework form or safeguarding concern (1.2, 2.1, 4.1, 4.2, 5.3, 6.2, 7.3);

- evidence working in partnership with parents (2.7, 4.3, 6.3);

- evidence listening and communicating and engaging in sustained shared thinking with children in this age group (2.4, 2.5);

- evidence your reflective practice: use your journal to record your progress through the stages of reflection, active experimentation and evaluation and present the rationale for this change and your evaluation of its impact, identifying what you could have done differently and will do next (4.5, 8.7).

Other factors can also influence the length of your placement. If, for example, your placement is with a staff team who know you well, or you already have good understanding of the needs of this age group, you may not need as much time on placement. If this is your first experience with this age group and you need time to build up your expertise before you can lead and support others, then you may need more time.

Choosing your placement

If you have chosen an additional early years placement, you may need to find this placement for yourself. This allows you to choose a setting that is convenient for you. There are several issues you need to consider when choosing your placement.

- Will you be able to address all the gaps in your practice in this setting? For example, if you need experience of working with other professionals for 5.5, 6.2 and 8.7, will this be possible here?

- Will you be able to observe examples of good practice?

- Will there be an opportunity for you to introduce a change in practice?

- Will there be opportunities for you to lead and support others?

- Is there an appropriate member of staff available to mentor and support you?

Before your placement

Once you have identified why you need a placement, you can start to prepare yourself. Remember that your placement will only last for a short period of time so you need to make sure that you gain the experiences you need while you are there.

The team cannot support you and help you make this possible if they do not understand what it is you have to achieve so it is your responsibility to make sure that those you work with are aware of the Initial Teacher Training Early Years requirements that you need to meet while you are with them.

Here are some suggestions to help you prepare for your placement and help your new team to support you:

- Make a list for your placement supervisor or mentor outlining what you need to achieve while you are there.

- Add a timeline, so everyone knows what you will be doing and when.

- Check with your colleagues that your plans will not interrupt anything that has already been planned.

- Discuss your plans with the team: make sure that what you are planning is relevant for the children and fits in with the overall plans for the room.

- Explain to your new colleagues that you need to introduce a 'change' and ask for their ideas: what areas do they think need refreshing?

- Ask in advance whether a colleague who knows your work well can provide a witness testimony.

Preparing to take on a leadership role in placement

It can feel difficult to imagine taking on a leadership role on your placement and how successful you are at this will depend on how well prepared you are. You may be nervous taking on a leadership role when you are working with an unfamiliar age group so you need to think about strategies you can use to boost your confidence and ensure that you appear knowledgeable and confident.

Here are some suggestions to help you prepare for your placement leadership role.

- One starting point would be to think about how you show your confidence through your body language. Do you appear too timid or overly confident? If you lack confidence, read up on the area you will be working in before you start. Then you have something worthwhile to share and your colleagues will pick up on this.

- You may have noticed in Chapter 10 on understanding 'personal practice' and 'leadership' that a great leader is one who inspires others and helps them identify for themselves what needs to be done. You can find your own way to do this, perhaps by talking to colleagues about something have you read and asking for their opinion.

- You need to think about how to balance the types of activities you engage in. You need to do your share of the routine tasks, such as clearing up after lunch. However, you also need enough time to focus on introducing your 'change' and to embed it in the practice of the room.

- The manager will have given permission for you to take the lead in some areas when they agreed your placement. However, if there are any problems with this, you need to contact your tutor or placement co-ordinator immediately.

Taking the lead on placement: preparation and strategies

There are several additional strategies you can consider when starting a placement with an unfamiliar age group and you are concerned about how to gain the trust of more experienced colleagues and take on a leadership role when you may lack experience.

1. Read up on this age group so that you can demonstrate your knowledge and understanding and don't appear to be a 'beginner'. *Key Times for Play: The First Three Years* by Julia Manning-Morton and Maggie Thorp (2003) is a good starting point if your placement is with younger children.

   Research archived *Nursery World* articles on this age range or search online for case studies and examples of good practice.

   If you can, visit another setting's provision for this age group as this will give you some ideas you can take with you to your placement.

2. Collaborate with your new colleagues. Explain that to achieve your Early Years Teacher Status you need to promote good practice by introducing a 'change' and ask them what 'change' would be most helpful. Your attitude will be the key to your success. You need to appear quietly confident, but keen to listen, to share expertise and work together to tackle a problem that the team have identified.

   The one thing you don't want to do is go in and say, 'I'm going to introduce treasure baskets as you don't have any!' If there are no treasure baskets in the baby room or you can see any 'obvious' gaps in practice, ask about it. There may be a very good reason why things are done this way.

3. Spend time observing practice in your setting and looking at how the children engage with the resources and areas in the room before you make any suggestions. If you complete a brief time sampling observation it can help you identify whether certain areas of the room needs attention and you can then share these observations with your new colleagues.

4. Extend your reading on leadership styles to help you find one you feel comfortable using in this situation.

7   School-based placement

Introduction

One of the key requirements for your Early Years Initial Teacher Training is that you complete a two-week placement in a primary school and demonstrate some understanding of how children learn and develop in Key Stages 1 and 2. This is because the National College for Teaching and Learning (NCTL) (**www.gov.uk/government/organisations/national-college-for-teaching-and-leadership**) believes that to be an effective teacher you need to appreciate how the stages of a child's education fit together.

All teachers need to have some understanding of the previous stage in a child's education and appreciate how children's current learning contributes to future learning and development, and this is no different for you as an Early Years Teacher. You will find this requirement reflected in 3.1, where you are asked to *Have a secure knowledge of early childhood development and how that leads to successful learning and development at school*, and in 3.3, where you are asked to *Demonstrate a critical understanding of the EYFS areas of learning and development and engage with the educational continuum of expectations, curricula and teaching of Key Stages 1 and 2*.

Your provider will give you guidance on how to structure, organise and evidence your experiences during your school-based placement, so in this chapter we will look at how to prepare yourself for this placement. This will enable you to use your time there wisely and to evidence any Standards that look at the learning and development of older children. You may find it helpful to look at the chapters on 3.1 and 3.3 after you have read this chapter as they will provide some additional guidance.

Understanding how the early years promote progress in Key Stages 1 and 2

The NCTL believes there is good reason for the emphasis on how the early years support a child's success in school that is reflected in 3.1. Information on the Government's Get into Teaching website (**www.education.gov.uk/get-into-teaching/subjects-age-groups/early-years**) reports that 94% of children who achieve a good level of development at age five go on to achieve the expected levels for reading at Key Stage 1 and are five times more likely to achieve the highest level (Department for Education, 2011).

They also report that pupils who start off in the bottom 20% of attainment at age five are six times more likely to be in the bottom 20% at Key Stage 1 compared to their peers. The website also refers to the *Evaluation of the Graduate Leader Fund: Final Report*, which claims that graduates have a positive impact on the delivery of quality early years education and the resulting improvements in outcomes for young children (Mathers et al., 2011).

Preparing for your school placement

According to the NCTL (Gov.uk, 2014):

> Trainee teachers must be trained to teach across the Early Years Foundation Stage (from birth to 5 years old). They must also understand how early education links to education beyond age 5 and into key stages 1 and 2 in school ... Your training programme will need to provide trainees with enough time in early years settings or schools to allow them to show they meet the standards. Placements should take place in at least 2 schools or early years settings and include at least 2 weeks in a school in key stage 1.

This means that as an Early Years Teacher trainee you will need to spend two weeks in a Key Stage 1 classroom at some point during your Early Years Initial Teacher Training. It does not mean, however, that you will be expected to teach the class, but you will be expected to support the activities the teacher has planned and become involved in planning activities whenever possible.

Your provider may have a structured timetable that you need to follow while you are on placement, but if they don't, this section contains some guidance on planning how best to use your time on placement before you even start. There are several ways that you can prepare yourself and your time on placement will be much more worthwhile and productive if you prepare well and know what you need to achieve while you are there.

Here are some suggestions to help you prepare yourself.

1. Read through the Standards and work out where your experience in school can help you evidence a particular Standard or indicator. For example, you may want to learn about the teaching of phonics in school to help you evidence 3.4.

2. Find out about how the school is structured and how the National Curriculum is delivered. Check whether the school is an academy or free school as they may not follow the National Curriculum. You will need to find another way to learn about this to help you evidence 3.3 if your provider allows this type of placement.

3. Read about how school-age children learn and develop. You can focus on child development from age five to 11 and look at the National Curriculum. This will help you to appreciate how early childhood development supports successful learning and development in school for 3.1. It will also help you to identify *the educational continuum of expectations, curricula and teaching* between the early years and Key Stages 1 and 2 for 3.3. You might also want to look at the terminology used within the National Curriculum and the formative and summative assessment methods used, such as the end of key stage tests, known as SATS.

4. If you have a particular skill you can share with children in Key Stage 1, you can suggest that you would like to lead a project in a Key Stage 1 classroom. Ellie, an Early Years Teacher Trainee, ran five yoga sessions in a year 3 class and five sessions on using sculpture with found materials in a year 1 class.

5. Identify some activities you would like to carry out, such as observations of a curriculum area such as phonics to help you evidence 3.4 or maths to help you evidence 3.5. You may wish to find out how the school supports children with English as an Additional Language or children with special needs.

6. Remember that you need to evidence some knowledge and understanding of Key Stage 2 for 3.3, so plan to observe some lessons in a Key Stage 2 class. If you find out how children are prepared for the transition between Key Stages 1 and 2 this can help you evidence 5.4 on supporting children through transitions.

7. Decide on a system for recording what you have learnt, as this will help you to evidence particular Standards. You can adapt the planner in Table 7.1 that Ellie has used to help you prepare for your placement.

Table 7.1 Preparing for placement

Requirements	My actions
My provider's requirements	I keep records of attendance
Standards I can evidence on placement	3.1, 3.3, 3.4, 3.5, 5.2, 5.3, 5.4, 8.2, 8.6.
Reading I need to do before I start my placement	Read about the National Curriculum and assessment methods
Information I need on Key Stage 1	Find out how the National Curriculum is delivered in Key Stage 1 and how children are supported in their transition into Key Stage 1
Information I need on Key Stage 2	Find out how the National Curriculum is delivered in Key Stage 2 and how children are supported in their transition into Key Stage 2 and then on to secondary school
Activities I need to carry out on placement	Observations, planned yoga and sculpture activities, speak to special educational needs (SEN) co-ordinator and teaching assistant who supports children with English as an Additional Language (EAL)
Questions I need to ask on placement	How are children with SEN identified?
	What strategies are used to support children with EAL?
	Can I attend a planning meeting?
Areas to reflect on in my journal	Transitions
	How the curriculum is delivered, teaching methods, assessment, support for children with SEN and EAL
	How I needed to adapt my early years teaching strategies to support older children

Evidencing your placement

Your provider may give you a handbook for you to record your evidence from your placement, but if not, you may find it helpful to think about what you need to record and how you can record it before you start. Table 7.2 can help you identify what you can evidence on placement and how you can record this evidence. Ellie has added her ideas to Table 7.2 to help you start.

Table 7.2 Evidencing your school placement

Standards and requirements to evidence	My actions	My evidence
3.1 Early childhood development and learning and development at school	Read about child development from five to 11 years and how learning in the early years 'leads to successful learning and development at school'	Reflections on my reading in my journal, e.g. on how learning in the early years prepares a child for school
3.3 Early Years Foundation Stage (EYFS) and the National Curriculum	Read about the National Curriculum and how this relates to EYFS: identify 'the educational continuum of expectations, curricula and teaching of Key Stages 1 and 2'	Assignment on EYFS and learning in school
3.4 Phonics activities in Key Stage 1 and Key Stage 2	Observe phonics activities in years 1 and 2 and then in Key Stage 2 so I can see the progression	Observations and reflections in my journal
3.5 Maths activities in Key Stage 1 and Key Stage 2	Observe maths activities in years 1 and 2 and then in Key Stage 2 so I can see the progression	Observations and reflections in my journal
5.1 Support children with English as an Additional Language (EAL)	Find out how children with EAL are supported at different stages within Key Stages 1 and 2 and compare this to the strategies we use: this will help me appreciate how I can prepare a child with EAL for school	Case study
3.1/5.2/5.3 Supporting children with special educational needs	Find out how children with special needs are supported at different stages within Key Stages 1 and 2 and compare this to the strategies we use: this will help me appreciate how I can prepare a child with SEN for school	Case study
5.4 'Support children through a range of transitions'	Think about different strategies we can use to support a child in the transition to school	Reflections in my journal
	Find out about the transition from reception class to Key Stage 1 and from Key Stage 1 to Key Stage 2	
8.2 'Make a positive contribution to the wider life of the setting'	Project: Through my yoga project and found materials sculpture sessions I can evidence how I contribute to the wider life of the setting for 8.2	Witness testimony from Key Stage 1 teachers
8.6/3.1 Reflective practice	Reflect on how early years prepare child for school: make notes in my journal to help me prepare for my assignment	Assignment on EYFS and learning in school
Additional requirements: record of two weeks in school		Attendance record
Additional requirements: observations		Observations in Key Stage 1 and Key Stage 2 classes
Additional requirements: witness testimony		Witness testimony

SUGGESTED READING

Your provider may suggest some reading to help you prepare for your school placement. If not, you might find some of these texts helpful.

Bayley, R, Featherstone, S and Hardy, M (2003) *Smooth Transitions: Ensuring Continuity from the Foundation Stage*. Featherstone Catalogue. London: Bloomsbury.

Blatchford, R (2013) *Taking Forward the Primary Curriculum: Applying the 2014 National Curriculum for KS1 and KS2*. Suffolk: John Catt Educational.

Boys, R, Spink, E, Macrory, G and Bowen, P (2008) *Primary Curriculum: Teaching the Foundation Subjects*. London: Continuum.

Constable, C (2012) *The Outdoor Classroom Ages 3–7: Using Ideas from Forest Schools to Enrich Learning*. London: Routledge.

Cox, R (2011) *Primary English Teaching: An Introduction to Language, Literacy and Learning*. London: SAGE.

Cremin, T and Arthur, J (2014) *Learning to Teach in the Primary School*. London: Routledge.

Doherty, J and Hughes, M (2013) *Child Development: Theory and Practice 0–11*. Essex: Pearsons.

Fisher, J (2010) *Moving on to Key Stage 1*. Berkshire: OUP McGraw-Hill Education.

Hayes, D (2008) *Primary Teaching Today: An Introduction*. London: Routledge.

Jones, R, Boys, R, Cooper, W and Sugarman, I (2008) *Primary Curriculum: Teaching the Core Subjects*. London: Continuum.

Lindon, J (2013) *Understanding Children's Behaviour: 0–11 Years* (Linking Theory and Practice). Oxon: Hodder.

Scholastic (2013) *The National Curriculum in England: Framework Document*. Oxfordshire: Scholastic.

Shurville Publishing and Department of Education (2013) *The 2014 Primary National Curriculum in England: Key Stage 1 & 2 Framework*. Available online at: **www.gov.dfe/nationalcurriculum** (accessed 20/10/2014).

8 Your action plan

Introduction

Your progress review and action plan are two of the key tools to help you successfully achieve your Early Years Teacher Status. As you need to evidence all the Standards and assessment requirements, such as demonstrating your work with each age group, you need to identify any areas where you lack experience or evidence as soon as possible and it is in your progress review and action plan that you will identify these gaps and plan how you will address them.

Many providers will arrange a progress review where you meet with your tutor, mentor or assessor. Together you will look at the evidence you have and identify any gaps in your practice or evidence and draw up an action plan to address these gaps. This action plan enables you to have the experiences you need and enough time to achieve your Early Years Teacher Status successfully. If your provider does not arrange this for you, the information in this chapter will give you the guidance you need to work through this process yourself.

Progress review

At some point in your Early Years Teacher Status programme you will have an opportunity to meet with your tutor, mentor or assessor to look in detail at each Standard and the assessment requirements. Some providers will refer to this process as your 'developmental progress review', but others will have their own name for this. However, whatever name this process is given, it will be designed to help you to evaluate your current practice against the Standards, decide whether you can evidence your previous practice, identify what counts as 'evidence' and plan your next steps.

Each provider will have their own system, but during this review you will be encouraged to think about how you can evidence each Standard and indicator, identify the evidence you already have, and most importantly, identify any gaps in your evidence or practice and plan how you will address these. This review will remind you that you need to evidence all Standards and meet all the assessment requirements before you can achieve your Early Years Teacher Status, so the sooner you identify any gaps, the easier it will be for you to address these in time.

Before you attend this review you will probably be required to complete a form where you evaluate your knowledge and understanding, your experience and your evidence against each Standard and indicator. It is important that you spend as much time as you can on this process as this will help you to understand each Standard and appreciate where your strengths lie and where you need to extend your practice or your knowledge.

This form will not usually form part of your final assessment, so you do not need to worry about making any mistakes in this. Instead you need to focus on using the form as a tool to help you analyse your practice and knowledge and think about how you can evidence these. Initially you will identify how your actions relate to specific indicators, for example, that carrying out a risk assessment relates to health and safety in 7.2. Gradually you will be able to appreciate how you can evidence your actions, for example, through a completed risk assessment form.

It is in the meeting with your tutor, mentor or assessor that you will turn your initial analysis of your skills and understanding into a list of concrete pieces of evidence that address each indicator. This list will be very useful later on when you are preparing for your final assessment.

At some point during this review meeting your tutor, mentor or assessor may complete a second form, based on your discussion, the information in your original form and the action points that you decided on together. On this form they will record everything you need to do to achieve a 'met' and you need to make sure that you remember to address all of these points. It is often during this discussion that trainees decide they need to complete an additional age-related placement to address gaps in their experience with a particular age range.

One of the most effective ways to ensure that you address all the points raised in the discussion is to make yourself a detailed and time-bound action plan. Then, you can plan when and how you will address all your gaps and make sure that you do not forget any of the action points.

Tutors' top tips for getting the most out of your progress review

Here are the top ten tips from tutors who regularly carry out progress reviews:

1. Give yourself plenty of time to prepare for your progress review and to complete the form you have been given.

2. Read the form carefully and if you don't understand anything, ask your tutor.

3. If you have any questions about the assessment process or any individual Standards, make a list of these queries and bring it with you to the progress review.

4. The more you embrace this process, the more you will learn about yourself and the more support your tutor can give you: take time to address each aspect of the form in detail.

5. When you are asked to analyse your knowledge and understanding for each indicator, avoid making general statements, such as 'good' or 'excellent'.

6. Instead, list the subject areas you need to evidence and give examples of where your understanding is strong and where you might need to extend your reading or attend training.

7. Don't be afraid to say you are not confident in a particular area. This process is designed to identify the areas where you are less confident and give you the opportunity to rectify this. If you try to hide a lack of understanding or practice now, it will show up later, when it is too late to address the problem.

8. You need to think about how each indicator relates to your practice and how you can evidence that you do this. For example, you can evidence your involvement in planning in a 'weekly planning sheet,' and how you support children's behaviour for 1.3 through the 'new behaviour management policy with my revisions included'.

9. When your tutor summarises the areas you need to address, use this to create a detailed and time-bound action plan for yourself.

10. Make sure you do not forget to address any of the action points that your tutor suggests.

Top ten action points

Your first task will be to list for yourself all the action points you need to carry out if you are to achieve your Early Years Teacher Status successfully. Here are some of the action points that trainees often add to their action plans.

1. Extend reading on a particular topic, such as the development of babies or learning in Key Stages 1 and 2.

2. Lead a change in the baby, toddler or pre-school rooms.

3. Arrange an additional age-related placement.

4. Attend training on multi-agency working.

5. Support a child with special educational needs (SEN).

6. Shadow an Area SEN co-ordinator (SENCO) or other professional.

7. Carry out actions to promote equality of opportunity and anti-discriminatory practice, such as leading a resources audit.

8. Review setting policies.

9. Lead and mentor colleagues and students and support an Early Years Educator.

10. Act to promote setting-wide good practice, such as encouraging practitioners to visit other settings to observe good practice or set up a peer observation programme.

Your action plan

Once you have identified all the actions identified in the progress review, you can draw up your action plan. Your provider may have a particular format that they suggest you use, but if not, you can adapt the action plan in Table 8.1 or create a format that suits you.

Table 8.1 Action plan

Action point	Standard/indicator/ assessment requirements	Stages in this action	Start date	Date this action must be completed by	Resources or support I will need
Understanding of babies' development	2.2	Extend my reading on babies' development by reading articles in *Nursery World* and texts on reading list	December	January, when my baby placement starts	Reading list Library card Copies of *Nursery World* from my manager
Baby placement: introduce a change	Requirement to work with babies and 1.1, 2.2, 2.5, 3.1, 4.5, 8.6	Visit baby drop-in for examples of good practice. Observe practice in baby placement so I can identify possible areas for development. In staff meeting introduce myself and ask colleagues if there is an area they feel needs developing. Prepare information on area for change to present in staff meeting	December	December: visit drop-in. January: arrange to speak in staff meeting	Placement supervisor to agree I can introduce a change in collaboration with colleagues

What is most important is that you draw up a timeline for each action as some actions will take longer to achieve than others. For example,' developing the garden area' will take longer than 'complete a risk assessment'. If you do not plan when you will achieve each action you risk ending up with a gap in your evidence as, for example, you cannot extend your practice with one age group if you have not given yourself enough time to find a suitable placement.

You may be familiar with designing targets that are SMART – specific, measurable, realistic and time-bound. You may find it helpful to make sure that your actions points are SMART, but what is most important is that you make sure they are time-bound.

Marion, an Early Years Teacher trainee, has added some of her action points to Table 8.1.

Your weekly planner

Once you have completed your action plan, adding dates for when you will start and complete each action, it can be very helpful to transfer this information to your diary, so that you can see clearly which actions you will be carrying out each week. This is particularly important when you are on placement as your time there will be limited.

You will need to provide your manager or placement supervisor with a list of these actions and dates and check whether this is appropriate. For example, you may want to deliver safeguarding training at the next staff meeting, but your manager may have already arranged to focus on something else in this session.

Marion created a weekly planner for her baby placement which she shared with her supervisor. You can adapt her planner, which is in Table 8.2, if this is helpful.

Table 8.2 *Your weekly planner*

Week	Action	Who else is involved	Evidence
Week 1	Visit baby drop-in session	Arrange with baby drop-in manager	
Week 2	Read about babies' development	Visit the library	
Weeks 3 and 4	Christmas break and reading about babies' development		Reflections in journal
Week 5	Start placement: speak to supervisor about introducing a change: observe a session and identify potential areas for development	Meet with supervisor	
Week 6	Introduce myself in staff meeting and discuss colleagues' ideas about potential areas for development	Staff meeting	
Week 7	Present information on developing practice in staff meeting, collaborate with colleagues and decide timeline for introducing changes	Staff meeting	Minutes of meeting
Week 8	Carry out 'before' observations, consult with parents	Involve colleagues in observations	Observations Parent feedback

Action planning – top ten tips

1. You may not be required to review your progress in this way, but a good action plan can be the key to your success.

2. You can use your progress review to evaluate your knowledge and understanding, personal practice, leadership, experience with babies, toddlers and young children, and your evidence for each Standard and indicator.

3. You can only achieve your Early Years Teacher Status if you meet all the requirements, so use your action plan to identify any gaps while you still have time to address them. Some indicators take longer to evidence than others, especially when events occur at set points during the year, such as parents' evenings.

4. To identify whether your evidence is strong enough, read through each indicator and note down where you feel your knowledge and understanding and practice are strong, where there is room for improvement and where there are significant gaps.

5. One way to identify any gaps is to use a chart or traffic lights system. Make yourself a list of the Standards and record next to each indicator either a green light or the comment 'I do this frequently and my evidence is … .', an amber light or the comment 'I only do this occasionally; if I do this more often my evidence will be … ', or a red light if 'I do not do this and need to … '.

6. You may need more than one action plan: a separate, smaller action plan can help you plan your activities during a placement.

7. You might need a short action plan to work out how to approach a Standard or group of indicators you find difficult to evidence, such as those involving working with other professionals.

8. Time is of the essence, so targets, or actions, need to be time-bound. Once you have set a date for an action, you need to put this information in your diary.

9. Once you have completed your action plan make yourself a list of the actions you plan to carry out. Use this to plan when you will carry out each activity and add this to your work diary. Remember you need time to check whether it is appropriate to carry out a certain activity at this time, especially when you are on placement, as you may not be aware that practitioners have other activities planned then.

10. You can then divide the tasks into groups of related actions. Some Early Years Teacher trainees list actions under the headings 'reading and research', 'placement activity', 'actions at work'. Others create lists according to the type of evidence required. They make lists of the activities they can record in their journal, those they need their mentor to observe and those they can ask a witness to record.

Planning for success

Your action plan doesn't need to be limited to the actions that help you meet certain Standards and assessment requirements. You can also use it to help you develop the personal and professional skills you need to support you through your Early Years Initial Teacher Training. In addition it can be helpful to set aside time for organising your portfolio, extending your reading or planning your weekly activity timetables. Any time spent organising yourself early on will pay dividends.

For example, Beth was concerned about her timekeeping so she added to her action plan that in weeks 1 and 2 she needed to read about strategies to support timekeeping. She also felt anxious about her school placement, so added to her action plan for term two that she would read about learning in school and find a book on assertiveness to help her with her confidence.

Rae, another Early Years Teacher trainee, felt she lacked confidence in writing at Level 6 so added to her action plan that she needed to attend the university study skills sessions. Maurice felt he lacked confidence in giving feedback and thought this could have a negative impact on his leadership role and evidence for Standard 8. He added to his action plan that he needed to attend a half-day training session on 'The do's and don'ts of effective feedback'.

Organising yourself – top ten tips

Here are Early Years Teacher trainees' top ten tips on planning for success.

1. Study timetable: create a weekly study timetable that includes your placement hours, lectures and designated time for reading and self-study. Don't forget to schedule in time for relaxation, as you will need this!

2. Extend your reading: reread your analysis of your knowledge and understanding for your progress review and identify areas where you need to extend your reading.

3. Find the right book: set time aside to browse relevant books in your library or online. Find one that you think will be useful and that you will find easy to read.

4. Choose the right time: timetable in periods for reading at a time of day when you still feel fresh, even if it is just 20 minutes on the train on your way to work.

5. Keep your reading focused: identify one section or chapter to concentrate on, study it for a fixed amount of time and photocopy the most useful sections for reference. Two or three days later, revise what you learned.

6. Keep records: make notes on everything you read and keep accurate references in case you want to refer back to your reading in an assignment. Your notes can also evidence your knowledge and understanding and can be cross-referenced to the relevant Standard/indicator, such as 2.2 on child development.

7. Action plan: co-ordinate your study timetable with your action plan so that you schedule in time to prepare for each new activity. Your action plan records the tasks you need to carry out in your setting, for example, setting up a role-play area. Use your timetable to help you plan to research the topic before you introduce it, so that you are well prepared and have knowledge and understanding you can share with your colleagues.

8. Develop your writing skills: if you are anxious about your writing skills, find a simple guide that you can refer to. If you need help with grammar and punctuation, *Eats, Shoots and Leaves: The Zero Tolerance Approach to Punctuation* by Lynne Truss (2003) is an excellent starting point.

9. Find out what online help is available: most universities have a section on their website with tips for writing assignments. You will not be writing an academic assignment for your Early Years Initial Teacher Training, but you may find some helpful tips here.

10. Ask for support: if you need support with your study skills, see if there any university study skills sessions you can attend. If you think you may be dyslexic or dyspraxic, find out if there is support available.

9 Guidance for mentors and mentees

One of the most interesting and rewarding requirements of the Early Years Initial Teacher Training is the relationship between mentor and mentee. It is worth making sure that this relationship is as good as it can be and the information in this chapter will help both you and your mentor to make the most of the time you have together.

In the first section of this chapter on guidance for mentees, you and your mentor will find answers to commonly asked questions on choosing your mentor and managing mentoring sessions. The second section, on guidance for mentors, looks at how a mentor can support a mentee to meet all the requirements of the Early Years Initial Teacher Training. Both sections look at the information that the mentee needs to provide for the mentor and the skills and aptitudes both mentee and mentor need to foster.

Guidance for mentees

Here are some common questions and answers you might find helpful. They will help you to understand the role of the mentor and appreciate how you can help your mentor to support you.

What is a mentor?

A mentor is a person who gives help and advice to someone who is less experienced. The original Mentor was mentioned in Homer's *Iliad*. He was the person to whom Odysseus entrusted the education of his son, Telemachus, while he was away fighting the Trojan War. Your mentor will be someone who will help you in working towards your Early Years Teacher Status. Your mentor will support you in setting appropriate goals and expectations, maintain ongoing and regular contact with you, support you to develop your reflective practice and help you to identify and solve problems for yourself.

Your mentor will offer regular face-to-face, telephone or email support and make sure that appropriate opportunities are available to you so that you can meet all the Standards, such as those involving contact with parents and other professionals.

What are the skills of a good mentor?

A good mentor is:

- a good listener who will give you constructive advice and feedback;
- approachable, supportive, enthusiastic, trustworthy and respectful;

- respectful of confidentiality and has clear expectations and boundaries;
- willing to share time with you;
- able to help you apply what you are learning;
- willing to ask open questions, encourage you in your reflective practice and explore difficult issues with you;
- prepared to support you in developing your work with each age group and taking a leadership role within your setting;
- not going to not teach you, but will help you to learn.

Who shall I choose to be my mentor?

The first decision you make will be who to choose as your mentor, so it is worth taking time to think about the support you will need and who can best provide this. One consideration is that your mentor needs to be someone who knows your work well, otherwise it will be difficult to discuss your practice in any detail with that person.

Another important consideration is whether this person is your line manager. Most mentoring relationships work best when they do not involve line management relationships. In a small setting you may have less choice, so you and your mentor will need to be clear about when they are acting as your mentor and when he or she is acting as your manager.

If you are a child minder, you might want to think about working alongside another practitioner who might be prepared to act as mentor. If you are a manager, you can ask your deputy to mentor you and this can be a very interesting experience for you both. You can also ask for support from outside your setting, for example, from a local authority advisor you work closely with.

When do we meet?

Your provider may suggest how often and for how long you need to meet with your mentor, though this is something you usually need to negotiate with your mentor. Usually half an hour a week or an hour a fortnight is an appropriate amount of time, although you may prefer an alternative arrangement if this suits you both better. However, if your mentor regularly observes your practice, these sessions will take longer. You do need to bear in mind that your mentor is a busy person who is prepared to share time with you, so you need to be reasonable about the amount of time you request.

What is most important is that you meet regularly so you can plan ahead and know what you will address in each session. Arranging regular times to meet ensures progression and continuity, but you do need to be flexible enough to respond to any last-minute changes to plans that are inevitable in a busy nursery.

Where do we meet?

You will need to arrange a quiet and private space for your meetings with your mentor, but you can be flexible about where and when you meet. For example, some

Early Years Teacher trainees prefer to communicate with their mentor through email or Skype. Some mentees have found that meeting outside their setting helps them reflect on their practice from a slightly different perspective.

What ground rules will we need?

It can be very helpful to discuss ground rules with your mentor before you start to meet. Your responsibilities include being punctual and reliable and that you accept that your assessor cannot give you answers or do your work for you. It is your responsibility to plan what you need to discuss in each meeting so that you use the time well.

In return, your mentor will meet regularly with you and listen to and support you, ensure that you have the experiences you need to meet all the Standards and requirements, and help you explore your understanding of an aspect of practice and explore any issues you are finding difficult. Your mentor cannot read or mark any of your assignments.

What does my mentor need to know?

You need to make sure that as early as possible you give your mentor information on the organisation of your Early Years Initial Teacher Training, and an overview of the Standards, the age range requirements, the role of leadership and personal practice and the assessment requirements.

Your mentor will be able to support you better if you can present this information clearly and concisely and as soon as possible. You may need to adapt and simplify the information you receive from your provider and draw your mentor's attention to the tasks you need to carry out, especially if they fall outside the remit of your role.

You are likely to find that as you progress through your Early Years Teacher training the issues you need to discuss with your mentor change, so it is up to you to make sure that your mentor understands the process and what you need to focus on at each stage. If you help prepare them for this process, they will be better able to help you.

What can I expect from my mentor?

Your mentor is there to give you support and encouragement at a pre-arranged time and to act as a sounding board if you need to explore a particular issue, for example, to extend your understanding of systematic synthetic phonics activities that are appropriate for toddlers.

Your mentor can help you explore issues and find solutions to your queries, but cannot provide the answers. Your mentor cannot mark your assignments or allow you to work on them during your work or placement hours.

How can I prepare for each mentor session?

You are asking your mentor to give up time for you so you need to make sure that you use this time well. Prepare one issue to discuss in each session and be clear about why you need to discuss this and what you want to come out of the discussion.

It is your responsibility to decide on the content and purpose of each session and you may find that as you progress through your Early Years Initial Teacher Training you need to use your time with your mentor differently. You can use the chart in Table 9.1 to help you prepare for your mentor sessions at each stage in the process. This will help you spend the time together effectively and avoid trying to cover everything in the last few weeks.

Table 9.1 *Planning your mentoring sessions*

When I start my Early Years Teacher Initial Teacher Training I will need support to help me …

When I decide whether I have enough experience with babies, toddlers and young children my mentor can …

When I need to extend my understanding of an area of early years practice, I can ask my mentor to …

When I cannot understand a Standard, I can ask my mentor to …

When I struggle to evidence a particular Standard, my mentor can …

When I think about how I can evidence leadership my mentor can …

When I plan a change in my setting, my mentor can …

When I prepare for my progress review, I can ask my mentor to …

When I have my action plan, my mentor can …

When I reflect on my practice in my journal, I can ask my mentor to …

When I am organising my portfolio and deciding what to include, I can ask my mentor to … .

When I am planning an assignment to help me evidence the Standards I can ask my mentor to …

When I need to be observed, I can ask my mentor to …

When I am reviewing my evidence, I can ask my mentor to …

What makes a good mentee?

The success of the mentor–mentee relationship depends on the skills and attitudes of both the mentee and mentor, so you can have a positive impact on the relationship if you think carefully about your role and responsibilities.

At the start of the mentoring process you need to be able to talk about your expectations and goals for the relationship. Find out what you mentor feels he or she can offer and check whether this matches the support you feel you need. If your mentor's expectations don't match your needs, you need to discuss this.

As mentee you are not a passive recipient of the knowledge your mentor pours into you. You need to collaborate with your mentor, engage actively in your learning and reflect on your experiences (Zachary and Fischler, 2009). You need to be eager to learn and open to advice and to value the time your mentor spends with you.

You need to demonstrate that you value and respect the mentor–mentee relationship by following the ground rules you established together and keeping in touch with your mentor regularly. You need to come to each session well prepared with questions and issues you want to discuss. You need to appreciate that your mentor cannot give you the answers, but can help you explore the issues.

Once you are meeting regularly with your mentor you need to review the mentoring process, and feel able to highlight what is going well for you and what is not working so well. This may seem difficult, but it is this honesty and open communication that is at the heart of the mentoring relationship.

Can I become a mentor?

In Standard 8 you are asked to demonstrate how you lead and support your team and mentoring a colleague can help you to evidence this. The experience of being mentored can help you to think about how you can become a mentor yourself. The questions in Table 9.2 can help you think about becoming a mentor yourself.

Table 9.2 Becoming a mentor

- Who has acted as a mentor for me in the past and what did they do that helped me the most? You can think of anyone who acted as a mentor for you, either in a formal mentoring relationship or because they were someone you respected and saw as a role model.
- What skills and qualities will my mentor need?
- Do I have any of these skills and qualities?
- Are there any ways in which I can use these skills to help others in my setting, for example, by asking 'what if … ' questions?
- I can find out more about mentoring skills by …
- One mentoring activity I can carry out tomorrow is …
- One mentoring activity I can carry out next week is …

Making the most of your mentoring sessions – top ten tips

1. Make a list of all the requirements, tasks you need to carry out and assessment methods for your Early Years Initial Teacher Training and share this with your mentor.

2. Prepare a list of the Standards for your mentor and use it to highlight where you may need support, either to understand the Standard or to gain the experience you need. If you are struggling to understand what you need to evidence for a particular indicator, you can read the chapter on this indicator in this book and carry out one of the activities with your mentor.

3. Review your practice against each Standard and indicator with your mentor so that your mentor can help you identify any gaps and consider strategies to address them.

4. You can use this review of the Standards to draw up an action plan that you can share with your mentor. You need to discuss the timetable for carrying out your actions with your mentor so that any changes you introduce are timed appropriately and fit in with any existing plans for the room.

5. If you need to extend your reading in a particular area, ask your mentor to recommend some reading. You can then discuss what you have read with your mentor to help you look at how to apply what you are learning.

6. Talk to your mentor about how to evidence your leadership so that you demonstrate this in the way that is appropriate for your role and useful for the setting.

7. Discuss with your mentor whether you need to extend your experience with babies, toddlers and/or young children. Your mentor will be able to help you make arrangements for an additional placement within your setting.

8. Discuss with your mentor how learning in the early years supports successful learning and development in school. This will help you to prepare for your school-based placement.

9. Ask your mentor to review the evidence you are planning to submit: your mentor cannot mark your assignments or your portfolio, but can help you identify where the evidence lacks clarity or relevance.

10. Ask your mentor to observe your practice and/or write a witness testimony. You will need to plan which indicators you would like your mentor to evidence, so that he or she can focus on observing particular aspects of your practice.

Guidance for mentors

Firstly, thank you for agreeing to mentor an Early Years Teacher trainee. Your encouragement and support will be invaluable to the trainee you guide.

Your mentee's provider should give you all the information you need on your role as mentor and on the Early Years Initial Teacher Training process. However, if you have any queries, you may find the information helpful in the section on guidance for mentees, above, and there is more detailed information on how you can support your trainee in this section. There is also information on each aspect of the Early Years Initial Teacher Training within this book that you can refer to.

You can find an overview of the EYTS requirements in Chapter 2, information on the progress review and action plan in Chapter 7, on assessment methods in Chapter 4, on placements in Chapters 5 and 6, and on personal practice and leadership in Chapter 10. If you need to help your trainee understand the requirements of a particular Standard or indicator, then the chapter on that Standard/indicator provides tips and activities that you can look at together.

Mentoring Early Years Teacher trainees – top 12 tips

1. Ground rules and when and where to meet

One of your first tasks needs to be to establish some ground rules and look at expectations and goals for the process, as it is easiest to iron out any misconceptions at this stage. You may want to think about issues of punctuality and confidentiality and the responsibility of the mentee to plan what will be covered in each session. If you are your mentee's line manager, you will have to find a way to clarify when you are acting as manager and when as mentor so as to keep these roles separate.

You can choose a time and place to meet that suit you both, but you do need to make sure that the time you offer is regular and reliable. You can choose whichever form of contact is appropriate for you both, and this could be face-to-face meetings, Skype or emails. However, you should expect to meet for approximately half an hour a week or an hour every fortnight with your mentee.

2. Planning each session
Your mentee is responsible for deciding what to cover in each session, and should let you know this beforehand so that you are prepared. Mentees can plan to discuss an area of practice, something they have been reading or how they can gain experience in a particular area, such as working with other professionals.

3. Mentor training
Each provider provides guidance on how you can support your mentee to meet the requirements of their Early Years Initial Teacher. However, you do need to think about your own continuing professional development (CPD), as to help others develop you need to value your own professional development. Many mentors find mentoring supports their own professional development and you may be able to access additional mentoring training, such as online university modules, that can contribute to your own CPD.

4. Early Years Initial Teacher Training requirements and the Standards
You will find it helpful to have an overview of the Early Years Initial Teacher Training requirements and you can ask your mentee to provide you with a list of the Standards and the assessment criteria. You can also ask your mentee to list all the activities and tasks they need to evidence if that would be helpful. For example, they might highlight that they need to work with a child with special needs or support a child through a transition.

It is not your responsibility to know the Standards in detail, but you may find it helpful to form an overview of the Standards, and Chapter 3 on getting to know the Standards can help you with this.

5. Action plan
You can help your mentee identify any gaps in their experience and evidence in relation to the Standards and look at strategies to address these gaps. Mentees need to add these actions to their action plan which they can share with you. Together you can plan a timetable showing which actions they plan to address each week.

6. Mentees on placement
If your mentee is on a temporary placement with you, you need to ask him or her to write down exactly what experiences he or she needs while on placement so that you can plan together when it is appropriate to carry out each activity. Mentees may also need to discuss with you how best to support children in this age group if they have not worked with this age range before. Mentees will make more progress on placement if they can attend team meetings and planning meetings, so you may wish to suggest this.

7. Promoting reflective practice
Mentees need to demonstrate that they are reflective practitioners so their discussions with you can evidence their reflective practice. They may reflect on these discussions in their journal or you can refer to your mentee's reflective practice in a

witness testimony. You can also provide evidence that evaluates your mentee's practice in relation to all or some of the Standards in a witness testimony.

8. Supporting your mentee's evidence

Although you cannot mark mentees' work, you can support them to prepare their evidence in other ways. For example, you can help trainees check that the documents they include in their document portfolio clearly demonstrate their own practice and are signed. You can also help your mentee to appreciate that one document can evidence several Standards.

9. Observations

You can provide evidence for mentees when you observe their practice. Your mentee's provider may ask you to carry out observations that are either formative or summative, i.e. that assess either ongoing progress or progress made by your mentee at the end of the programme. In both cases your mentee's provider will give you guidance on how to cross-reference your observations to the Standards.

Some providers will ask mentors to grade a trainee's practice against each Standard and/or indicator. They will provide you with detailed guidance and information on what strong, adequate and weak evidence would look like for each indicator. These descriptions are referred to as level descriptors.

If your mentee is a member of your staff, you will probably also want to use your observations to develop that person's practice and this will be very helpful for him or her. You can discuss each observation with your mentee and look at how this helps them to evidence a particular Standard or whether it identifies a gap in practice that they need to address.

10. Leadership requirements

Your mentee needs to demonstrate leadership for Standard 8 and support practice with babies, toddlers and pre-school children. It will be very helpful if you can support mentees in demonstrating leadership, even if leadership is not part of their job description. They will need to think about using a range of appropriate facilitative and collaborative leadership styles, and you can find information on this in Chapter 10, on understanding 'personal practice' and 'leadership'. You might find it helpful to read this chapter and discuss it with mentees to help prepare them for their leadership role.

11. Using this text

You can use the information in this book to support mentees if they struggle, for example, to understand assessment requirements or how to use their journal, prepare for placement or put together a document portfolio. If mentees find it hard to understand a particular standard or indicator, you can suggest they look at the appropriate chapter in this book for an explanation of the indicator and activities to help them evidence this.

12. Mentoring and coaching skills

There is much that has been written about mentoring and coaching and you might find it helpful to read further on this topic. You might also wish to read about active listening and reflective practice. There are many general introductory guides to mentoring and coaching skills available, but Alison Robin's (2006) text looks specifically at

Mentoring in the Early Years. The top 12 tips below can also help you to extend your mentoring skills.

Mentoring skills – top 12 tips

1. Establish the parameters of your relationship
According to Kram (1988), every mentoring relationship progresses through a series of stages known as initiation, cultivation, separation and redefinition. The initiation stage is important as it establishes the foundations for the later stages. Spending time establishing open communication and setting goals and expectations together at this early stage can have a positive impact on the effectiveness of the mentoring relationship over time.

2. Identify the qualities of a successful mentor–mentee relationship
According to Allen and Poteet (1999), successful mentor–mentee relationships establish open communication, provide reciprocal feedback and trust, set goals and expectations whilst appreciating constraints, allow mistakes, demonstrate flexibility and promote work on common tasks. Successful mentor–mentee relationships are open and comfortable, and both parties care for and learn from each other.

3. Be prepared to spend time helping someone
You need to have the desire to help someone and be willing to spend time with that person and remain positive even when you are under pressure yourself.

4. Focus on your own professional development
You need to be motivated to continue developing and growing yourself if you are to help others to develop and grow.

5. Build your mentee's confidence
You need to have a confident and reassuring manner, so that you can support mentees when they lack confidence whilst helping them identify areas for development. You need to be able to challenge mentees in a way that is non-threatening and helps them look at a situation from a new perspective, as an important part of your role is to build both confidence and competence.

6. Ask open questions
The key to supporting your mentee is to ask the right question at the right time. You need to ask questions that help mentees find the answers themselves. You can ask open questions or more direct questions that offer several answer options. Then you can ask mentees why they chose that particular answer.

7. Listen actively
When you listen actively you can observe your mentee's body language and maintain eye contact. This will help you see which topics are difficult for the mentee to discuss. Active listening shows that you value what your mentee has to say and he or she will appreciate that you listen without interruption and judgement.

8. Provide feedback
You need to provide feedback that accurately and objectively summarises what you've heard, and interprets what you have heard in a way that shows that you understand

what your mentee was thinking and helps that person to see a situation from another perspective. You can also choose what to focus on in your feedback as you don't have to cover everything at once.

9. Set regular mentoring meetings

Although there will be times when you have to postpone a meeting due to circumstances that are out of your control, arranging a regular time to meet can be very helpful as you will find that continuity builds trust and respect and leads by example. Although you will foster an informal atmosphere in the mentoring sessions, you need to make the arrangements with formality and professionalism. If you can, try to meet away from the workplace, as a change of environment can help mentees to look at their situation from a new perspective.

10. Establish procedures for your meetings

If you establish some procedures for each meeting, such as introducing agenda items or performance goals, the sessions will be more successful as one of the most common reasons why mentoring fails is that there is a misunderstanding about what is expected.

11. Be honest and open

Without honesty, the mentoring relationship will not succeed. You do need to discuss any concerns you have, but do this in a way that encourages mentees to challenge themselves and does not undermine their confidence.

12. Focus on sustainable improvements, not quick fixes

You cannot address all areas for development in one session and you don't have to give immediate answers to a problem. Your role is to help your mentee explore one issue at a time and learn how to approach similar problems in the future.

10 Understanding 'personal practice' and 'leadership'

Introduction

What makes achieving your Early Years Initial Teacher Training so different from other Early Years programmes is that you have to demonstrate both your own practice and how you lead and support your colleagues.

To do this well, you need to understand what is meant by 'leadership' and 'personal practice' in this context.

- *Personal practice* is everything you do to meet the needs of the children, such as following Early Years Foundation Stage (EYFS) requirements and your setting's policies and procedures.

- *Leadership* is the way in which you support your colleagues to develop their practice. This can include asking questions, modelling new activities, mentoring students and staff and leading a staff training session or appraisal.

- *Leadership* is also how you introduce changes. This includes changes to the organisation of the setting, such as planning systems, and physical changes to the environment, such as creating an outdoor area for babies.

You need to have a clear understanding of the difference between the two concepts. For example, leading an activity does not count as *leadership*; it is an example of *personal practice*. However, if you were *modelling* a new activity for a colleague, then it is *leadership* and *personal practice*.

If you have management responsibilities some of your role is *leadership* and other aspects are *management*, so you need to understand the difference between the two. For example, checking the rotas is *management*, but helping staff understand the EYFS ratios requirements is *leadership*. We will look at this in more detail in the section on understanding leadership and management, below.

To achieve your Early Years Initial Teacher Training you also need to be clear about what to evidence. In the following section on 'Understanding personal practice' you will explore the personal practice you need to evidence in relation to the Standards, where you can evidence it and how. Similarly, in the sections on 'Leadership', and 'Staff development opportunities' you will identify how to evidence your leadership.

Understanding 'personal practice'

Personal practice refers to your work with individual children and groups of children and how you follow setting policy and procedure. For example, it includes carrying out an observation, attending staff training, planning a group activity or completing a risk assessment or profile book.

You will need to evidence personal practice in Standards 1–7 and parts of Standard 8. Read through these Standards and identify the actions that you carry out that demonstrate your personal practice in relation to a specific Standard/indicator. If you are a manager, this activity will help you identify whether you need to extend your personal practice.

ACTIVITY 10.1

Personal practice evidence checklist

If you want to achieve your Early Years Initial Teacher Training you have to plan carefully. You need to read the Standards and identify any gaps in your personal practice and plan in advance how you will address them.

Some gaps will take time to fix. For example, Standard 5.5 asks you to Support children through a range of transitions, so you will need to plan in advance to work with the pre-school children when they prepare to transfer to school.

If you are a manager or child minder or run drop-in sessions, this activity will be particularly useful. Debbie, who is a room leader, has added her comments to the chart in Table 10.1.

Table 10.1 Identifying gaps in personal practice

Standards	Experience	Evidence
1 Set high expectations which inspire, motivate and challenge all children	I am room leader so am responsible for overseeing weekly plans, organising the room and garden and planning projects that meet my key children's interests, e.g. bus project and role-play area. I encourage team members to have high expectations of all children	My display on Early Years Foundation Stage areas of learning in the garden. My plans for bus project and role-play area. My profile book entries for child 'P'. Minutes of staff meetings. *I need evidence of motivating children
1.1 Establish and sustain a safe and stimulating environment where children feel confident and are able to learn and develop	I introduced garden risk assessments. Promoting healthy-eating project. Circle time activities to promote children's confidence. Involving children in planning. Projects based on children's interests	Completed risk assessment forms. Peer observation of circle time. Reflection in journal on children and planning. Bus project planning notes and observations
1.2 Set goals that stretch and challenge children of all backgrounds, abilities and dispositions	Observations and next steps for all my key children, including 'B' with special educational needs, 'J' from Roma family, and 'S' who learns best through 'hands-on' exploratory activities	Observations Profile books Individualised education plan

Draw a chart in your journal similar to Table 10.1 and use it to:

- List the Standards and indicators in the first column.

- Use the second and third columns to assess your experience and evidence against each Standard and indicator.

- Identify any gaps in your practice or evidence.

- Make an action plan to address these gaps.

Addressing gaps in your practice – top ten tips

In Table 10.1, you identified any gaps in your personal practice, such as supporting children through transitions. Once you have identified a gap, you need to plan how you will address this. These top ten tips will help you approach this methodically and you can find further information in Chapter 8, on your action plan.

1. Know where you are going
You can't tackle gaps in your evidence unless you know exactly what they are. Activity 10.1 and Table 10.1 will help you do this.

2. Be specific
You need to be specific in two ways. You need to be clear which aspect of a Standard you need to meet; then you need to create very specific tasks or steps to ensure that you address that gap.

3. Break large tasks into manageable chunks
If your aim is to support children through transitions, break this down into small achievable steps.

4. Create milestones
Once you have a clear picture of what you need to achieve, you can identify the steps and the timescale. If you have identified a set of small steps, set yourself a milestone for the completion of each task.

5. Make a timeline
The key to an effective action plan is the timeline. Record every milestone on your timeline alongside a proposed completion date. Make sure you stick to your deadlines, otherwise you may run out of time.

6. Create a visual representation of your plan
You can use a flow chart, a timeline, a chart or a spreadsheet, which ever is easier for you.

7. Share your timeline with your team
If you are evidencing your personal practice on placement, make sure your new colleagues know what you need to be doing and when.

8. Make sure that anyone who is involved in these tasks with you knows the schedule and what their responsibilities are

You cannot expect your colleagues to work alongside you and support you in your actions if they do not know what their responsibilities are.

9. Take some action every day to achieve your milestones

Do not deviate from your plan; however, you can revise it when you need to. If you need to revise your plan or change the date for an action, you can do this as long as you do not give up on the action.

10. Celebrate each time you achieve a milestone!

Examples of personal practice

Here are some examples of personal practice that you can reference to specific indicators to help you understand how an activity can evidence your personal practice.

- Follow health and safety procedures, including risk assessments, accident forms and ensuring all visitors sign in.

- Follow safeguarding procedures to act to protect a child from harm.

- Conduct regular observations of key children and use them to inform your planning.

- Plan next steps based on children's needs and interests.

- Work closely with professionals from outside the setting to support a child with special educational needs (SEN).

- Plan and set up activities indoors and outdoors that reflect EYFS requirements.

- Provide healthy snacks.

- Create a timetable that is flexible and responsive to individual children's needs.

- Communicate appropriately with children, demonstrating that you are listening carefully, and engage in sustained shared thinking.

- Model appropriate, positive behaviours.

Evidencing your personal practice

Now that we have looked at the personal practice you need to evidence (Table 10.1), and identified any gaps in your practice (Table 10.1 and your action plan in Chapter 8), we can think about how you will evidence this. We will look in detail at how to record your evidence of personal practice in an assignment and how to check that you are evidencing your practice equally across all sources of evidence.

For more information on how to evidence your personal practice in your reflective journal, document portfolio, observations and witness testimonies, see Chapter 4 on assessment methods and the 'evidence' section at the end of each chapter on the Standards.

Referencing personal practice in your written assignments

An assignment is one of the most useful sources of evidence for personal practice. It enables you to highlight your strengths and your reflective practice in detail, explaining 'why' you acted in this way as well as 'what' you did and 'how' you did it. Even if your provider does not require you to write an assignment, you might choose to write one as this is such an effective way to evidence your practice.

Where you describe an example of your personal practice, you will write '(P)' at the end of the sentence, to alert your assessor to the fact that this is a good example of personal practice. You will also identify which Standard you are addressing in that sentence and insert the number of the Standard/indicator next to your 'P' symbol.

For example: 'I checked the list of children with food allergies before choosing which ingredients to use in the cooking activity (P, S7.2).'

You will use a similar system for recording examples of your leadership, with the symbol (L) representing 'leadership'.

For example: 'C said she was not confident speaking in the meeting between the parents of J and the SENCO, so we arranged that I would lead this meeting and she could shadow me. We talked about her concerns and practised ways she could lead the conversation in the next meeting (8.3, 8.4, L).'

Tracking your personal practice and leadership across the five sources of evidence

You will be able to evidence your personal practice across all sources of evidence, including your assignments, reflective journal, document portfolio, witness testimonies and observations and any other methods that your provider allows.

When all your evidence is assessed at the end of your Early Years Initial Teacher Training, you assessor will use a chart to track your evidence across the different sources. This will give your assessor an overview to help him or her see whether there are any gaps in your evidence and to check whether you have a balance between personal practice and leadership across your evidence.

If this is so useful for your assessor, why not use this yourself?

You can create a simple chart (Table 10.2) and use it to record where you evidence personal practice (P) and leadership (L). You then have a visual representation of your evidence and can make a judgement as to whether it is sufficient.

Debbie has added her comments to Table 10.2 to help you start.

Table 10.2 *Tracking your evidence*

Standard	Written assignments	Journal	Observation	Document portfolio	Witness testimony
1.1 Establish and sustain a safe and stimulating environment where children feel confident and are able to learn and develop	L: I will describe how I introduced a sensory room for babies and led a ten-minute session in staff meeting about why sensory rooms are important	L: I reflect on how I led the developments of the sensory room and changes to the garden area	P: I will be observed leading a session in the sensory room and praising the children, to help them develop their confidence	L: notes from INSET day where I led training on planning for EYFS areas of learning outdoors	P: Ask my manager to describe how I follow health and safety procedures
1.2 Set goals that stretch and challenge children of all backgrounds, abilities and dispositions	P: In my assignment I will describe how I differentiated the cooking activity	P: Reflect on how I use the Profile Books for my key children to help me set challenging goals	P: I can be observed leading a cookery activity and my plans will show how I have differentiated the activity	P: Copies of my observations and next steps for key children	Ask my colleague to describe how I set goals for my key children
1.3 Demonstrate and model the positive values, attitudes and behaviours expected from children					

INSET, in-service training; EYFS, Early Years Foundation Stage.

Understanding 'leadership'

To achieve the leadership requirements of Early Years Initial Teacher Training you will need to evidence leadership. Leadership refers to your role in supporting staff development and reviewing and extending practice within your setting. You will need to demonstrate your leadership role in your evidence for Standard 8, but you can (and should) evidence leadership in relation to other Standards as well, as this will strengthen your evidence. For example, if you deliver training on safeguarding this will evidence your knowledge and understanding of child protection procedures for 7.3 as well as your support for staff development for 8.5.

However, you need a good understanding of the meaning of leadership in this context, particularly the differences between leadership and management, and leadership and personal practice. For example, leading an activity is an example of personal practice, not leadership, unless you are modelling the activity for a colleague. If you are a manager, you only demonstrate leadership when you support staff development and promote good practice.

Leadership in your Early Years Initial Teacher Training is about how you inspire and support your colleagues to develop their own practice, whereas *personal practice* is about how you engage with individual children and groups of children.

In this section we will look first at understanding what is meant by leadership within your Early Years Initial Teacher Training and then look in detail at how you can evidence this.

Introducing a 'change'

Some providers will encourage you to evidence your leadership through introducing a change. These changes can relate to either practice within the setting (for example, a new planning system) or the physical organisation of the setting itself (for example, changes to the book corner). You will need to demonstrate how you work co-operatively with colleagues, share your rationale for the change and support colleagues to develop their practice.

Defining 'leadership'

ACTIVITY **10.2**

Definitions of leadership

If you are to demonstrate effective leadership skills, you need to appreciate what it is that makes a good leader. Ask yourself these questions:

- *Can you name someone who you think is a good or great leader?*
- *What is it that that person does that makes him or her so good or great?*
- *Can you define what 'leadership' is?*

Leadership is an elusive quality, so here are some definitions you can use to help you visualise what leadership means for you.

> *Leadership is like the Abominable Snowman, whose footprints are everywhere but who is nowhere to be seen*
>
> (Bennis and Nanus, 1985)

> *A leader is best when people barely know that he exists, not so good when people obey and acclaim him, worst when they despise him … a good leader, who talks little, when his work is done, his aim fulfilled, they will all say, 'We did this ourselves'.*
>
> (Lao Tzu, Chinese founder of Taoism, author, sixth century BC)

> *A leader shapes and shares a vision which gives point to the work of others.*
>
> (Charles Handy, 1992)

> *A leader takes people where they want to go. A great leader takes people where they don't necessarily want to go, but ought to be.*
>
> (Rosalynn Carter, US First Lady, b. 1927)

> *As we look ahead into the next century, leaders will be those who empower others.*
>
> (Bill Gates)

> *Leadership and learning are indispensable to each other.*
>
> (John F. Kennedy)

'Leadership' methods in your Early Years Initial Teacher Training

Now you have formed an idea of what makes good leadership, you need to think about what good leadership looks like in this context. There are two components to your leadership: the leadership methods you use, which we will look at here, and your leadership style, which we examine later on. You leadership will be most effective if you think about both these components and choose strategies that are appropriate for each situation.

If you read Standard 8, you will see that you are asked to evidence leadership using a range of methods, such as modelling activities and mentoring colleagues. Your evidence of leadership will be strengthened if you can demonstrate your confidence in using a range of these leadership methods.

Here are several common leadership methods to give you some ideas:

- mentoring new members of staff and students;
- leading appraisals;
- leading in-service training (INSET);

- delivering a short piece of training in a staff meeting;

- identifying and supporting colleagues' training needs;

- asking questions, such as 'what if … ?';

- modelling new activities;

- providing prompt cards, such as sample open questions above the role-play area;

- enabling colleagues to shadow you, for example, during a parents' evening;

- being available for colleagues to ask you questions when they need support;

- reading up on good practice and sharing these ideas with colleagues.

ACTIVITY 10.3

Personal leadership audit

This activity will help you identify your leadership strengths and any aspects of leadership you need to develop.

You can use your answers to these questions to help identify action points which you can add to your action plan (see Chapter 8 on your action plan).

- *What do you know about different leadership styles and methods?*

  You may need to find out more about leadership methods and styles and can add this to your action plan.

- *What do you know about the Standards and leadership?*

- *In what areas of your work or personal life do you already demonstrate leadership skills?*

  What skills are you using when you are most effective?

- *If you demonstrate effective leadership skills in your personal life, can you transfer these skills to your working life?*

- *If you find the concept of leadership difficult, what is it that holds you back from taking on this role?*

- *Are there any personal barriers you need to overcome, or are there practical issues to deal with before you can take on a leadership role, for example, if you are on placement?*

- *If you demonstrate leadership skills in your personal life, for example, when you support your children, what holds you back from transferring these skills to the workplace?*

- *In what areas do you feel you need to develop your leadership skills and why?*

- *What specific skill would you like to develop first?*

(Continued)

ACTIVITY 10.3 *continued*

- *What strategies could you use to do this?*

- *What leadership methods and styles do you prefer to use or use most frequently?*

  For example, do you prefer to mentor colleagues and students/support colleagues one to one or in groups/model good practice/lead staff development/ask coaching questions, such as 'what if … '?

- *Which method do you feel least comfortable using? Can you identify why?*

- *Can you choose one new leadership method to try this month?*

  If you reflect on this experience in your journal, you will learn more from this, and it will evidence your leadership skills and that you are a reflective practitioner.

Leadership on placement: overcoming obstacles

In Activity 10.3 you may have identified that you find some leadership methods daunting or that you feel uncomfortable taking on a leadership role if it is not part of your job description. These are really common concerns, especially if you are new to early years or are starting a placement.

It can be hard to imagine taking on a leadership role if you are working with colleagues who you feel are more experienced than you are, but there are strategies that can help you. The most helpful strategy is to think about how best to phrase what you want to say. If you read the section on leadership styles, below, you will see how you can adopt a collaborative approach through the language you choose. Your role is not to tell colleagues what needs to be done, but to foster a reflective environment so that the team can engage in discussions about their provision.

For example, you might find that asking coaching questions gives you a 'way in' to your leadership role. We are aware of the benefits of asking children open questions, but this can be just as useful with colleagues. If you find some information to read on asking coaching questions it will help you to think about asking prompt questions. For example, if you feel something needs changing, you could ask: 'what if … ?'

Preparing for your leadership role on placement

If you are starting a placement in a new setting, you need to think about what you can do to ensure that the placement goes smoothly. It can be hard to start a placement when you need to develop your practice and demonstrate appropriate leadership. These tips will help you identify the strategies you can use to make this more manageable.

- Read as much as you can about the age range you will be working with.

- Visit another setting to see examples of good practice before you start this placement.

- Get to know the requirements of the Standards so that you can clearly explain what you need to cover during the placement.

- Make sure each member of staff knows something about what you need to cover during the placement. They can't help you if they don't know what it is that you need to do.

- Think about your confidence and how you convey this through your body language.

- Read up on leadership styles to find one that suits you and is appropriate for this situation.

- Find out about some simple coaching techniques you can use, such as asking 'what if … ?'

For more information, see Chapter 5 on age range requirements.

Leadership styles

You may automatically associate leadership with a particular, directive style. However, there are a range of leadership styles available, and they run along a continuum, so you can experiment until you find a style that suits you.

There have been significant changes in our understanding of leadership over recent years. In the last century the focus was on behaviour-based leadership styles, which relied on rewarding people for reaching goals. This was developed from the work of Skinner and other behaviourists.

Current research into leadership promotes the idea of a leadership toolbox, where you have access to a range of styles, behaviours and traits, and you can choose whichever are most appropriate in each situation.

Tannenbaum and Schmidt and the leadership continuum

The Tannenbaum and Schmidt model of delegation and team development intro-duced the idea of a collaboration continuum. If you have found the idea of exer-cising leadership difficult, this may be because you have preconceptions of what leadership involves. The work of Tannenbaum and Schmidt shows that leadership can be collaborative: it can be those invisible footprints in the snow (Bennis and Nanus, 1985).

Tannenbaum and Schmidt believed in democratic styles of leadership and devised a continuum of *levels of delegated freedom*. If you read through the statements in Table 10.3 you can identify where you are on the continuum and choose an approach that is suitable for a particular situation.

According to Tannenbaum and Schmidt (for more information, see **www.elizabeth jarmantraining.co.uk**), over time, a manager should aim to take the team from the top of the scale down to number 7 and allocate time to foster potential successors from the team to take over from the manager.

Table 10.3 Tannenbaum and Schmidt's levels of delegated freedom

1. The manager decides and announces the decision.
2. The manager decides and then 'sells' the decision to the group.
3. The manager presents the decision with background ideas and invites questions.
4. The manager suggests a provisional decision and invites discussion about it.
5. The manager presents the situation or problem, gets suggestions, then decides.
6. The manager explains the situation, defines the parameters and asks the team to decide.
7. The manager allows the team to identify the problem, develop the options and decide on the action, within the manager's received limits.

For more information see: **www.businessballs.com/tannenbaum.htm.**

Their advice is that this process can take time, so be patient with yourself and your team. Explain what you are doing and why and be constantly aware of how your team is responding and developing.

They also remind us that delegating freedom and decision making to a team does not absolve the manager of accountability.

The Tannenbaum and Schmidt continuum is often shown as a simple graph, as in Figure 10.1.

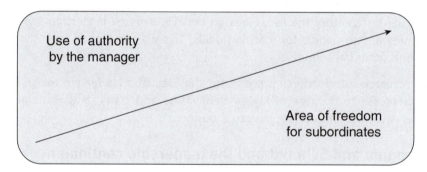

Figure 10.1 The Tannenbaum and Schmidt continuum

ACTIVITY **10.4**

The Tannenbaum and Schmidt continuum

It can be very helpful to identify where you are now on the Tannenbaum and Schmidt continuum and consider where it might be helpful to place yourself in relation to a specific situation and the questions below can help you in this. You can refer to the levels of delegated freedom in Table 10.3 (above) or try to position yourself on the image of the continuum (see above).

- *If you are a manager: where are you on this continuum?*

- *If you are not a manager: what point on the continuum would be a comfortable starting point?*

- *Looking at the levels of delegated freedom in Table 10.3, which approach have you used before?*
- *Which approach is most suitable for you now?*
- *Think about a leadership action you are planning: where would be the most suitable place on the continuum for this particular intervention?*

Goleman: emotionally intelligent leadership styles

Another helpful model of leadership styles comes from Daniel Goleman, a science reporter at the *New York Times*. In his best-selling book, *Emotional Intelligence and Social Intelligence: The New Science of Human Relationships* Goleman (1995) highlights the importance of emotionally intelligent leaders.

He defined emotional intelligence as the ability to manage yourself and others effectively and he listed six styles linked to emotionally intelligent leadership:

1. the coercive leader who demands compliance;
2. the authoritative leader who moves the team towards a vision;
3. the affiliative leader who thinks about the emotional climate;
4. the democratic leader who ensures everyone has a chance to contribute ideas;
5. the pacesetting leader who expects self-direction towards meeting goals;
6. the coaching leader who develops future leaders.

Choosing your own style of leadership

You might find it helpful to review your leadership style in relation to these six styles as well as (or instead of) the model proposed by Tannenbaum and Schmidt.

It doesn't matter what model you use, but it is important is that you think about the strategies you use and decide whether they are appropriate in all situations or whether you need to adjust your approach according to the circumstances. Making a conscious decision to choose the most appropriate style for a situation can also help you to overcome any anxiety you have about demonstrating leadership.

You may notice a resonance between Goleman's emotionally intelligent leader and the role of the Early Years Teacher and Early Years Practitioner whose roles have been to inspire and support their colleagues. You may find it helpful to ask yourself the following:

- How does your role as Early Years Teacher relate to Goleman's ideas about emotionally intelligent leadership?
- Think about a recent experience you have had with a member of staff and try to identify which leadership style you used and why.

89

- Does the style you use depend on the person and situation?

- If so, what can you learn from this?

- Does Goleman's list of leadership styles suggest any additional strategies you can use, for example, when you are on placement?

- If you are to extend your use of leadership styles, will you need any support?

If you explore these questions in your journal, this may help you to evidence your leadership and reflective practice for Standard 8.

Understanding leadership and management

In the introduction to this chapter you were reminded that if you have a management role in your setting, you will need to appreciate the difference between leadership and management in this context, so that you only evidence your leadership role. You might find it helpful to read about the difference between leadership and management. There are several excellent texts available on leadership in the early years and you can find some useful references in the sections on 'Suggested reading' for 8.4 and 8.5.

Early Years Teacher trainees who are managers often find it difficult to separate out their leadership and management responsibilities, but this is important as you only need to evidence your leadership role. The two quotations below and the statements in Activity 10.5 may help you in this process.

> 'You manage things, you lead people.'

> (Admiral Grace Murray Hooper, US naval officer, 1906–1992)

> Management is efficiency in climbing the ladder of success; leadership determines whether the ladder is leaning against the right wall.

> (Stephen R. Covey)

Management is *what* you have to do to achieve the goals and aspirations of your organisation, such as setting up systems and structures and roles and responsibilities.

Leadership is *how* you support and inspire your colleagues and ensure that they are committed to the organisation's aspirations.

Do you agree?

ACTIVITY *10.5*

Leadership or management?

If you have management responsibilities in your setting, you need a clear understanding of which aspects of your role evidence your leadership, and which evidence your management skills and make sure that you only evidence your leadership role.

The questions in this section will help you understand the difference between leadership and management and identify which aspects of your practice you can evidence. Complete the following statements and if you can, record your answers in your journal.

- *When someone is managing me, it feels like …*

  When someone is leading me, it feels like …

- *Management is …*

  Leadership is …

- *The difference between my tasks as a leader and my tasks as a manager are …*

- *My regular management activities are …*

  My leadership activities* are …

*Any activities you list here can be evidenced as part of your leadership role for Standard 8

Leadership methods and strategies

If you are not in a management position you might be anxious about taking on a leadership role, but you do need to do this to meet Standard 8. Even if you are a manager, you might realise that you have overly relied on a few 'tried and tested' methods.

Reading about leadership styles can help you find a style that feels natural and comfortable.

However, you might find it helpful to focus on leadership methods as well, as you can choose a method or activity that feels comfortable for you. These methods range from asking stimulating questions and contributing to staff meetings right through to mentoring and modelling good practice and leading formal staff INSET events.

You can extend the range of methods or strategies you rely on if you:

- find one new method to use this week, one you feel comfortable with so that you build up your confidence;

- write down in your journal what method or strategy you have chosen, why you chose it, and how you will carry out a leadership activity using this method;

- plan to try out a new method every few weeks.

Opportunities for leading staff development

You will find it easier to evidence the breadth of your leadership if you think carefully about the range of opportunities that might be available to you. If you read through the questions below, they may help you identify opportunities for leading practice that you had not previously considered.

- What is your area of expertise?

  This could be something that relates to early years or a personal skill, such as gardening.

- What skills are you most confident using and can you support others in learning these skills?

  These might be practical skills, such as cookery, or relate to an area of early years practice, such as asking open questions.

- Do you have any hobbies you could introduce to the children and model for colleagues, such as craft activities?

- Do you have any ideas about early years practice that you could share with your team?

- Is there anything that a colleague has asked you about? Could you offer that person more support on this topic?

- Does anyone in your team have any skills they could share with the children and model for colleagues, such as dance or yoga?

  Can you encourage them to share their expertise?

ACTIVITY *10.6*

Identify opportunities for leading staff development

In Table 10.4 there is a list of leadership methods or strategies that other Early Years Teacher trainees have used to evidence their leadership. Read through this list and decide which of these methods you could adapt and use in your setting.

Table 10.4 Leadership methods

Leadership methods/strategies	How I can demonstrate this in my setting	Standards this will meet
Share an article or information		
Display information, e.g. a display of safeguarding procedures		
Ask coaching questions, such as 'what if … ?'		
One-to-one mentoring, e.g. of new colleague or student		
Model a new activity		
Support a student		
Lead a change in the environment, e.g. introducing a sensory area		
Introduce a project or scheme, such as Every Child A Talker (ECAT) or a quality improvement scheme		

Leadership methods/strategies	How I can demonstrate this in my setting	Standards this will meet
Support practice within your room, for example, by supporting colleagues in observations and planning		
Introduce a topic in a staff meeting or lead a discussion on, for example, changes to Early Years Foundation Stage		
Lead a short or full-day training event, for example on carrying out the progress checks at age two		
Identify staff development needs, e.g. finding appropriate courses for colleagues		
Lead staff appraisals		
Work with local authority advisor to develop practice		
Address areas for development identified in the self-evaluation form or Ofsted report		

Remember, that you must not introduce a change in practice just to evidence your leadership; it must be relevant to your setting and address an area where you, your colleagues, Ofsted or the self-evaluation form (SEF) have identified a need to enhance practice.

Start with the methods you feel most comfortable with and as you gain confidence, gradually introduce some of the other strategies.

Promoting good practice

You have looked in detail in Activity 10.6 at the strategies you could use to promote good practice within your setting. However, there may be certain issues you need to consider before you can introduce a change in practice. This may be because there is a lack of consensus on what good practice is, or because there are practical considerations such as cost.

In this section we will look at evidence-based practice in early years and any organisational barriers you may experience and suggest some discussion points you can explore with your team or in your journal.

Discussion point: evidence-based practice

We have looked at how you can demonstrate your leadership and explored some of the issues you may face when taking on a leadership role. We now need to consider some other issues that can impact on your ability to lead.

Leaders in medicine, such as senior doctors, can only lead and suggest changes in clinical practice if they can justify these changes using evidence, from either clinical trials or epidemiology, which rely on quantitative or qualitative research such as standardised observations or interviews. This approach is termed evidence-based medicine or evidence-based health care. It can be helpful to hold this model in mind for a moment and ask yourself the following questions:

- In early years how do we use evidence to justify changes in practice?

- Do we define evidence in the same way?

- What types of evidence are available to you?

- How do we reach a definition of good practice and what are the implications of this for your practice as leader?

Discussion point: organisational barriers

We have looked briefly at some of the personal barriers you may need to overcome when taking on a new leadership role, but we also need to think about the organisational barriers you may experience.

- You may plan an excellent training session for colleagues which addresses an area where they requested support, but what if your setting will only provide training during annual INSET events and the focus for these sessions has already been decided?

- What if you feel it is important to revise one of your setting's policies, but your setting is part of a chain of nurseries and changes can only be made at head office?

- What if the changes you wish to promote, which you feel are in the children's best interests, carry a financial cost?

- What if the changes you suggest are rejected as your setting promotes an alternative approach to good practice?

- How can you justify your beliefs and explain where your ideas regarding good practice come from?

- Do you have access to evidence to back up your ideas?

Evidencing leadership

There are Standards where you must evidence leadership, such as Standard 8, and others where you could evidence it. For example, you could evidence your leadership for Standard 6.1, 'Understand and lead assessment within the framework of the EYFS framework' if you led staff training on EYFS and assessment. It will strengthen your evidence if you demonstrate as much leadership as possible. Activity 10.7 will help you to identify and evaluate the evidence you do have and see where there may be gaps in your practice that you need to address.

ACTIVITY 10.7

Identify your evidence of leadership

Make yourself two lists of Standards, one where you have to evidence leadership and the other where you could evidence leadership. Then, identify the evidence you have and any gaps that you need to address. Beth has added some examples to help you start.

You may recognise, as Beth did, that your evidence for Standard 8 can help you to evidence other Standards.

Table 10.5 *Evidence of leadership*

Standards where I have to evidence leadership			Standards where I could evidence leadership		
Standard	My actions and evidence	Gaps in my practice	Standard	My actions and evidence	Gaps in my practice
8.4	'Support and lead other practitioners including Early Years Educators': one-to-one meeting with student to discuss observation methods. Evidence: student's witness testimony	Support for an Early Years Educator	4.1	Mentor student on how to 'Observe and assess children's development and learning'. Evidence: student's witness testimony	

In Activity 10.7 you will have identified that you can evidence your leadership across all sources of evidence, including your assignments, your journal, your document portfolio, witness testimonies and observations. Here are some tips to help you make the most of each source of evidence.

Written assignments

The advantage of a written assignment is that you can record the leadership strategies you use in detail, step by step.

For example, if you write:

'I led a staff development session on EYFS and assessment,'

this tells your assessor almost nothing about the depth of your knowledge or how well you supported your colleagues.

If, on the other hand, you describe your actions and words as if you were writing a film script, your assessor will be able to visualise what you did, said and know. Rae wrote an effective description of her leadership role in an assignment on supporting young children:

C, a new member of staff, came up to me after the staff meeting and said she wasn't sure if she was making observations on her key children in the right way. We arranged that we would spend an hour together to discuss this on the following day.

When we met we spent half an hour observing C's key children together and then compared our written observations. We then looked at these children's profile books and identified some next steps for each key child.

We agreed that next week she would observe the children on her own, but we would still discuss next steps together.

Document portfolio

You can evidence your leadership role in your document portfolio when you include any document that shows how you support staff development and practice. For example, you could include copies of policies you developed or the materials you prepared for a staff development event.

However, you need to examine each document carefully to check whether it actually evidences what you think it does. Read through each document and ask yourself these questions. If you are not sure of an answer, ask a friend to read the document.

- How clearly does this document state what it is that you know or said or did?

- Is it clear that you wrote the document and/or that your words or actions promote good practice?

- If you prepared materials for colleagues, does your evidence show whether your colleagues actually read them, or how you used the materials to support them?

Observation

You can arrange to be observed leading an activity of your choice. Remember that leading an activity with a group of children does not count as evidence of *leadership*, but if you model the activity for a colleague or student, it will evidence *leadership*.

You can also choose to be observed in a mentoring session with a student or colleague and you can also use an activity to showcase any changes you have introduced, for example, by promoting maths and literacy activities outdoors.

You can use your plans for an observation to highlight your leadership role. For example, you can explain why this colleague asked you to model this activity and how you will then support him or her when s/he delivers a similar activity.

You can find more information on using each source of evidence in Chapter 4 on assessment methods.

Some examples of leading changes

Here are ten examples of changes that Early Years Teachers have introduced and used to evidence their leadership. They are not here for you to imitate, as what made these examples so memorable was that the practitioners had identified exactly what was needed in their settings at that time. These ideas are here to inspire you, and to help you think more widely about what is possible and what your setting might need right now.

1. Bringing the outdoors into the baby room
This included an indoors mini-beasts and planting area and filling the sand tray with mud for digging.

2. Treasure baskets, heuristic play and a sensory room
for the babies and toddlers
This practitioner led training for her colleagues on the benefits of treasure baskets, heuristic play and how to use the sensory room.

3. Extending the garden area

This practitioner involved parents in developing the garden and creating different areas for the children. Parents brought in tree trunks to create climbing areas, developed a planting area and built a low-level tree house.

4. Building a garden area

This nursery teacher identified that most children in her class lived in the local tower blocks and had no access to a safe outdoor area. She oversaw the landscaping of a garden area in an old playground space.

She introduced guinea pigs and rabbits for the children to care for and created a large planting area. She ensured that all children had wellington boots and access to low-level outdoor taps so that they could water the garden themselves.

5. Purpose-built baby unit

This nursery teacher identified that many of her children had younger siblings who had no access to early years provision. She worked alongside an architect and designed a purpose-built baby and toddler unit. She recognised that many of the children came from single-parent families, so she recruited a male practitioner to run the unit.

6. Involving fathers

This practitioner recognised that her team rarely had contact with children's fathers and she wanted to encourage fathers to read to their sons to promote boys' literacy skills. She set up a Saturday club for fathers and their children, called Men Behaving Dadly.

7. Communication-friendly spaces

This practitioner attended training on communication-friendly spaces (for more information, see **www.elizabethjarmantraining.co.uk**) and was so inspired that she worked with her colleagues to introduce communication-friendly spaces that the children helped design.

One space was a small cream and brown tent with cushions, hanging mobiles, books and plastic flowers. Another was a large tent that children could choose the focus for and design themselves. The current theme was Spiderman and it contained resources the children had designed and made.

8. Literacy, maths and role play outside

This practitioner was concerned that the boys in her group were not accessing literacy and maths activities indoors so she worked with her colleagues to promote maths and literacy opportunities outside. The current focus was the children's interest in transport.

The children created 'bus station' and 'train station' areas in the garden and used playground chalk to draw the train tracks and bus route. They made the timetables, tickets and money for the role-play area and the staff used these to introduce mathematical language and encourage mark making.

9. Makaton

This practitioner introduced Makaton in the baby and toddler rooms. She ran sessions for staff and parents to teach them songs with Makaton signs that they could share with their children.

10. Rolling snack and free flow

This practitioner identified the need for a flexible approach to setting routines. She introduced rolling snack and organised staffing so as to make free flow indoors and outdoors possible.

She encouraged staff to take advantage of the smaller snack time groups to engage in more one-to-one conversations and led training on how to plan for all EYFS areas of learning outdoors.

Standard 1: **Set high expectations which inspire, motivate and challenge all children**

Introduction

Standard 1 asks you to evidence how you set high expectations for all children and motivate, inspire and challenge them. There are three indicators in Standard 1 that narrow down the context for your *high expectations*. These three indicators, 1.1, 1.2 and 1.3, ask you to evidence how you set *high expectations* in relation to three specific areas. These include how you create a safe and stimulating environment (1.1), set goals that stretch and challenge children (1.2) and model positive values, behaviours and attitudes for children (1.3).

The introduction to the Standards states that: *Early Years Teachers make the education and care of children their first concern and are accountable for achieving the highest possible standards in work and conduct.*

Standard 1, with its focus on the *high expectations* you set, is where you begin to evidence the positive impact that you, as an Early Years Teacher trainee, have on the children in your care. You must evidence how you set expectations and how they inspire, motivate and challenge children. You must demonstrate how you do this for all children, including children of different ages, interests and needs, who have special educational needs (SEN) or a disability.

As mentioned above, Standard 1 includes three supporting statements which you must also evidence. These are the indicators 1.1, 1.2 and 1.3. Your evidence for these indicators will contribute to your evidence for the opening statement of Standard 1, as they enable you to look at your actions one step at a time and explore what it is that you do to motivate all children and set high expectations.

Your evidence must highlight what you do, how you do it, show why you act in this way and evaluate how well you do it.

Understanding holistic assessment

Your evidence for your Early Years Teacher Status will be assessed 'holistically'. This means that your evidence for each Standard will be judged as a whole. You are not expected to evidence every word and phrase in each indicator equally strongly, but to provide evidence that addresses most areas within each Standard in enough detail and depth so that your professionalism can be seen and assessed.

It is advisable to look at each Standard and indicator carefully and attempt to evidence each aspect as well as you possibly can. As you must provide good evidence for every Standard to achieve your Early Years Teacher Status, you will be taking a serious risk if you do not attempt to evidence each aspect of every Standard and indicator.

This is a risk because some of the evidence you include may not be as strong or relevant as you think it is and if you have not provided additional evidence for that Standard or indicator you could be left with an evidence gap which results in you not achieving your Early Years Teacher Status.

Standard 1 as an introduction to the Standards as a whole

It is worth taking your time getting to know Standard 1 well as possible as it is your introduction to the Standards as a whole and provides the context for them all. It sets the scene for all the following Standards through its commitment to safe and stimulating high-quality provision for all children.

If you see how this focus on excellence develops through the Standards, you will begin to identify progression and patterns between Standards and this will make it easier for you to form an overview of the Standards as a whole.

Identifying 'high expectations'

Before you look in detail at the indicators for a Standard, you need to appreciate the Standard as a whole as it provides the context for the indicators. This context is expressed in the opening statement of the Standard.

Looking at the statement as a whole will help you develop a 'holistic' understanding of the Standard, where you identify the main areas and themes that you are to evidence.

Figure S1.1 shows a mind map that, when you work through it, will help you both to form an overview of the Standard and consider it in more detail.

ACTIVITY S1.1

Mind map: 'Set high expectations'

If you read the statement for Standard 1 and use a mind map similar to the one shown in Figure S1.1 you can identify each of the high expectations *that you set.*

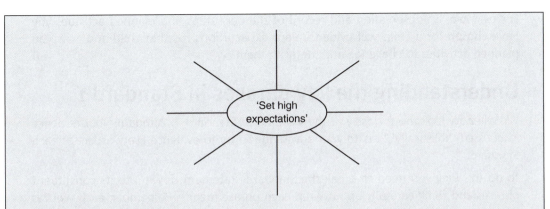

Figure S1.1 *High expectations*

You can use a mind map to identify the range of expectations you have. These high expectations can relate to your setting as a whole, the room that you work in or an individual child.

You can now think about how these expectations inspire, motivate and challenge children. As you must demonstrate how you do this for all children, you can use a table such as Table S1.1 and focus on identifying individual children who you have motivated and set high expectations for.

Table S1.1 *'Inspire, motivate and challenge all children'*

My 'high expectations'	How I 'inspire, motivate and challenge'	My evidence: 'all children'

Identifying actions to evidence for Standard 1

Once you have identified your *high expectations* and how you motivate individual children, you can look at your actions in more detail.

Use the prompts below to record everything you do that contributes to setting high expectations and motivates and challenges children.

I set high expectations when I …

I motivate and challenge children when I …

This will help you identify which of the actions you regularly carry out as part of your routine practice relate to Standard 1.

The next step is to think about where you can find specific pieces of evidence that demonstrate how you have carried out these actions.

For example, an observation and record of the next steps and planned activities you have chosen for a child will evidence your expectations for that child and how you planned activities to challenge and motivate them.

Understanding the key phrases in Standard 1

We will now look more closely at the wording of Standard 1. Although your evidence is assessed 'holistically', it is to your advantage to try to evidence every aspect of each Standard.

To do this well you need to break the Standard statement down into its constituent phrases and think carefully about what each phrase means. Remember, each word is there for a reason.

We will look in detail at this here as this is your first Standard. If you have any difficulties understanding the remaining Standards, then you can look back at this section to remind yourself of strategies that can help you.

One of the simplest strategies you can use is to break up the Standard statement into its constituent phrases and look at what each word or phrase may mean and consider the implications for your evidence (Figure S1.2).

Set high expectations:

which inspire:

motivate:

and challenge:

all children:

Figure S1.2 *Breaking up the Standard statement*

This process will help you identify the questions you need to ask yourself when you evaluate your evidence. Choosing which questions to ask yourself is key to your success as good questions encourage you to evaluate your evidence and identify any gaps in your practice.

If you break the statement for Standard 1 down in this way you will see that you need to do the following:

- *Set* high expectations: this means that you need to *set*, or establish expectations within your setting.

- Set expectations that are *high*: how can you judge whether the expectations that are set are high?

- How can you evidence your responsibility for the level at which expectations are *set*?

- Evaluate your expectations: how can you tell whether they are appropriately *high*?

  Have you lowered your expectations for any child without realising this? If so, what can you do about this?

- Think about how you motivate children.

  Can you provide an example to illustrate how you motivated a child?

- Consider how you know when you have challenged a child.

  How can you evaluate and then evidence this?

- Ensure that you and your colleagues do this for all children.

  You need to evidence how you have high expectations for all children, including children with SEN, and how you motivate all children, including the able children who may not always be noticed.

  How do you ensure that all staff have high expectations and know how to motivate and challenge children?

Discussion points for you and your team

If you are to demonstrate your responsibility for setting *high expectations* across your setting, it may be helpful to explore and evaluate these expectations with your team.

In Standard 8 you must evidence how you reflect on practice and have responsibility for improving the quality of your provision. If you lead a staff discussion on setting high expectations, records of this discussion will help you evidence Standard 8 as well as your leadership role for Standard 1.

Questions to share with your team

Asking yourself and your team challenging questions helps you to clarify your thinking and reflect on your practice. You may have your own questions to discuss with your colleagues and reflect on yourself, but here are some suggestions to help you start this process.

- How do we express our expectations?

  Are they the same for all children?

  Is this a good thing?

  Do we express our expectations unconsciously as well as consciously?

  Are the expectations we express unconsciously the same as those we consciously hold?

- How do we *set* our expectations?

  Do we set expectations through the process of differentiation?

  If we have different expectations for one child, what impact does this have on the others, particularly if this is an expectation around acceptable behaviour?

- Can we identify specific examples of motivating and challenging a child?

  Do we motivate all children adequately?

  Are there some children we find it harder to motivate?

Do we leave some children to motivate themselves, for example, when a child is quiet or self-absorbed?

How do we motivate children with SEN?

If we are following the targets on a child's individualised education plan (IEP), how do we know that the child feels challenged in a positive way?

- What evidence do we, as individuals and a team, have of creating an inspiring environment?

Is there any evidence in your Ofsted report? Or parent surveys or a report from your local advisory teacher?

If any of these documents explicitly mention your actions, then you can use this as evidence for Standard 1.

How can we, as individuals and as a team, move practice forwards from this point?

Cross-referencing evidence: EYFS, Standard 8.6 and your reflective journal

Once you begin to see the patterns between the Standards you will understand how evidence for one Standard may help you to evidence another. This process is called 'cross-referencing' your evidence. To cross-reference your evidence effectively, you need to be aware of the differences as well as similarities so that you can see whether you need to emphasise aspects of your evidence differently for each Standard that you cross-reference.

In the introduction to Standard 1 you were asked to form a picture of the overall meaning of this Standard and you will have identified that it is about creating a high-quality environment that stimulates and challenges all children and relates to all the positive ways in which you affect your environment.

As you will discover as you work your way through the Standards, there are many ways in which they overlap. If you evidence how you provide an environment that challenges all children for Standard 1, you will also provide evidence for 8.6, as in 8.6 you are asked to *reflect on the effectiveness of the provision, and shape and support good practice*. The process of thinking through your evidence for Standard 1 helps you evidence 8.6 as it provides you with a focus for your reflections on the quality of your provision.

You can use your reflective journal (see Chapter 4, Assessment methods, for guidance) to explore some of the issues in the questions below. These questions relate to Standard 1 and its three indicators, 1.1–1.3, as you will evaluate how the environment your provide is appropriately challenging, safe and stimulating for all the children in your care. As mentioned above, they will also help you to evidence 8.5 since by answering these questions you will reflect on practice.

Some questions you might ask yourself are:

- How do I evaluate our provision?
- What are the signs of high-quality provision?

- What does Early Years Foundation Stage (EYFS) say about high-quality provision that challenges every child?

- How do I promote the EYFS principles and how do they relate to Standard 1, for example, that every child is unique and the importance of enabling environments?

- If I have concerns about how stimulating an area of provision is, what procedures do I need to follow to address these?

- This might include using observations to evidence your concern, reading up on good practice, sharing information and ideas, speaking to your manager, especially if there are cost implications, and collaborating with your colleagues to explore possible ways forwards.

- Does my setting have a culture of continuous improvement, and if not, what can I do to foster this?

- What can I do to support the reflective practice of my colleagues?

- Does my setting belong to a quality improvement or assurance scheme and if so, how does this relate to the requirements in Standard 1?

- If not, is this something we could consider joining?

- Can I work with the local authority advisor to develop stimulating and challenging practice in my setting?

Applying these strategies to other Standards

In this introduction to Standard 1 we have identified several strategies that can help you understand the meaning of Standard 1 and how you can evidence each aspect or phrase within it. You use these strategies again to help you understand other Standards and their indicators, so here is a list of these strategies with suggestions on how to adapt them.

- Think about how you can evidence each Standard holistically, by evidencing your practice in relation to the main themes of the Standard.

  To do this you must look at each statement as a whole and identify all the ways in which this relates to your practice. Activity S1.1 (above), where you follow up an initial mind-mapping activity with a chart to identify your evidence, can help you do this.

  This process helps you to identify your 'holistic understanding' of a Standard and the context it sets for the Standard's indicators.

- You then need to look at each Standard or indicator in detail, to make sure that you can evidence every aspect of it.

  You can list every phrase within a Standard or indicator and identify the ways in which it relates to your practice.

- Read a key phrase within a Standard and ask yourself, 'how do I do this?'

- Identify which Standards overlap and, where you can, cross-reference your evidence.

- Choose prompt questions to help you evaluate your evidence and identify any gaps, for example, 'how do I know when I am doing this well?'

- Use your reflective journal to explore the meaning of any phrases you find difficult to understand and help you identify how they relate to your practice.

- Lead a discussion with your team on one or two of the key phrases or themes within a Standard or indicator. This will help you evidence your leadership for Standard 8 and help you clarify your own thoughts.

Standard 1 and the three indicators, 1.1, 1.2 and 1.3

Each Standard consists of a main statement and a series of bullet points, or indicators, and you need to address both the main statement and each indicator in your evidence. When you read the main statement and the bullet points together, you will form a clear understanding of the Standard and how you can evidence it.

Standard 1 has three indicators and you must evidence each of these indicators at least once. Your provider will tell you more about how you need to do this as individual providers have their own systems.

1. Set high expectations which inspire, motivate and challenge all children

1.1 Establish and sustain a safe and stimulating environment where children feel confident and are able to learn and develop.

1.2 Set goals that stretch and challenge children of all backgrounds, abilities and dispositions.

1.3 Demonstrate and model the positive values, attitudes and behaviours expected of children.

This may seem daunting at first, but if you look in more depth at the three indicators below you will see that they clarify and extend the opening statement and that your evidence for one statement can overlap with another.

It is also helpful to look at the patterns between, as well as within, each Standard as you will see that many statements relate to each other and there is a logic to them. Once you can grasp that logic, you will find it much easier to remember each Standard and recognise when a piece of your work provides good evidence for one of them.

Standard 1.1: Establish and sustain a safe and stimulating environment where children feel confident and are able to learn and develop

Indicator 1.1 revisits the concepts introduced in the opening statement for Standard 1 as you are asked to create a stimulating environment where children are able to learn and develop. However, 1.1 extends the scope of the opening statement as you are asked to evidence how you provide a safe as well as a stimulating environment and promote children's confidence as well as their learning and development. This means that you must look at the quality of the environment you provide, your role in establishing it and how this has a positive impact on children's learning, development and confidence.

As this is the first Standard, we are going to look at 1.1 in more detail than we will for the other indicators, so that you can identify and try out strategies to help you get to know what each indicator requires.

If you read 1.1 aloud to yourself, you will soon see that it is a complex sentence with several clauses. Your first job is to break this statement down into its constituent parts as if you try to evidence this statement as a whole, you may end up overlooking one or two points in your evidence.

In Table S1.2 is a strategy that you can use to identify each phrase in an indicator and how you can evidence this and some examples have been added to help you. However, if you can find another way to identify each phrase that suits you better, then use this method instead.

Standard 1.1 has been separated out into its constituent phrases in Table S1.2. Read each phrase in the box and note down what you think it means, how it relates to your practice and how you could evidence this.

Table S1.2 *Understanding 1.1*

'Establish a safe environment':	I introduced risk assessments for the garden area
'Sustain a safe environment':	I trained my colleagues in using the risk assessment form
'Establish a stimulating environment':	I can show how I developed the construction area so as to involve more girls in construction activities
'Sustain a stimulating environment':	Ongoing observations that I use to plan activities according to children's interests
'Where children feel confident':	
'And are able to learn and develop':	
'Establish a safe environment':	I introduced risk assessments for the garden area
'Sustain a safe environment':	I trained my colleagues in using the risk assessment form
'Establish a stimulating environment':	I can show how I developed the construction area so as to involve more girls in construction activities
'Sustain a stimulating environment':	Ongoing observations that I use to plan activities according to children's interests
'Where children feel confident':	
'And are able to learn and develop':	

Questions to help you plan and organise your evidence for 1.1

We have identified the importance of asking yourself questions to clarify your thinking and reflect on your practice. Below are some questions you can ask yourself to help you identify sources of evidence for 1.1.

These questions will help you identify how each phrase in 1.1 relates to your practice, how you can evidence each phrase and where you can find or record this evidence, for example, in a written assignment.

What is the difference between 'establish' and 'sustain'?

How do you evidence *establish* and *sustain* and how might your evidence for each differ?

If you *establish* a practice, you are setting it up for the first time. For example, you could introduce a risk assessment form for the garden area. A completed copy of the new form and an explanation of why this form was needed could evidence how you *established* a safe environment.

If you *sustain* a practice, you are ensuring that it becomes part of your setting's routine practice and that you and your colleagues regularly adhere to this system. So, if you then wanted to use your new risk assessment form to evidence how you *sustain a safe environment* as well as *establish* one, you would need to describe how you embedded this form into the practice of your setting. For example, you may have trained other staff to use this new form and regularly monitor that it is being completed correctly.

What is the difference between a 'safe' and 'stimulating' environment?

You need to be really clear about the difference between a *safe* and a *stimulating* environment. A *safe* environment relates to health and safety procedures, such as signing in visitors and using stair gates. It can also refer to following safeguarding procedures.

A *stimulating* environment, however, refers to everything you do to promote children's learning and development in line with the EYFS (2014) and 'enabling environments'. It can include, for example, how you create communication-friendly spaces or use your observations to plan activities based on children's interests.

So you need to evidence both *safe* and *stimulating* and the evidence for each looks very different. Evidence for a safe environment could include an accident form you completed, an allergy list you devised and records of a fire drill you led. Evidence of a stimulating environment might include planning sheets and your reflections on the changes you introduced to the environment, for example, by setting up forest school activities or a train station role-play area the children had requested.

How do you evaluate what makes an environment 'stimulating'?

If you are to evidence how you establish a *stimulating environment*, you need to consider how you know whether the children do actually find it stimulating. Here are some suggestions on how you can evaluate and evidence how *stimulating* your environment is.

- Involving children and parents in your planning and evaluation of the environment.

  Can you involve the children in planning and evaluating activities?

  Do you have feedback from parents and children on the quality of environment?

- Seeing the room from the child's point of view.

  Try to go down to the children's level and see what the setting looks like from their height. You can write about what you observe in your reflective journal and then use this piece of reflective writing as evidence.

- Using observation to inform your evaluation.

  You can use an observation to evaluate how stimulating an activity or area of the room is for children. You can observe an area you suspect may be underused using a time sampling or narrative observation to help you evaluate how effectively children use the area. You can then use your journal to explore what this tells you about how stimulating children find a particular activity.

  If you then introduce changes to areas you felt were underused, you can repeat the process of observation and reflection and compare the results to identify the impact of your actions.

How can you evidence how you promote children's 'confidence'?

In 1.1 you are asked to establish an environment *where children feel confident*. You need to consider how you define 'confidence' and then evaluate the impact of the environment that you have established on individual children's confidence. You can adapt the process of observation and reflection mentioned above to help you evaluate the impact of your environment on individual children's confidence. You can also use your own observations of individual children and peer observations of your interactions with children to evaluate the strategies you use to promote confidence.

Any work you do to help children identify and talk about their emotions can provide evidence of promoting children's confidence, as does any evidence you have of involving children in the evaluation of activities and their own progress.

How can you evidence what you do to enable 'children ... to learn and develop'?

This phrase asks you to evidence what you do to help children *learn and develop*. This means you need to evidence how you follow the EYFS (2014) requirements to support learning and development, and how you differentiate your provision to ensure that all children are able to learn and develop.

You can include evidence of planning for specific children and groups of children, and demonstrate how you plan activities that children can succeed in, and that are not too difficult for them to achieve, or too dull or too easy. This is particularly important for children with SEN or disability.

As you must evidence that the environment you provide enables children to *learn and develop*, you need to demonstrate that children do make progress and highlight the relationship between this progress and your actions. For example, observation of a child engaging in an activity you planned for that child may demonstrate how your planning promotes the child's learning. If you observe children taking part in an activity you have introduced, such as planting vegetables, then you can evidence how the stimulating environment you provide supports children's learning and development.

How can you evidence that an environment that promotes diversity support's children's learning and development?

If you want to evidence that all children feel confident and able to learn, you need to show how you promote a positive approach to diversity. Imagine a child who has two Daddies, but does not feel that her family is fully accepted in the setting. Perhaps her key person referred to one of her fathers as 'uncle' or she has been asked to make a Mothers' Day card. How confident and able to learn will she be if she does not feel she is accepted?

Presenting your evidence

You can present your evidence for each Standard in several formats, and the choice of format will largely depend on your provider.

Most Early Years Teacher trainees will be able to evidence their practice in written assignments and case studies, a reflective journal, a document portfolio and a series of observations of their practice that can be completed by peers, a mentor or a tutor. These are the sources of evidence that we will consider in the 'evidence' section for each indicator. If some of these sources of evidence do not apply to you, then you can ignore or adapt the suggestions in that section. You may also be able to include a series of witness testimonies in your document portfolio. We don't look at these in any detail here, but the main point to bear in mind is that your witness needs to have seen your practice often enough to be able to describe examples of your practice in detail.

Your aim is to provide at least two good sources of evidence for every indicator, but you must check this with your provider as different providers have different systems. Even if your provider only requires two sources of evidence for each Standard, for example, rather than two for each indicator, you would be wise to provide additional evidence that relates to each indicator, just in case your evidence isn't strong enough or has significant gaps.

Evaluating your evidence

The evidence you provide will be judged according to its strength and relevance. This means that you need to look at each piece of evidence and ask yourself these questions:

- Does this piece of evidence clearly demonstrate my actions or my knowledge and understanding?

- If it doesn't, can I add a note to explain my actions, for example, to highlight my contributions to a setting policy?

- Am I sure that this piece of evidence matches the indicator/s I have claimed? Does this evidence address the topic of the indicator in depth, or does it just refer to the topic in passing?

- Have I claimed that this piece of evidence meets too many Standards? You only want to cross-reference a piece of evidence to a small number of Standards as it needs to provide evidence that is detailed and in depth for each indicator you claim.

Organising your evidence

As you need to make sure that your evidence addresses all the major themes or topics within a Standard and you don't have too much evidence for one aspect of a Standard and not enough for another, you can use the information on the website on tracking your evidence to help you organise and record the evidence you have for each indicator. This will help you identify any gaps in your evidence and make sure that your evidence covers the breadth of each Standard.

CASE STUDY

Joseph's evidence for 1.1

Here is an excerpt from the journal of Joseph, an Early Years Teacher trainee who has used a list of the key phrases in indicator 1.1 to help him plan and organise his evidence.

Establish

I need an example of how I set up a health and safety system, e.g. accessible allergy lists, and how I made the environment more stimulating, for example, by introducing the baby garden area and quiet corner.

Sustain

I need to record in my journal how I ensure that we all follow health and safety procedures and how I regularly observe the room to check that the setting is stimulating.

Safe

I can evidence how I set up and follow health and safety procedures by setting up a food allergy poster and ensuring new staff are aware of it.

Stimulating

I can include my observations and reflections on the sand area when I observed it over a week to check that the area was stimulating. I can use a case study to talk about how I follow our planning systems to make sure we set out activities that interest children.

Environment

I need to evidence the changes I've made to the indoors and outdoors areas, such as the science table and new book corner display. I can include children's comments on how much they like the new planting area I set up and the observations of child K joining in a group activity (planting bulbs) for the first time.

Where children feel confident

I can ask a colleague for a peer observation of helping child K join in a group activity and of using the persona dolls with child P.

(Continued)

(Continued)

And are able to learn and develop

I can include excerpts from profile books and highlight the children's progression and how I supported them through my planning and include examples of engaging in sustained shared thinking in the new planting area.

Your evidence for 1.1

Written assignments, case studies and your reflective journal

If your provider encourages you to write a series of assignments to help you evidence each Standard, then you can choose the topics for each assignment carefully and plan to evidence every Standard and indicator at least once across all the assignments.

As Standard 1 asks about your practice in relation to *all children*, you need to evidence your work with children of different ages, including babies, toddlers and pre-school children. In each case you can describe the changes you introduced to ensure that the environment was safe and stimulating for that age group.

You can use an assignment or case study to provide examples of promoting health and safety and a *stimulating environment* and show that you have evaluated the impact of the changes you introduce, especially in relation to children's confidence and learning and development. If you also describe the impact of these changes on children's motivation, then you are providing evidence for the opening statement for Standard 1.

If you have written a case study reflecting on your work to support a specific child, you can highlight how you ensured that the environment was safe for this child, how you set up stimulating activities that helped the child develop and learn and engaged with the child to promote confidence.

You can use excerpts from your reflective journal to help you evidence 1.1. If, for example, you carried out a health and safety audit and use your journal to reflect on your findings and identify possible improvements, then this will help you evidence 1.1. If you reflect on your observations of the environment and the impact of any changes you introduced, then this too will help you evidence 1.1.

Document portfolio

You can include a series of work products and other documents in your document portfolio. Here are some suggestions:

- a new risk assessment form you introduced (provide information on how you trained staff to use it and carry out checks to ensure it is used regularly);

- an allergy list you designed;

- a reminder lists you produced for your colleagues on following food hygiene regulations;

- copies of the signing-in sheets you use and of fire evacuation drills you have led;

- your plans for any changes you introduced, a summary of your rationale for these changes and copies of the observations you carried out to assess their effectiveness to evidence how you *establish ... a stimulating environment*;

- notes from any relevant staff training you have delivered, such as sessions on developing children's confidence or creating a safe environment;

- excerpts from a child's profile book if it demonstrates how the environment you established had a positive impact on the child's learning and development or confidence.

Look carefully at each document before you include it to check whether it is clear what your actions were. For example, if you have contributed to a health and safety policy, outline the sections or sentences that reflect your contribution. If you have included a list of children's allergies with photos, add a note to explain that there had been a previous list of children with allergies, but you added the photographs to ensure that agency staff could recognise each child on the list.

Observations

If your sources of evidence include observations you will be able to decide which activity your mentor or tutor will observe you leading and you can choose an activity or area that relates to 1.1. You could be observed:

- leading circle time activities to promote children's confidence;

- working with children in a planting area in the garden that you set up.

Include information on how and why you set up each activity and how it relates to 1.1 in your planning notes, which you can send to your mentor or tutor before the observation takes place. If your setting encourages peer observations, then you can ask a colleague to observe you in an activity that can help you evidence 1.1, for example, encouraging a child to risk assess an activity.

You can also demonstrate any practices you have introduced that *establish and sustain a safe ... environment* and demonstrate the changes you introduced to make the environment more stimulating, for example, by setting up a new baby garden area. You can highlight how you ensure that children feel confident, for example, through circle time activities with persona dolls or through your introduction of key times either in your plans for the activity or in a discussion with your mentor or tutor after the observation. You can demonstrate the impact of your actions on children's learning and development if you then show your mentor or tutor some relevant entries in children's profile books.

SUGGESTED READING

Green, S and Hughes, C (2008) *Protection, Safety and Welfare for the Early Years.* Dulwich: Step Forward Publishing.

Hodgman, L (2012) *Enabling Environments in the Early Years.* London: Practical Pre-school Books.

Miller, L and Devereux, J (2004) *Supporting Children's Learning in the Early Years.* London: David Fulton.

Parker, L (2012) *The Early Years Health and Safety Handbook.* Oxon: Routledge.

Parker, L (2013) *How to do a Health and Safety Audit (Health and Safety for Early Years Settings).* Chiswick: David Fulton.

Thornton, L and Brunton, P (2014) *Bringing the Reggio Approach to your Early Years Practice.* London: Routledge.

Standard 1.2: Set goals that stretch and challenge children of all backgrounds, abilities and dispositions

In 1.2 you are asked to take this process one step further and evidence how you stretch and challenge individual children, including children with different abilities, dispositions and starting points.

This section will help you understand 1.2 in more detail. Adapt the strategies you read about here to suit you best and to help you get to know other Standards.

A mind map for 1.2

As mentioned earlier in this chapter, it can be really helpful to break down each indicator into its constituent phrases. Then you can then note down all the ideas that come to you that relate to each phrase within the indicator to help you understand how it relates to your practice.

Joseph, an Early Years Teacher trainee, has added some of his thoughts to the mind map in Figure S1.3.

You can use your list or mind map to record:

- the key phrases in 1.2;

- what each phrase means to you;

- how each phrase relates to your practice;

- any activities you carry out that provide evidence for a key phrase;

- any evidence you have for parts or all of 1.2;

- any queries that you have or gaps in your practice that you need to address;

- any areas that you need to research further, such as the impact of dispositions on learning.

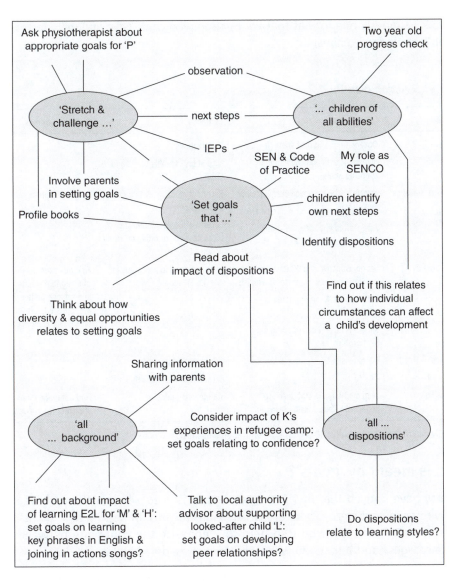

Figure S1.3 *Key phrases in 1.2.*

Creating an action plan

You can use the points you recorded in your list or mind map to draw up a brief action plan for yourself to help you organise how you will evidence 1.2. Your action plan can record the evidence you have, where you can find it and how you will address any gaps in your practice or understanding.

In the mind map shown in Figure S1.3, Joseph reminds himself to check out what is meant by 'dispositions' and how best to support the learning of a looked-after child. If you need more information on action planning, you can read Chapter 8 (Your action plan).

Table S1.3 suggests one format that your action plan could take and includes some of Joseph's reminders to himself.

Table S1.3 Action plan for 1.2

Key phrase	My activities	Evidence	Areas to address
'Set goals'	Observations and next steps Involve parents and children in choosing goals	Observations Next steps in profile books and IEPs	
'Stretch and challenge'	Involve children in setting their next steps Involve parents in choosing next steps Advice from physiotherapist on appropriate goals for 'P'	Record of meetings with parents and physiotherapist Records of goals children choose for themselves recorded on sticky notes	Talk to 'P's physiotherapist
'all backgrounds'	Set goals for 'M' and 'H' to support development of key phrases in English. Set goals for 'K' on promoting confidence. Set goals for 'L' on supporting peer relationships	Observations and next steps for 'M', 'L', 'H' and 'K'	Find out more about impact of being looked-after child and refugee on learning and appropriate goals that focus on social and emotional skills
'all abilities'	My role as SENCO	Completed IEPs Records of meetings with parents	
'all dispositions'	Lead discussion in staff meeting on impact of dispositions on learning	Staff meeting minutes	Find out more about impact of dispositions on learning

IEPs, individualised education plans; SENCO, special educational needs co-ordinator.

What is meant by 'goals'?

You may have noticed that in 1.2 the term *goals* is used when in the early years we usually refer to *next steps*. There are two reasons for this. In Key Stage 1 'goals' is the preferred term, so it is introduced here to emphasise the continuity between EYFS and Key Stages 1 and 2 that you will examine in more detail in 3.1 and 3.3.

The term 'goals' is also used in Development Matters in EYFS (2012), with its emphasis on the *early learning goals*.

- Can you identify any differences between the terms 'goals' and 'next steps'?
- Do you have a preference for one term over the other, and if so, why?

Identifying your evidence for each key phrase in 1.2

In this section we will look at how you can look at each key phrase in 1 and ask yourself prompt questions to help you identify the best ways to evidence each phrase.

The first example below considers the phrase *stretch and challenge children*.

Evidence how you 'stretch and challenge' children
You may consider that you always stretch and challenge children, but for 1.2 you must identify the methods you use and then evaluate and evidence how you do this.

Firstly, you need to identify all the ways that you *stretch and challenge children*. Complete this phrase: I stretch and challenge children when I . . .

Now, think about how you can evidence this. Some suggestions are shown in Table S1.4.

Table S1.4 Stretching and challenging

Evidence of stretching and challenging children
Profile books for my key children that show goals I set with input from parents and children
Profile books with children's evaluations of how interesting they found an activity
Observations and next steps for my key children
Individualised education plan for child 'P'
Goals developed with physiotherapists in report for child 'P'
Discussion on setting goals for child 'L' in staff meeting minutes

If you find it hard to identify evidence for this key phrase, try to ask yourself the following questions:

- Has a colleague observed you doing this and could s/he record this in a witness testimony?

- Do your key children's profile books demonstrate how you do this?

  If the profile book records a child's progress, does it explicitly highlight how your input had an impact on that child's learning?

- What tells you that a child found a goal challenging and is this something you can record or measure?

  For example, can you monitor a child's level of engagement during an activity you planned to support that child towards a specific goal?

- Can you analyse your observations of your key children to help you identify which of the goals you set effectively stretched and challenged a child?

Evidencing 1.2 if you are a manager
If you are a manger and do not work directly with any key children, you may find it difficult to evidence how you *set goals* for individual children for 1.2.

You may need to complete a placement to build up experience that you can then evidence for 1.2. For more information on deciding whether you need to take on a placement, you can look at Chapter 6 (Preparing for placement).

Evidence how you set goals that stretch and challenge children of 'all backgrounds'
In Standard 1 you are asked to *challenge all children* and in 1.2 you are specifically asked to evidence that you stretch and challenge *children of all backgrounds, abilities and dispositions*. This means that you also need to provide examples that demonstrate how you set goals that stretch and challenge children and highlight how you take into account their different backgrounds, abilities and dispositions.

Remind yourself to provide evidence for each of these three categories, perhaps by placing a reminder in your action plan for this Standard. However, before you can evidence each category you need to check that you understand each term well enough that you can reflect on their potential impact on a child's learning and development.

Ask yourself questions to help you clarify your understanding in relation to children's 'backgrounds'. For example:

Why might children's background affect their learning and the goals you set for them?

If you are to evidence goal setting for children with different backgrounds, you need a good understanding of how and why their background can affect the goals you set for them.

Make a list of the different backgrounds of some of the children in your setting and try to identify any ways in which a child's background can influence the goals or 'next steps' you plan for them.

For example, you might have thought about setting goals relating to sharing and understanding emotions when a child struggled after the birth of a new sibling. If you are settling in a child who speaks no English, your goal might be to share key words with her in English and her home language.

CASE STUDY

Polly's understanding of the impact of children's backgrounds on their learning and goal setting

Polly is an Early Years Teacher trainee working in a school nursery class in a deprived area of an otherwise leafy outer London borough. Polly was new to the area and her role as teacher. She recorded in her journal that she soon realised that, although there were several large parks near the school, most children lived in the six high-rise tower blocks. She described how parents told her that they did not feel safe using the communal play area below the flats and found it too difficult to get on the bus with several young children and their buggies to get to the larger parks.

Once Polly realised that many of the children in her group had limited access to outdoor play and opportunities to develop gross motor skills climbing and riding bikes, she made developing the outdoor area a priority.

Because she worked in a school that had traditional tarmac playgrounds, she had to persuade senior management that the nursery class needed something very different. She was given a small budget and used it to provide a homely 'garden' area.

She created raised beds where the children planted the vegetables that were later used in their lunch. She provided wellington boots, small watering cans and low-level outdoor taps so that the children could water the plants independently. She created a large area with opportunities for climbing and space to ride bikes. Her priority was to give the children a 'home'-like environment so she set up a pets' area with rabbits and guinea pigs.

Polly had identified how these children's individual circumstances had an impact on their learning so created an environment where she would be able to set goals that were appropriate and relevant for the children in her group.

Evidence how you stretch and challenge children of 'all abilities'

You must evidence your ability to *stretch and challenge children of all ... abilities* in 1.2. Think about all the ways that you do this and how you can evidence how you have done this to support a range of children of *all abilities*, including children with SEN or disabilities.

You may find that there is some overlap here with Standard 4, where you are asked to provide further evidence of your ability to differentiate provision for all children.

Make a list of possible sources of evidence. Your list might include planning notes for your focus children, IEPs, and observations and next steps for children of different abilities.

Understanding 'dispositions' and their impact on learning

In 'A mind map for 1.2' (see pp. 114–15), Joseph is not sure how he will evidence how he sets goals to challenge children *of all dispositions*. He has made a note on the mind map in Table S1.3 to remind himself to find out about children's dispositions.

You must understand what a disposition is, how it relates to EYFS (2012) characteristics of effective learning and how a disposition can affect a child's learning. You will then be able to evidence how this affects your planning for a child. Below is some insight into how Joseph researched this.

(see pp. 114–15)

CASE STUDY

Joseph's research into dispositions

Joseph, an Early Years Teacher trainee, was concerned that he did not fully understand how a child's disposition matters so decided to do some research on this and then present his findings to his team to help him evidence his leadership role for Standard 8.

(Continued)

(Continued)

He found one article was particularly helpful, and this was Why Children's Dispositions Should Matter to All Teachers, written by Denise Da Ros-Voseles and Sally Fowler-Haughey. He found this article online at **www.naeyc.org/files/yc/file/200709/DaRos-Voseles.pdf.**

He explained to his colleagues that this article looks at what a disposition is, how it affects a child's learning and the strategies that can best support children. He highlighted several points he found interesting, such as what practitioners can do to foster certain dispositions and the long-term impact of this. He explained that the article identified three types of disposition: inborn, social and intellectual.

He explained to his team that an important characteristic of children's dispositions is that they are environmentally sensitive and this means that they are acquired, supported or weakened by interactive experiences in an environment with significant adults and peers (Bertram and Pascal, 2002). He felt that these significant adults include practitioners in early childhood settings. He gave an example from the article about a Reggio Emilia-inspired school where teachers purposely integrate materials from nature into activities (Da Ros-Voseles and Fowler-Haughey, 2007). 'A large, ordinary tree branch can become the core for cooperative ribbon weaving ... [which] supports children's dispositions, such as co-operation, creativity, problem solving, and inventiveness'.

Quoting from the article, he stressed that educators can pass on messages about whether a disposition is desirable or undesirable. This means that dispositions such as resourcefulness, curiosity and persistence can be strengthened. On the other hand, practitioners can try to reduce undesirable dispositions, such as selfishness, impatience and intolerance, by modelling good practice.

Leading practice on setting goals

Part of your role as Early Years Teacher is to demonstrate leadership and develop practice within your setting. Below are some questions to help you plan how to evidence your personal practice and leadership for 1.2 and your leadership role for Standard 8. Read through them and discuss with your team how you can set goals and evaluate the impact of these on the quality of your provision.

Discuss with your team:

- What areas of your practice are associated with goal setting (for example, observations that inform next steps)?

- What is the process you follow when you set goals or next steps?

- Could this process be improved in any way?

- Do all staff understand and follow these goal-setting procedures (including students and agency staff)?

- How can you identify any gaps in colleagues' understanding and plan group or individual training to address these gaps?

Cross-referencing your evidence: links between 1.2 and 5.2

In 5.2 you are required *to have a secure understanding of how a range of factors can inhibit children's ability to learn, and how best to overcome these*. There is some overlap between this statement and 1.2, but you need to be clear about the similarities and differences between 1.2 and 5.2.

You need to ask yourself:

- Do you have any evidence for 5.2 that you can use for 1.2 as well?
- What is the difference between these two indicators?
- What is the impact of these differences on your evidence for each?
- Will you need to adapt the evidence in any way, for example, to highlight why a specific factor in a child's background affected the goals you set for that child?

Evidence for 1.2

You should now have a clear idea of the breadth and depth of evidence that is required for1.2. Now you need to look in more detail at where and how you can provide this evidence. You need to organise your evidence, check whether you have any gaps and think about where and how you can best evidence each aspect of 1.2.

Written assignments, case studies and your reflective journal

You can evidence every aspect of 1.2 in a written assignment or case study if you plan this carefully. Provide examples that highlight how you set and differentiate goals to challenge children of different ages and abilities. You can reflect on the goals you have set for individual children and how you adapted the goals you set according to the ability, background and disposition of each child.

You could include:

- a case study to evidence your work with a child with an SEN or disability that can include examples of the goals you set to stretch and challenge the child. Make sure your evidence is detailed. Describe specific examples of goals you have set and relate them to what you have observed about the child, her needs and possible next steps. Explain how these goals stretch the child and how you have taken account of the child's background, ability and disposition;
- any entries in your reflective journal that relate to setting goals and understanding the impact of children's background and disposition on their learning. You might find it helpful to use your journal to reflect on your provision for a specific child to explore the possible impact of that child's background or disposition.

Document portfolio

You can provide a significant amount of evidence for 1.2 in your document portfolio and you will be able to cross-reference some of this against other Standards that require evidence of differentiation, such as Standards 4, 5 and 6.

You could include:

- copies of observations and next steps and entries on planning sheets and in profile books (make sure they highlight the goals you have set for specific children);

- completed Common Assessment Framework (CAF) forms and individual educational plan (IEP) that you have contributed to. Anonymise documents releating to specific children and ensure you highlight why you set these goals and how you took account of each child's background, ability and disposition;

- handouts from any training you have delivered on setting goals;

- notes or minutes taken during the goal-setting training;

- staff evaluation forms (if they evidence the quality of your support).

Make sure, however, that this evidence clearly relates to the key phrases in 1.2. You will also be able to cross-reference this evidence to Standard 8, where you are asked to evidence your leadership role.

Look at each piece of documentary evidence and ask yourself if it explicitly evidences all the key phrases in 1.2. If it doesn't, add an additional note to set the context and provide the missing information. For example, you can add a note to a planning sheet to explain that you have chosen to lead a session on action songs to support two key children who are learning English as a second language (ESL).

Observations

When you are observed by your mentor or tutor leading an activity with the children, you can record the individual goals you set in your planning notes and explain to your observer why you chose these goals and how they take account of a specific child's ability, background and disposition.

You could be observed:

- delivering training on setting goals, perhaps to a new member of staff or a student;

- meeting with parents to discuss setting goals for their child, perhaps for an IEP (with informed consent).

You may be able to show your mentor or tutor the goals you have set for individual children, for example, in their profile books. You can explain the context and describe how you took account of a child's background, ability and disposition. You can show examples of your support for children of different ages and abilities if you share examples of your planning in the different rooms in your setting. You can also share the goals you have set in an IEP or CAF forms that you have contributed to.

Bertram, T and Pascal, C (2002) What counts in early learning. In: ON Saracho and B Spodek (eds) *Contemporary Perspectives in Early Childhood Curriculum* (pp. 41–56). Greenwich, CT: Information Age.

Da Ros-Voseles, D and Fowler-Haughey, S (2007) *Why Children's Dispositions Should Matter to all Teachers. Beyond the Journal: Young Children on the Web: September 2007*. National Association for the Education of Young Children. Available online at: **www.naeyc.org/files/yc/file/200709/DaRos-Voseles.pdf** (accessed 20/10/2014).

Drifte, C (2014) *Early Learning Goals for Children with Special Needs: Learning Through Play.* London: Routledge.

Stewart, N and Moylett, H (2011) *How Children Learn: The Characteristics of Effective Early Learning.* London: British Association of Early Childhood Education.

Wilcock, L (2013) *The Early Learning Goals in Practice.* London: Practical Pre-school Books.

Wilford, S (2008) *Nurturing Young Children's Disposition to Learn.*. Minnesota: Redleaf Press.

Standard 1.3: Demonstrate and model the positive values, attitudes and behaviours expected of children

To evidence 1.3 you must identify the five key phrases in this statement and appreciate how these fit within the context of EYFS (2014). In the previous sections on 1.1 and 1.2, you looked at a range of strategies to help you identify the key phrases within each indicator and you can adapt these strategies to help you identify the meaning of the key phrases in 1.3.

The five phrases in 1.3 are *demonstrate*, *model*, *positive values*, *positive attitudes* and *positive behaviours* and you will need to relate each phrase to your practice and find a way to evidence this. Table S1.5 can help you identify the meaning of each phrase, how it relates to your practice and how you can best evidence it. Some examples have been added to help you.

Table S1.5 *Planning your evidence for 1.3*

1.3	Meaning	How this relates to my practice	My evidence
'Demonstrate'			Mentor observation
'Model'			Peer observation
'Positive values'		'I model positive values when I ... '	Record of discussion with pre-school children on choosing our Golden Rules
'Positive attitudes'		'I demonstrate positive attitudes when I ... '	
'Positive behaviours'	I model how to share resources during activities		

Identifying your strategies

You must consider how these requirements relate to your setting's behaviour management policy and EYFS (2014) requirements around modelling positive behaviours and using positive behaviour management strategies.

The questions below will help you identify the links between each phrase and your practice:

- What is the difference between *demonstrate* and *model*?

- How can I evidence that I *demonstrate* positive values, attitudes and behaviours?

- How can I evidence that I *model* positive values, attitudes and behaviours?

- How do I adapt these strategies to support a child with SEN or a disability?

- What are the EYFS requirements in relation to positive values, attitudes and behaviours?

- How does 1.3 relate to my setting's behaviour management policy?

Discussion points on positive values, attitudes and behaviours

Here are some questions that you can reflect on in your journal or use in a discussion with your colleagues if, for example, you lead a staff development session on behaviour management.

If your record of this discussion evidences your understanding and practice, then this can contribute to your evidence for 1.3. If you have evidence of leading a staff discussion, perhaps through the staff meeting minutes, then this can help you evidence your leadership role for Standard 8.

- What are the *positive values, attitudes* and *behaviours* that you are expected to model for the children?

- Do these vary according to the ages of the children?

- Does everyone in the team agree about what needs to be modelled?

- How do you know if there is a consensus?

- Is this consensus recorded in a policy?

  If not, why not? Can you create a policy to address this?

- Can you identify how you each demonstrate and model *positive values, attitudes and behaviours*?

- Can you explain why you do it this way?

- Are there any resources that could help you, for example, persona dolls or puppets?
- Can you think of any ways in which you could develop your team's practice in this area?

Promoting positive behaviours

The reference in 1.3 to modelling *positive ... behaviours* provides an opportunity for you to reflect on your setting's behaviour management policy and practise you and your team's *understanding of effective behaviour management strategies.*

Consider and ask your team what strategies can promote positive values, attitudes and behaviours. If you find that you need to provide training for colleagues on positive behaviour strategies and behaviour management, you can keep a record of this and use it to help you evidence your leadership role for Standard 8.

Evidence for 1.3

In 1.3 you are asked to evidence how you *demonstrate and model the positive values, attitudes and behaviours expected of children*.

This means that your evidence needs to demonstrate:

- how you demonstrate and model values, attitudes and behaviours;

- your rationale for choosing these behaviours, values and attitudes to model;

- your understanding of the impact of this approach;

- how you adapt these strategies to support children with SEN;

- how this relates to EYFS (2014) and your setting's behaviour management policy.

Written assignments, case studies and your reflective journal

You can use a written assignment to record examples of modelling positive behaviours, attitudes and values and the impact this has on individual children. You can describe your rationale and actions in detail and address values, attitudes and behaviours separately if this feels appropriate. Include examples of modelling positive behaviours in a case study that focuses on a specific child or on developing your setting's behaviour management strategies and policy.

You can include examples of modelling these behaviours with children of different ages, so that you also evidence your understanding of the developmental needs of children at different ages, for example, for 2.2 and 3.1. In each example, you need to describe your rationale in detail and give practical examples so that it is possible to form a picture of the purpose of your actions, your actions themselves and how children respond.

CASE STUDY

Polly's journal

Polly, an Early Years Teacher trainee who extended children's opportunities for physical play in the case study in 1.2, wanted to find out about how she could encourage the positive behaviour of 'L', a child with SEN through the targets she set for him in his IEP.

She found some tips she could use in the Guidance for Identifying and Supporting Young Children with Special Educational Needs for Early Years Settings, Schools & Support Services (Oxfordshire County Council, Children's Centres and Sure Start, *2010) that she found online.*

She identified some strategies that she could use, including regularly monitoring how 'L' responded to certain activities, interactions and strategies and sharing this information with parents and carers so that they could consistently use the most successful strategies.

She used her reflective journal to help her reflect on what she had learnt and then presented these strategies in a staff meeting and led a discussion on how to create goals for 'L' to support his behaviour management. She then arranged a meeting with 'L's parents to discuss this new approach.

Polly used her journal to reflect on the outcomes of the staff meeting and 'L's parents' response. She found it also helped her to think about the goals that would best support 'L' in managing his behaviour.

Document portfolio

You can include excerpts from your reflective journal to evidence your rationale for modelling certain behaviours in your document portfolio. As you need some objective evidence of your practice, you could also ask a colleague to complete a peer observation or witness testimony to evidence the behaviours you demonstrate and model in different situations and with children of different ages.

If you lead a training session on modelling appropriate behaviours you can include records of this, such as handouts and minutes of the meeting, if you can judge that they relate directly to 1.3. If you have been involved in revising your setting's behaviour management policy, then you can include a copy of this in your document portfolio as long as you highlight what your contributions were.

Observations

When you are observed engaging with a group of children, either in a peer observation or by your mentor or tutor, you need to remind yourself to think about how you can model positive values, behaviours and attitudes during the activity. You could add a brief comment on your behaviour management strategies to the planning notes that you share with your observer.

You may also be able to show your mentor or tutor any practices or resources you have introduced to support children in managing their behaviour and promoting positive values and attitudes. You can describe how you model the activities and any other ways you support the children. For example, you could point out the resources you bought to support sharing and turn-taking and the Golden Rules you established with the pre-school children. You might also be able to describe or demonstrate how you use puppets to model appropriate behaviours at meal times and circle time.

SUGGESTED READING

Bullock, EE and Brownhill, S (2014) *A Quick Guide to Behaviour Management in the Early Years.* London: SAGE.

Drifte, C (2014) *Encouraging Positive Behaviour in the Early Years: A Practical Guide.* London: SAGE.

Harding-Swale, J (2006) *Setting the Scene for Positive Behaviour in the Early Years: A Framework for Good Practice.* Oxon: Routledge.

Oxfordshire County Council, Children's Centres and Sure Start (2010) *Guidance for Identifying and Supporting Young Children with Special Educational Needs for Early Years Settings, Schools & Support Services.* Available online at: **http://schools.oxfordshire.gov.uk/cms/sites/schools/files/folders/folders/documents/SEN/guidance/EY_SEN_guidance_leaflet.pdf** (accessed 20/10/2014).

Rogers, B and McPherson, E (2014) *Behaviour Management with Young Children* (2nd edn). *Crucial First Steps with Children 3–7 Years.* London: SAGE.

Standard 2: **Promote good progress and outcomes by children**

Introduction

In Standard 1 you will have evidenced how you set high expectations for all children and provide a high-quality, stimulating environment. Now in Standard 2 you will evidence how you create this stimulating environment through your interactions with children, your partnerships with parents and by applying your understanding of child development.

The opening statement for Standard 2 asks you to evidence how you promote children's progress and outcomes. The seven indicators then identify the knowledge, skills and practice you will need to demonstrate to evidence how you promote *progress and outcomes*, for example, how you work in partnership with parents and promote children's confidence and social skills.

Before we look at a summary of these seven indicators, you need to identify all the ways in which you promote children's progress and outcomes.

Identifying how you 'promote good progress and outcomes by children'

Here are some questions to help you reflect on your practice and identify how you promote children's progress and outcomes.

- What are your first thoughts when you consider how you *promote good progress and outcomes by children*?

- Can you identify what it is that you do that promotes good outcomes, such as plan according to children's interests and use observations to identify 'next steps' or goals?

- How do you demonstrate this for children of different ages and abilities?

- How can you judge whether the progress you *promote* is *good*?

- How can you evidence the quality of your practice?

Standard 2: the wider context

Although you need to understand Standard 2 primarily in the context of your role as a practitioner, it can be helpful to think about this Standard in its wider context. Recent Government initiatives have introduced changes to early years provision, hoping to reduce inequalities between children. From the Ten-Year Strategy, Every Child Matters and the introduction of graduate practitioners right through to More Great Childcare and beyond, the focus has been on improving the life chances of the most disadvantaged children.

There is a list of recent policy documents below which you can use to explore the links between these initiatives and Standard 2. Standard 2 relates to this agenda because of its focus on how you, as practitioner, promote children's outcomes.

Promoting good outcomes: the political context and your practice

Successive UK Governments have demonstrated a commitment to raising the life chances of all children through a series of policy documents, strategies and legislation that have had an impact on early years provision. Here is a list of some of the most significant of these, but this is not an exhaustive list and you need to identify other and more recent documents that affect your practice.

You can identify how these policies and strategies impact on your practice and support you in promoting positive outcomes for children. If you reflect on this in your journal then this can help you evidence Standard 2.

Ten-year strategy for childcare (2004) (**http://webarchive.nationalarchives.gov.uk/20130401151715/www.education.gov.uk/publications/standard/_arc_SOP/Page9/DCSF-00173-2009**);

The Children Act (2004) (**www.legislation.gov.uk/ukpga/2004/31**);

Childcare Act (2006) (**www.legislation.gov.uk/ukpga/2006/21/pdfs/ukpga_20060021_en.pdf**);

Next Steps for Early Learning and Childcare, Building on the 10-Year Strategy (Department for Education, 2009);

The Early Years Foundation Stage (Tickell Review): Report on the Evidence (Gov.uk, 2011)

Supporting Families in the Foundation Years (July 2011) (**www.familyandchildcaretrust.org/Page/index/research-and-policy**);

The Education Act (2011) (**www.legislation.gov.uk/ukpga/2011/21/contents/enacted**);

Northern Ireland Children and Young People's Plan 2011–2014 (**www.cypsp.org/publications/cypsp/action-plan/cypsp_action_plan_2011-2014.pdf**);

Foundations for Quality: the Independent Review of Early Education and Childcare Qualifications – Nutbrown Review (**www.gov.uk/government/publications/nut-brown-review-foundations-for-quality**);

More Great Childcare – Raising Quality and Giving Parents More Choice (2013) (**www.gov.uk/government/publications/more-great-childcare-raising-quality-and-giving-parents-more-choice**);

Building a Brighter Future: Early Years and Childcare Plan (*Wales*) (2013) (**wales.gov.uk/docs/dcells/publications/130716-building-brighter-future-en.pdf**).

Your leadership role and the Graduate Leader Fund Report

The Graduate Leader Fund Final Report (Mathers et al., 2011) noted that Early Years Professionals had a stronger influence over the quality of practice within their room than on the quality of provision across the setting as a whole. As an Early Years Teacher trainee you need not only to ensure that you raise the quality of practice in your room, but also enhance provision across your setting.

It is the actions you take to raise quality and outcomes that you can relate to Standard 2 and cross-reference to Standard 8. To ensure that you have a positive impact across your setting you can model good practice and support colleagues in developing their practice, perhaps through providing training and mentoring. You will find that you can evidence your leadership role through a range of activities, including modelling a new activity for colleagues or leading circle time. This relates to Standard 2 because the focus is on ensuring good outcomes for all children. For example, Sue, an Early Years Teacher trainee, led a ten-minute discussion on promoting children's thinking skills in a staff meeting and provided a handout to summarise the main points.

ACTIVITY **S2.1**

Getting to know the indicators for Standard 2

Read through the questions below and consider your responses. These introduce you to the key concepts addressed in the seven indicators for Standard 2 and help you to consider how your evidence for 2.1 to 2.7 relates to how you promote children's progress and outcomes, as required by Standard 2.

- *What is your role in promoting children's progress, attainment and outcomes, and improving their life chances? (2.1)*

- *How does your knowledge of child development help you to support children's progress in ways that are developmentally appropriate? (2.1, 2.2)*

(Continued)

ACTIVITY S2.1 continued

- Can you think of a situation where your knowledge of child development helped you in your practice, for example, when working with parents to identify when their child is developmentally ready for toilet training? (2.2)

- Do you feel confident enough in your knowledge of attachment theory to share your understanding of the work of, for example, Bowlby and Ainsworth and more recent writers on attachment? (2.3)

- Can you explain to a colleague the ways in which attachment theory informs your practice, for example, through key person relationships and settling-in procedures? (2.3)

- Why do children need to develop critical thinking skills? (2.4)

- What strategies do you use to promote these skills? (2.4)

- What is the difference between asking open questions and engaging in sustained shared thinking? (2.4)

- How can you model these strategies for colleagues and what impact might this have on how you promote good progress and outcomes for children? (2.4)

- Why is it important to focus on our own listening skills when we communicate with children? (2.5)

- What will the quality of our listening teach children about the value of what they have to say? (2.5)

- Can you describe the communication skills you use with each age group – babies, toddlers and pre-school children? (2.5)

- How do you adapt the communication strategies and your responses according to the age of the child? (2.5)

- Can you identify the strategies you use to help children develop their confidence? (2.6)

- How does your use of constructive feedback, positive behaviour management strategies, circle time, key times and focus group activities promote children's confidence? (2.6)

- Can you identify the strategies you use to promote communication and social skills through group activities? (2.6)

- How do you use circle times and focus group activities to promote social skills? (2.6)

- Can you describe how you use routines such as snack time and changing times to promote communication? (2.6)

- Can you identify all the ways in which you believe that parents/carers have a positive impact on the development of their child? (2.6)

- Can you describe how you form partnerships with parents and demonstrate that you recognise their positive impact? (2.7)

- *How do you build on your partnerships with parents to support their child's progress? (2.7)*

- *Can you identify the strategies that you use to promote partnerships with parents, such as introducing home link books, daily handovers, inviting parents to open days or in to share stories with the children? (2.7)*

Identifying how you 'promote good progress and outcomes'

Now that you have looked at the areas addressed in the indicators for Standard 2, you may find it helpful to look in more detail at the strategies you use to *promote good progress and outcomes*. You can use or adapt the chart in Table S2.1 to record your initial thoughts and then identify how you can evidence your actions. An example has been added to help you.

Table S2.1 Standard 2: Promote good progress and good outcomes for children

Promote …	… good progress and …	… good outcomes for children
You can record:	You can consider:	You can record:
– examples of your practice	– how you judge that progress is 'good'	– how you evaluate outcomes and decide if they are 'good enough'
– your leadership actions	– how you promote 'good progress'	– how you record children's outcomes
– how you can evidence your actions	– how can you evidence this	
I observe my key children daily and plan next steps	I assess whether children have reached their next steps through regular observations	If they don't progress against next steps then I discuss this with my manager and consider other strategies
My evidence:	**My evidence:**	**My evidence:**
Observations	Profile books	Staff meeting minutes
Profile books	Observations	Two-year check
I do this with:		Profile books
– babies ☐		
– toddlers ☐		
– pre-school children ☐		

Although your evidence for each Standard will be evaluated 'holistically' (see section on holistic assessment in Chapter 4, Assessment methods), taking time to understand Standard 2 in detail will help you make informed decisions about what evidence would be most appropriate.

If you are a manager in your setting or only work with one age group, you can use the chart to help you judge whether you have adequate evidence of promoting the progress of individual children in each age group – babies, toddlers and pre-school children.

If you feel that you may need an additional age-related placement, then Chapter 5 on age range requirements will give you some guidance.

CASE STUDY

Sue's reflective journal

Sue is a toddler room practitioner who has recently embarked on her Early Years Teacher Status. Sue uses her reflective journal to record key incidents and reflect on what she can learn from each situation and she links her statements to the Standards and indicators. She has annotated this excerpt from her journal to help her develop her understanding of the indicators for Standard 2.1. She will then be able to use this extract to help her evidence the indicators she identified. Sue has summarised a conversation she had with two-year-old Aaron's pregnant mother, Julie, as she had some concerns about how Aaron was managing the changes the pregnancy has brought about.

Unlike her observations of children, which need to be objective, Sam uses her journal to explore how she responds in a situation and explores what this might tell her about the other person's point of view.

I noticed Aaron's mum arrived later than usual to collect him and I thought she looked tired. She didn't go straight over to Aaron as usual, but sat in the corner. As we've had some problems with Aaron's behaviour, I said to him, 'look, your mummy is here! Shall we go and tell her how kind you were to Ellie when she was upset today?'

He smiled and ran over to his mum. He tugged her arm but it was a moment before she responded. This is really not like her and I noticed she was rubbing her back. Together Aaron and I told Julie how he shared a doll's buggy in the garden with Ellie when she was upset she didn't have one for her doll. I reiterated how good it is to share and how Aaron had made Ellie smile. I had a feeling that Julie was relieved that I wasn't coming to her with another biting incident.

> S2.6 'Develop children's confidence'

I then showed her Aaron's painting and he tried to tell her how he'd been mixing colours. When he struggled to find words I encouraged Julie to give him time to find his words and model the words he needs, like 'it was runny?!'

> 2.5 'Communicate effectively with children'
> S2.6 'Develop children's communication skills'

> S2.2 Knowledge and understanding of how children ... develop

When Aaron ran off to play I asked Julie how she was. She said she has problems with her pregnancy and spent last night in Accident and Emergency and had to leave Aaron with a neighbour. She said she needs Aaron to go to bed earlier so she can rest and asked if we could stop his sleep time after lunch. We spoke about Aaron's need to sleep and the impact of stopping this before he's ready, that if he's tired there might be more problems with his behaviour. We talked about strategies

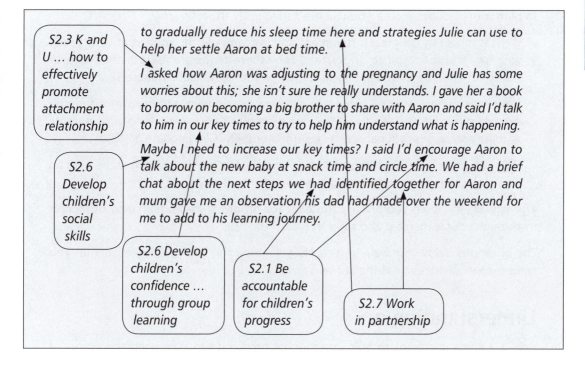

S2.3 K and U ... how to effectively promote attachment relationship

to gradually reduce his sleep time here and strategies Julie can use to help her settle Aaron at bed time.

I asked how Aaron was adjusting to the pregnancy and Julie has some worries about this; she isn't sure he really understands. I gave her a book to borrow on becoming a big brother to share with Aaron and said I'd talk to him in our key times to try to help him understand what is happening.

S2.6 Develop children's social skills

Maybe I need to increase our key times? I said I'd encourage Aaron to talk about the new baby at snack time and circle time. We had a brief chat about the next steps we had identified together for Aaron and mum gave me an observation his dad had made over the weekend for me to add to his learning journey.

S2.6 Develop children's confidence ... through group learning

S2.1 Be accountable for children's progress

S2.7 Work in partnership

Standard 2.1: Be accountable for children's progress, attainment and outcomes

Introduction

In Standard 1 you are asked to evidence how you promote a stimulating environment for all children and in Standard 2 you are asked to take this one step further and identify how you do this when you promote children's *good progress and outcomes*.

In 2.1 you need to evidence this in more detail and identify how you are accountable for individual children's progress, attainment and outcomes. There is a clear relationship between 2.1 and the main statement for Standard 2 as both emphasise your responsibility for progress and outcomes. However, 2.1 takes your role one step further by asking you to evidence how you are *accountable* for promoting children's *attainment* as well as their *progress and outcomes*.

This means that you need to evidence all the ways in which you have accountability for promoting children's progress; for example, by completing two-year-old progress checks, following targets on an individual education programme (IEP) or leading staff training on planning and assessment.

To plan your evidence for 2.1 you will need to identify the following:

- What is meant by progress, attainment and outcomes in the context of early years: you may find it helpful to understand how these terms are used in the National Curriculum and by Ofsted and information on this is available in Table S2.2.

- How your routine practice promotes progress, attainment and outcomes for children of different ages and abilities, for example, through working with parents and the special educational needs co-ordinator (SENCO) to update an IEP.

- How you judge whether these strategies are effective, for example, by reflecting on how well children are progressing towards their next steps.

- The ways in which you are accountable for progress, attainment and outcomes through your leadership and support role.

The questions below can help you clarify your thoughts and identify strategies you can use to evidence each of the above points.

Understanding 2.1

Here are some questions to help you identify how you can evidence each aspect of 2.1. Although this Standard will be assessed holistically, your evidence will be much stronger if you have considered each aspect of every indicator.

What is my 'accountability' and how does my job role define this?

If you are a room leader or manager you will have overall accountability for children's progress, and if you are a key person, your accountability will be for your key children's progress.

Therefore, your role has some implications for how you evidence your accountability. Whatever your role, you need to consider how you can evidence both promoting individual children's progress and supporting staff development in this area.

Questions of meaning: what is the difference between 'attainment', 'progress' and 'outcomes'?

The precise meanings of the terms *attainment, progress* and *outcomes* can vary according to the context and there is further information on this in Table S2.2.

Generally, *attainment* records a 'score', such as the child's level in relation to early learning goals, *progress* refers to a child's movement from one level to the next, such as between levels in the National Curriculum (although this becomes optional from 2015) and *outcomes* refers to levels reached in a summative assessment process, such as an Early Years Foundation Stage (EYFS) Profile.

If you can develop a good working knowledge of the meaning of each term it will help you to evidence 2.1 well.

Table S2.2 *Progress, attainment and outcomes*

	National Curriculum	Ofsted	Early years
Progress	A child's movement from one level to another in the National Curriculum to another	The extent to which pupils have progressed in their learning, given their starting points and capabilities	Children's movement from one level to another with reference to their next steps and early years outcomes.
			Progress can be recorded and evidenced in profile books, the two-year-old progress checks, IEPs and EYFS Profiles.
Attainment	The National Curriculum level a child has achieved.	The standard of academic attainment typically shown by test and examination results.	If children have SEN their progress needs to be reviewed at least twice a year EYFS (2012) 2.7: 'Each child's level of development must be assessed against the early learning goals. Practitioners must indicate whether children are meeting expected levels of development, or if they are exceeding expected levels, or not yet reaching expected levels ("emerging"). This is the EYFS Profile.'
	Children's scores in their end of Key Stage statutory national tests.	A 'raw score' expressed in numbers or letters, either GCSE results or National Curriculum levels achieved	
	League tables track and compare 'attainment levels' in schools		Attainment can be recorded against the early years outcomes and early learning goals in a child's learning journey, two-year-old progress check and EYFS Profile.
Outcomes	Programmes of study are designed to help pupils reach desired goals.	Ofsted use 'outcomes' to describe their findings, such as in the phrase, 'inspection outcomes'.	Every Child Matters outcomes can be used to identify a child's progress/lack of progress against the five outcomes. This can be recorded in a Common Assessment Framework.
	Outcomes can refer to children's level at the end of a key stage or their performance in an area of the curriculum, such as 'cognitive outcomes' or 'social/behavioural outcomes' (Sammons et al., 2008).	If you are a manager, you may be able to evidence your impact on the outcomes Ofsted identifies for your setting	Outcomes can be summarised in the EYFS Profile.
	It can also be applied more generally, as in *Outcomes for Children Looked After by Local Authorities* (Gov.uk, 2013e).		You may identify the 'learning outcomes' for a child or specific activity.
	'Assessment outcomes' are published in school league tables.		
	The National Strategies: Attainment and Progress for Pupils with SEN/LDD (2008) suggests use of Every Child Matters outcomes instead of National Curriculum levels for some children with SEN (**www.gmsen.co.uk/fileuploads/targets/assessment/general/NSAttainmentandProgress.pdf**)		

IEPs, individual education plans; EYFS, Early Years Foundation Stage; SEN, special educational needs.

How do I evidence my accountability for attainment, progress and outcomes?

What do you do to promote attainment, progress and outcomes? How can you demonstrate your accountability? This refers both to your role in supporting your key child's learning and development and any ways in which you promote the attainment of all children in your setting.

How can you evidence all this? You need to evidence all the ways in which you promote progress and attainment and ensure that your evidence demonstrates your accountability.

If you work with other professionals to support a child with SEN, any records of your contributions to the child's IEP and discussions at Early Years Action and Action Plus stages will highlight your role in promoting this child's progress.

If you complete a two-year-old progress check or EYFS Profile for a key child, or you identify an area of concern and share this with parents and other professionals, this evidences your accountability as practitioner. If you have designed the two-year check for your setting, then you are demonstrating your accountability in relation to leading practice across your setting.

How do I record children's attainment and progress?

Consider how you contribute to observations, next steps, planning sheets, focus group activities, profile books, two-year checks and EYFS Profiles. You may also contribute to an IEP or Common Assessment Framework (CAF) form.

How can I evidence this?

You will have records of promoting progress in your observations, next steps, IEPs and profile books. If you then relate these observations and next steps to Development Matters and the early learning goals or two-year-old progress checks, then you are recording *attainment*. If you complete an EYFS Profile then you are recording a child's *outcomes* in relation to EYFS (2012). If you complete a CAF form then you are recording children's *outcomes* in relation to Every Child Matters.

How am I accountable for promoting good practice in my setting?

You need to evidence how you are responsible for promoting the progress, attainment and outcomes of your own key children, for example:

- through observations, planning and next steps (4.1);

- providing activities that interest and stimulate each child (1.1, 4.3);

- engaging in conversations that promote confidence, social skills and thinking skills (2.4, 2.6);

- using your knowledge of child development (2.2);

- the strength of your key person relationship to support children in their learning and development (2.3).

To evidence your leadership for 2.1, think about how you have you promoted systems for observation, planning and assessment and record keeping. You may have designed the two-year-old progress check for your setting and delivered training on how to complete the check. You may have helped individual colleagues understand the planning and assessment cycle or led staff training on aspects of this. If you have supported staff in planning for children's interests or in working with parents to promote children's progress, then this is also evidence of your accountability.

How can I lead practice in observation, assessment and planning across my setting?

Find out where colleagues feel they need some support in relation to observation, planning and assessment and offer to support and mentor them. Model good practice or lead a professional discussion or training session.

'Attainment', 'progress' and 'outcomes' in EYFS, the National Curriculum and Ofsted

To evidence 2.1 well, you need to understand the meaning of *attainment*, *progress* and *outcomes* in this context. One reason for the use of these terms in the Early Years Teacher Standards is to provide continuity between EYFS and the National Curriculum and Ofsted.

Table S2.2 looks at how the phrases *attainment, progress and outcomes* are used in Key Stages 1 and 2 and by Ofsted and compares this to how these terms are used in the early years. This will help you identify what it is you need to evidence for 2.1.

How to evidence your role in promoting 'progress, attainment and outcomes'

If you measure how children progress against a scale, such as EYFS and Every Child Matters outcomes, then this measures their *attainment*. Their *progress* can be described as their movement from one level in the scale to the next, so you can evidence *progress* alongside *attainment*.

You can evidence your role in promoting both *progress* and *attainment* in the two-year-old progress checks and EYFS Profiles that you complete, records of your intervention at Early Years Action stage and your routine observations and next steps that relate to Development Matters and early outcomes.

You can also evidence how you promote *progress* in its more general sense when you document the ways in which you extend children's learning and development, such as widening their experiences in your evidence for 3.2 and promoting thinking skills in your evidence for 2.4.

You can record *outcomes* in several ways – through summative assessment and reference to the Good Level of Development measure in the EYFS Profile or assessment against Every Child Matters outcomes in a CAF. You may be able to use an Ofsted report to evidence your role in promoting more general positive outcomes for your setting.

Leadership opportunities: the planning cycle

One of the key strategies for ensuring that your provision effectively promotes each child's learning and development is the planning cycle and you may find that reviewing the effectiveness of your planning cycle can provide a starting point for evidencing your accountability for 2.1.

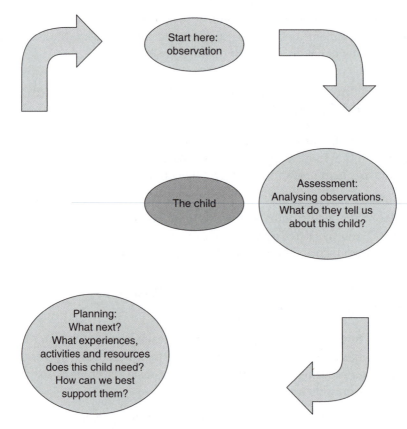

Figure S2.1 *The planning cycle*

You can evaluate the effectiveness of the planning cycle in your setting and find out whether all colleagues understand the cycle of observation, assessment and planning and how to implement this in practice. Figure S2.1 reminds you of the stages in this cycle.

If you identify any gaps in practitioners' understanding or practice, such as how to assess progress against the early learning goals, and you support practitioners with this, then you have evidence of leadership and support for 2.1 as you will have demonstrated your accountability.

Evidence for 2.1

Here are some examples of evidence you can use for 2.1. You can use this list to help you identify where you may have appropriate evidence and any gaps in your evidence. Remember that all references to individual children need to be carefully anonymised.

Written assignments, case studies and your reflective journal

- a written assignment describing how you developed systems for planning and assessment and/or supported colleagues in using these;
- a written assignment or case study describing how you supported the attainment, progress and outcomes for a specific child;
- entries in your reflective journal looking at, for example, your role in assessing a child against the Every Child Matters outcomes and contributing to a CAF for that child.

Document portfolio

- profile books containing your own annotated observations and next steps for a child;
- planning records that identify activities you have planned to promote a child's next steps;
- evidence of helping colleagues to understand and follow the planning cycle, such as records of meetings with them or notes you prepared for them;
- two-year-old progress check you have completed for your own key children;
- records of the system for two-year-old progress checks that you designed and introduced;
- records of training you provided for colleagues in completing two-year-old progress checks;
- a child's IEP with your contributions carefully highlighted and evidence of your own role in supporting the child so that she makes progress and/or meets these targets;
- copy of a CAF and/or records of a Team Around the Child (TAC) meeting to promote a child's outcomes (anonymised) and that highlight your contributions;
- records of meetings with other professionals to promote a child's outcomes;
- records of assessing a child against Every Child Matters outcomes;

- staff minute meetings recording discussions on promoting a child's progress;

- records of one-to-one meetings with colleagues to support them in promoting children's progress;

- peer or mentor observations of you working with a child to support his progress in an area identified as his next step in, for example, an IEP;

- records of following the stages of the Special Needs Code of Practice for one of your key children;

- records of your interventions as SENCO to promote individual children's progress, attainment and outcomes.

Observations

Arrange for a peer observation or for your mentor or tutor to observe you leading an activity with a child that will help that child progress towards identified goals or next steps. Share your planning notes to explain why and how this activity will support a child's progress.

You may also be able to share your general planning notes, contributions to an IEP and entries in a child's profile book with your tutor or mentor.

CASE STUDY

Sheena evidences her leadership for 2.1

Sheena is room leader in room with both toddler and pre-school children. She is an Early Years Teacher trainee and as she wanted to evidence her leadership and support for 2.1 she devised a questionnaire for her colleagues on how to identify a child's next steps. She was concerned that the results of her questionnaire revealed that her colleagues were not clear about how to plan clear and appropriate next steps for children and she felt that this could impact on children's progress. She decided that if she led some training on next steps and how to promote children's progress, this would provide some evidence of her accountability for progress, attainment and outcomes.

She attended training on SEN run by her local authority, and the trainer presented excerpts from Including all Children in Early Years Settings: A Guide to Implementing the Special Needs Code of Practice by Leicestershire County Council (2011).

She decided to use some of these materials to cascade what she had learnt in this training. She planned a training session for her colleagues on designing next steps that are SMART (specific, measurable, achievable, relevant and time-bound) and offered to support colleagues one to one after the session to plan next steps for their key children and assess their progress.

She recorded evidence of her leadership in her reflective journal, where she examined what she had learnt on the training and how it had had a positive impact on her practice. Alongside this in her document portfolio she included copies of pages from her key child's *profile book so as to demonstrate her personal practice and show how she used the strategies she learnt to promote this child's progress.*

To evidence her leadership role she also provided a copy of her rationale for the support she gave her colleagues and copies of the materials she provided for the training session. Finally, she included copies of staff evaluations that recorded how she had helped them identify how to design next steps that are SMART so as to measure and evaluate progress and attainment.

Here are the materials Sheena shared with colleagues, adapted from Including all Children in Early Years Settings: A Guide to Implementing the Special Needs Code of Practice *(Leicestershire County Council, 2011) (Table S2.3).*

Table S2.3 SMART means …

Specific	Be specific about the child's needs, current skill level and the provision to be put in place
Measurable	Next steps should always be observable.
	Can you clearly answer yes or no if someone asks if the child has achieved the next step?
	Are you able to see/hear evidence of achievement?
	In many cases, it is also desirable to set measurable next steps,
	e.g. 'Sita will remain on a carpet square for 10 minutes at story time with an adult alongside her'
Achievable	Next steps must be manageable for your setting. Is it possible for the child to meet the next step by the date you are aiming for?
Relevant	Relate the next step to the child's learning ability. Success is more likely if the next steps are easy to remember, realistic and seen as part of the everyday routine for that particular child
Time-bound	Next steps need a timescale. The Special Educational Needs Code of Practice recommends that individual education programmes are reviewed at least three times a year

Can you identify a next step for one of your key children that is SMART?

Can you use the Table S2.4 to check whether your next step really is SMART?

Table S2.4 SMART or not SMART?

Next steps that are not SMART	Next steps that are SMART
1. Joanne will recognise some letters of the alphabet	1. Joanne will recognise the first letter of her name, J, used in her name and in five other words
2. Sunita will be able to catch a ball	2. Sunita will catch a large beach ball when thrown to her from a distance of one metre
3. To improve Ryan's concentration	3. Ryan will participate in an adult-chosen activity for one minute. Sand timer to be used

(Continued)

CASE STUDY *continued*

Criteria for success: how will you know when your key child has made progress?

All next steps need to have criteria for success to enable us to observe the progress made. Otherwise, how will you know when your key child has made progress?

When setting a next step, think about how you will know that what you have been working on with the child has made a difference. Describe what you will see the child doing when she has achieved that step.

A child might not always achieve a skill 100% of the time. You might want to say that you will see the child achieve the target three out of five times or eight out of ten times.

SUGGESTED READING

Here is some additional reading on promoting children's progress and assessment.

There is further information on Government policy documents in the section on 'Promoting good outcomes: the political context and your practice', above.

Carr, M (2003) *Assessment in Early Childhood Settings: Learning Stories.* London: SAGE.

Drake, J (2000) *Planning Children's Play and Learning in the Foundation Stage.* London: David Fulton.

Gallow, C (2007) *Trackers 0–5: Tracking Children's Progress Through the Early Years Foundation Stage.* London: QED Publishing.

Harding, J and Meldon-Smith, L (2001) *How to Make Observations and Assessments Work.* London: Hodder & Stoughton.

Hobart, C and Frankel, J. (2004) *A Practical Guide to Child Observation and Assessment* (3rd edn). Cheltenham: Nelson Thornes.

Hutchin, V (2007) *Supporting Every Child's Learning Across the Early Years Foundation Stage.* London: Hodder Education.

Welch, S, Whalley, ME, Goodriffe, G and Trodd, L (2008) *Leading Practice in Early Years Settings (Achieving EYPS).* Exeter: Learning Matters.

Standard 2.2: Demonstrate knowledge and understanding of how babies and children learn and develop

Introduction

Standard 2.2 addresses one of the major strands in the Standards, which is your knowledge of child development and how this informs your practice. It is also one of the few Standards that ask you to evidence your work with *babies* and children and relates to the emphasis within Early Years Teacher Status on understanding child development right through from birth.

In 2.2 you are asked to evidence your *knowledge and understanding* of child development and theories relating to how children learn. However, as you are asked to *demonstrate* this knowledge, you need to evidence how your knowledge and understanding inform your practice. This means that you could, for example, explain how your understanding of Vygotsky's zone of proximal development influences the way you support a child. Or you could emphasise that your understanding of the work of Bowlby and Ainsworth has helped you develop the settling-in policy for your setting.

Similarities and differences: 2.2 and other Standards that relate to child development

It can be helpful, at this stage, to identify the other Standards that ask you to evidence your knowledge of child development. If you can identify how each Standard asks you to evidence your understanding of child development from a different perspective, you will understand how to evidence your knowledge of child development in 2.2. Figure S2.2 identifies some similarities and differences to help you start.

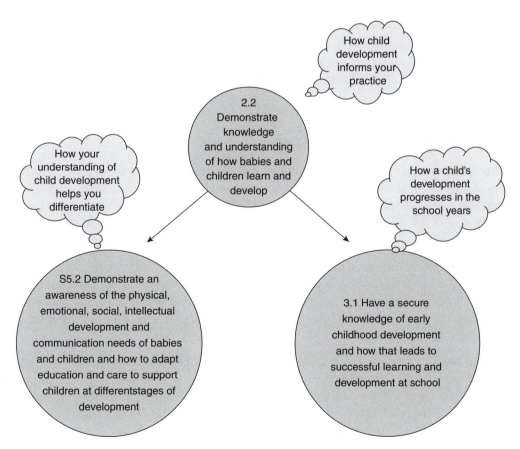

Figure S2.2 *Similarities and differences*

145

Getting to know the requirements of 2.2

Standard 2.2 asks you to *demonstrate* your knowledge of how babies and children learn and develop. The use of the verb *demonstrate* in this indicator means that you need to evidence your knowledge and understanding of child development through your actions (and the rationale for your actions). For example, your understanding of attachment theory and how children learn through positive relationships underpins your interactions with your key children.

As this is one of the few Standards which explicitly refer to babies as well as children, you will need to demonstrate your knowledge and understanding of child development from birth right through to five years and demonstrate this through your practice. If you do not have recent experience of working with any of the three age groups, babies, toddlers and pre-school children, you may find it helpful to read the section in Chapter 5 on deciding whether to take on an age-related placement.

'Learn and develop'

You are asked to evidence how you support children to *learn and develop*. This emphasis on how your knowledge of how children *learn* as well as how they *develop* means that you need to consider both your understanding of child development theory and of theories of learning.

You can relate your understanding of how children learn and develop to EYFS principles, themes and requirements and how these impact on your practice. You can refer to EYFS principles, areas of learning, early years outcomes and early learning goals in your evidence for 2.2.

Extending your reading

You need to evaluate your knowledge of child development theory from birth onwards and consider whether there are areas where you need to extend your reading. Although you will evidence your knowledge and understanding through your actions, you still need to demonstrate a thorough understanding of child development theory.

If you feel you are weaker in one area, such as babies' development, you need to extend your reading on this. If you lack confidence or experience with the younger age groups, *Key Times for Play* by Manning-Morton and Thorp (2003) is an excellent starting point as it highlights how you can use your knowledge to inform your practice.

As you need to evidence your understanding of how children learn as well as how they develop, you may need to extend your reading in this area too. You might choose to look at a history of theories of learning or, for example, consider the writings of Tina Bruce (1991) on block play or Gerhardt (2004) on the ways in which affection shapes a baby's brain.

The impact of a child's environment

As children learn from everything, not just from the experiences we explicitly plan for them, your evidence can reflect your understanding of this. So, as well as demonstrating your understanding of different perspectives on child development, theories of learning and the EYFS framework, you can evidence your understanding of the impact of the environment and the children's social world on their learning and development.

Leading and supporting your colleagues

An effective way to demonstrate your understanding of how children learn and develop is to lead and support your colleagues and deliver training on this. If you lead a training session on an aspect of child development and the implications for practice, then this will evidence of your own knowledge and understanding and your leadership.

You may have noticed in discussions with colleagues that some members of your team struggled to understand an area of child development and its implications for their actions and you could plan to support them in this. Jo, an Early Years Teacher trainee, realised her colleagues needed support in understanding the importance of an enabling environment and active learning. She then led a short training session in a staff meeting where she discussed the EYFS requirements for an enabling environment, provided hand outs on strategies for promoting active learning and gave a new colleague one-to-one mentoring on how to promote active learning with toddlers.

Remember that any evidence you can present of leading and supporting colleagues will help you evidence 2.2 and will also help you evidence your leadership role for Standard 8.

Evidence for 2.2

You need to check that your evidence for 2.2 addresses all of these points:

- your knowledge and understanding of how children develop from birth to five;

- your knowledge of how children learn, also from birth to five, with reference to EYFS;

- practical examples of applying your knowledge of child development with babies, toddlers and pre-school children; for example, how your understanding of Vygotsky's zone of proximal development and scaffolding (in Wood and Middleton, 1975) informs your support for a child in a problem-solving activity, such as how to balance the large blue block on top of the small yellow block;

- your knowledge and understanding and how you apply this in practice with each age group in detail, step by step, for example, by looking at how you introduced Every Child a Talker (ECAT) and helped colleagues understand how to introduce communication-friendly spaces with different age groups;

- your understanding that everything children experience has an impact on their learning and development.

You will be able to evidence these points through examples of your practice that you record in your various sources of evidence and in the following section you can find some examples. Jo's evidence in the case study below demonstrates how she addresses the points listed above across a range of sources of evidence.

CASE STUDY

Jo's evidence for her baby room placement

Jo, an Early Years Teacher trainee, presented evidence of her work with the babies and the baby room team on her placement in a small private nursery. She made sure that her evidence demonstrated her knowledge and understanding of babies' development for 2.2.

She presented her initial observations and reflections on practice in the baby room and a written rationale for the changes she suggested. She also provided copies of her plans for the development of the baby room home corner and treasure basket area and the minutes of the staff meeting where she gave a presentation on the work of Elinor Goldschmied and the team then discussed the plans for change.

Jo then provided a series of her observations of individual babies engaging with resources, both before and after the changes she introduced so as to evidence their positive impact.

She also included a peer observation of her interactions with a non-mobile baby to record how she promotes communication and language: listening and attention through encouraging playfulness, turn-taking and responses, including peek-a-boo and rhymes, as required in Development Matters (EYFS 2012). The peer observation evidenced how Jo uses a lively voice with the babies, uses songs and rhymes in everyday routines such as changing babies and repeats sounds and phrases so that babies can begin to recognise particular sounds.

Jo recorded in her journal how she provided support for a student who was new to the baby room and this student has written a witness testimony that outlines how Jo helped her understand babies' development. In the witness testimony the student notes that Jo helped her to understand the EYFS characteristics of effective learning, such as finding out and exploring, *and follow the guidance for babies in Development Matters, such as* tune in sensitively to babies, *and provide warm, loving, consistent care, responding quickly to babies' needs, and* hold and handle babies, *since sensitive touch helps to build security and attachment.*

Jo also evidenced her understanding of babies' development through the entries in babies' profile books, her contributions to planning for the week and the training hand-outs on treasure baskets that she prepared for her colleagues.

Taken together, these pieces of evidence demonstrate Jo's understanding of how babies learn and develop to evidence 2.2. They also evidence how Jo's understanding of babies' development broadened as she spent more time reading about babies' development and working in the baby room.

Written assignments, case studies and your reflective journal

You can describe your experiences in the baby, toddler and pre-school rooms in a series of case studies or written assignments. In each assignment you can outline your understanding of child development at that stage and its implications for practice; for example, how your understanding of attachment theory leads you to promote settling-in procedures and key person relationships. Assignments and case studies provide you with an opportunity to evidence your understanding of theory and its implications for practice in depth, and to relate this to the work of key theorists.

CASE STUDY

Shahnaz's assignment

Shahnaz is an Early Years Teacher trainee who works in a pre-school room. She decided to use a written assignment to describe a treasure hunt she organised to evidence her under-standing of how pre-school children develop and learn. She chose to evidence her work in an assignment as she felt this would give her the scope she needed to evidence her knowledge and understanding of how pre-school children learn and develop and how she applies this in practice, step by step.

In her assignment she described how the children had been on many trips in the local environment, to shops, the post office, the park and a local café. She felt that they needed a more stimulating approach for their next outing, and wanted to choose an activity that built on their interest in nature, such as collecting leaves and stones, and their recent interest in maps.

She explained how the previous week she had created a treasure map activity, hiding objects in the sand tray in the garden and giving children a map to help them find the

(Continued)

149

(Continued)

'buried treasure'. After observing how interested children were in this activity and how the activity promoted their problem-solving skills, she decided to create a map for a treasure hunt in the local area.

In her assignment she described how she had a meeting with the staff team and explained how each child would have a map to help them find the 'treasure'. It would be a visual map with photographs, for example the café on the corner, the bus stop and the statue in the park. There would be a 'tick box' on their map so that they could make marks when they had seen them, and then move on to the next clue.

On the day, Shahnaz hid the 'treasure' and other clues and explained that the adults needed to support and encourage the children, and reinforce letters and numbers in the environment, and problem-solving and reasoning.

In her evaluation of the activity, Shahnaz analysed the observations she made during the treasure hunt and identified the EYFS (2014) areas of learning that the activity addressed. She identified the benefits of active learning and learning through first-hand experiences. She then analysed the conversations colleagues had with individual children and demonstrated how the scaffolding her colleagues provided enabled the children to problem solve at a higher level than they were able to do on their own. She made links to the work of Donaldson (1978) when she described examples of children making sense of abstract concepts in a situation that made human sense to them, for example, when staff asked the children, 'where would Teddy hide in the shop so that we can't see him?'

You can use your reflective journal in several ways to help you evidence 2.2. You can use it to record your understanding of various theories of learning and development, or to relate your understanding of these theories to the needs of a particular child. You can also use your journal to reflect on how your understanding of theory helps you understand how to organise your setting. This can include the implications of theories of learning and development for planning, resources, routines and setting policies.

You can use a case study to analyse an individual child's development against EYFS requirements and your understanding of a particular area of child development. In the case study below Jo has used her reflective journal to identify an area for improvement and the strategies she can use.

CASE STUDY

Jo's reflective journal

I spent the first day in my baby room placement observing how the babies interacted with the resources provided for them. Many of the resources I could see were plastic and the babies would pick them up for a moment and then discard them.

I thought about what I know about enabling environment and think that maybe I could support the team to introduce some improvements in this area. According to EYFS, an enabling environment needs stimulating resources, relevant to all the children's cultures and communities, rich learning opportunities through play and playful teaching and support for children to take risks and explore.

I thought about Goldschmied and Jackson's (2005) use of natural, household and recycled resources and decided to speak to my new colleagues about Goldschmied, treasure baskets, heuristic play and using natural resources and see if they felt that any of these ideas would be useful. I would need to demonstrate how these resources provide the babies with opportunities to explore a wide range of real objects.

From my observation I noted that the children in the room were at different stages of development, with seated, crawling and walking babies, so I need to ensure that the resources are varied enough. For example, the seated babies will have supporting cushions, bowls of wooden and real fruit and vegetables and materials of different textures to explore with their mouth and hands. The crawling babies will need space to move around the area and we will need to provide larger objects on the mats for them to explore, such as household utensils, and we can ask parents to bring these in from home.

I thought about how children need time to adjust to transitions and change, so I decided that we would need to make gradual, small changes first, perhaps asking each parent to bring in one item from home for the treasure basket.

I observed colleagues' interaction with the babies and identified that, although many babies were not yet verbal, the babies were able to communicate in different ways and adults paid careful attention to them and responded with care, using eye contact, following the child's gaze and repeating the sounds that the child made.

I have started to look at EYFS requirements for babies in more depth and I found it helpful to read about how every child is unique. I realised that treating children equally does not mean providing them with the same things. Rather, the provision must be differentiated according to individual needs, interests and development stages if outcomes are to be positive. I feel that it is important to work with parents to incorporate their child's personal experiences and familiar objects in the home corner and treasure baskets.

Document portfolio

You will be able to include a range of documents or work products in your document portfolio to evidence 2.2. Here are some suggestions:

- If your planning notes for different age groups are detailed enough then they can provide evidence of differentiation, demonstrating how you apply your knowledge of child development. For example, if you work in a room with toddlers and pre-school children you can evidence how you differentiate a particular activity for children in each age group to demonstrate your understanding of their developmental needs at each stage.

- Your observations and 'next steps' for your key children can demonstrate how you apply your knowledge of child development and how children learn, especially if you relate these to EYFS early learning goals and early outcomes.

- The strategies you use to support an individual child can demonstrate your understanding of how children learn. For example, your understanding of Piaget may prompt you to provide first-hand exploratory experiences for young children.

- A record of your concerns about a child's development in a CAF form or an IEP demonstrates that you are aware that this child's development is delayed or not following the expected trajectories.

- A two-year-old progress check or EYFS Profile is evidence of assessing a child against developmental norms.

- Supply a witness testimony where a colleague describes how you use your knowledge of child development to inform your practice. Your colleague could provide examples of how you use your understanding to inform your practice.

- Planning sheets for different age groups can demonstrate that you appreciate the differing learning needs of each age group.

- Settling-in documents can demonstrate your understanding of attachment theory. If you have reviewed or contributed to setting policies, such as a behaviour management policy which refers to children's developmental needs, then this too can provide some evidence.

- Records of conversations with parents and other professionals about a child's development, such as emails or minutes of meetings, can also provide good evidence.

Observations

You will be able to ask a colleague or your mentor or tutor to observe you supporting a child in a particular activity you have planned to support that child. They can refer to your planning notes where you can evidence your understanding of child development and EYFS requirements for a child of that age.

If you have related your observations of that individual child to EYFS early outcomes then you can share these with your observer to demonstrate why you chose this activity as this will demonstrate your knowledge of child development and learning for 2.1.

If you have the opportunity to share with your mentor how your understanding of child development informs your practice, you can show:

- how you organise each room to support the children's developmental needs;

- the activities you plan that are appropriate for a particular age group, such as heuristic play with toddlers;

- how you have introduced changes in each room to support the developmental needs of a particular age group, such as black and white areas for non-mobile babies.

Evidencing your leadership role

You can also use a case study or entries in your journal and a selection of documents to evidence your leadership and support for colleagues as these will allow you to record in detail:

- your rationale for the training you provide on, for example, why children need an enabling environment and the areas where your colleagues need support to promote this;

- the handouts you produced to support your colleagues and the notes you prepared for yourself;

- the areas of child development you addressed and the practical strategies you suggested;

- how you engaged with your colleagues;

- a summary of any one-to-one mentoring conversations you had with colleagues;

- your colleague's evaluation of the support you gave in an evaluation form or witness testimony.

In the case study below, Joshua uses a series of documents to evidence his leadership role for 2.2 and Standard 8. He uses his journal to record his rationale for leading change and how this relates to his understanding of the developmental needs of the toddlers in a play and stay session.

CASE STUDY

Joshua's work documents evidence his leadership role

Joshua is an Early Years Teacher trainee who is the lead teacher at a children's centre and he supports the staff who have set up a new play and stay session. He decided to use his reflective journal and a series of work documents to evidence his understanding of how toddlers develop and learn. The documents he included were a rationale for his intervention, his plan for a training session with the stay and play team, minutes from the training session and his annotated observations of the stay and play sessions after the training.

In his journal Joshua describes his findings from his initial observations of a messy play session in the toddlers' stay and play group and presents his rationale for the changes he plans to introduce:

> The staff were newly qualified and didn't seem confident enough to let the children explore freely. Perhaps this was from a lack of knowledge or their concerns about safe

(Continued)

(Continued)

practice and how parents would react if their children get messy. Also I observed that a lot of parents were reluctant to let their children play outside, saying it was too cold.

I planned to train staff to be more confident and knowledgeable about the positive learning opportunities for toddlers inside and out and encourage them to support parents and talk to them about their concerns.

I observed a few play and stay sessions with a range of parents to see what areas could be changed and how to help staff and parents feel more confident in letting the children play outside and take part in messy play.

When I observed parents I found that they had a real concern about their children playing outside in the cold and would encourage them to stay inside. One explained: 'he's always getting colds so I have to keep him inside.' I saw that staff were agreeing with this and were happy to shut the door to the outside area, explaining it was probably too cold! While all this was happening some children were at the doors asking to go out and parents were struggling to get them involved in other activities.

Joshua used his document portfolio to present his plans for the training session and the handouts he prepared to prompt discussion amongst the team. In these plans and hand-outs he highlighted the emphasis in the work of Susan Isaacs and EYFS (2012) on providing opportunities for learning outdoors and that while playing children can express fears and re-live anxious experiences. They can try things out, solve problems and be creative and can take risks and use trial and error to find things out (Department for Education and Skills, 2003a).

He also included in his evidence for 2.2 a series of plans that the team drew up during the training session that looked at:

- *how it would be possible to set up role-play areas in the garden to promote early literacy and numeracy activities, such as bus station with tickets, timetable, etc.;*

- *activities to support toddlers' developmental needs, particularly opportunities to develop gross motor skills, heuristic play, messy play and how we need to talk to parents about the importance of these activities;*

- *extending opportunities for messy play and explaining to parents how toddlers learn through heuristic play.*

Joshua attached the minutes of the training session to his plan, to show how he promoted discussion of toddlers' developmental needs.

He then included observations he carried out after the training session and his reflections in his journal to summarise what he had observed:

- *The number of adults outside nearly doubled in one week.*

- *Staff were encouraging parents to come out: staff appeared more confident and seemed happier to be outside and this had an impact on how parents felt about going outside with their children.*

- *One parent came to me and told me that she had taken my advice and now bought spare clothes so 'he can get as wet and messy as he likes!'*

- *The level and variety of activities outside increased and staff are now regularly planning activities for the outside area and talk to parents about why these activities support toddlers' development.*

Bee, H (1997) *The Developing Child*. Harlow: Longman.

Donaldson, M (1978) *Children's Minds*. London: Fontana.

Gerhardt, S (2004) Why *Love Matters: How Affection Shapes a Baby's Brain*. London: Routledge.

Goldschmied, E and Jackson, S (2005) *People Under Three: Young Children in Day Care*. London: Routledge.

Gopnik, A, Khul, P and Meltzoff, A (2001) *How Babies Think: The Science of Childhood*. London: Phoenix.

Lindon, J (2008) *Understanding Child Development: Linking Theory and Practice* (2nd edn). London: Hodder Arnold.

Manning-Morton, J and Thorp, M (2003) *Key Times For Play*. Maidenhead: Open University Press, McGraw-Hill Educational.

Nutbrown, C (2006) *The Threads of Thinking: Young Children Learning and the Role of Early Education*. London: SAGE.

Smith, PK, Cowie, H and Blades, M (2003) *Understanding Children's Development*. Oxford: Blackwells.

Standard 2.3: Know and understand attachment theories, their significance and how effectively to promote secure attachments

Introduction

Standard 2.3 asks you to focus on your understanding of attachment theories and how this informs your practice. You are asked to evidence your understanding of the work of key theorists and explain how this helps you to promote secure attachment relationships in your setting.

The key phrases in this indicator that you need to note are:

- *know and understand*: this means that you need to evidence your knowledge as well as your practice;

- *attachment theories*: you need to evidence your understanding of more than one attachment theory and the work of two or more relevant theorists;

- *promote*: you need to evidence the actions you take to promote attachments, for example, between parents/carers and their child or the key person relationships within your setting;

- *effectively*: you need to evaluate your actions to find out whether they were, in fact, effective;

- *secure attachments*: if you are to promote secure attachments, you need to understand the characteristics of a secure attachment and the different forms that an insecure attachment can take.

In this section we will look in some detail at the ideas of the main attachment theorists and at the implications for your practice, as well as providing information on further reading and how to evidence 2.3.

Attachment theory

Cathy's introduction to attachment theory

Cathy is an Early Years Teacher trainee working in a private nursery. She was responsible for developing her setting's settling-in policy and, while leading discussion on this in a staff meeting, she discovered that several members of the team lacked confidence in their understanding of attachment theory and how to apply it.

Cathy decided to lead a staff training session on attachment theories and promoting secure attachments to support her team and help her evidence 2.3. She created a handout for the team that summarised the main ideas of the key theorists and included a copy of this in her document portfolio. Cathy also developed a chart that the team could complete during the training session to help them identify the implications for practice of each theorist. (You can find a copy of this chart in Table S2.5, below.)

Cathy's handout for staff training on attachment theorists

Bowlby (1969) and attachment theory

Bowlby's theory of attachment maintains that children come into the world biologically pre-programmed to form attachments, because in evolutionary terms this helps them to survive. They are born with the ability to display innate behaviours that promote proximity to their mother or mother figure, such as crying and smiling, and these instinctive attachment behaviours are activated if a situation appears to threaten this proximity.

Bowlby suggested that a child would initially form only one attachment, with the mother, and that this attachment figure acted as a secure base for exploring the world, and that the fear of strangers represents an important survival mechanism.

Bowlby's ideas have had a great influence on the way researchers approach attachment and much of the disagreement with them has focused on his belief in 'monotropy', that the attachment with the mother is unique.

You can find more information on Bowlby at **www.simplypsychology.org/bowlby.html**.

Schaffer and Emerson (1964)

Schaffer and Emerson disagreed with Bowlby's ideas on monotropy, as they identified that babies form specific attachments to one person from about 8 months and soon afterwards become attached to other people. By 18 months very few children (13%) were attached to only one person and some had five or more attachments. This provides a rationale for the importance of the key person role.

Mary Ainsworth (1970, 1978) and the strange situation

Researchers following on from Bowlby identified individual differences in the quality of children's attachments and the psychologist Mary Ainsworth provided the most well-known exploration of these differences. She devised an assessment technique called the Strange Situation Classification (SSC) in order to investigate how attachments might vary between children.

For more information, see **www.simplypsychology.org/mary-ainsworth.html**.

Michael Rutter and Maternal Deprivation Reassessed

Bowlby used the term maternal deprivation to refer to separation from or loss of the mother and the failure to develop an attachment to her. Rutter (1981) in Maternal Deprivation Reassessed suggested that Bowlby had oversimplified this concept, as failure to develop attachment, separation from an attached figure and loss of the attached figure each has different effects.

For more information, see **www.simplypsychology.org/bowlby.html**.

Anna Freud and the Hampstead War Nursery

After the outbreak of the Second World War, Anna Freud, daughter of Sigmund Freud, set up the Hampstead War Nursery to provide foster care for over 80 children from single-parent families to help them develop attachments through their ongoing ties with the helpers at the nursery and by encouraging their mothers to visit as often as possible. With her colleague Dorothy Burlingham, she published a study of these children under stress in Young Children in War-Time and Infants Without Families (Freud and Burlingham, 1942b, 1944).

After the war, Anna Freud was able to observe more extreme parental deprivation when she conducted a series of case studies on a group of orphans from the Theresienstadt concentration camp. In 'An experiment in group upbringing' (Freud and Dann, 1951) she describes how the children found attachment to adults difficult after their experiences in the concentration camp, but they supported each other so that their peers became their

(Continued)

157

(Continued)

central attachment figures. Anna Freud believed this indicates that bonding with the mother is not always necessary for successful attachment and socialisation.

For more information, see **www.freud.org.uk/education/topic/40053/anna-freud/**.

Judy Dunn and Young Children's Close Relationships: Beyond Attachment

Judy Dunn (1993, 2004) examines current research and explores children's relationships with their parents, siblings and friends and the connections between these. She stresses the need to broaden research into children's close relationships as attachment theory has been useful in illuminating aspects of the parent child relationship and [its] significance in later life, and hypothesizing about what processes may be important, however its typology is limited and limiting *(Dunn, 1993: 14). She demonstrates how siblings and friends as well as parents, childcare providers and educators influence children's social understanding and relationships.*

Heather Geddes and Attachment in the Classroom

Geddes (2006) developed a model that relates patterns of early attachment to their impact on learning and relationships in the classroom, and on children's long-term future, including work and social inclusion. She demonstrates how patterns of early attachment (forming 'memory templates') are directly linked to children's expectations and responses to adults in school.

Cathy developed a chart to help her team identify the implications of the work of the attachment theorists mentioned in the case study. Table S2.5 has adapted Cathy's chart and you can use this to identify the ways in which attachment theories have an impact on your practice and how you can evidence this.

Some of Cathy's team's entries are added to the boxes to help you, but you need to complete this yourself, in relation to your own understanding and practice, as this will help you to identify your evidence.

Secure and insecure attachments

If you are to identify how you promote secure attachments, you need to have a good understanding of what makes an attachment secure or not secure, such as anxious-ambivalent attachment, anxious-avoidant attachment and disorganised attachment.

Use your journal to identify the qualities of a secure attachment and reflect on the different types of attachment, their implications for a child's well-being and how you can evaluate the quality of the attachment relationships of your key children.

Table S2.5 Attachment theory and examples of practice, leadership and evidence

Ideas of theorist	Implications for practice	Evidence of your practice	Evidence of your leadership
A child has an innate need to attach to one main attachment figure (Bowlby's monotropy) or a small number of key attachment figures (Schaffer, Rutter, A Freud, Dunn)	Low staff turnover	Key person observations	Training handouts and minutes of staff meeting on attachment theory and how it relates to our settling-in policy
	Promote key person relationship	Order forms for books and puppets to support children through loss of attachment figure	Records of exit interviews to identify reasons for high staff turnover
	Support child during separations from attachment figure, e.g. if parent is in hospital	Hospital role-play area to support child with parent in hospital	
		Photo display of family for child to refer to in parent's absence	
Children use their attachment figure as a secure base for exploring the world (Bowlby)	Settling-in procedures need to take account of children's need to move away from their attachment figure gradually	Settling-in forms and observations	Contributions to settling-in policy
		Finding out child's favourite activities from parents	
		Providing photos and comforters from home to provide a secure base when parent is absent	
A breakdown of the primary attachment relationship can lead to serious negative consequences (Bowlby and Rutter)	Support parents in promoting attachment relationships	Completed Common Assessment Framework form and minutes of meeting recording discussion with mother about how postnatal depression affected her bonding with child	Set up systems for allocating or changing key person so as to take account of bonds children form naturally with practitioners
	Promote alternative attachment relationships, including the key person relationship	Referral form for mother to see children's centre psychologist	Arrangements for and minutes from meeting where invited psychologist to talk about how we can promote attachment relationships
		Settling-in records and records of key times to demonstrate strategies key person uses to develop attachment relationship with key child	

(Continued)

Table S2.5 (Continued)

Ideas of theorist	Implications for practice	Evidence of your practice	Evidence of your leadership
Children should receive continuous care from their most important attachment figure for approximately the first two years of life (Bowlby)	Avoid high staff turnover	Observations of key child and records of key times	Identify reasons for staff leaving and introduce exit interviews
	Provide system for second key person for each child to provide support if key person is away	Observations of visiting toddler room with key child and plans for transition from baby room to toddler room	Set up system for additional key person to cover when key person is away or if key person is part-time
	Introduction of key times so key person is responsible for changing own key child and has one-to-one times with key children throughout day		Handouts from training on importance of key times
Children's attachment relationship with their primary caregiver leads to the development of an internal working model with three main features:	Key person models positive internal working model	Peer observations of key times with child where listen carefully, respond consistently and provide reliable, positive feedback to child	Deliver training on how key person can present alternative internal working model for a child without a secure attachment, e.g. by listening and consistently responding sensitively, providing positive feedback
1. a model of others as being trustworthy;	Consider implications for looked-after children		
2. a model of self as valuable;			Training notes on impact of being a looked-after child
3. a model of self as effective when interacting with others.			
This mental representation guides future social and emotional behaviour (Bowlby)			
Children can form more than one attachment relationship (Rutter and Schaffer)	Find out about children's attachment relationships, for example, with foster carer, single father or grandparents	Plans for Mothers' Day celebrations that include all key attachment figures, e.g. making cards for grandparents	Plans for activities including child's wider family members
	Support relationships with wider family members		
Children can form attachment relationships with siblings and peers (Dunn)	Set up systems to promote peer and sibling attachment relationships , particularly with older siblings	Photo displays of family that include siblings	Set up times where older siblings can visit younger siblings, for example, after rest time, or to visit for snack time
	If a child is going into foster care, stress the need to keep the child together with his siblings	Observations of interactions between siblings when have encouraged older siblings to visit younger siblings in the playground	

In 2.3 you are asked to evidence how you promote attachment relationships 'effectively', so you now need to think about how you can evaluate your actions to promote secure attachments. How can you judge whether they were effective?

Evidence for 2.3

You need to evidence three areas for 2.3 – your understanding of attachment theory, why promoting secure attachments is so important in the early years, and how you promote secure attachment relationships, for example, through organising ratios to provide regular key times.

You need to provide practical examples of how you effectively promote attachment relationships and why this is important. Remember, that as you have to evidence that you *effectively* promote secure attachments, your evidence needs to demonstrate how or why your actions were effective.

If you are a manager rather than a practitioner, your evidence of promoting secure attachments may be different. You may have more evidence of setting up systems to promote attachment relationships within the setting rather than of working with a specific parent to support her relationship with her child or forming attachment relationships yourself with your key children. You will need to judge whether the evidence you do have is sufficient or whether you need to consider taking on a placement where you can address this. The introductory chapter on age-related placements can help you decide this.

You may find that you can cross-reference some of your evidence for 2.2 on child development to 2.3 on attachment. However, you need to make sure that this evidence clearly addresses the requirements of each Standard.

Written assignments, case studies and your reflective journal

A case study or written assignment provides you with the scope to explore your knowledge and understanding of more than one attachment theory in depth and evidence how your understanding informs your practice. You can evidence your practice by including documents in your document portfolio; however, you do need to elaborate on how the documents demonstrate that your actions are informed by theory and how you have evaluated the effectiveness of your actions and a written assignment, case study or entry in your journal can provide the scope you need for this.

You could also lead a staff development session on attachment. You can use an assignment, case study or a series of journal entries to record the ways in which you share your understanding of attachment theories with you colleagues as a group, or one to one.

CASE STUDY

Sue and Aaron

I noticed Aaron's mum, Julie, arrived later than usual to collect him and I thought she looked tired. She didn't go straight over to Aaron as usual, but sat in the corner. As we've had some problems with Aaron's behaviour, I said to him, 'Look, your mummy is here! Shall we go and tell her how kind you were to Ellie when she was upset today?'

He smiled and ran over to his mum. He tugged her arm but it was a moment before she responded. This is really not like her and I noticed she was rubbing her back.

When Aaron ran off to play I asked Julie how she was. She said she has problems with her pregnancy and spent last night in Accident and Emergency and had to leave Aaron with a neighbour. She said she needs Aaron to go to bed earlier so she can rest and asked if we could stop his sleep time after lunch. We spoke about Aaron's need to sleep and the impact of stopping this before he's ready, and that if he's tired there might be more problems with his behaviour. We talked about strategies to reduce his sleep time here gradually and strategies Julie can use to help her settle Aaron at bed time.

In the case study in the introduction to Standard 1 we met Sue, a toddler room practitioner who has recently embarked on her Early Years Teacher Status. Sue has used her journal to reflect on her concerns about Aaron and how he was responding to his mother's pregnancy and these reflections provide good evidence for 2.3.

> *I asked how Aaron was adjusting to the pregnancy and Julie has some worries about this; she isn't sure he really understands. I gave her a book to borrow on becoming a big brother to share with Aaron and said I'd talk to him in our key times to try to help him understand what is happening.*
>
> *Maybe I need to increase our key times? I also said to Julie that I'd encourage Aaron to talk about the new baby at snack time and circle time.*

Sue observed that as Aaron's mum, Julie, was tired and had been in hospital, she was not as responsive to Aaron as usual and Sue was concerned that Aaron might be aware of this. They had been managing his behavioural issues and Sue's concern was that the lack of his mother's attention and her need for him not to sleep after his lunch would put him under stress and this might affect his behaviour.

She was also worried about his understanding of his mother's pregnancy and wondered whether she needed to extend her key times with Aaron so that he would have more access to one of his attachment figures.

In her next journal entry Sue reflected on some of the strategies she had been carrying out to support Aaron's attachment relationship with his mother and her own key relationship with him. She also focused on giving Aaron the words to describe and manage his emotions.

As Sue was concerned that children need their attachment figures to respond consistently and positively to provide them with a sense of their own worth, her journal entry provides good evidence of applying her knowledge of attachment theory in her work with Julie and Aaron.

CASE STUDY

Sue's reflective journal

Today Julie has asked to collect Aaron an hour later than usual in the afternoon. I explained that I understood that she needs the rest, but I was concerned that at Aaron's age, and because he is unsettled, this is a long time for him to be without his mum. I wonder if I need to talk to Julie about attachment relationships next time we speak?

I explained that I've been spending one-to-one times with Aaron, sharing books and activities with his favourite truck that he brings in from home. I suggested that maybe it would help him if he could regularly bring in a comfort object from home. I asked for some photos of him at home with his mum so we could make these into a book with him as this might comfort him when he misses her.

I asked mum about other people he is close to and she mentioned that his granny looks after him at the weekends when she does the shopping. I asked if his grandma could collect him, perhaps twice a week at his normal time, so that he'd have more time at home with one of his important attachment figures? Then, if he stayed later the other three days it might not be so hard for him.

Document portfolio

There are many routine practices in your setting that you contribute to that are influenced by attachment theory and you can evidence these in your document portfolio. Make sure that any documents you include clearly highlight your knowledge or understanding and/or actions. If this is not clear, you can add a note to explain how this piece of evidence demonstrates your understanding and its implications for your practice.

These documents can include:

- records of completing a home visit;
- routine observations of children to support their settling in;
- your settling-in records and the settling-in policy if you have contributed to it;
- records of supporting a child through a transition to another room or through other separations from an attachment figure;
- completed 'all about me' forms to help you plan for a child's interests and create continuity between a child's home and your setting;
- reminders of key words from the child's home language;
- peer observations of key times with your key child;
- observations of your key children interacting with their parent or carer and your reflections on their attachment relationship;

163

- records of creating photo displays and books of the child and family;

- records of creating a system for children to bring in comfort objects from home;

- plans for activities you introduced to support a child during a separation from his attachment figure;

- records of buying books on separation or loss to use with a child;

- peer observations that highlight how you provide a consistent attachment relationship and a positive internal working model for a child, for example, by using positive feedback to help children appreciate that they are effective when interacting with others;

- including objects from home in treasure baskets and role-play area;

- records of conversations with parents that relate to attachment issues, such as supporting a child through his parents' separation or a bereavement;

- records of promoting contact between the setting and the parent that a child does not live with, for example, by sending the parent copies of your setting newsletter and feedback on the child's progress;

- an anonymised CAF form and records of conversations with other professionals that relate to a child's attachment relationships or separations from attachment figures.

Observations

You can arrange to be observed in an activity that promotes a child's secure attachments. This could be an activity where you support a child who is settling in or moving between rooms to evidence how you apply your understanding of attachment theory. You can use your plans for the activity to highlight your understanding of attachment theory and its implications for your practice.

You could also arrange to be observed leading an activity that involves a child's parent or carer, perhaps cooking or sharing stories and songs in the child's home language. If you are working in a school nursery, you may be in a position where you can be observed inviting children's older siblings to visit the nursery for a particular occasion, such as a birthday celebration.

You could also arrange for your mentor or tutor to observe you creating a photo book with a child about her family or sharing a book about separation to support a child who no longer lives with one of their parents. You could also demonstrate how you have ordered books that reflect the full range of attachment relationships that the children in your room have.

SUGGESTED READING

Ainsworth, MDS and Bell, SM (1970) Attachment, exploration, and separation: Illustrated by the behaviour of one-year-olds in a strange situation. *Child Development*, 41: 49–67.

Ainsworth, MDS, Blehar, MC, Waters, E and Wall, S (1978) *Patterns of Attachment: A Psychological Study of the Strange Situation.* Hillsdale, NJ: Erlbaum.

Bowlby, J (1951) *Maternal Care and Mental Health.* Geneva: World Health Organization.

Bowlby, J (1953) *Child Care and the Growth of Love.* London: Penguin Books.

Bowlby, J (1969) *Attachment and Loss, Vol.1, Attachment.* New York: Basic Books.

Bowlby, J (1973) *Attachment and Loss, Vol. 2, Separation: Anxiety and Anger.* New York: Basic Books.

Bowlby, J (1980) *Attachment and Loss, Vol. 3, Loss: Sadness and Depression.* International Psycho-analytical library no. 109. London: Hogarth Press.

Bretherton, I and Ainsworth, MDS (1974) One-year-olds in the Strange Situation. In: M Lewis and L Rosenblum (eds) *The Origins of Fear* (pp. 134–164). New York: Wiley.

Bretherton, I and Waters, E (1985) Growing points of attachment theory and research. *Monographs of the Society for Research in Child Development,* 50 (1-2, Serial No, 209).

Bretherton, I, Biringen, Z, Ridgeway, D, Maslin, M, and Sherman, M (1989) Attachment: the parental perspective. *Infant Mental Health Journal* (Special Issue), 10: 203–220.

Bretherton, I, Ridgeway, D and Cassidy, J (1990) Assessing internal working models in the attachment relationship: An attachment story completion task for 3-year-olds. In: MT Greenberg, D Cicchetti and EM Cummings (eds) *Attachment During the Preschool Years* (pp. 272–308). Chicago: University of Chicago Press.

Dunn, J (1993) *Young Children's Close Relationships: Beyond Attachment.* London: SAGE.

Dunn, J (2004) *Children's Friendships: The Beginnings of Intimacy.* Oxford: Blackwell.

Dunn, J and Kenrick, C (1982) *Siblings: Love, Envy and Understanding.* London: Grant McIntyre.

Erikson, F (1950) *Childhood and Society.* New York: Norton.

Freud, A and Burlingham, D (1942) *War and Children.* New York: International Universities Press.

Freud, A and Burlingham, D (1944) *Infants without Families.* New York: International Universities Press.

Geddes, H (2006) *Attachment in the Classroom: The links Between Children's Early Experience, Emotional Well-being and Performance.* London: Worth.

Jacobsen, T and Hoffman, V (1997) Children's attachment representations: longitudinal relations to school behaviour and academic competency in middle childhood and adolescence. *Developmental Psychology,* 33: 703–710.

Lamb, ME (1977) The development of mother–infant and father–infant attachments in the second year of life. *Developmental Psychology,* 13: 637–648.

Larose, S and Bernier, A (2001) Social support processes: mediators of attachment state of mind and adjustment in later late adolescence. *Attachment and Human Development,* 3: 96–120.

Main, M and Solomon, J (1990) Procedures for identifying infants as disorganized/disoriented during the Ainsworth Strange Situation. In: MT Greenberg, D Cicchetti and EM Cummings (eds) *Attachment in the Preschool Years* (pp. 121–160). Chicago: University of Chicago Press.

McLeod, SA (2008) *Mary Ainsworth: Attachment Styles – Simply Psychology.* Available at: **www.simplypsychology.org/mary-ainsworth.html** (accessed 20/10/2014).

Robertson, J and Bowlby, J (1952) Responses of young children to separation from their mothers. *Courrier of the International Children's Centre. Paris,* 2: 131–140.

Rutter, M (1979) Maternal deprivation, 1972–1978: New findings, new concepts, new approaches. *Child Development,* 283–305.

Rutter, M (1981) *Maternal Deprivation Reassessed* (2nd edn). Harmondsworth: Penguin.

Schaffer, HR and Emerson, PE (1964) The development of social attachments in infancy. *Monographs of the Society for Research in Child Development,* 29 (3), serial number 94.

Standard 2.4: Lead and model effective strategies to develop and extend children's learning and thinking, including sustained shared thinking

Introduction

Standard 2.4 asks you to demonstrate how you lead and model strategies to promote children's thinking and learning and engage in sustained shared thinking (SST is often used as an abbreviation for this). Your evidence of promoting children's learning may overlap with your evidence for other Standards that relate to children's learning, such as Standard 4. However, what makes 2.4 different from the other Standards that promote children's learning is that you need to evidence this in relation to how you support children's thinking skills and engage in sustained shared thinking, and this is the area we will explore in this chapter.

We will look at definitions of thinking skills and why they are important, explore strategies suggested in EYFS to promote children's thinking skills, how to evidence these strategies and how to model these strategies for colleagues. We will then consider how to promote sustained shared thinking. As this can all be difficult to evidence we will look at how to provide detailed examples of your interactions with children to demonstrate, step by step, how you engaged with them to extend their thinking skills and how you adapt these strategies with children of different ages.

The key phrases you will need to evidence in 2.4 are:

- *lead and model*: you will need to evidence how you provide training and mentoring and model strategies to extend children's thinking and learning.

- *effective strategies*: you need to identify strategies that are most effective and find a way to evaluate how effective the strategies you use actually are.

- *develop and extend*: you will need to evidence how your actions promote children's progress, for example, through ongoing observations that record your interventions and the impact they have: you also have to consider the difference between *develop* and *extend* and make sure that you evidence how you do both of these.

- *children's learning and thinking*: you need to identify the difference between *learning* and *thinking* and identify strategies to promote both of these with children of different ages. Your evidence of promoting children's learning needs to relate to EYFS requirements and you can cross-reference some of this evidence to other Standards that relate to children's learning, such as Standard 3.

- *sustained shared thinking*: you need to identify what is meant by sustained shared thinking and how it relates to children's thinking skills: your evidence of engaging in sustained shared thinking needs to be detailed enough to identify your input and the impact it has on that child's thinking.

Thinking skills

In recent years, as a result of research into how the brain works and how we learn, there has been growing interest in how to foster children's thinking and learning skills (Fisher, 2005). Thinking skills are defined as how we apply our minds to solving problems. Researchers have suggested that thinking skills are essential to effective learning because if thinking is how children make sense of learning, then developing their thinking skills will help them learn throughout their life.

Thinking skills include how a person applies processes such as remembering, questioning, forming concepts, planning, reasoning, imagining, solving problems, making decisions and judgements and translating thoughts into words.

A skill is frequently defined as a practical ability in a particular context, such as being 'good at playing an instrument', but it can be applied to the processes involved in thinking as, for example, being able to memorise can be seen as a skill.

Children can be supported to learn ways to 'think' that are most effective and they can learn these strategies if they are given opportunities to practise these skills.

CASE STUDY

Cathy and Bloom's taxonomy (www.thinkingclassroom. co.uk/ThinkingClassroom/ThinkingSkills.aspx)

Cathy is an Early Years Teacher trainee who we met in the case study in 2.3. She felt that she did not understand enough about theories of thinking skills so she decided to find out more about this and share what she learnt with her colleagues, to see if this might help them develop strategies to promote children's thinking skills. She realised that if she could model and lead practice in this area it would help her to evidence 2.4.

Cathy found that many researchers have attempted to identify our key thinking skills, but the most famous of these is Bloom, whose work builds on the ideas of Piaget and Vygotsky.

Bloom identifies a range of basic, lower-order cognitive skills (knowledge, comprehension and application) and higher-order skills (analysis, synthesis and evaluation) and stresses the importance of providing opportunities to develop the full range of higher- and lower-order skills. Cathy learnt that we need to challenge children to think deeply and widely and in more systematic and sustained ways.

(Continued)

(Continued)

She decided that looking at Bloom's model in detail could help her team to identify ways in which they could promote children's lower- and higher-order thinking skills through planned activities and identify when it is appropriate to focus on each skill. For example, she thought that one way they could help a child feel more confident contributing to circle time would be to ask them a simple lower-order question, such as 'what is our teddy called?', so that they have experience of success.

She prepared the chart in Table S2.6 to identify how she and her team could promote children's thinking skills at each level. She introduced this chart to her team by saying that when they next share a story with a child they could ask any of these questions:

1. *Knowledge: What happened in the story?*

2. *Comprehension: Why did it happen that way?*

3. *Application: What would you have done?*

4. *Analysis: Which part did you like best?*

5. *Synthesis: Can you think of a different ending?*

6. *Evaluation: What did you think of the story? Why?*

Table S2.6 *Using Bloom's taxonomy to identify practice and plan evidence*

Cognitive goal	Thinking cues	Examples of your practice	Sources of evidence
1. Knowledge	Ask child: what do you know, or remember?		
	Child can: describe, identify, tell who, when, which, where, what		
2. Comprehension	Ask child: describe in your own words how you feel about something		
	Child can: interpret, show understanding, explain, compare, relate		
3. Application	Ask child: how can you use it? Where does it lead?		
	Child can apply and use what he knows, use it to solve problems, demonstrate		
4. Analysis	Ask child: what are the parts, the order, the reasons why?		
	Child can: take apart, make judgements about causes/problems/solutions/consequences		
5. Synthesis	Ask child: how might it be different? How else? What if?		
	Child can: connect, be creative, suppose, put together, develop, improve, create her own		
6. Evaluation	Ask child: how would you judge this? Does it succeed? Will it work? What would you prefer? Why do you think so?		
	Child can: judge and assess		

EYFS (2012) and strategies to extend children's learning and thinking

If you are to evidence how you promote children's thinking and learning effectively you need to know how this relates to EYFS requirements. EYFS (2012) explicitly promotes children's thinking skills and the section on 'characteristics of effective learning' includes a category called 'creating and thinking critically'.

Development Matters (Early Education, 2012: 7) also suggests ways in which adults can promote children's thinking skills and if you can evidence how you model and implement these strategies, this can help you to evidence 2.4.

Table S2.7 lists some strategies that EYFS (2012) suggests using to promote children's thinking skills. If you record examples of your practice in the central column and your evidence in the right-hand column this will help you plan your evidence and identify any gaps in your practice. Cathy's suggestions have been added to help you start, but you need to identify your own examples and evidence.

Table S2.7 *EYFS 'Creating and critically thinking: thinking'*

EYFS 'Positive Relationships What adults could do'	Examples of my strategies	Evidence
Use the language of thinking and learning: think, know, remember, forget, idea, makes sense, plan, learn, find out, confused, figure out, trying to do	Record key phrases to use to promote thinking skills on focus activity plans, e.g. 'can you remember when … ' and 'can we find out … ?'	Peer or mentor observation of using this language during focus group activity
Model being a thinker, showing that you don't always know, are curious and sometimes puzzled, and can think and find out	Use phrases when engaging in sustained shared thinking with a child, such as: 'Hmm, I'm not sure … .how can we find that out?'	Peer or mentor observation Plans for modelling activity for student
Encourage open-ended thinking by not settling on the first ideas: what else is possible?	Put list on wall for colleagues as reminder of key prompts they can use, such as 'what if … ?' Deliver training session in staff meeting on using open questions	Colleagues' evaluations of training session on promoting open-ended questions
Always respect children's efforts and ideas, so they feel safe to take a risk with a new idea	Take photos of children's 'work in progress' as well as finished pieces and ask them to explain to their peers in circle time what they were creating	Peer or mentor observation of circle time
Talking aloud helps children to think and control what they do. Model self-talk, describing your actions in play	Demonstrate how I model self-talk to support a child learning something new and supporting child-initiated activity, for example, 'I wonder, shall I put the big block here? I wonder if it will balance … it might fall down?'	Peer or mentor observation Plans to model engaging in child-initiated activities
Give children time to talk and think	Ensure that at circle time children know they have time to respond: use the puppet, so the child with the puppet can't be interrupted	Observations of circle time with and without puppet to compare quality of children's interactions
Value questions, talk and many possible responses, without rushing toward answers too quickly	Use rolling snack to promote conversations in small groups	Plans to introduce rolling snack with focus on small-group conversations and sharing songs

(Continued)

Table S2.7 (Continued)

EYFS 'Positive Relationships What adults could do'	Examples of my strategies	Evidence
Support children's interests over time, reminding them of previous approaches and encouraging them to make connections between their experiences	Introduce 'children's interests' column on planning sheet	Planning sheets
Model the creative process, showing your thinking about some of the many possible ways forward		
Sustained shared thinking helps children to explore ideas and make links. Follow children's lead in conversation, and think about things together		
Encourage children to describe problems they encounter, and to suggest ways to solve the problem		
Show and talk about strategies – how to do things – including problem solving, thinking and learning		
Give feedback and help children to review their own progress and learning. Talk with children about what they are doing, how they plan to do it, what worked well and what they would change next time		
Model the plan–do–review process yourself		

At the end of this chapter is a section on suggested reading which contains several texts that can help you to understand how to promote children's thinking skills. Here are three texts you might also like to consider:

Costello, PJM (2000)*Thinking Skills and Early Childhood Education (Early Years and Primary)*. London: David Fulton.

Eysenck, MW and Keane, MT (2010) *Cognitive Psychology: A Student's Handbook*. Sussex: Psychology Press.

Wallace, B (2002) *Teaching Thinking Skills across the Early Years: A Practical approach for children aged 4 to 7*. London: NACE/David Fulton.

Sustained shared thinking

Standard 2.4 asks you to *lead and model effective strategies to develop and extend children's thinking … including sustained shared thinking*. So, you need to understand exactly what sustained shared thinking is, and what it isn't. If you were asked to define sustained shared thinking, what would you say?

Sustained shared thinking is not …

It can be helpful to look at what sustained shared thinking isn't before we look at what it is. An adult-initiated activity ('we are making pizza today'), involving questions that test a child's knowledge or understanding ('what is pizza?') or factual, closed questions ('is the dough yellow or white?) may extend children's thinking, but it is not sustained shared thinking.

Sustained shared thinking is ...

- *An episode in which two or more individuals 'work together' in an intellectual way to solve a problem, clarify a concept, evaluate activities, extend a narrative etc. Both parties must contribute to the thinking and it must develop and extend* (Siraj-Blatchford et al., 2002).

- *Those wonderful times that you get when you are totally absorbed with a child, whether it is in conversation or in an activity, with a genuine interest on both parts to find out more* (Kathy Brodie, 2009: **www.kathybrodie.com/viewpoint/ sustained-shared-thinking-important/**)

- An opportunity for the practitioner to *learn extensive amounts about how the child sees the world, their level of cognitive development, schemas, community and self-esteem (to name but a few!). The child may learn things such as social interaction techniques, how to think creatively, cause and effect and factual information* (Kathy Brodie, 2009: **www.kathybrodie.com/viewpoint/sustained-shared-thinking-important/**).

- *Sustained shared thinking helps children to explore ideas and make links. Follow children's lead in conversation, and think about things together* (Early Education, 2012).

Sustained shared thinking is also ...

- related to the ideas of theorists who promote learning through social interaction, such as Vygotsky and his ideas on scaffolding and Bruner with his focus on discovery learning;

- a spontaneously occurring conversation where a child introduces a topic that is of interest to her and your role is to help her explore and extend her understanding of the concepts involved: you will learn about the child's level of understanding and thinking skills and help her extend these through an absorbing and stimulating two-way conversation;

- not an event you can plan, but if you are aware of a child's particular interests, such as 'what do worms eat?', and you provide resources to help the child explore his interests, such as a magnifying glass and wormery kit, then sustained shared thinking is more likely to occur.

Three aspects of sustained shared thinking that you can evidence

As it can be hard to evidence sustained shared thinking in enough detail, we will now look at some strategies you can use to help you evidence this.

You will be able to judge whether a piece of evidence adequately evidences sustained shared thinking if you look at your evidence in the light of the three words, *sustained*, *shared* and *thinking*. These three words will tell you what it is that you need to evidence.

1. You need to evidence a conversation that is *sustained*, where you take time to explore with a child something he said in conversation with you.

2. It needs to be a conversation that is *shared*, absorbing and interesting both of you. You are acting as scientists exploring the issue together as equals.

3. You use this opportunity to support and extend the child's *thinking* skills, perhaps using the strategies identified in EYFS (2012) (Table S2.7) and Bloom's taxonomy (Table S2.6). You can demonstrate how you encourage thinking skills such as problem solving, creative thinking, evaluation, reasoning, enquiry and information processing.

Promoting sustained shared thinking: two case studies

Often Early Years Teacher trainees find it difficult to choose appropriate and detailed enough pieces of evidence for 2.4. You can use the following two examples to help you identify the qualities of sustained shared thinking that your evidence needs to demonstrate, the role of the adult in promoting sustained shared thinking and what a good piece of evidence looks like.

You may want to discuss these examples with your colleagues to promote their understanding of sustained shared thinking, as in 2.4 you need to demonstrate how you lead and model good practice. These two examples come from an article by Iram Siraj-Blatchford et al. (2009) and you may find it helpful to read the whole article and share it with your colleagues.

CASE STUDY

Case study: example 1

In the following example a nursery officer was observed supporting sustained shared thinking that was initiated by a child and entirely unrelated to the activity that the adult had planned:

Boy 3 (3:11) has finished his cake and starts to sing 'Happy Birthday' to Nursery officer 1.

Nursery officer 1 pretends to blow out the candles. 'Do I have a present?'

Boy 3 (3:11) hands her a ball of playdough.

Nursery officer 1: 'I wonder what's inside? I'll unwrap it.' She quickly makes the ball into a thumb pot and holds it out to Boy 3 (3:11), 'It's empty!'

Boy 3 (3:11) takes a pinch of playdough and drops it into the thumb pot. 'It's an egg.'

Nursery officer 1, picking it out gingerly, 'It's a strange shape.'

Boy 1 (4:0) tries to take the 'egg'.

Nursery officer 1: 'Be very, very careful. It's an egg.' To Boy 3 (3:11): 'What's it going to hatch into?'

Boy 3 (3:11): 'A lion.'

Nursery officer 1: 'A lion? … I can see why it might hatch into a lion, it's got little hairy bits on it.'

She sends Boy 3 (3:11) to put the egg somewhere safe to hatch. He takes the egg and goes into the bathroom …

Boy 3 (3:11) returns to the group.

Nursery officer 1: 'Has the egg hatched?'

Boy 3 (3:11): 'Yes.'

Nursery officer 1: 'What was it?'

Boy 3 (3:11): 'A bird.'

Nursery officer 1: 'A bird? We'll have to take it outside at playtime and put it in a tree so it can fly away.'

CASE STUDY

Case study: example 2

We can borrow a short dialogue cited by Donaldson (1992), who uses it to illustrate what she refers to as children's spontaneous wonderings (p. 44). Jamie (3 years 11 months) was standing in a lane beside a house in the English countryside. It was a warm and dry day, and a car was parked on a concrete drive nearby:

Jamie:	Why is it [the car] on – that metal thing?
Adult:	It's not metal, it's concrete.
Jamie:	Why is it on the concrete thing?
Adult:	Well, when it rains the ground gets soft and muddy, doesn't it?
	[Jamie nods, bends down and scratches the dry earth.]
Adult:	So the wheels would sink into the mud.
	But the concrete's hard, you see.
Jamie [excitedly]:	But the concrete's soft in the mix!
	Why is it soft in the mix?

When you read the examples above you may have identified some of the skills you can use to engage in rich conversations and sustained shared thinking with children. You need to ensure that you can identify and describe these skills and demonstrate this understanding when you support your colleagues.

You can extend your knowledge by reading Iram Siraj-Blatchford's article in full or looking at practical ideas to promote sustained shared thinking in Marianne Sargent's *Using Projects to Promote Sustained Shared Thinking* (2011).

You can also use these texts to inform your discussions with colleagues on the full range of skills involved in sustained shared thinking, such as supporting child-initiated activities, following the child's train of thought, active listening, asking open questions, making it clear that there is no right or wrong answer, expressing genuine interest and modelling problem-solving strategies.

Strategies for supporting sustained shared thinking in your setting

There are many ways in which you can promote sustained shared thinking in your setting and you may have identified some strategies in the sections on 'EYFS (2012) and strategies to extend children's learning and thinking' and 'Case study: example 1', above. Here are some additional ideas you can consider.

- You can model sustained shared thinking to show practitioners how to take the lead from children and help them explore their ideas at their own pace.

- You can model how you take time, ask prompt questions, provide resources to explore further, recap what the child has stated, elaborate when necessary, ask 'what if … ?' questions, suggest strategies and, most importantly, show genuine interest.

- You can lead a staff development session on sustained shared thinking and provide examples of scenarios where it is more likely to occur and how this relates to EYFS requirements for an enabling and stimulating environment.

- You can lead a discussion on how to employ different strategies when you engage in sustained shared thinking with children of different ages.

- You could highlight, for example, that if you are engaging in sustained shared thinking with a baby, you will be responding to the baby's gaze and will provide the resources the baby is interested in to help him explore using his senses.

You can provide a list of prompt questions for colleagues, such as

- 'tell me about … ';

- 'what if … ?';

- 'what can we do when … ?';

- 'do you think we could … ?';

- 'what do you think will happen if … ?'

Evidence for 2.4

In your evidence for 2.4 you will need to address how you promote children's learning and thinking and engage in sustained shared thinking, where possible, with children of different ages. Your evidence of promoting children's learning may overlap with your evidence for other Standards that relate to children's learning, such as Standard 3.

Some of your evidence of extending children's learning and of thinking skills and engaging in sustained shared thinking may also overlap, but some will not, so you need to evaluate each piece of evidence carefully.

There are many ways to evidence how you promote children's learning and thinking skills, but evidencing how you engage in sustained shared thinking can be more difficult. You need to be able to record a conversation you have with a child in enough detail so that if someone were to read your record of the conversation, that person would be able to judge whether this was an example of sustained shared thinking or an example of a conversation where you asked closed, factual questions. The reader can only do this if you provide as detailed a record of the conversation as possible, as close to verbatim as you can manage.

You need to be prepared. If you keep your reflective journal with you at your setting, whenever you have unexpectedly engaged in sustained shared thinking with a child, your journal will be there for you to record the conversation immediately while it is still fresh in your mind, as well as your thoughts on what this told you about the child and the child's next steps. You can then include these excerpts from your journal in a case study or written assignment.

When you record a conversation in detail you need to demonstrate how you evaluate and respond to the child's comments and interject in a way that helps the child extend her understanding. This will help you evidence how you promote children's learning and thinking skills and it can be helpful if you set the context for this conversation and highlight how your previous knowledge of this child influenced how you responded in this situation and how this conversation will inform your planning for this child.

You also need to evidence how you lead and model good practice in 2.4, so you need to check that the pieces of evidence you include demonstrate your leadership skills and evidence how you lead and how you model good practice.

If you are a manager rather than a practitioner, you need to think carefully about how you can evidence 2.4. You may have some good evidence of developing an environment that promotes children's thinking skills and provides opportunities for engaging in stimulating problem-solving activities. You may also have evidence of modelling good practice or leading a staff development event on promoting children's thinking skills. However, you still need to evidence how you promote thinking skills and sustained shared thinking with individual children.

You may find that you can cross-reference some of your evidence for 2.4 to other Standards and, if you can evidence how you engage with children in each age group in 2.4, this will strengthen your evidence for other Standards. For example, if you can record examples of engaging in sustained shared thinking with children of different ages you will also be evidencing your understanding of child development from birth to five for 2.2 and your communication with babies, toddlers and pre-school children for 2.5.

Written assignments, case studies and your reflective journal

You can use a written assignment or case study to examine in detail how you have acted to promote a child's thinking and learning. These will provide the scope to set the context for the activities you describe and how you use your knowledge of a child's learning and development to stretch and challenge them. You can describe how you use an activity or a spontaneous conversation to promote learning and thinking and record a conversation where you engaged in sustained shared thinking in detail. You can also explain how you will use what you have learnt about that child's learning and development from the exchanges you described to help you plan the child's next steps.

If you have led the development of areas of provision so as to promote children's learning and opportunities to develop their thinking skills, then you can write about this in detail in an assignment or case study.

Document portfolio

You may have evidence of promoting children's thinking skills through your observations, plans and next steps for each child. You may have records of conversations that demonstrate sustained shared thinking that you have added to children's profile books and learning journeys. You can also include relevant sections from a child's profile book, two-year-old progress check, IEP or EYFS Profile if they demonstrate what it is that you did to promote that child's thinking and learning.

If you have led a training event on promoting learning and thinking or engaging in sustained shared thinking you may have some relevant evidence in your training handouts, the minutes of the meeting, a colleague's witness testimony or evaluations of your training.

In 2.4 you are asked to model good practice and you may be able to evidence this through your plans for the session, a witness testimony or evaluation or a record of your discussion with the colleague you modelled the activity for. You can also use your reflective journey to record the steps you take when modelling an activity for a colleague.

You may have records of resources you have ordered to support a child in exploring his interests or schemas and you can include this in your document portfolio if you highlight how you then used these resources.

If you have been involved in promoting an enabling environment to support children's thinking and learning, then you may have some evidence you can include in your document portfolio, such as plans for Forest School or science activities.

Observations

You may find that you have evidence of promoting thinking and learning in peer or mentor observations of your practice as well as in your own observations of your key children. If you can't find any strong enough examples in existing observations you can arrange to be observed leading an activity or engaging. You can ask your observer to record in detail any conversations where you engage in sustained shared thinking and the strategies you use to promote a child's thinking and learning. You may also be able to record a discussion with your observer about how effective the strategies you used were.

You can also arrange to be observed leading an activity you have planned and resourced to support children's thinking and learning. This could involve preparing resources to support children in exploring their schema further, providing gardening equipment and a selection of beans and seeds to support a child's interest in how things grow or creating communication-friendly spaces that reflect children's current interests in, for example, superhero play.

SUGGESTED READING

Athey, C (2007) *Extending Thought in Young Children: A Parent–Teacher Partnership* (2nd edn). London: Paul Chapman.

Bayley, R and Broadbent, L (2002) *Helping Young Children to Think Creatively*. Walsall: Lawrence Educational Publications.

Charlesworth, V (2005) *Critical Skills in the Early Years*. Stafford: Network Educational Press.

Clarke, J (2007) *Sustaining Shared Thinking*. Lutterworth: Featherstone Education.

Costello, PJM (2000) *Thinking Skills and Early Childhood Education (Early Years and Primary)*. London: David Fulton.

Dowling, M (2005) *Supporting Young Children's Sustained Shared Thinking* (Training Materials). Available at: **www.early-education.org.uk** (accessed 20/10/2014).

Dowling, M (2008). *Exploring Young Children's Thinking Through Their Self-Chosen Activities* (Training Materials). Available at **www.early-education.org.uk** (accessed 20/10/2014).

Eysenck, MW and Keane, MT (2010) *Cognitive Psychology: A Student's Handbook*. Sussex: Psychology Press.

Featherstone, S and Featherstone, P (eds) (2008) *Like Bees not Butterflies – Child-Initiated Learning in the Early Years*. London: A & C Black.

Fein, G (1991) The self-building potential of pretend play, or 'I got a fish, all by myself'. In: M Woodhead, R Carr, and P Light (eds) *Becoming a Person*, pp. 328–346. London: Routledge.

Fisher, R (2005) *Teaching Children to Think* (2nd edn). Cheltenham: Nelson Thornes.

Garton, AF (2004) *Exploring Cognitive Development: The Child as Problem Solver*. Oxford: Blackwell.

Jarvis, P, George, J and Holland, W (2013) *Early Years Professional's Complete Companion*. Harlow: Pearsons.

Robson, S (2006) *Developing Thinking and Understanding in Young Children: An Introduction for* Garton, AF (2004) Exploring Cognitive Development: the Child as Problem Solver. Oxford: Blackwell.

Siraj-Blatchford, I (2007) *Creativity, Communication and Collaboration: The Identification of Pedagogic Progression in Sustained Shared Thinking*. London: Institute of Education.

Siraj-Blatchford, I (2009) Conceptualising progression in the pedagogy of play and sustained shared thinking in early childhood education: A Vygotskian perspective. *Educational and Child Psychology*, 26: (2) June.

Siraj-Blatchford, I and Sylva, K (2004) Researching pedagogy in English pre-schools. *British Educational Research Journal*, 30(5): 713–730.

Siraj-Blatchford, I, Sylva K, Melhuish, E et al. (2004) *EPPE: Final Report*. London: DfES and Institute of Education, University of London.

Thornton, S (1995) *Children Solving Problems*. Massachusetts: Harvard University Press.

Thornton, S (2002) *Growing Minds: An Introduction to Cognitive Development*. New York: Palgrave Macmillan.

Tizard, B and Hughes, M (1986) *Young Children Learning: Talking and Thinking at Home and at School* (Fontana Developing Child) London: Fontana.

Wallace, B (2002) *Teaching Thinking Skills Across the Early Years: A Practical Approach for Children Aged 4 to 7*. London: NACE/David Fulton.

WEB-BASED RESOURCES

http://little-blossoms-childminding.blogspot.com.es/2010/04/what-is-sustained-shared-thinking.html

This is an accessible article on promoting sustained shared thinking by Jennifer Williams.

www.atl.org.uk/Images/Playing%20to%20learn%20%20-%20Feb%202012.pdf

Playing to Learn: A Guide to Child-led Play and its Importance for Thinking and Learning

www.kathybrodie.com/viewpoint/sustained-shared-thinking-important/

A useful reminder of the key qualities of sustained shared thinking by Kathy Brodie.

Standard 2.5: Communicate effectively with children from birth to age five, listening and responding sensitively

Introduction

Standard 2.5 is about your communication with children. You are asked how and why you communicate in different ways with children of different ages and to demonstrate the quality of your listening skills. You need to identify whether and how the children know you are listening carefully to what they say and evidence how you respond appropriately and with sensitivity.

The key phrases in 2.5 that you must evidence are:

- *Communicate effectively*: you need to evidence all the ways that you communicate, both verbally and non-verbally, and evaluate whether these methods are effective.

- *Children from birth to age five*: you need to evidence your communication with each age group and how you adapt your communication strategies according to a child's age and stage of development.

- *Listening and responding sensitively*: you need to evidence both how you listen and how you respond and consider how you can do this with appropriate sensitivity.

  You must think about EYFS requirements in relation to communicating with and listening to children and identify the skills involved in communication and active listening and make sure that you demonstrate these.

You need to think about how you adapt your communication strategies with children of different ages and with children with special needs, including those who rely on augmentative and alternative communication strategies and/or technology.

You may find that members of your team would appreciate some support to help them develop their communication and listening skills, perhaps with children in a particular age range, such as babies.

'Children from birth to age five': age range requirement

Standard 2.5 is one of the indicators that requires evidence of your work with each age group, so you must evidence your communication with babies, toddlers and pre-school children. This means that you need significant practical experience with children in each of these age groups that you can record and evidence in detail.

If you are a manager or a practitioner with limited experience with one age range, you may need to consider taking on an age-related placement. You can find information on this in the introductory chapter on age-related placements. The questions below can also help you identify whether the evidence you do have with each age group is sufficient.

How do you communicate with and demonstrate that you are listening to babies? Do you need to adapt these strategies with mobile/non-mobile babies? Can you evidence these strategies?

- How do you communicate effectively with toddlers?
- Can you provide examples of your communication with toddlers?
- Can you describe an example of listening to more than one pre-school child and responding with sensitivity?

If you need guidance on how to identify the ways in which you adapt your communication with different age groups, you can refer to Development Matters (Early Education, 2012), which suggests differentiated strategies, and the sections below on 'EYFS (2007) requirements: Language for communication and thinking' (Department for Education and Skills, 2007) and 'Communication and language evidence audit' (Department for Education, 2012).

'Listening and responding sensitively'
Why listening matters

Listening matters for a wide range of reasons and if you can identify some of these reasons it will help you to broaden your evidence for 2.5. When you listen to children you are showing them that they are worthy of attention and that what they say is important. You may remember from 2.3 that showing children they are valued is one of the key roles of an attachment figure so your careful listening promotes positive relationships, as required by EYFS (2012).

When you are listening you are also modelling what it is that makes a conversation and the strategies children can use to keep a conversation flowing. When you communicate with toddlers you will carefully model the words and phrases they need and help them to gain control in their lives in a range of ways, from asking for a drink to managing their emotions.

As these examples show, how you respond to a child is important and has an impact on their development and this is something you can refer to in your evidence for 2.5. For example, when you engage in proto-conversations with a baby, repeating the sounds that he makes, you are teaching the child about how a conversation is structured, but you are also promoting his self-esteem and confidence.

You may find it helpful to address in your evidence the range of ways in which children communicate and how you can support these through your active listening. Children communicate their ideas through making marks and creative activities and part of your role as listener and observer is to provide the resources they need, when they need them. Children will learn that we communicate through books and telephones and even the television and will start to show interest in these. Your role as listener is to identify and build on these interests, providing resources and asking prompt questions.

Identifying listening behaviours

To evidence effective listening, it can be helpful to identify the range of behaviours that demonstrate that you are listening. These include eye contact, body language, gestures and verbal and non-verbal communication. Consider how you respond in different ways according to the age of the child, such as repeating babbling noises and following the gaze of a baby and repeating key words and phrases with a toddler.

Active listening skills audit

The National Strategies (Early Years) document, *Challenging Practice to Further Improve Learning, Playing and Interacting in the Early Years Foundation Stage* (Department for Children, Schools and Families, 2010) looks at strategies to improve practice in the early years. The section on active listening focuses on developing these skills between team members, but these principles can equally be applied to communication with children.

ACTIVITY S2.2

Consider how you evidence each of the components of active listening when you are modelling practice for a colleague and when you are actively listening to a child. Some examples have been added to Table S2.8 to help you identify how you use these skills in practice and how you can adapt them according to the age of the child.

Table S2.8 Active listening skills audit

Active listening skill	I do this when I ...
Eye contact	'I maintain eye contact with babies and follow their gaze'
Attention to seating positions and body language	'During activities I make sure I am sitting down at a child's eye level'
Affirmation	'When I give feedback it is constructive and specific, for example, "you were very kind to Charlie when you said, 'you can share my bike'"'
Recognition of what is being said	'I repeat some of the words the child says, to show I'm taking on board what she wants, even if it's not possible right now'
Reflecting feelings	'I know you are sad Mummy has gone to work: shall we look at some pictures of Mummy in your special book?'
Encouraging, acknowledging, checking and clarifying	'I repeat some of the words the child says, to check I understood correctly, for example, "you want the red paint for your picture?"'
Showing empathy	'I know you really wanted to take your doll on the bike right now, and it's really hard that you have to wait for your turn. Maybe we can take your doll for a walk while we wait?'
Asking open-ended questions	Ask 'what if ... ?' and 'what do you think we can now ... ?' and 'How could we find out?' questions
Brief, accurate summary of the points put forward	'So, you want the big bricks to build a wall round the cars?'

Responding sensitively: cross-referencing your evidence to 2.4

If you have provided strong evidence of engaging in sustained shared thinking for 2.4, then you already have some good evidence of responding sensitively for 2.5. Listening, responding sensitively and communicating effectively are key attributes of sustained shared thinking where the key factor is the way in which you respond to what the child says.

If you are to cross-reference your evidence of engaging in sustained shared thinking to 2.5 as well, however, you need to ensure that you have evidence of your conversations with a child that are recorded in enough detail so that it is possible to identify the quality of your listening and your responses.

What also makes 2.5 differ from 2.4 is that you must evidence communication with each age group – babies, toddlers and pre-school children.

Communicate effectively

To evidence that you communicate effectively you must understand what effective communication consists of, understand EYFS requirements in relation to communication and evaluate the effectiveness of your own communication.

EYFS (2007) requirements: language for communication and thinking

If you are to evidence effective communication for 2.5 you must take account of EYFS (2012) requirements in relation to communicating with children.

The EYFS Principles into Practice card on Communication, Language and Literacy (2007) **(http://earlyyearsmatters.co.uk/wp-content/uploads/2011/02/eyfs_res_comm_lang_lit1.pdf)**, summarised below, highlights the importance of communication and compares language for communication with language to promote thinking. This separation of the purpose of communication can help you plan how to identify and evidence all aspects of your communication with children and relate some of your evidence to 2.4, where you are asked to promote children's thinking skills.

'Language for communication' (Principles into practice: EYFS, 2007)
'Language for communication' is about how children become communicators. The skills of learning to listen and speak emerge from methods of non-verbal communication, which include facial expression, eye contact and hand gestures. These skills develop as children interact with others, listen to and use language, extend their vocabulary and experience stories, songs, poems and rhymes.

'Language for thinking' (Principles into practice: EYFS, 2007)
'Language for thinking' is about how children learn to use language to imagine and recreate roles and experiences and how they use talk to clarify their thinking and ideas or to refer to events they have observed or are curious about.

'Communication and language' evidence audit

EYFS (2012) promotes effective communication with children. 'Communication and language' includes the strands 'Listening and attention', 'Understanding' and 'Speaking', and if you can demonstrate how you promote each of these strands then you will strengthen your evidence of effective communication for 2.5.

You can use the strategies suggested under 'positive relationships' and 'enabling environment' in Development Matters to help you organise your evidence for 2.5. Each strand illustrates strategies for children at different ages and this can help you evidence your practice with each of the required age ranges. Use Table S2.9 to help you reflect on how you can use the EYFS (2012) categories and statements to identify your evidence for 2.5.

The strategies you use in relation to 'Communication and language' (Table S2.9) enable you to evidence how you *communicate effectively with children from birth to age five*. The strategies you follow in relation to 'listening and attention 'will enable you to evidence how you *listen* and *respond sensitively*.

Remember that in 2.5 you need to evidence effective communication, so this activity can help you evaluate the effectiveness of your own communication with children in each age group.

Table S2.9 EYFS (2012) 'Communication and language' evidence audit

EYFS Communication and language	My strategies	Leadership	Evidence
Speaking			
Babies			
Find out from parents how they like to communicate with their baby, noting especially the chosen language	When settling a child ask parents about how they communicate with their baby		'All about me' form completed with parents
Ensure parents understand the importance of talking with babies in their home language	Booklet for parents on communicating with your baby		Booklet for parents
Encourage babies' sounds and babbling by copying their sounds in a turn-taking 'conversation'		Model copying babies' sounds for new practitioner	
Communicate with parents to exchange and update information about babies' personal words		Records of babies' personal words on wall for all practitioners to use	Display of personal words Minutes of staff meeting where discuss using these
Toddlers			
Build vocabulary by giving choices, e.g. 'apple or satsuma?'	Identify key words in focus activity plans	Lead training for colleagues on promoting toddlers' vocabulary	Handouts from training
Model building sentences by repeating what the child says and adding another word, e.g. child says 'car', say 'mummy's car' or 'blue car'	Use key times to extend child's vocabulary		Peer observations on promoting communication
Show children how to pronounce or use words by responding and repeating what they say in the correct way, rather than saying they are wrong	Introduce dual-language books using key words in child's home language and English	Introduce list of key phrases in children's home languages for staff	Booklet for parents on promoting toddlers' communication skills
Accept and praise words and phrases in home language, saying English alternatives and encouraging their use			Handout for staff on using Makaton
Encourage parents whose children are learning English as an Additional Language to continue to encourage use of the first language at home	Booklet for parents on promoting toddlers' communication skills		
Support children in using a variety of communication strategies, including signing, where appropriate	Using Makaton signs at circle time and Makaton signs in songs and rhymes	Introduce Makaton sign of the week	Poster with Makaton sign of the week

Effective communication with children with diverse needs

Birth to Three Matters (Department for Education and Skills, 2003b) 'A skilful communicator: listening and responding' addresses issues of equality of opportunity and diversity in relation to communication and you must to consider these issues in relation to your evidence for 2.5.

If you can demonstrate how you promote and adapt communication to meet the needs of individual children, then you may also be able to cross-reference this evidence to 8.1, where you are asked to *promote equality of opportunity and anti-discriminatory practice*. Children with severe communication difficulties should be encouraged to use non-verbal ways of making contact, and feel that their attempts to listen and respond are being valued.

Communication and safeguarding

Promoting communication skills with children with severe communication difficulties can also be a safeguarding issue and will relate to your evidence for 7.3.

Children who have difficulty communicating can be of heightened risk of abuse, especially if they have multiple carers carrying out intimate acts of care. The fact that the child has many carers makes it less likely that the child can communicate well with all of them, making it harder for the child to disclose information about what might be happening to her.

Communication: extending your knowledge and understanding

Communication and listening are significant areas of practice and you may find it helpful to develop your understanding in relation to children and communication. Here are some topics you can explore. Use your journal to reflect on your reading and evidence your knowledge and understanding and how this informs your practice.

You can also discuss these ideas and their implications for practice with colleagues to evidence your leadership role for Standard 8.

- Explore ideas of key theorists on communicating with children: Chomsky, Brunner, Vygotsky, Stern, Meek.

- Explore the EYFS (2012) guidance on communication.

- Discuss how to promote the use of open questions and sustained shared thinking.

- Explore the concept of 'active listening'.

- Explore Magaluzzi's *Hundred Languages of Childhood* (Thornton and Brunton, 2006, in Jarvis et al., 2013: 175).

- Introduce peer observation to analyse communication with children.

- Create a display of opening statements to promote communication, such as 'what if … ?'.

- Consider ECAT training and developing communication-friendly areas.

- Identify the reasons why we listen to children (Jarvis et al., 2013: 175), such as:

  - Children are entitled to have their views and experiences respected.

  - We learn children's real interests and concerns and how they feel about themselves.

  - It makes us more reflective.

  - Listening is a vital part of establishing a trusting and respectful relationship.

  - It helps practitioners develop sensitivity to how children perceive the world.

  - We provide children with a model of how to listen and take turns in a conversation.

  - It helps us provide an environment in which all children feel confident. Children will know that their thoughts, feelings and ideas will be taken seriously.

Leadership and support opportunities in 2.5

As communicating with children is such a priority for practitioners, there is scope for you to demonstrate your leadership in relation to 2.5, for example, by encouraging your team to evaluate their communication with children and by leading and developing practice in relation to listening to children.

If you have delivered training on communicating with children, you may be able to provide evidence of this through a written assignment or records of the event, such as your plans, the handouts you produced and staff evaluations of the session. Read through any evidence you wish to include and check whether it provides enough relevant and detailed evidence of your input.

If you have promoted communication skills by supporting colleagues one to one or modelling good practice, then you may be able to evidence this through peer observations, records of meetings, materials you prepared or a witness testimony from a colleague you supported.

You may find it helpful to combine training events and one-to-one support with a particular focus. For example, you may have led an audit of opportunities for communication in your setting, with colleagues sharing their observations of communication at certain times of the day or in particular areas in the setting so as to evaluate the quality of child–adult interactions.

Another way you can evidence your leadership role would be to take on responsibility for attending ECAT training and cascading this to your colleagues and supporting some colleagues on a one-to-one basis. You could then, perhaps, facilitate the development of communication-friendly spaces in each room. In this scenario you will have evidence of improving your own practice, leading training, facilitating practical changes to the environment, supporting colleagues one to one and modelling good practice.

If you plan to address communication with your staff team, you may consider starting with a discussion of what makes a conversation effective and what the characteristics are of an effective conversation with children in each age range.

Another starting point might involve introducing peer observations within your team so that you can analyse and build on strengths in relation to adult–child interactions. For example, if you find that too many conversations are focused on giving instructions or organising and disciplining children, this gives you a starting point to move practice forwards.

Developing opportunities for communication

As you are asked to demonstrate effective communication, 2.5 provides you with an opportunity to demonstrate how you promote communication as part of your leadership role. Here are some ways Surrey County Council use to help parents and practitioners support children's communication (**www.surreycc.gov.uk/learning/ early-years-and-childcare-service/early-years-practitioners-and-providers/commu- nication-and-language-in-early-years**).

CASE STUDY

Communication case study: trying new things (www. surreycc.gov.uk/ecat)

Helen Strange, from Teddies on a Rainbow in New Haw, explains how they are developing children's communication and language skills at their nursery.

Art exhibition

We recently held an art exhibition, which gave children a chance to talk and arrange their own work as well as tell their families about their art. Above all, it values what the child is doing.

On the spur of the moment we moved the artwork outside. If children have made butterflies, what better place to show them than hanging than in nearby trees? It was wonderful as the dog walkers stopped to have a peep!

Walk 'n' talk

This was something I learnt about at ECAT training [that Surrey Early Years and Childcare Service ran]. We sent a letter to families telling them that every day we take a small group of children for a walk with a specific topic to chat about, such as circles or bugs, and parents and siblings can come too. We model good ideas and things to talk about.

It has shown parents how rewarding a walk and chat can be with their child. No equipment needed, just a willingness to chat and get involved.

Dads' Story Sacks

We handed out leaflets to dads or via the mums inviting them to use the Dads' Story Sack with their child. It's a simple story with puppets and dads can keep them as long as they need.

Dads love having a connection with their child's nursery, especially if they don't get to come in. Many dads feel awkward coming into nursery so this is a great icebreaker!

Evidence for 2.5

Written assignments, case studies and your reflective journal

To evidence 2.5 well you need to provide detailed examples of conversations with individual children. It is not enough to say, 'I listened to what Alberta was saying.' Instead, you need to provide an almost verbatim account of a conversation with Alberta which demonstrates how you responded so that it is possible to evaluate whether you were *listening and responding sensitively*. As you are asked to demonstrate effective communication you can use your journal to reflect on the quality of your communication with individual children of different ages.

Because you need this level of detail, you may choose to evidence your practice for 2.5 through an extended piece of writing, such as an assignment or case study or through your reflections on a conversation in your journal. Using a series of assignments, journal entries or case studies will make it possible for you to evidence your communication with children of different ages and provide examples of adapting your communication with a child with special needs or a disability.

You will be able to highlight your understanding of the communication needs of a child of that age and ability and describe and reflect on a conversation where you demonstrated appropriate language and tone in relation to the child's age, and responded sensitively and appropriately. You need to make sure that you highlight the different ways in which you communicate with babies, toddlers and pre-school children.

Document portfolio

There are several documents that you can include in your document portfolio. These can include work products that evidence your practice, such as observations which demonstrate your listening skills, entries in profile books that record a conversation with a child or a witness testimony from a colleague of parents who has observed you communicating with a child.

Check that every document you reference to 2.5 to evidence your own practice records a specific conversation in enough detail and highlights the context and presents the rationale for your responses. Your rationale will explain that you respond in a certain way with a particular child because of the child's age and stage of development and because you are focusing on their next steps.

Documents that can evidence your leadership role include training handouts on communicating with children of different ages, posters displaying 'prompt' questions for colleagues or minutes of meetings where you support colleagues to develop their communication skills. Other documents may relate to your role in the introduction of ECAT or a peer visiting programme that focuses on developing communication skills.

Observations

One of the most appropriate ways to evidence your communication with children is through an observation of your practice. You can ask a colleague or your tutor or mentor to observe you engaging in activities with groups of children in each of the three age ranges. You can ask your tutor or mentor to focus the observation on how you communicate with individual children and record how you listen and respond appropriately.

ACTIVITY S2.3

Evaluating your evidence of effective communication

Here is an excerpt from a conversation between a nursery officer and a boy aged 3 years and 11 months that we previously looked at on page 172. Read through the conversation and consider whether this evidences:

- *how the practitioner communicates with the child;*

- *how the practitioner demonstrates that her or she is listening;*

- *how the practitioner responds sensitively;*

- *how the practitioner communicates with babies from birth to five.*

  Boy 3 (3:11) has finished his cake and starts to sing 'Happy Birthday' to Nursery officer 1.

  Nursery officer 1 pretends to blow out the candles. 'Do I have a present?'

  Boy 3 (3:11) hands her a ball of playdough.

  Nursery officer 1: 'I wonder what's inside? I'll unwrap it.' She quickly makes the ball into a thumb pot and holds it out to Boy 3 (3:11), 'It's empty!'

  Boy 3 (3:11) takes a pinch of playdough and drops it into the thumb pot: 'It's an egg.'

  Nursery officer 1 picking it out gingerly, 'It's a strange shape.'

  Boy 1 (4:0) tries to take the 'egg'.

> Nursery officer 1: 'Be very, very careful. It's an egg.' To Boy 3 (3:11) 'What's it going to hatch into?'
>
> Boy 3 (3:11): 'A lion.'
>
> Nursery officer 1: 'A lion? … I can see why it might hatch into a lion, it's got little hairy bits on it.'
>
> She sends Boy 3 (3:11) to put the egg somewhere safe to hatch. He takes the egg and goes into the bathroom.
>
> Boy 3 (3:11) returns to the group.
>
> Nursery officer 1: 'Has the egg hatched?'
>
> Boy 3 (3:11): 'Yes.'
>
> Nursery officer 1: 'What was it?'
>
> Boy 3 (3:11): 'A bird.'
>
> Nursery officer 1: 'A bird? We'll have to take it outside at playtime and put it in a tree so it can fly away.'

If you reflect on the following questions it will help you identify some of the questions you can ask yourself to evaluate your own evidence of effective communication for 2.5.

- How could this practitioner add additional comments to the above transcript so that it more clearly evidences all aspects of 2.5?

What could this practitioner have done differently to demonstrate that s/he is listening and to extend their communication with this child? You may have identified that this practitioner could:

- highlight how s/he used actions and body language to emphasise that s/he was listening;

- extend comments to support the child's next steps;

- build on Boy 3's interest in birthday cakes, perhaps using knowledge that he is looking forward to his fourth birthday next month: the practitioner could, for example, talk about numbers of candles: 'Can we put three candles on the cake because you are three now? How old will you be on your next birthday? How many candles will we need when you are four? Shall we put them on the cake?';

- include examples of conversations with children of different ages so as to demonstrate how the practitioner differentiates communication skills according to the needs and stage of development of the child.

SUGGESTED READING

Adam, AJ (1990) *Listening to Learn: A Handbook for Parents of a Hearing-Impaired Child.* Washington, DC: The Alexander Bell Association/Tucker-Maxon.

Close, N (2002) *Listening to Children: Talking with Children about Difficult Issues.* London: Alleyn and Bacon.

Cooper, J (2013) *The Early Years Communication Handbook.* London: Practical Pre-School Books.

Cousins, J (2003) *Listening to Four Year Olds: How They Can Help Us Plan Their Care and Education*, 2nd edn. London: National Early Years Network.

Davies, B (2014) *Listening to Children: Being and becoming.* (Contesting Early Childhood). London: Routledge.

De Boo, M (1999) *Enquiring Children, Challenging Teaching.* Maidenhead: Open University Press.

Edwards, C, Gandini, L and Foreman, GE (eds.) (1998) *The Hundred Languages of Children: The Reggio Emilia Approach – Advanced Reflections.* Westport, CT: Ablex.

Goldschmied, E and Jackson, S (2004) *People under Three,* 2nd edn. Abingdon: Routledge.

Knowles, G (2006) *Supporting Inclusive Practice.* Abingdon: Routledge.

Lancaster, P and Broadbent, V (2003) *Listening to Young Children.* Buckingham: Open University Press.

Lewis, A and Lindsay, G (eds.) (2000) *Researching Children's Perspectives.* Buckingham: Open University Press.

McLeod, A (2008) *Listening to Children: A Practitioner's Guide.* London: Jessica Kingsley.

O'Quigley, A (2000) *Listening to Children's Views: The Findings and Recommendations of Recent Research.* York: York Publishing Services/ Joseph Rowntree Foundation.

Pound, L (2005) *How Children Learn: From Montessori to Vygotsky – Educational Theories and Approaches Made Easy.* Warwickshire: Step Forward.

Roffey, S (1999) *Special Needs in the Early Years: Collaboration, Communication and Coordination.* London: David Fulton.

Roper, D and Hardy, M (2004) *The Little Book of Circle Time: Making the Most of Circle Time. The Foundation Stage.* Leicestershire: Featherstone Education.

WEB-BASED RESOURCES

Communication, Language and Literacy Development, Sure Start: **www.ness.bbk.ac.uk/support/ documents/1057.pdf**

Every Child a Talker: **www.foundationyears.org.uk/2011/10/every-child-a-talker-guidance-for-early-language-lead-practitioners/**

'I Can' resources: www.ican.org.uk/: The I CAN national charity website provides resources and advice for practitioners to enable them to engage effectively with children who struggle with communication.

National Literacy Trust: **www.literacytrust.org.uk/early_years**: The National Literacy Trust has a website with a wide range of resources and ideas for communication skills in the early years which you can share with colleagues.

Standard 2.6: Develop children's confidence, social and communication skills through group learning

Introduction

Standard 2.6 asks you to evidence the ways in which you support children's confidence, social skills and communication and that you do this through group learning experiences. You need to provide evidence of promoting each of these three aspects of children's development – their confidence, their social skills and their communication skills – and do this by providing appropriate group activities. Your evidence will be stronger if you identify and reflect on each of these areas in turn before you prepare your evidence.

To evidence 2.6 well, you need to think about how you adapt your strategies to support children of different ages and with a range of needs. The strategies you use to support the confidence of a toddler with a physical disability may be different from those you use to support the confidence of a pre-school child on the autism spectrum. Other issues you can consider for 2.6 include working in partnership with parents and understanding the impact of children's home circumstances on, for example, the development of their confidence.

Group learning

Standard 2.6 asks you to evidence how you promote children's communication and social skills through group learning, so you may find it helpful to reflect on this focus on group learning. You can ask yourself questions, such as:

- What group learning activities do I lead?

- How do they promote children's confidence, communication and social skills?

- How do I differentiate and adapt group activities according to the age and needs of the child?

- Are group learning activities always the most effective way to promote these skills? For example, are group learning activities the most effective way to develop a child's confidence when working with babies or when a child is settling in?

- Do I promote confidence, social skills and communication through the same activities or do I need to evidence different activities for each of the three?

Demonstrating your knowledge and understanding

Ask yourself how confident you are in your understanding of how children develop confidence, social skills and communication skills. You may feel that you know what to do, but need to clarify your understanding of why you do this and develop your understanding of the theory behind your practice. If that is the case, you can extend your reading on this topic and there are some suggestions on how you can do this in the 'Guidance on developing children's communication skills' and 'Suggested reading' sections below.

Once you have extended your understanding of theory, you can share what you have learnt with your colleagues. Remember, as an Early Years Teacher your role is to develop practice across your setting, so if you lead a staff training session on, for example, developing children's confidence, you will be supporting colleagues and evidencing your knowledge and understanding for 2.6 as well as your leadership skills for Standard 8.

STANDARD 2

Developing children's confidence

To evidence that you develop children's confidence you must demonstrate your understanding of *confidence* in the context of early years, how you apply this in practice, how you plan group learning activities to promote confidence and lead and support your colleagues.

Start by thinking about definitions of *confidence* and how practitioners can promote this. One starting point might be to explore the difference between children's *confidence* and their self-esteem and how these relate to each other. You can then look at how your setting's policies and procedures promote both confidence and self-esteem.

It can be useful to talk with your colleagues about what you understand by *confidence* and how they believe the setting promotes this. This would provide you with an opportunity to share strategies and create a bank of practical ideas to share with new colleagues and use to create a consistent approach within the setting.

You may also wish to consider how you:

- promote confidence and self-esteem in children who are learning English;

- encourage parents to support their children's self-esteem and confidence;

- identify the components of high self-esteem and confidence and consider practical strategies to promote these;

- identify signs of low self-esteem and confidence and think of some effective, practical strategies to address low self-esteem;

- identify ways that you can promote confidence through group learning;

- identify EYFS (2012) requirements in relation to confidence (see section on 'EYFS and developing children's confidence', below).

CASE STUDY

Cathy's work on developing an understanding self-esteem and confidence

Cathy, an Early Years Teacher trainee, decided that she needed to develop her understanding of the relationship between self-esteem and confidence and reflect on how this can inform her practice.

She found an online article that helped her identify how children's confidence develops over time and how confidence relates to self-esteem (www.earlychildhoodaustralia.org.au/learning-hub/). She adapted this article to create a short handout for her colleagues and briefly spoke about the issues it raised in a staff meeting.

Understanding self-esteem and self-confidence

Supporting self-confidence birth to 12 months

Babies develop self-confidence when they feel safe and secure. This means that our role is to foster their sense of safety and security and help them to feel good about themselves. When we support them to become good problem solvers this builds their self-confidence.

Supporting self-confidence 12–24 months

Toddlers develop self-confidence alongside their self-awareness. We can help them develop self-awareness and become confident when we recognise their progress and achievements and allow them to make new discoveries.

Supporting self-confidence 24–36 months

Older toddlers are capable and we support their confidence when we recognise how capable they are. We need to allow them to be independent, try new things and make mistakes as this supports their confidence.

Self-esteem in languages other than English

We need to think about how we can help children build positive self-esteem when they are speaking languages other than English. We need to think about cultural considerations in relation to self-esteem.

Nurturing a positive self-esteem

Young children's self-esteem is shaped by their early experiences, so it is crucially important that they trust the adults who care for them, and have a supportive and safe environment to explore independently.

Text from: **www.earlychildhoodaustralia.org.au/emotional_foundations_for_learning/ building_trust_and_self_esteem/self_esteem_and_confidence.html.**

EYFS and developing children's confidence

Another way to approach 2.6 is to research EYFS requirements around developing children's confidence and how you can apply this in practice. You can examine references to *confidence* within 'Personal, social and emotional development' (Department for Education , 2012) and the EYFS Principles, as these also refer to confidence.

In a 'Unique child' there is the statement that *Every child is a competent learner from birth who can be resilient, capable, confident and self-assured* and the principle of 'Positive relationships' addresses how children develop strength and confidence through the relationships they form.

In the section on the characteristics of effective teaching and learning there is a reference to children's active learning, the importance of persevering when they encounter difficulties and the enjoyment of their eventual achievement, and you can consider how this relates to *confidence*.

Developing children's social skills

To evidence 2.6 well you need to think about your theoretical understanding of how children develop their social skills and the practical strategies you use to support them. You may find that you have addressed some of this in your evidence for 2.2 on child development. However, if you do not feel confident in your understanding or practice in this area, or in relation to developing social skills with a particular age group, you need to extend your reading. Any of the texts mentioned under 'Suggested reading' in the section on 2.2 will have a section on developing social skills that you can refer to.

Strategies for developing children's social skills

You may find it helpful to relate your understanding of how children's social skills develop from birth to examples of your practice and the strategies you use, for example, how you promote social skills using group learning activities, such as circle time.

Use Table S2.10 to make notes on your understanding of how children develop social skills and the strategies and activities you have introduced to promote these skills. You can also use Table S2.10 to identify examples of your personal practice and leadership, how you differentiate the strategies you use and how you can evidence these. This will help you identify any gaps in your evidence and reflect on how you adapt your strategies to support children at different ages and with a range of needs.

Table S2.10 Evidence of promoting children's social skills

Knowledge and understanding	Group learning activities	Personal practice	Differentiation	Leadership and support	Sources of evidence
Bronfenbrenner's ecological theory and emphasis on social development. 'Bronfenbrenner (1979) saw children's social environments as a series of circles, or systems, one nesting inside the other. He believed that the interactions children had with people close to them had a strong impact on their ability to understand others and their emotions and relationships with others are crucial to children's social development'	Circle time Persona dolls Story time Cooking activities Designing and building 'tree house'	Circle time activities with pre-school Persona dolls Sharing stories that emphasise prosocial behaviours Cooking activities: emphasise turn taking Communication with parents Parents' evening presentation on developing social skills	Next steps in individual education programme re social skills for child 'P' Encouraging all children to use Makaton to promote the social inclusion of child 'J'	Leading discussion in staff meeting Modelling emphasis on turn taking in group activities Model praising children for prosocial behaviours Training session on the relationship between attachment relationships and developing social skills (Bronfenbrenner)	Peer observations Reflective journal Case study

The strategies you use to develop the social skills of a child learning English may differ from the strategies you use to support the social skills of a child with a disability. Likewise, the strategies you use to support the social skills of an only child of a single parent may differ from the strategies you use to support a child from a large family.

Some examples have been added to Table S2.10 to help you. These are the ideas recorded by Cathy, the Early Years Teacher trainee in the case study above.

Leading practice to develop children's social skills

If you model good practice and support your colleagues to understand how to promote children's social skills, this will help you to demonstrate leadership for 2.6 and Standard 8.

You would be able to evidence your leadership for 2.6 and Standard 8 if, for example, you:

- discuss with colleagues, in a team meeting or one to one, their understanding of how children develop social skills and the strategies they use to promote these;

- share information on what EYFS (2012) requires in relation to promoting social skills through group activities;

- compare theories of social development and look at their implications for practice;

- review group learning activities and identify opportunities for promoting children's social skills;

- identify strategies used by colleagues to build up a bank of practical ideas and strategies.

Developing children's communication skills

You will have identified some of the strategies you use to promote children's communication skills in your evidence for 2.4, 2.5 and 5.2. What makes your evidence for 2.6 differ, however, is that for 2.6 you need to evidence how you promote children's communication skills *through group learning*.

Think about the reasons for this emphasis on promoting children's communication skills across the Standards. Cathy, the Early Years Teacher trainee in the case study above, suggested that 'it is through communication skills that children develop relationships with the people that matter to them and the internal language they need to think and learn'.

According to Reardon (2013: 94; cited in Brock and Rankin, 2008), your role is to help your colleagues understand:

> how babies', toddlers' and young children's listening, speaking, pre-reading and pre-writing skills develop ... early communication, language and literacy, play and learning activities should be fun. As a leader your setting should be bursting with opportunities for baby babble, talking, listening, singing, rhyming and storytelling.

These are the building blocks of literacy and make the difference to how quickly and easily they acquire language.

(Brock and Rankin, 2008: 7)

Many of these activities that Reardon mentions here involve group learning, so if you identify your role in promoting these activities, you will have some appropriate evidence for 2.6.

You are given some guidance on supporting children's communication skills in EYFS (2012), where you are encouraged to plan a range of appropriate and enjoyable activities to promote children's communication. Here is a list of some of the skills children need to practise from EYFS (2012). You need to think about how you can evidence the strategies you use to promote the development of these skills *through group learning*.

- listen to stories, music and rhymes;
- respond to what they hear;
- make relevant comments and ask questions;
- ask and answer 'how' and 'why' questions;
- pay attention to what others say;
- explore ideas;
- understand how to follow instructions;
- give explanations;
- talk about what interests them, what is going on in their lives and their likes and dislikes;
- talk about events that have happened or are due to happen in the future.

Promoting non-verbal communication skills

Be aware that communication involves more than just spoken language. You can use your journal to reflect on how you develop the communication skills of babies and children who do not engage in spoken communication.

This might involve supporting babies' non-verbal communication skills, such as gestures, how you model the use of body language and how you promote communication skills of children with special needs, for example, by using Makaton signs, Picture Exchange Communication System (PECS) cards or augmentative communication.

Developing communication skills with children of different ages

Reflect on how you promote communication skills differently according to the age of the child. Gestures and shared gaze are important communication tools for babies, but may not be the skills that you foster and model with toddlers or pre-school children.

Guidance on developing children's communication skills

You can find more guidance on developing children's communication skills in several other government publications produced by the Department for Education, Department for Education and Skills and Department for Children, Schools and Families. Helpful documents are listed below.

Progression in Phonics: Materials for Whole-class Teaching, produced in 1999 and 2000 by the Department for Education for the National Literacy Strategy. This is aimed at children in the Foundation Stage.

Playing with Sounds, a supplement produced by the Department for Education and Skills in 2004 gives practical examples of activities for developing 'sound awareness'.

I Can's Early Talk Programme by the Department for Children, Schools and Families and Department of Health in 2007 addressed speech, communication and language needs in Sure Start Children's Centres.

Every Child a Talker (ECAT), published by the Department for Children, Schools and Families in 2008 and 2009, was introduced to help practitioners create a developmentally appropriate and stimulating environment where children could experiment with language and which involved parents in their children's language development.

The Bercow Report: a Review of Services for Children and Young People (0–19) with Speech, Language and Communication Needs, published by the Department for Children, Schools and Families in 2008, makes several recommendations. These include an emphasis on the importance of communication, that early identification and intervention are important, and that joint working between services is needed.

Evidence for 2.6

Planning your evidence for 2.6

You might find it helpful to map your understanding of each of the three skills against your practice and any leadership actions you have taken.

You can adapt and use Table S2.11 to help you identify your knowledge and understanding, examples of your practice and leadership and possible sources of evidence for each of the three strands of 2.6 – confidence, social skills and communication skills.

Some examples have been added to help you identify how you can use this table.

Table S2.11 Planning your evidence for 2.6

	Knowledge and understanding	Personal practice	Leadership and support	Sources of evidence
Confidence		Persona dolls with pre-school	Modelling group activity with persona dolls	Peer observations reflective journal
				Written assignment
Social skills	Bronfenbrenner	Circle time activities with pre-school		Peer observation
		Record of conversation with parent		Reflective journal

(Continued)

Table S2.11 (Continued)

	Knowledge and understanding	Personal practice	Leadership and support	Sources of evidence
Communication skills	PECS cards and Makaton for 'P' in toddler room		Introducing ECAT	Emails to and from speech and language therapist
				'P's IEP and plans for group activities involving 'P'

PECS, Picture Exchange Communication System; ECAT, Every Child a Talker; IEP, indivual education plan.

Written assignments, case studies and your reflective journal

A written assignment and entries in your reflective journal can provide you with an opportunity to demonstrate your knowledge and understanding and evidence the strategies you use to promote children's confidence and social and communication skills during group activities.

A case study will provide an opportunity to describe in detail the strategies you use to promote the confidence, social and communication skills of a particular child. You may have planned to write a case study to evidence how you have supported one particular child to evidence aspects of Standards 4, 5 and 6. If you describe how you used group activities to promote this child's confidence, social or communication skills, then you can cross-reference the case study to 2.6 as well.

Document portfolio

There may be several planning documents that you could include in your portfolio to evidence 2.6, especially if you have identified on the plans why you need to focus on a particular skill with a specific child. However, planning documents are not always detailed enough to demonstrate how you interacted with each child, adapted your strategies and differentiated the activity. If you can include records of your next steps for a particular child and an observation from the activity, then your evidence will be strengthened.

If you have produced information for colleagues or led a staff development session on children's confidence, social or communication skills, you can include evidence of this in your document portfolio.

If you have worked with another professional, such as a speech and language therapist, to promote a child's social development or communication skills, you can include any records of these conversations in your portfolio.

Observations

Observations are one of the most effective sources of evidence for 2.6. A detailed observation can record your verbal interactions with a child and demonstrate how you support a child's communication skills, provide positive feedback to increase a child's confidence and model appropriate behaviours to promote social skills.

SUGGESTED READING

Broadhead, P (2014) *Early Years Play and Learning: Developing Social Skills and Cooperation.* London: Routledge Falmer.

Cooper, J (2013) *The Early Years Communication Handbook: A Practical Guide to Creating a Communication Friendly Setting.* London: Practical Pre-School Books.

Freeman, K (2011) *Babbling Babies: Activities to Build Babies' Language Development* (cards). Available online at: **https://shop.ican.org.uk/chattingwithchildrenpb** (accessed 31/10/2014).

Freeman, K (2011) *Toddler Talk 2011: Activities to Build Toddlers' Language Development* (cards). Available online at: **https://shop.ican.org.uk/chattingwithchildrenpb** (accessed 31/10/2014).

Freeman, K (2012) *Babbling Babies, Toddler Talk and Chatting with Children* (cards). Available online at: **https://shop.ican.org.uk/chattingwithchildrenpb** (accessed 31/10/2014).

Frydenberg, E, O'Brien, K and Deans, J (2012) *Developing Everyday Coping Skills in the Early Years: Proactive Strategies for Supporting Social and Emotional Development.* London: Continuum International Publishing Group.

MacKay, T, Knott, F and Dunlop, AW (2007) Developing social interaction and understanding in individuals with autism spectrum disorder: a groupwork intervention. *Journal of Intellectual and Developmental Disability*, 32(4): 279–290.

Mathieson, K (2004) *Social Skills in the Early Years: Supporting Social and Behavioural Learning.* London: Paul Chapman Publishing.

Robinson, M (2014) *The Feeling Child: Laying the Foundations of Confidence and Resilience.* London: Routledge.

Roffey, S and Parry, J (2013) *Special Needs in the Early Years: Supporting Collaboration, Communication and Co-ordination.* London: Routledge.

Sutherland, M, Hancock, N and Armstrong, N (2003) *Helping Children with Low Self-Esteem: A Guidebook.* (Helping Children with Feelings). Buckinghamshire: Speechmark Publishing.

Standard 2.7: Understand the important influence of parents and/ or carers, working in partnership with them to support the child's well-being, learning and development

Introduction

Standard 2.7 is one of the main indicators where you evidence your work with parents and/or carers so you need to identify all aspects of your work with parents to make sure that your evidence demonstrates the breadth of your practice.

There are two sections in 2.7 that you need to address. You need to evidence your understanding of the important influence parents and carers have on their child. This reference to *parents and/or carers* means that you can focus on the influence of extended family members as well as parents, such as grandparents or foster carers.

You also need to evidence the ways in which you work in partnership with parents and carers to support their child's development, well-being and learning. You need to understand the difference between *development, well-being* and *learning* and think about the ways in which you work with parents in relation to each of the three terms. For example, sharing a two-year-old progress check with a parent may provide evidence of working together to support a child's learning and development, but a meeting with a parent to complete a CAF form may focus on the child's well-being.

You need to evidence that you understand that children learn and develop best when there is consistency between home and their setting and practitioners form active partnerships with parents. You could evidence the ways in which you establish respectful partnerships with parents when you lead open-day activities or speak to them about how children learn through play.

There are many ways to evidence your work with parents for 2.7. You could describe how you foster communication with parents and share information with each other about the child's interests, likes and dislikes and their learning and development. You could demonstrate how you use the information parents share with you to inform your planning and how you share your observations with parents to help them support their child. You can evidence how you support colleagues so that they feel confident in their interactions with parents.

'Understand the important influence of parents and/or carers'

This statement asks you to evidence your understanding of the importance of parents and carers and their influence on their child's development. This influence is significant for many reasons and you need to identify these in your evidence. Parents and carers are a child's first educator and introduce that child to the culture s/he is growing up in. You may have to consider some of the less positive influences on a child, too, for example, when you identify the impact of a parent who has problems with addiction.

One way you can evidence this understanding is by providing a rationale for your actions. Describe how and why you work alongside parents, sharing information and helping parents support their child, and demonstrate how you learn about the child from the parents. Activities you could evidence include:

- home visits;

- working with a parent to complete an 'all about me' form;

- encouraging parents to add their observations to their child's profile book and home link book.

Understanding the important influence of parents and/or carers also involves identifying and celebrating the child's background, represented by their parents. This might include inviting in a parent to share stories in their home language or lead a cooking activity. It can also involve asking parents to share their specific skills with the children.

Another way you can evidence your understanding of the important influence of parents and carers is to create an environment that is welcoming for them as well as their children. This might include displaying signs in the family's home language as well as English and asking parents to bring in familiar resources from home to include in displays and the home corner. Even your choice of menu will say something to parents about how you value their child's background.

Guidance on working with parents

Recent Government policies have attempted to support the role of parents. Reading these documents can inform your practice and reflecting on them can evidence that you *Understand the important influence of parents and/or carers.*

These documents include:

- *The Children's Plan – Building Brighter Futures* (Department for Children, Schools and Families, 2007), which emphasises that the role of the Government is to support parents: services need to respond to the needs of families, rather than be designed around professional boundaries.

- Every Child Matters (Department for Education and Skills, 2003a) has implications for how settings work with parents.

- *Supporting Families in the Foundation Years* (Department for Education, 2011b) acknowledges the role of parents, but considers the other people who play a role in a child's development, such as grandparents and professionals.

- EYFS (2012) introduced the two-year-old developmental checks which must be shared with parents.

- The Effective Provision of Pre-School Education (EPPE) Project (Siraj-Blatchford et al., 2004) found that settings which had developed strong partnerships with parents, share information and involve parents in decision making were most effective.

  Review some of these documents and see how they impact on your practice and what you can learn from them.

'Working in partnership'

To evidence the breadth of your practice for 2.7, you need to identify all the ways in which you work in partnership with parents and think about how you can evidence each of your actions. You may have evidence of working with parents when their child starts in your setting and can evidence this through your settling-in records and your observations. You may also have evidence of engaging with parents to share feedback on their child's progress and development and set goals together. You may have records of informal conversations with parents at the end of the day and of more formal meetings, such as parents' evenings and meetings to discuss an IEP or complete a CAF form.

'To support the child's well-being, learning and development'

This statement asks you to evidence the formal and informal ways in which you work in partnership with parents to promote their child's well-being, learning and development.

You need to understand the differences between these three terms. Check that you focus on each of these in your interactions with parents and that the evidence you have addresses each term adequately. For example, a conversation about toilet training may support a child's development and well-being, but may not promote a child's learning.

'Well-being, learning and development'

If you are to evidence how you work with parents to promote their child's well-being, learning and development, you need to understand the meaning of each term and how you can best evidence it.

Use Table S2.12 to record what you understand by each of these terms, how you promote each in practice and how you can evidence this. Some examples have been added to the table to help you start.

Table S2.12 'Well-being, learning and development'

	Definition	Personal practice	Evidence
Well-being		Regular meetings with child's foster carer to support 'J' through transitions	Records of meetings with 'J's foster carers
Learning		Termly meetings with parents to discuss individual education programme	
Development			Observations
			Two year old progress check

If you identify your own definition of each term, *well-being, learning and development*, this will help you identify the type of evidence you need.

Learning relates to progress against EYFS, so if you discuss with parents 'next steps' for their child that relate to EYFS and Development Matters, then this would provide good evidence.

Development refers to how a child is progressing against developmental norms, so if you share a two-year-old progress check that records a child's development against these norms, then this would provide good evidence.

Well-being is used to refer to a child's emotional and physical state. EYFS (2012) identifies the importance of a child's well-being in the principles and commitments. For example, *Children's health is an integral part of their emotional, mental, social, and spiritual well-being and is supported by attention to these aspects* (Commitment 1.4 Health and Wellbeing: **www.teachingexpertise.com/articles/early-years-pip-cards-1-4-health-and-well-being-3351**)

As EYFS (2012) identifies the importance of both physical and emotional well-being, you must evidence how you work with parents to support a child's physical as well as emotional well-being, perhaps through discussions about healthy snacks and the importance of spending time outdoors.

Evaluating your partnerships with parents

You are asked to evidence *working in partnership with [parents] to support the child's well-being, learning and development.* So, how will you know if the partnerships you have formed with parents are effective, and whether they do, in fact, support the child's well-being, learning and development?

Although you are not directly asked to evaluate your working relationships with parents in 2.7, if you reflect on the questions below, this will provide evidence for 2.7.

You may find it helpful to use your journal to reflect on some of these questions as they will help you to consider some of the barriers you may face when working with parents.

- Do you evaluate your settling-in procedures to see whether they promote effective relationships with parents?

  Do you learn about children's culture and background and their interests and preferences from their parents and carers when they first enter your setting?

  Does your settling-in period set the right tone for future communication with parents?

- Do you communicate effectively with parents?

  What are the signs of effective communication that you can look out for?

  Do you try to hold the parent's gaze and make eye contact?

  Do you pay attention to parents' body language when speaking with them?

  Are parents able to communicate freely with you, for example, if there is a language barrier?

- Do you engage effectively with all parents?

  How do you engage with parents who may be reluctant to come into your setting, for example because they are working or because they lack confidence?

  If you have had a difficult conversation on one occasion, does this parent avoid you in the future or did this incident build trust between you?

- Are there any practical strategies that can help you improve your partnerships with parents?

  Do you organise ratios so that it is possible for each key person to speak to parents on a daily basis when they drop off and collect their children?

  Do you use an interpreter when needed?

- If it is a child minder who regularly collects a child, how do you establish contact with a parent you rarely see?

  Do you have regular contact with other carers of the child, such as grandparents?

  How do you have regular contact with the carers of a 'looked-after' child?

- If you are establishing an open day for parents, will parents who are working be able to attend?

- Do you have a comfortable, private space you can use when discussing difficult issues with a parent?

- Some settings have introduced email communication with parents who are working and can't collect their child in person.

  Is this something you might consider introducing?

- Is there an area where parents can mingle and make themselves a cup of tea in the morning when they drop off their children?

- Every Child Matters introduced an emphasis on families' financial well-being and providing opportunities for parents to develop their skills. Many settings, especially children's centres, provide a mixture of parenting classes, English for Speakers of Other Languages (ESOL) and vocational training. Those settings that do not have scope for this provide information for parents on local training opportunities.

  Can you evaluate how well your setting provides this support?

- How effectively does your setting engage with fathers?

  One Early Years Teacher trainee set up Saturday clubs for children and fathers and established a programme to encourage fathers to read to their children.

Leadership role: working with parents

Effective partnerships with parents are a priority as consistency between home and the setting has such a positive impact on children's well-being. Engaging with parents can be difficult, especially for new members of staff who may lack confidence, or for students who are not sure what they are and aren't allowed to communicate. So 2.7 provides you with opportunities to demonstrate your leadership role.

You can evidence the ways in which you support colleagues to ensure that they work with parents to support their child's learning, well-being and development, perhaps through leading a staff training event on developing communication with parents, or introducing a parents' open day or home link book and modelling how to engage with parents. You can also evidence your leadership for 2.7 by encouraging colleagues to shadow you and by modelling good practice during meetings with parents.

You could lead an evaluation of your settling-in procedures with colleagues. Ask colleagues to consider how they use the settling-in period to establish working relationships with parents. Cathy, the Early Years Teacher trainee, asked her colleagues to imagine what it must be like for parents to bring their child to nursery if they have unhappy memories of their own education. This helped them to evaluate their settling-in process from the point of view of a parent.

Colleagues may appreciate a forum for discussions on working with parents that addresses some of the complexities involved. It could be helpful to discuss issues such as how to identify the impact of children's individual circumstances on their development and discuss this with parents without leaving them feeling that they are failing their child.

Another issue to explore with colleagues is how much support it is appropriate to give to parents. You can pose questions such as:

- How do you maintain professional relationships and boundaries with parents? Can you identify the boundaries of your role and when is it more appropriate to refer a parent elsewhere for support?

- How can you respond sensitively and offer guidance and support and motivate parents to support their children's development when parents may be dealing with a wide range of issues?

- How do you support parents experiencing personal difficulties, such as separation or domestic violence at the same time as promoting their child's well-being and dealing with complex developmental issues, such as a child's speech and language delay?

- How do you ensure that parents/carers in non-traditional families feel that their influence is regarded as positive?

- How can you prepare yourself to deal with challenging conversations that can occur at any time?

Evidence for 2.7

Your evidence for 2.7 will need to address your understanding of the important influence of parents and carers and how you work with parents to support their child's learning, development and well-being. Review the evidence you have chosen to check whether it addresses each phrase in this indicator. For example, as 2.7 refers to parents and/or carers, you can make sure that you include examples relating to parents and to other carers, such as grandparents.

When you evidence your work with parents, describe how effectively this partnership supports their child's learning, development and well-being and identify a range of ways in which you work with parents to promote their child's progress. You may be able to evidence how you support colleagues in developing respectful and active partnerships with parents.

Evidence audit

Table S2.13 can help you identify the activities you can carry out to help you evidence 2.7.

You can record examples of your personal practice and leadership and identify any gaps in your evidence. Some examples of activities have been added.

Table S2.13 Evidence audit

Activity	How can I evidence my understanding of the important influence of parents/carers?	How do I work in partnership with parents to support learning/well-being/ development?	How do I support my colleagues?	How can I evidence this?
Home visits				
Settling-in process				
Daily feedback				
Home link and profile book recording parents' comments				
Inviting parents in for Book Week				
Asking parents to share their skills				
Sharing information from two-year-old checks and EYFS Profile				
Parents' evenings				
Open days				
International evenings				
Activities to involve fathers				
Working in partnership with carers				
Working with carers of looked-after children				
Working with parents/carers to support child's well-being during family bereavements and transitions				
Working with parents on IEP				
Working with parents and other professionals, e.g. CAF form, SLT				

EYFS, Early Years Foundation Stage; IEP, individual education plan; CAF, Common Assessment Framework; SLT, speech and language therapist.

Written assignments, case studies and your reflective journal

Written assignments and case studies allow you to explore the relationships you form with particular parents in detail and outline how you work in partnership with other carers to support the child's well-being, learning and development. Assignments and case studies also give you scope to describe how you adapt the environment to make sure that parents and children feel welcome.

You can use your journal to reflect on the quality and effectiveness of these partnerships and your appreciation of the important influence of parents and carers. You can also use it to explore some of the more complex issues involved in partnerships with parents.

Document portfolio

You can include evidence in your document portfolio, but you need to check that it records the quality of your engagement with parents and how you work together to support a child's progress. You also need to check that this evidence is carefully anonymised.

If you have worked closely with a particular parent or carer, you may be able to ask that person to complete a witness testimony for you. Other documents you could include are records of home visits and settling in, parents' contributions to home link or profile books and parents' evenings or meetings. Think carefully about including documents such as a newsletter as these only record your communication to the parent and 2.7 asks you to evidence effective, two-way engagement.

You may be able to evidence your understanding of the important influence of parents through any records you have of involving parents in the life of the setting, perhaps by making story sacks together or inviting parents into the setting to find out more about how their children learn.

If you have worked with parents on an IEP or a CAF form, then you can include these documents as long as they are anonymised and you highlight how the process of completing them evidences your partnership with the parent.

Observations

You can arrange to be observed by your tutor or mentor when you are interacting with parents as you welcome children when they arrive, help a new child settle in or in a one-to-one meeting. However, you need to check that the parents are fully informed and happy to be observed.

During an observation you can demonstrate how you support your relationships with parents, ensure that they feel welcome and discuss their child's learning, well-being and development. You can also invite parents in to share their skills and provide both formal and informal opportunities for feedback.

SUGGESTED READING

Fitzgerald, D (2004) *Parent Partnerships in the Early Years.* London: Continuum.

Lindon, J (2012) *Parents as Partners* (Positive Relationships in the Early Years). London: Practical Pre-School Books.

Siraj-Blatchford, J and Morgan, A (2013) *Using ICT in the Early Years: Parents and Practitioners in Partnership.* London: Practical Pre-School Books.

Ward, U (2013) *Working with Parents in the Early Years.* (Early Childhood Studies Series). London: SAGE.

Standard 3: **Demonstrate good knowledge of Early Learning and EYFS**

Introduction

In Standard 3 you will evidence your understanding of learning and development in relation to Early Years Foundation Stage (EYFS) (2014) and how children's learning progresses through Key Stages 1 and 2. You will demonstrate your understanding of the EYFS areas of learning, early phonics and maths activities and how you prepare children for learning in primary school. You will also demonstrate how you widen children's experiences and raise their expectations.

To prepare children for learning in school, you will need some understanding of the continuity between EYFS and Key Stage 1 and Key Stage 2. Any experience you have of preparing children for school will help you evidence this Standard and you can plan to develop your understanding of Key Stage 1 and Key Stage 2 during your school-based placement.

To evidence this Standard well, you must review your understanding of child development, EYFS, learning in school and early maths and literacy activities, including the use of systematic synthetic phonics in the teaching of reading. You need to identify any gaps in your understanding or practice and plan how you can address these. Your action plan will help you record these gaps and organise how you will address them. You can use your action plan to record all the indicators in Standard 3 that relate to learning in school and plan to research these areas during your school placement.

Although this Standard does not require evidence of leadership, there are opportunities for you to demonstrate your leadership role. As you are expected to *Demonstrate good knowledge of Early Learning and EYFS*, one of the most effective ways to demonstrate this knowledge is to share it with your team.

Overlapping Standards

As you read through Standard 3 you may recognise some concepts and phrases from Standards 1 and 2. However, you must identify the differences between these Standards as well as the similarities. For example, as you are asked to relate your understanding of EYFS to your knowledge of children's development in Standard 3, some of your evidence will overlap with 2.2, but you must be very clear about how Standard 3 differs from 2.2. For example, in 2.2 you need to demonstrate your understanding of child development through your actions, but in Standard 3 you will evidence your understanding of child development in relation to EYFS and learning in school.

The Venn diagrams in Figure S3.1 give you a visual representation to help you identify the areas of overlap between Standards 1, 2 and 3. Use this to help you identify the similarities and differences between any sets of Standards. You can then look at what makes each Standard different and consider how to reflect this in your evidence.

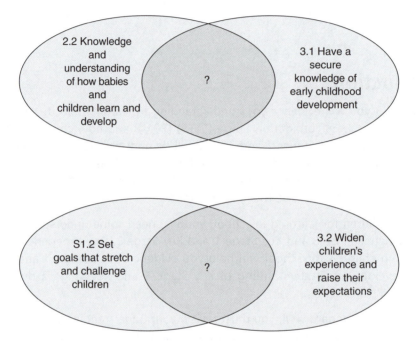

Figure S3.1 *Similarities and differences between Standards 1, 2 and 3*

Standard 3.1: Have a secure knowledge of early childhood development and how that leads to successful learning and development at school

Introduction to 3.1

Standard 3.1 asks you to evidence *a secure knowledge of early childhood development*, which includes an understanding of how children develop and learn. If you have looked at the first Venn diagram in Figure S3.1 you will have considered the overlaps between Standards 3.1 and 2.2 which asks you to *demonstrate understanding of how children learn and develop*. However, there are important differences that you need to bear in mind when you plan your evidence. In 2.2 you are asked to demonstrate your knowledge of child development through your practice, for example, by evidencing how your understanding of attachment theory informs your settling-in procedures. In 3.1, however, you are firstly asked to demonstrate your knowledge of child development in relation to EYFS, and secondly, through your understanding of the relationship between learning in the early years and at school.

This means that in 3.1 you need to evidence your understanding of how children learn and develop at school and the continuity between early years and EYFS and Key Stages 1 and 2. If you have completed your school-based placement this will help you to understand and evidence how children learn in school, but you also need to think about extending your reading about Key Stages 1 and 2. You can look in the 'Suggested reading' section, below, for some texts that can help you.

'Successful learning and development at school'

Standard 3.1 is the Standard that asks you to look forward, to ensure that your provision will support a child's progress in the future as well as during the early years. You must consider a child's development through to Key Stages 1 and 2 at school and how a child's learning and development in the early years can support a child's *successful learning and development at school.*

You need to evidence that you understand how children progress from the early years and EYFS through to Key Stages 1 and 2, and demonstrate how your understanding of early childhood development informs your understanding of learning at school. Your evidence must highlight how you promote children's development in ways that will help prepare them for and contribute to *successful learning and development* at school.

Preparing children for successful learning and development at school: your evidence

The focus in 3.1 on the early years as the preparation for future learning relates to the current Government's emphasis on school-readiness. This emphasis has proved controversial and some early years professionals have argued that it is important to focus on children's developmental needs in the present rather than focus on preparing them for the future. For example, creating a toddler room environment that is rich in opportunities for early literacy activities may be more useful than prematurely teaching reading skills. (In an open letter to *The Daily Telegraph* on Thursday 12 September 2013 signed by 126 leading early years academics, charity leaders, teachers and authors and reported by Graeme Paton, Education Editor, it was claimed that the current system *puts too much emphasis on formal learning in areas such as the three Rs at a young age ... [and] warns that the Coalition is now ratcheting up the requirements with policies that prioritise 'school readiness' over free play.*)

Whatever your personal views, you will have to evidence the ways in which you prepare children for *successful learning and development at school*. There are many ways in which you prepare children for success at school, and you may not even label these as 'preparation'. For 3.1 you need to identify all the strategies that you use so that you can evidence them adequately.

You prepare children in many ways, using strategies that are explicit and others that are less obvious. In the months before children leave to start school you may encourage them to write their name, dress independently and sit still for short periods during circle time. You might share stories about going to school and invite their reception teacher to visit your setting. These are some of the explicit ways in which you prepare a child for school and you can evidence your role in any of these activities to help you meet 3.1.

You can also evidence the less explicit ways in which you help prepare a child for school. Here are just a few examples:

- Help children develop strategies to manage transitions, such as transitions between rooms.

- Set up stimulating activities and resources to promote children's curiosity and interest in the world around them.

- Give children opportunities to be listened to and have their ideas valued so that they gain confidence in speaking in groups and sharing their ideas.

- Engage in sustained shared thinking to promote children's problem-solving skills.

- Provide opportunities for children to pursue their interests and engage in an activity over time to foster concentration skills and love of learning.

- Use constructive feedback to help children to identify their achievements and choose their own next steps.

- Help children learn how to manage their behaviour and understand their feelings, for example, through choosing Golden Rules and using persona dolls.

- Model positive behaviours and support children to identify and develop appropriate social skills through their experiences in group activities.

To evidence 3.1 adequately you must highlight how these strategies and activities prepare children for success in school.

Your school placement

You must complete a school placement for at least two weeks to achieve your Early Years Teacher Status. You can use this placement to help you evidence 3.1 as you can compare the ways in which learning and development are promoted in the early years and in primary school and how delivering EYFS (2014) provides children with the building blocks they need to support their learning in Key Stages 1 and 2.

You can use this time to explore the continuity between learning in the early years and in school, particularly if you focus on one aspect of learning and compare EYFS requirements to those in Key Stages 1 and 2. You could also compare the ways that activities are structured, the styles of teaching and learning and methods of observation and assessment.

You could compare strategies to support children with special needs and children learning English or reflect on how early literacy activities support and prepare children when learning to read in school. You might also find it helpful to reflect on how the social skills, independence and positive behaviour strategies promoted in the early years help a child to manage the demands of a primary school.

Evidence for 3.1

Planning your evidence for 3.1

To evidence 3.1 you must demonstrate how both your practice and your secure knowledge of early childhood development prepare children for successful learning and development in school. You must evidence your understanding of the progression and continuity between your early years practice and successful development at school and demonstrate some understanding of how children learn and develop in Key Stages 1 and 2. If you can visit a local school and read information on the National Curriculum for Key Stages 1 and 2 (Gov.uk, 2014), this will give you the knowledge you need for 3.1. Your school placement will also help you to understand the continuity between early years and learning in school.

Cross-referencing your evidence to 3.3

If you extend your understanding of systematic synthetic phonics and maths activities in Key Stages 1 and 2 this will help you to evidence 3.3, 3.4 and 3.5.

As the requirements for 3.1 are complex, you may find it helpful to use Table S3.1 to identify and organise your evidence.

Use the columns along the top to identify which areas to focus on in your reading and your school-based placement. Explore each area in detail and record your thoughts in Table S3.1. This can help you plan what to focus on in your placement and to record your evidence and identify any gaps. Some examples from Kelly, an Early Years Teacher trainee, have been added to two of the columns to help you start.

Written assignments, case studies and your reflective journal

As you need to evidence your understanding of how children learn and develop from birth through to Key Stages 1 and 2, a written assignment or case study will give you the scope to evidence this understanding in depth. It will also provide you with the breadth you need to compare learning in EYFS to learning in school and outline how you believe that activities in the early years prepare a child for successful learning in school.

You may find it helpful to plan an assignment based on your school placement and you can use this to address the issues outlined in Table S3.1. If you also explore Key Stages 1 and 2 and children's learning of phonics and maths in this assignment then it will help you to evidence 3.3, 3.4 and 3.5 as well.

Table S3.1 Planning your evidence for 3.1

3.1	Attachment	Systematic synthetic phonics	(Add your own topic/s here)	My evidence	Gaps in my practice/evidence
Knowledge of early childhood development	The importance of attachment: the attachments children form in the early years can create 'templates' for attachment relationships in the future	Understanding of development of early literacy skills		Assignment	
				Case study on supporting child settling in	
Early years activities that help prepare a child for school	Supporting secure attachment relationships: key person relationships and supporting relationship with parents/carers	Early literacy and listening skills activities: songs, rhymes, stories, mark-making activities in role-play areas		Observations	
		Print-rich environment		Planning sheets, home visit and settling-in case study	
	Settling-in period				
How this leads to successful learning in school	Early Years Foundation Stage principle 'positive relationships' and Geddes (2006): positive relationships support a child's learning and development	Opportunities for children to choose books Prepares children for listening out for letter sounds in words and understanding that print has meaning		Assignment Case study	Find out how school promotes attachment relationships, especially in reception class
Additional activities to prepare children for success at school	Making a book using photos children have taken of the school and new teacher	Book-borrowing scheme: to introduce children to taking a book home each night		Assignment on school placement	
What successful learning and development in school look like	Confidence in relationship with teacher	Confidence handling books Enjoys choosing books to read		Assignment on school placement	Find out about how school promotes positive relationships
How I promote continuity between setting and school	Geddes (2006) on the learning triangle (teacher–pupil–task): take children to visit reception class and spend time with teacher so that they feel secure in this relationship	Confidence trying out new strategies Help children gain confidence in listening out for initial letter sounds, handling books and sharing their own stories		Observation and planning sheets (literacy activities)	
		Introduce book-borrowing scheme		Plans for 'we went to see our new school' book and activities	
My understanding of Key Stages 1 and 2				Assignment on school placement	I need to find out about literacy in Key Stage 1

Your reflective journal will be a useful tool on your school placement. You can use it to reflect on what you observe and relate this to children's learning in the early years.

Document portfolio

You could include a plan for a group problem-solving maths activity, highlighting how this will help children to develop the mathematical understanding and language they need to support mathematical learning in Key Stage 1, or how problem-solving skills will help them to become effective learners and that working in a group will help them develop the co-operative and social skills they will need in school.

You may have made books with the children about preparing for school and you can include these in your portfolio.

Records from your school placement, such as a witness testimony, can be included if relevant, or observations of practice in school that you can annotate with your reflections on how practice in the early years prepares children for this area of learning in school.

You may have evidence of your leadership role, such as notes from a training session you led on preparing children for school. You can include documents that evidence your understanding of child development from birth through to primary school, such as a leaflet for parents or handouts for colleagues.

Observations

If you can identify a series of activities that you feel help prepare children to become successful learners at school then you can arrange to be observed leading these activities. You could highlight how the activity promotes the skills a child will need in school, such as independence, listening skills and self-esteem. Explain how the activity prepares a child for learning in school, for example, by introducing mathematical language or science activities. You must make sure that your rationale for each activity clearly highlights how this helps you to evidence 3.1.

SUGGESTED READING

Bayley, R, Featherstone, S and Hardy, M (2003) *Smooth Transitions: Ensuring Continuity from the Foundation Stage.* London: Featherstone Catalogue Bloomsbury.

Constable, C (2012) *The Outdoor Classroom Ages 3–7: Using Ideas from Forest Schools to Enrich Learning.* London: Routledge.

Cremin, T and Arthur, J (2014) *Learning to Teach in the Primary School.* London: Routledge.

Doherty, J and Hughes, M (2013) *Child Development: Theory and Practice 0–11.* Essex: Pearsons.

Fisher, J (2010) *Moving On To Key Stage 1.* Berks: OUP McGraw-Hill Education.

Lindon, J (2013) *Understanding Children's Behaviour: 0–11 Years* (Linking Theory and Practice). Oxon: Hodder.

Standard 3.2: Demonstrate a clear understanding of how to widen children's experience and raise their expectations

Introduction to 3.2

In Standard 3.2 you are asked to demonstrate your understanding of how to widen children's experiences and raise their expectations. Widening children's experience and raising expectations are significant issues and you may find it helpful to reflect on your understanding of these concepts and ask yourself some questions before you start gathering your evidence for 3.2.

Consider how widening children's experience relates to EYFS areas of learning such as *Understanding of the world* and *Expressive arts and design* and raising children's expectation relates to *Self-confidence and self-awareness* in *Personal, social and emotional development.* Ask yourself how you can raise the expectations of all children, including, for example, babies and children with special needs. How can you involve parents in this process and how does widening experiences relate to providing first-hand experiences, both in and out of the setting?

Before you start to organise your evidence for 3.2 you must clarify your understanding of the terms used and the issues raised. You must do the following:

- Demonstrate a clear *understanding*: review your understanding and identify any areas where you need to extend your reading.

- Consider how you can *demonstrate* this understanding, for example, through outlining your understanding in a written assignment or showing how your knowledge informs your practice, as you did in 2.2.

- Identify what is meant by *widen children's experience* and decide whether you widen experiences through routine planned activities or through the additional, new activities that you introduce in your setting: for example, do you *widen children's experience* when you plan routine and focus group activities, such as cooking, and/or when you introduce a new topic or take children on a local outing?

- Identify all the ways in which you *widen children's experience*. You widen children's experience when you look at worms through a magnifying glass, plant vegetables, read stories, bake cakes, try new fruits at snack time and visit the local shop before you set up a shop-keeping role-play area. All the first-hand experiences you provide for children, such as an outing on the bus or a visit from the local fire fighters, widen their experience.

- Reflect on how widening children's experiences and raising their expectations relates to specific areas in EYFS (2014), such as *Self-confidence and self-awareness* and *The world*.

- Reflect on how you *widen children's experience* when you observe children and use your observations to plan 'next steps' according to their skills and interests.

- Evaluate the environment and activities you provide to review how they *widen children's experience* and complement the experiences their families provide.

- Consider how you can work in partnership with parents to raise a child's expectations.

- Appreciate that raising expectations is particularly important if a child has a special need or disability or has the experience of being part of a minority group: you need to think about the impact of an illness, special need or disability on the child's own expectations and those of their parents who may feel that the expectations they had for their child before s/he was born cannot now be fulfilled.

- Understand what is meant by *raising expectations* in the context of early years, and particularly in relation to the youngest children.

- Identify cultural and gender issues in relation to families' expectations for their children and be prepared to challenge any discriminatory practice: this will also help you to evidence 8.1.

'Widening children's experiences'

Before you organise your evidence for 3.2 take time to identify and evaluate the strategies you use and activities you plan to *widen children's experience*. Think about what is meant by 'widening experience', how the experiences you provide relate to EYFS requirements and to the experiences children have with their families.

Ask yourself:

- Does *widening children's experience* refer to providing the resources and experiences children need in relation to their next steps, interests and schemas?

- Does it include new experiences that you introduce, such as music and movement sessions or baby yoga?

- Does it involve experiences outside the setting, through outings?

- How do you widen the experiences of children of different ages?

Use Table S3.2 to help you identify and organise your evidence for 3.2. Kelly, the Early Years Teacher trainee who we will meet in the case studies, has added some ideas, to help you start.

Table S3.2 'Widening children's experience'

Activities	Age range	These widen children's experiences because …	My evidence	Gaps in my practice/evidence
Introduce baby yoga sessions	Babies	Extends their experience of physical activities and contact with their parent	Witness testimony from parent	
Cascading training on schemas	Toddlers	We will be able to provide more suitable activities and richer resources for children to explore and plan to support children' schemas	Handouts from training I deliver on schemas and minutes of discussion on providing appropriate resources to support schemas	
Introduce planting area	Pre-school children	Building on children's interest in natural world, providing new hands-on experiences		

CASE STUDY

Every Child Matters and raising children's expectations

Kelly, an Early Years Teacher trainee working with pre-school children, wanted to think about how Every Child Matters (ECM, 2004) outcomes relate to raising expectations to help her understand and evidence 3.2. She wondered whether the ECM outcomes could help her to identify ways she and her team could raise children's expectations.

She read that the ECM outcomes were designed to achieve better outcomes for all children and young people, and narrow the gap between children who do well and those who do not. She read that early years providers and other professionals were encouraged to help children realise how much they are capable of and appreciate that they are entitled to their own place in the world. Kelly read that, although the current Government is not actively promoting ECM outcomes, they are still supported by Ofsted, so she decided to learn about them in more detail to help her identify some strategies for 3.2.

Kelly used her journal to reflect on her findings.

Kelly's journal

Outcome four: 'make a positive contribution'

This relates to children's expectations as it focuses on encouraging children to realise they can have a positive impact on their environment.

*I discovered (**http://webarchive.nationalarchives.gov.uk/+/dcsf.gov.uk/everychildmatters/**) that providers need to focus on helping children learn how to:*

- *Engage in decision making and support the community and environment*
- *Engage in law-abiding and positive behaviour in and out of school*
- *Develop positive relationships and choose not to bully and discriminate*
- *Develop self-confidence and successfully deal with significant life changes and challenges*
- *Develop enterprising behaviour.*

These suggestions seem designed to support school-age children, but we can discuss these in a team meeting and think about how to adapt them for young children.

Does our project to bake cakes which the children will sell at a stall on our open day count as promoting enterprising behaviour?

Will it widen the children's experiences and raise their expectations for 3.2?

CASE STUDY

Gender and cultural issues

Kelly wanted to raise her awareness of the issues involved in raising children's expectations to help her to evidence 3.2. She felt that children's expectations are likely to be influenced by the expectations their family has for them and wanted to find out about the influence of gender and cultural assumptions on children's expectations for themselves. She read an article on 'Sex role expectations in children's vocational aspirations and perceptions of occupations' (Franken, 1983).

This article raised several issues around aspirations in the early years so Kelly shared the article with her team and designed a series of questions to promote a discussion on how to raise the expectations of the children in their care:

- *Can we identify the characteristics that children with high expectations have? If we can identify these characteristics, is it possible or appropriate for us to promote them?*

- *Are there cultural and gender issues around expectations that we need to think about? Can we identify any cultural or gender assumptions that we make that could have a negative effect on a child's expectations?*

- *How should we deal with a situation where a parent/carer/student/volunteer expresses a cultural or gender assumption that could have a negative impact on a child's expectations? For example, if a family has low aspirations for their girl children, what is our role in challenging this?*

- *What strategies can we use to promote anti-discriminatory practice? What role should we take in promoting positive expectations?*

Evidence for 3.2

You need to prepare your evidence for 3.2 carefully as you must ensure that it demonstrates both how you widen children's experiences and raise their expectations. You need to review your evidence and check that it relates to a range of different situations and evidences your work with children of different ages. The strategies that you use to widen the experiences of a baby are different to those that you use with a pre-school child, so your evidence needs to demonstrate your understanding in relation to each age range.

Written assignments, case studies and your reflective journal

You can use a written assignment or case study to explore the issues involved in raising children's expectations and widening their experiences alongside your description and analysis of your actions. You could:

- describe an initiative to increase girls' involvement in construction activities alongside your rationale for introducing this project so as to increase girls' expectations and to widen their experiences;

- describe how you invited a team of women in construction to plan and build a structure in the garden with the girls and make sure that your resources and books reflect positive images of women and men in non-traditional roles.

You can also use an assignment, case study or entry in your journal to explore complex issues, such as raising the expectations of a child with a disability or low self-esteem and the strategies you can use to widen that child's experiences. Any reflections on promoting positive expectations through anti-discriminatory practice can also help you to evidence 8.1.

If you have introduced a project that widens children's experiences then you can use an assignment or entries in your journal to describe these. You might have led a project to introduce Forest School activities or regular visits to the library and other community resources. Describe the activities you introduced and highlight the ways in which these activities widen the experiences of specific children.

Document portfolio

Your planning documents will demonstrate how you widen children's experiences in line with EYFS requirements. You may have evidence of widening children's experiences in your observations, planning, next steps and contributions to profile books and your plans for any projects you have introduced, such as baby yoga or cooking activities. You may also have plans for developing an area in your setting that can help you evidence 3.2, such as introducing communication-friendly spaces or a planting area. You must explain the rationale for your actions and highlight how and why these experiences will widen the experience of a particular child at that moment.

You can also evidence how you raise children's expectations through documents in your portfolio. You may have peer observations of a series of conversations with a child where you support that child to raise her expectations, for example, when looking through her profile book with her and encouraging her to recognise her achievements.

You might also have records of the strategies you use, such as persona dolls and positive feedback, to promote children's expectations. You may also have a witness statement from a colleague or parent that highlights how you supported a particular child, but you need to check that it is detailed and specific enough to evidence 3.2.

If you have led a staff discussion on strategies to widen children's experiences and raise their expectations then you may have records of these sessions that you can include in your portfolio. These discussions might involve, for example, widening children's experience through science activities, or raising their expectations through visits from parents who work in non-traditional roles.

Observations

When you are observed working with a group of children, you can plan an activity that will *widen children's experience* and in which you interact with children in ways that will help raise their expectations. You must make sure that the plans you share with your observer highlight how this activity will widen the experiences of the individual children involved.

SUGGESTED READING

Archer, L and Francis, B (2006) *Understanding Minority Ethnic Achievement in Schools.* London: Routledge.

Browne, N (2004) *Gender Equity in the Early Years.* Berkshire: OUP McGraw Hill Education.

Constable, C (2012) *The Outdoor Classroom Ages 3–7: Using Ideas from Forest Schools to Enrich Learning.* London: Routledge.

Louis, S (2012) *Knowledge and Understanding of the World in the Early Years Foundation Stage (Practical Guidance in the EYFS).* London: Routledge.

Martin, B (2011) *Children at Play: Learning Gender in the Early Years.* Sterling, VA: Trentham.

Sheppy, S (2012) *Personal, Social and Emotional Development in the Early Years Foundation Stage* (Practical Guidance in the EYFS). London: Routledge.

Thwaites, A (2008) *100 Ideas for Teaching Knowledge and Understanding of the World* (100 Ideas for the Early Years). London: Continuum.

Winter, J (2006) *Breakthrough Parenting for Children with Special Needs: Raising the Bar of Expectations.* San Francisco: Jossey-Bass.

Standard 3.3: Demonstrate a critical understanding of the EYFS areas of learning and development and engage with the educational continuum of expectations, curricula and teaching of Key Stages 1 and 2

Introduction to 3.3

In Standard 3.3 you will evidence your understanding of EYFS areas of learning and development and demonstrate how this informs your practice. What makes 3.3 different from the other Standards that relate to EYFS is that you will demonstrate your understanding that EYFS is one stage in a continuum of children's learning experiences, right through to Key Stages 1 and 2. This emphasis on how children learn in school means that your experiences during your school-based placement will help you evidence 3.3. (For more information see Chapter 7, School-based placement.)

To meet 3.3 well you must demonstrate:

- a *critical understanding* of EYFS areas of learning and development;
- an appreciation of the continuum between EYFS and learning in school;
- an understanding of the continuum of expectations, curriculum and teaching methods children will experience through EYFS and into Key Stages 1 and 2;
- familiarity with the key features of Key Stages 1 and 2.

Although the reference to Keys Stages 1 and 2 may initially appear daunting, if you plan your time carefully during your school-based placement you will have plenty of opportunities to develop the understanding you need to meet these requirements.

Standard 3.3 is a complex indicator, but if you pay close attention to each key phrase then you will be able to evidence it well. We will look at the key phrases in more detail in the sections below.

Similarities and differences: Standard 3

You will recognise that there are significant overlaps between the indicators in Standard 3, especially between 3.1, 3.3, 3.4 and 3.5. If you identify these areas of overlap now, it will help you plan the focus for your research for 3.3 and your school-based placement. If you are reading about the continuum between EYFS and Key Stages 1 and 2 for 3.3, this reading will help you prepare to evidence 3.1 as well. If you can identify how the Key Stages 1 and 2 requirements for maths and phonics build on the maths and phonics strategies in EYFS, this will help you to evidence 3.4 and 3.5 as well as 3.3.

'Demonstrate a critical understanding'

In 3.3 you are asked to *Demonstrate a critical understanding of the EYFS areas of learning and development*. The requirement to *demonstrate* your understanding means that you need to evidence this understanding through your actions (and your rationale for your actions), showing how you apply your knowledge of *EYFS areas of learning and development* in practice.

You are also asked to demonstrate a *critical* understanding. Think for a moment about what exactly is meant by *critical understanding* and how you can evidence this. Demonstrating a *critical understanding* does not mean that you are expected to criticise EYFS, but that you have a sound knowledge that you can apply to help you analyse a variety of situations. It involves having a good working knowledge of all significant EYFS principles and requirements that you can rely on to inform your practice. You need to demonstrate how this understanding informs the decisions you make about a child's next steps or helps you to review the quality of your provision.

Think about how you can evidence *critical understanding*. You may find that using your reflective journal to analyse the rationale for your actions enables you to practise this style of writing. A series of journal entries, then, would enable you to build up evidence of your *critical understanding*. For example, you could review an observation of an area of learning in relation to a specific child's development or reflect on EYFS requirements when you review an area of your provision. If you regularly reflect on your practice in relation to EYFS requirements you will be able to build up your confidence gradually, expressing and analysing different positions and ideas.

Definitions of 'critical understanding'

There are many accepted definitions of *critical understanding.* One defines this as *an intellectually defensible opinion that shows a clear grasp of the issues* (Thornton, 2008). The following questions may help you to explore what *critical understanding* means to you and how you can evidence this.

- Can you use these definitions to help you identify what it is that you do when you demonstrate *critical understanding*?
- Can you form your own definition of *critical understanding*?
- Can you identify examples of demonstrating a critical understanding of EYFS areas of learning and development?
- How can you evidence this process?

'EYFS areas of learning and development'

In 3.3 you are asked *to demonstrate a critical understanding of EYFS areas of learning and development*. This means that you need to demonstrate how your understanding of EYFS areas of learning informs your practice and evidence 3.3 through examples of your practice.

In your evidence for other Standards, such as 6.1 and 7.1, you are asked to demonstrate your understanding of one particular aspect of EYFS. In 3.3 you are also asked to evidence your understanding of one aspect of EYFS, and this is the *EYFS areas of learning and development*. You need to make sure that you address all areas of learning and demonstrate an in-depth understanding in each area. This is not as daunting as it may appear, as you will be able to cross-reference your evidence to other Standards, such as 3.4 and 3.5, where you evidence your understanding of promoting early phonics and maths activities. Several work products will provide evidence of applying your understanding of the areas of learning and development. These could include a completed two-year-old progress check or entries in a child's profile book. If you include a completed individual education plan (IEP) and write a case study about a particular child you will be able to analyse your support for that child's development and areas of learning in detail.

'Engage with the educational continuum of expectations, curricula and teaching of Key Stages 1 and 2'

The 1988 Education Act introduced the National Curriculum and divided primary school education from year 1 upwards into Key Stages 1 and 2. Key Stage 1 refers to years 1 and 2 in maintained schools in England and Wales, and years 3 and 4 in Northern Ireland. Children are aged between five and seven and some schools refer to this time period as 'infant school'.

In Key Stage 1 pupils follow Programmes of Study for the National Curriculum core and foundation subjects. From September 2014, a new National Curriculum is being taught in Key Stage 1. The new programmes of study for all subjects are available on the **www.gov.uk** website (**http://webarchive.nationalarchives.gov.uk/ tna/20110208160107/http://curriculum.qcda.gov.uk/** and **www.education.gov. uk/schools/teachingandlearning/curriculum/primary**). Free schools and academies are exempt from the National Curriculum, but are required to provide a broad and balanced curriculum that includes English, maths, science and religious education, and they may choose to teach the National Curriculum. At the end of Key Stage 1, when children are aged seven, they are assessed as part of the national programme of assessment, known as SATs.

Key Stage 2 refers to the four years in maintained schools in England and Wales when children are between the ages of seven and eleven, and these are known as years 3, 4, 5 and 6. In Northern Ireland Key Stage 2 refers to children in years 5, 6 and 7 only, so pupils in Key Stage 2 are aged eight to 11. Children in maintained schools in Key Stage 2 also follow programmes of study from the National Curriculum and, at the end of this stage, pupils aged 11, in year 6, are tested again. The SATS tests are marked externally and the results for each school are published in Department for Education and Skills (DfES) performance tables.

In 3.3 you must demonstrate an understanding of these key features of Key Stages 1 and 2 and the continuum between EYFS and Key Stages 1 and 2. You do not need to understand Key Stages 1 and 2 in the same depth as EYFS, but you do need to form an overview of the expectations, the content of the curriculum and the teaching methods used in primary schools.

You will be able to learn about these aspects of Key Stages 1 and 2 during your school-based placement, but you may find it helpful to introduce yourself to some of the key elements beforehand so that you are better prepared. You may be able to visit the local primary school with your pre-school children to prepare them for this transition or invite the reception teacher to visit your setting. Both these situations will enable you to start forming an understanding of the expectations and possibly the curriculum and teaching methods used in Key Stage 1.

You can prepare yourself for your school placement and 3.3 by reading about learning in school and the National Curriculum. There are several texts in the section on 'Suggested reading' for 3.3 that can help you, and the government website at **www. gov.uk** provides regularly updated information. The DfES website provides information on the revised National Curriculum (2014) and includes the programmes of study, attainment targets and assessment guidance for all Key Stages 1 and 2 subjects (**www. education.gov.uk/schools/teachingandlearning/curriculum/primary**). You will also be able to find additional information available at the National Archives pages for Key Stages 1 and 2 (**http://webarchive.nationalarchives.gov.uk/tna/20110208160107/ http://curriculum.qcda.gov.uk/key-stages-1-and-2/index.aspx**).

In your evidence for 3.3 you must demonstrate that you appreciate the educational continuum between EYFS Key Stages 1 and 2. However, 3.3 is very specific, as it asks you to address three particular areas of the continuum between EYFS and Key Stages 1 and 2. These are the continuum of *expectations, curricula and teaching*.

You can identify the continuum of *curricula* when you examine a specific EYFS area of learning and compare this to the equivalent area of learning, or subject, in Key Stages 1 and 2, and if you look at the continuum between maths and phonics in EYFS and Key Stages 1 and 2 this will help you to evidence 3.4 and 3.5. You can use a series of observations of teaching methods during your school-based placement to identify the continuum of *teaching* between EYFS and Key Stages 1 and 2 and you can analyse the professional discussions you have with your own colleagues and colleagues on your school-based placement to help you identify the continuum of *expectations*.

Evidence for 3.3

In 3.3 you need to evidence your understanding of EYFS areas of learning and development and include examples that relate to children of different ages and abilities. You must evidence *a critical understanding* so your evidence needs to reflect a process of analysing and applying your understanding of each area of learning in a variety of situations.

You do not need to demonstrate *critical understanding* in each piece of evidence, but make sure you that you build up your experience of analysing your understanding, perhaps in your journal or when you deliver training on EYFS. You must gather a significant amount of evidence that highlights your depth of understanding of EYFS areas and how you use them to assess and plan for individual children. Fortunately you will find that this also helps you to evidence several other Standards, such as Standard 6.

If you use your action plan to help you prepare for your school-based placement you can identify the requirements of 3.3 and plan how to use your placement to develop the understanding you need. You will be able to use this experience in the records you keep during the placement. However, 3.3 asks you to identify the continuum of expectations, curricula and teaching between EYFS and Key Stages 1 and 2, so you need to make sure that you clearly highlight your understanding of each of these three areas in this evidence.

Written assignments, case studies and your reflective journal

You can evidence your critical understanding of EYFS areas of learning in a written assignment or case study. You could use an assignment to describe how you have enhanced provision in one area of learning or use a case study to analyse the ways in which you support the development of a child with special educational needs (SEN) or a disability.

You can use your reflective journal to develop your skills of critical thinking and reflect on your observations on, for example, the continuum of expectations between EYFS and Key Stages 1 and 2 or the teaching methods you have seen demonstrated in a year 1 class.

An assignment also provides you with enough scope to analyse your understanding of the Key Stages 1 and 2 curriculum and how this extends EYFS areas of learning and development. You could also use a case study to evidence how you prepare a child with SEN or a disability for the demands of Key Stage 1.

Document portfolio

Many documents and work products can be used in your portfolio to evidence 3.3. Make sure that each piece of evidence clearly relates to the requirements of this indicator. For example, if you have written a general assignment on the National Curriculum you would need to check that you highlight the educational continuum between EYFS, Key Stage 1 and Key Stage 2.

You will be able to demonstrate your critical understanding of EYFS areas of learning and development in your plans, your observations and next steps for children of different ages and abilities, entries in children's profile books, IEPs or a completed two-year-old progress check or EYFS Profile. If you have reviewed an area of learning or delivered training on EYFS areas of learning, then any notes you have made may provide appropriate evidence.

If you have created a leaflet for parents on EYFS areas of learning or preparing their child for the expectations and curricula in school, then you can include these in your portfolio. Any observations and reflections you make during your school-based placement may also provide some relevant evidence. You may also be able to include an observation of your practice in school or a witness testimony from a colleague who has observed you during the placement. Review all your documentary evidence and decide whether you need to annotate this to highlight how it relates to the requirements in 3.3.

Observations

When your tutor or mentor observes you working with a group of children, you can provide him or her with your plans for the session where you have identified the EYFS areas of learning that you plan to address during the activity. You can even provide personalised plans, outlining the EYFS areas you plan to focus on with a particular child and why.

You can arrange to be observed delivering a training or mentoring session to support a colleague in understanding EYFS areas of learning and development and the implications for practice.

You can be observed reviewing a child's progress with the child's parent or carer, as long as the parent or carer has given informed consent and within the meeting you focus on the child's progress in relation to specific areas of learning and development.

SUGGESTED READING

Bayley, R, Featherstone, S and Hardy, M (2003) *Smooth Transitions: Ensuring Continuity from the Foundation Stage.* Featherstone Catalogue. London: Bloomsbury.

Blatchford, R (2013) *Taking Forward the Primary Curriculum: Applying the 2014 National Curriculum for KS1 and KS2.* Suffolk: John Catt Educational.

Boys, R, Spink, E, Macrory, G and Bowen, P (2008) *Primary Curriculum: Teaching the Foundation Subjects.* London: Continuum.

Cremin, T and Arthur, J (2014) *Learning to Teach in the Primary School*. London: Routledge.

Fisher, J (2010) *Moving on to Key Stage 1*. Berkshire: OUP McGraw-Hill Education.

Hutchin, V (2013) *The EYFS: A Practical Guide for Students and Professionals*. Oxon: Hodder Education.

Jones, R, Boys, R, Cooper, W and Sugarman, I (2008) *Primary Curriculum: Teaching the Core Subjects*. London: Continuum.

Moyles, J, Payler, J and Georgeson, J (2014) *Early Years Foundations: Critical Issues*. Berkshire: OUP McGraw Hill Education.

Palaiologou, I (2013) *The Early Years Foundation Stage: Theory and Practice*. London: SAGE.

Scholastic (2013) *The National Curriculum in England: Framework Document*. Oxfordshire: Scholastic.

Shurville Publishing and Department of Education (2013) *The 2014 Primary National Curriculum in England: Key Stage 1 & 2 Framework*. Available online at: **www.gov.dfe/nationalcurriculum** (accessed 20/10/2014).

Standard 3.4: Demonstrate a clear understanding of systematic synthetic phonics in the teaching of early reading

Introduction to 3.4

Standard 3.4 can appear a little daunting at first. It can be hard to appreciate how much knowledge you already have when you look at phrases like *systematic synthetic phonics* and *the teaching of early reading*. However, all this indicator asks you to evidence are the early literacy activities you already provide for babies, toddlers and pre-school children and then relate these to the teaching of phonics in school. You need to demonstrate an understanding of the requirements of EYFS and the National Curriculum in relation to the role of phonics in the teaching of reading, but your school-based placement will provide you with opportunities to research this.

This chapter will help you form an overview of what is meant by *systematic synthetic phonics* and how this relates to your own practice. It will also help you to understand the historical context for the current emphasis on teaching phonics and relate school-based phonics activities to your role in promoting early literacy skills.

What is 'phonics'?

Phonics is about the relationship between letters and the sounds they make. The early literacy activities that we engage in with young children are the building blocks for learning to read in school as they help children learn to hear and identify sounds. Initially these are the sounds children hear in rhymes, songs and stories, and our job is to help children gradually learn to identify discrete sounds. Until children can hear the difference between, for example, 'bad' and 'dad', they will not be able to understand the difference between the sounds made by letters 'b' and 'd'.

To evidence 3.4 well you must evidence your role in promoting these early literacy activities and identify the progression from the phonics activities you engage in with babies, toddlers and pre-school children to the more formal methods of teaching reading in school. You will be able to observe a range of strategies for teaching reading during your school placement and this and your reading on the subject will help you understand what is meant by *systematic synthetic phonics*.

Phonics in EYFS and the National Curriculum

You can compare the strategies to promote reading that you observe in your school placement, such as their choice of reading scheme or use of guided reading, to the strategies you use to develop an awareness of phonics with babies, toddlers and pre-school children (EYFS). If you can identify the continuity between phonics activities and strategies in EYFS and Key Stage 1 you will be able to cross-reference this evidence to 3.1 and 3.3.

'Demonstrate a clear understanding'

To begin, you need to *demonstrate a clear understanding,* evidence the impact of your understanding on your practice. This can include you plans for early literacy activities, such as songs and rhymes or sound lotto games, and the understanding that you demonstrate through your reflective writing and your leadership role. You evidence *a clear understanding* when you use your journal to reflect on the reading activities that you observed in school, or produce a handout for colleagues on appropriate phonics activities for children in the early years.

'Systematic synthetic phonics'

You need a good understanding of what is meant by *systematic synthetic phonics* before you can organise your evidence for 3.4. Reading definitions of *systematic synthetic phonics* and discussions on how children learn to read through phonics will help you form this understanding.

This definition is from a briefing paper published by the Institute of Education (National Priority Briefing Paper: Teaching early reading using systematic synthetic phonics (SSP)', **www.ioe.ac.uk/study/documents/Study_Teacher_Training/Phonics_BriefingPaperv1.pdf**)

> **Systematic phonics** *refers to phonics teaching that is done regularly, discretely, explicitly and in an agreed and rational sequence.*
>
> **Synthetic phonics** *has nothing to do with the word 'artificial'; the reference is to the process of blending (synthesising) the individual sounds in a word together, working from left to right, to read them.*

Synthetic phonics work can begin simply with oral blending, that is, the children listen to sounds and then blend them. They also learn to say sounds, in order, that are represented by individual letters and pronounce these together to say a word (e.g. the sounds /c/, then /a/ and then /t/, blended together to say /cat/).

Synthetic phonics also teaches children to break down (segment) a word they hear into its individual sounds, starting from the first sound and working systematically through the word. For each sound they hear, they choose the letter (or combination of letters, such as 'ch' or 'ai' or 'th') to represent that sound in order to spell the word.

Systematic synthetic phonics programmes bring these two definitions together.

The difference between synthetic and analytic phonics

In a Government press release, 'Reading at an early age – the key to success' (Department for Education, 2010), the Government put forward its rationale for promoting systematic synthetic phonics. In the section on 'How phonics works' there is an explanation of the term 'systematic synthetic phonics':

Phonics focuses on sounds rather than, for example, having children try to recognise whole words.

In analytic phonics, words are broken down into their beginning and end parts, such as 'str-' and 'eet', with an emphasis on 'seeing' the words and analogy with other words.

In synthetic phonics, children start by sequencing the individual sounds in words – for example, 's-t-r-ee-t', with an emphasis on blending them together.

Once they have learned all these, they progress to reading books.

The 'synthetic' part comes from the word 'synthesise', meaning to assemble or blend together.

Children who learn using synthetic phonics are able to have a go at new words working from sound alone, whereas those using analytic phonics are more dependent on having prior knowledge of families of words.

'The teaching of early reading'

You must *demonstrate* an understanding of the *teaching of early reading*. You will *demonstrate* this understanding when you highlight the ways in which your practice is informed by your understanding of how children learn to read in school and how the experiences you provide in the early years prepares them for this. You can use your time on placement in school to find out about the methods that are used to teach reading in reception and Key Stage 1.

Standard 3.4 asks you to focus on the teaching of *systematic synthetic phonics*. However, there are other issues and strategies involved in the teaching of reading and you can use your time on your school placement to find out more about these.

You could, perhaps, look at the strategies that are used to support readers who are learning English as a second language (ESL) and children with special needs, or consider how the school responds to issues of reading in a digital age. You could focus on the school's choice of learning aids such as cards and alphabet guides, their choice of texts that engage children's interests, or their use of reading schemes such as Jolly Phonics or the Oxford Reading Tree. You can look in detail at the particular strategies used with each age group, such as 'cvc' ('consonant, vowel, consonant'), where individual letters and sounds are introduced gradually to children in the reception class and they are encouraged through books, games and readers to put these sounds together to form three-letter words such as, 'ant' and 'bee'.

The reference to *early reading* means you must relate your understanding of how reading is taught in school to EYFS requirements. You can find information on EYFS requirements in *Development Matters* (Early Education, 2012) and 'Communication and language' and 'Literacy: reading' and 'literacy: writing'. You will notice that *Development Matters* highlights a wide range of appropriate phonics activities for children from babies through to the end of the Foundation Stage.

CASE STUDY

Understanding phonics in context

Vanessa, an Early Years Teacher trainee, felt that, although she understood how to promote early literacy skills in her setting, she did not understand the relationship between these activities and the teaching of reading in school. She also did not really understand what was meant by systematic synthetic phonics.

She decided to find out as much as she could about phonics teaching and see what other methods have been used to teach children to read. She used her journal to record the information she found on how children are taught to read in school and tried to relate this to her own practice.

Vanessa's journal

'I found an article on the history of teaching reading in an online article in the BBC News magazine (Westcott, 2012). It looked at the history of reading in this country and helped me to put the discussion of synthetic phonics in context. It made me think about how I was taught to read and I realised I need to share what I've learnt with my team and with the parents of the children who are starting school soon.

The article outlined five key points about phonics and I can adapt some of these in a leaflet for parents:

1. *A phonics approach teaches children to use sounds to decode words so they do not have to recognise a word as a whole to be able to read it. In the approach called 'synthetic phonics', words are broken up into their smallest sounds, called 'phonemes'.*

The letters that represent phonemes are called 'graphemes' and children are taught to blend these into words. This is how I was taught to read, sounding out 'd-o-g' to make the word 'dog'.

What makes this more complicated is that in English we can represent one phoneme using one, two, three or four letters, like 'ough' in 'cough'.

We teach children approximately 40 phonic sounds and how to combine letters to represent each sound. However, we can spell many sounds in more than one way. 'Cough' and 'bough' (bough of a tree) are spelt using the same phoneme, but sound different, and 'bow' and 'bough', which use different phonemes, sound the same.

Children are tested on their ability to read groups of graphemes in their SATS tests at the end of year 1.

2. Although this government promotes phonics as they feel that this approach will boost reading standards, not all professionals agree. The 'phonics-only' approach is controversial as some teachers suggest a more balanced approach that includes other reading strategies is more helpful for some children because English is not always written phonetically and that 'decoding' text is not the same as reading for pleasure and to make meaning.

3. There are other methods of teaching reading that have been used in the past and methods for teaching children how to read have been debated since the nineteenth century – so now I don't feel so bad about my own lack of understanding!

Until the nineteenth century reading was taught by the 'alphabetic method', not phonics. Children were taught to recognise and name the letters of the alphabet, in order, in upper and lower case.

The phonics approach is not new as it was first used after 1850, according to 'Sounds familiar: the history of phonics teaching' (Cove, 2006), but it was often combined with other strategies, so that children could use the context of a story or the syntax within a passage to help them predict the next word.

The 'look and say' method became popular in the 1940s. It was also called the 'whole word method' and was introduced by an American psychologist, Edmund Huey, in 1908. In this approach children are introduced early to pictures and stories and learn to recognise complete words.

In the 1950s and 1960s, when my mother was at school, books with stories based on the lives of two children called Janet and John were popular. The idea of the 'whole word' approach was that children would repeat the words on each page so many times that they memorised them. Mum said that she found the stories repetitive and dull and the stories emphasised very stereotypical gender roles. She said she only enjoyed reading once she could choose her own books.

(Continued)

231

(Continued)

4. *The debates on reading continue*

   The reading debate has continued over the years, with opinion moving in one direction, and then back in the other. In the 1970s and 1980s the approach to reading was less polarised as a range of schemes were used and teachers could choose which methods they felt were most helpful.

   There was also an emphasis on the importance of giving children access to books of their own choosing, with rich and complex stories so that they could appreciate the purpose of reading. I remember my nephew in the 1990s bringing books home from school. They had beautiful, bright pictures and as he had chosen each book himself he was really keen for us to share the story with him.

5. *Learning about phonics is just one part of learning to read and we need to remember this when we promote early reading skills. One of the most important ways to promote reading skills is to encourage parents to share books with their children. I remember reading that boys, in particular, benefit from sharing books with their dads. This is something we can focus on when we work with our parents.*

I think I have learnt from my research that, for children to benefit from the 'systematic synthetic phonics' approach, we need to promote all the skills that contribute to reading in the early years. We need to provide an environment that is print-rich, and encourage children to handle books and appreciate the wonderful stories they contain and we can encourage parents to share books with their children. We need to really focus on helping children to listen out for sounds, through rhymes and songs and activities like sound lotto, and when they are older, encourage children to listen out for initial letter sounds in the words that mean something to them, like their names.

Systematic synthetic phonics and EYFS

Once you understand what is meant by *systematic synthetic phonics*, how it fits into the context of the history of teaching reading and the reasons for this choice of approach, you can think about extending the strategies you use to promote phonics in the early years.

You must identify how EYFS (2012, 2014) promotes systematic synthetic phonics. In *Development Matters* (Early Education, 2012), for example, there is a requirement that when children are ready, possibly in reception class, they need regular sessions in systematic synthetic phonics, but the sessions need to be 'multisensory' to capture their interests and motivation. Review the strategies suggested in 'Communication and language: listening and attention' from babies through to the end of EYFS and 'Literacy: reading' and 'Literacy: writing' and consider how these requirements relate to the activities you plan to promote children's early literacy skills.

Progression routes from early years phonics activities to systematic synthetic phonics in school

In 3.1, you are asked to demonstrate understanding of how children's learning progresses from the early years through to Key Stages 1 and 2. You need to follow a similar process in 3.4 to identify the early literacy activities that are the precursors of systematic, synthetic phonics, and be able to explain how you move from one activity to another, and how each step prepares a child for the more formal learning of phonics in school.

Read about activities to promote early literacy, particularly those that promote listening to sounds, like sound lotto games. You can use EYFS *Development Matters* (Early Education, 2012) and the National Curriculum to help you to identify the progression routes from early literacy listening activities to teaching phonics.

You may find it helpful to read through EYFS (2014) requirements for 'Communication and language' and 'Literacy' that relate to early reading and phonics and list all the related activities that you provide in your setting, starting with those involving babies, then looking at toddlers, and finally, pre-school children.

You can then take this chart with you to your school placement and use it to identify how each early years activity you identified supports children with phonics activities when they are learning to read at school and how EYFS supports the requirements of the National Curriculum.

One example that looks at activities to promote children's familiarity with books has been added to Table S3.3 to help you start.

Table S3.3 Progression routes from early years phonics activities to systematic synthetic phonics in school

Early Years Foundation Stage requirements	Early years activities	This helps children in school when they ...	Reception class (EYFS)	Key Stage 1 strategies and activities	Key Stage 2 strategies and activities
Babies	**Babies**		**Reception class**	**Year 1**	**Year 3**
'Communication and language: listening and attention': Listens to familiar sounds, words, or finger plays	Sharing books, songs and rhymes during key times Book library for parents to borrow books to share with their child	→	Taking a book of their choice home to share	Taking a reading-scheme book home	Regular times to read with their class teacher or teaching assistant
Toddlers	**Toddlers**				
'Communication and language: listening and attention': 'Recognises and responds to many familiar sounds, e.g. turning to a knock on the door, looking at or going to the door'	Encourage children to talk about the different sounds they hear, like the ringing of the bell and squeak of the gate	→			
Pre-school children	**Pre-school children**	→			

Systematic synthetic phonics: leadership opportunities

Any Standard that requires you to demonstrate your understanding can be evidenced through leadership activities as when you mentor colleagues or deliver training you demonstrate the depth of your knowledge. If you can support your team in developing their understanding of systematic synthetic phonics and other strategies that can support children when they learn to read, then you will *demonstrate a clear understanding,* as required in 3.4.

If you highlight the continuity between early literacy activities and learning to read at school and how the strategies you use in the early years support children when they learn to read in school, this will help you to evidence 3.1 and 3.3 as well. You can demonstrate how learning progresses from the early years into Key Stages 1 and 2 and explain why it is important that you focus on early literacy skills and appropriate phonics activities to provide the building blocks for systematic synthetic phonics in school.

When you deliver training on early reading and systematic synthetic phonics you must present a good understanding of the arguments for and against this method. You might emphasise that *systematic synthetic phonics* introduces consistency and that children benefit from a consistent approach. You could also address your concern that there are drawbacks when following only one approach and emphasise the importance of providing a range of rich early literacy experiences for children from babies through to the end of the Foundation Stage.

You could emphasise other strategies that complement a phonics approach to learning to read, such as the importance of developing children's love of books and of reading for meaning, of providing a print-rich environment and of involving parents in sharing books with their children. You can discuss the importance of creating a print-rich environment, and opportunities for emergent writing in role-play areas both inside and outside, to help children to appreciate that print has meaning and is a useful way for them to communicate. You must stress that phonics activities need to be meaningful, engaging, active and multisensory and capture the child's interest (so worksheets are not really suitable), with opportunities to learn through play and concrete experiences and where they can try out new rules as they learn them.

Evidence for 3.4

In 3.4 you are asked to demonstrate your understanding of the approach to the teaching of reading known as systematic synthetic phonics.

Written assignments, case studies and your reflective journal

You need evidence of introducing early literacy activities that help children hear and identify different sounds, such as songs and rhymes, and you can use a written assignment to describe how you plan appropriate activities for groups of children of a specific age or stage of development and highlight how these early phonics activities relate to the teaching of systematic synthetic phonics in school.

You can use a case study to describe how you have adapted phonics activities for a particular child, perhaps because s/he has a special need or disability, such as speech delay or hearing loss. You might also want to outline how you have adapted phonics activities to support a child who is learning English.

You can use your reflective journal to explore your understanding of phonics and the teaching of reading in school and how the strategies you use to support children's early language and literacy support learning in school. You can also use your journal to reflect the phonics sessions you observe during your school placement and the progression from EYFS phonics activities in the reception class and the teaching of phonics in Key Stage 1.

You may find it helpful to write an assignment on your experiences during your school-based placement and you can organise the assignment so that it helps you to evidence the indicators in Standard 3. If you describe and analyse what you have learnt about phonics and the teaching of reading in school and how EYFS (2014) requirements for 'communication and language' and 'literacy' prepare children for the related requirements of the National Curriculum, then this will help you to evidence 3.4.

Document portfolio

You can include a range of documentary evidence for 3.4 in your portfolio. This could include your training notes for a staff meeting on adapting phonics activities for children of different ages or an information booklet for parents highlighting the benefits of exploring sounds with their child, enjoying rhyming words and patterns of nonsense words or sharing songs together.

You may have activity plans for phonics activities with children of different ages and evidence of differentiating phonics activities to support a child with special needs. Each document must clearly highlight your understanding.

Observations

You can arrange to lead a phonics activity when you are observed by your mentor or tutor and include your rationale in your planning notes. You can plan to be observed leading an activity that promotes listening skills, such as home lotto, or a circle time activity where you encourage children to listen out for rhyming sounds or to identify the initial sound of their key words, such as their name.

SUGGESTED READING

Bryce-Clegg, A (2013) *50 Fantastic Ideas for Teaching Phonics*. London: Bloomsbury.

Campbell, R (2002) *Reading in the Early Years: Handbook*. Bucks: OUP.

Coulson, G and Cousins, L (2013) *Games, Ideas and Activities for Early Years Phonics*. Harlow: Pearsons.

Department for Education (2010) 'Reading at an early age: the key to success'. Available online at: **www.gov.uk/government/news/reading-at-an-early-age-the-key-to-success** (accessed 13/11/2014).

Dombey, H and colleagues in the United Kingdom Literary Association. (2010) *Teaching Reading: What the Evidence Says*. United Kingdom Literacy Association and the International Reading Association. Available online at: **www.teachers.org.uk/files/UKLATeachingReading[1].pdf** (accessed 21/10/2014).

Featherstone, S, Persse, L and Hardy, M (2013) *The Little Book of Phonics: Little Books with Big Ideas (4)*. London: Featherstone Bloomsbury.

Glazzard, J and Stokoe, J (2013) *Teaching Systematic Synthetic Phonics and Early English (Critical Teaching)*. Northwich: Critical Publishing.

Jolliffe, W and Waugh, D (2012) *Teaching Systematic Synthetic Phonics in Primary Schools*. London: Learning Matters, SAGE Publications.

Rose, J (2006) *Independent Review of the Teaching of Early Reading: Final Report* (Rose Review). Available online at: http://webarchive.nationalarchives.gov.uk/20100526143644/http:/standards.dcsf. gov.uk/phonics/report.pdf (accessed 13/11/2014).

Soler, J and Openshaw, R (2012) *Literacy Crises and Reading Policies: Children Still Can't Read!* London: Routledge.

Walt, M (1998) *Teaching Reading and Spelling to Dyslexic Children: Getting to Grips with Words*. Oxon: David Fulton.

Standard 3.5: Demonstrate a clear understanding of appropriate strategies in the teaching of early mathematics

Introduction to 3.5

In Standard 3.5 you will evidence your understanding of early mathematics and the strategies you use to promote young children's understanding of key mathematical concepts. You are asked to evidence *appropriate strategies in the teaching of early mathematics* and this refers to the range of mathematical activities you provide and your understanding of children's mathematical development, that children's understanding of abstract concepts develops though their repeated experiences in meaningful concrete situations. You will find that the work of Piaget, Hughes and Donaldson, amongst others, will help you identify the key features of early mathematical learning and relate these to your practice

Strategies also refers to the range of activities you provide and how you adapt and differentiate these according to a child's age and stage of development. You will use many, varied strategies to promote children's mathematical understanding and the key to evidencing 3.5 well is to identify all these strategies, and evidence the unplanned, spontaneous strategies as well as the planned ones.

You may have planned a cooking activity where you will introduce certain mathematical language and children will measure out the ingredients. Later in the day you might encourage children to count the steps down to the garden or sing counting songs while waiting to brush their teeth.

These activities all promote mathematical understanding and you need to make sure that you identify your role in all these activities. This includes the strategies you use to introduce maths activities outdoors as well as indoors and the resources you provide to encourage mathematical learning in role-play areas, such as making tickets for the 'bus station' in the garden. *Strategies* also includes the methods you use to support the mathematical development of children who are learning English as a second language. You might, for example, learn the number names in your key child's home language and display the numerals 1 to 10 in different scripts.

Mathematics in EYFS and the National Curriculum

As Standard 3 asks you to *demonstrate good knowledge of early learning and EYFS*, you need to relate your *understanding of appropriate strategies in the teaching of early mathematics* to your understanding of early learning and EYFS requirements. You will demonstrate your understanding of *early learning* when you plan activities that are appropriate for children at different ages and stages of development and appreciate that young children learn abstract concepts through concrete, first-hand experiences that make 'human sense' (Donaldson, 1987). You also need to demonstrate your understanding of EYFS requirements in the specific area of learning 'mathematics' and the strands, 'mathematics: numbers' and 'mathematics: shape, space and measures'.

To demonstrate this knowledge of EYFS requirements you can evidence how you use *Development Matters* (Early Education, 2012) to assess children's progress and provide appropriate and differentiated strategies that promote children's understanding of specific mathematical concepts. For the strategies you evidence to be 'appropriate' for babies, toddlers and pre-school children you will also need to show how they are developmentally appropriate, and that they are practical and stimulating and build on children's interests and support their 'next steps'.

You can then compare these strategies to the maths activities you observe in Key Stages 1 and 2 during your school placement and the requirements of the National Curriculum for mathematics. You can also identify the continuity between the strategies you promote in the early years, such as the importance of learning through first-hand, concrete experiences, and the strategies you observe in school.

'The teaching of early mathematics'

There is a reference to *the teaching of early mathematics* in 3.5, but you do not need to be concerned by the use of the term *teaching*. Teaching in this context refers to teaching strategies that are appropriate in the early years. You will only need to evidence the range of *appropriate strategies* that you are currently using, such as introducing the mathematical language of 'full' and 'empty' when a child is pouring water in and out of containers at the water tray.

For example, if you look at the section on 'Using this guidance to support each child's learning and development' in EYFS (2012) you will find that it recommends that practitioners follow the cycle of observation, assessment and planning with the support of *Development Matters* (Early Education, 2012) and states that, *This way of teaching is particularly appropriate to support learning in early years settings.*

EYFS: 'appropriate strategies in the teaching of early mathematics'

You must evidence *appropriate strategies* that you use to support children's understanding of the mathematical concepts outlined in EYFS (2012), 'mathematics: numbers' and 'mathematics: shape, space and measures'. The strategies and activities you introduce to support children's growing understanding of each of these concepts need to be 'appropriate', which means that they need to be differentiated, concrete and meaningful enough to make what Donaldson (1987) referred to as 'human sense'. For example, to encourage pre-school children to count reliably with numbers from 1 to 20 and place them in order, you would not give them a worksheet to complete. Instead you might encourage them to count the numbers of children present that day and then count out the cups and plates needed for snack time.

You can evidence the strategies you use through the activities you plan and the language you model during the activities, particularly when you involve children in problem solving. If you involve children in designing an obstacle course you will have opportunities to model positional language, such as, 'we walk *along* the beam and then we jump *down* and wriggle *through* the tunnel'.

You will be able to *demonstrate* your understanding of *appropriate strategies* if you arrange to be observed leading a mathematical activity you have planned and highlight how you adapt and differentiate the activity and when you lead and support the practice of your colleagues. You can *demonstrate … appropriate strategies* when you mentor a colleague or encourage your co-worker to shadow you when you introduce mathematical language into the daily routines or when you deliver training on, for example, extending opportunities for maths activities outdoors.

You may find it helpful to remind yourself of the mathematical concepts that are introduced in EYFS (2012), 'Mathematics' (capacity, position, distance and time).

Observing mathematics in Key Stages 1 and 2

Standard 3.5 is unlike indicators 3.1, 3.3 and 3.4 as it does not ask you to evidence your understanding of how mathematics is taught in school. However, it may be helpful to use some of your time on your school placement looking at the strategies used in teaching mathematics in Key Stages 1 and 2 as this will help you appreciate how the activities you plan support a child in learning in school.

CASE STUDY

Promoting Mathematical Understanding

David, an Early Years Teacher trainee, used his time on his school placement to find out about strategies for teaching mathematics in the reception class and Key Stages 1 and 2. He decided to share his understanding of strategies to promote mathematics in the reception class with his colleagues and the parents of two of his key children 'P' and 'T' as they were due to start school the following term. He encouraged the parents of 'P' and 'T' to appreciate the progression in their children's mathematical understanding from the early years through into school. This also helped David to evidence 3.1 and 3.3, which look at the continuity between learning in the early years and at school.

Appropriate strategies in the teaching of early mathematics: leadership opportunities

As you need to *demonstrate a clear understanding of appropriate strategies in the teaching of early mathematics,* you can evidence this through your leadership role as you will demonstrate this understanding when you mentor a colleague or encourage them to shadow you during a maths activity. If you lead a training day on how young children learn mathematical concepts, or on differentiating maths activities, or 'maths for babies', then this will evidence your understanding of *appropriate strategies in the teaching of early mathematics.*

Evidence of 'appropriate strategies in the teaching of early mathematics'

As Standard 3 asks you to *demonstrate good knowledge of early learning and EYFS,* you need to evidence your understanding of EYFS and early learning in relation to mathematics in your evidence for 3.5. You must evidence a good understanding of the EYFS requirements for mathematics and provide examples of strategies you use to promote children's understanding of the mathematical concepts outlined in 'mathematics: number' and 'mathematics: shape, space and measures'.

Complete Table S3.4 to help you to identify EYFS requirements and all the strategies you use to meet these, both those that you plan and the opportunities that occur naturally, so that you can evidence a balanced cross-section of your practice.

Some examples have been added to help you start.

Evidence for 3.5
Written assignments, case studies and your reflective journal

You can use a written assignment to review your role in developing mathematical learning in your setting in line with EYFS requirements and your understanding of how young children learn. You can describe and reflect on your role in, for example, developing early maths activities for toddlers in the garden area and analyse the impact of any changes you introduced to support the mathematical development of specific children.

You can use a case study to explore in detail how you adapt activities to support the mathematical development of a child with special needs or a disability or who is learning English as a second language. You can cross-reference any evidence of

Table S3.4 *Evidence of appropriate strategies in the teaching of early mathematics*

Age range	EYFS: 'mathematics: numbers'	My activities	EYFS: 'mathematics: shape, space and measure'	My activities	My evidence	Strategies in reception class, Key Stages 1 and 2
Babies			• 'Recognises big things and small things in meaningful contexts'	Include similar objects of different sizes in the treasure baskets and talk to the babies about the 'big ball and little ball' and point out big things and little things in picture books	Observations Session plans Assignment on developing treasure baskets	
Toddlers	• 'Beginning to organise and categorise objects, e.g. putting all the teddy bears together or teddies and cars in separate piles'	Place picture labels on to the boxes for cars, trucks and trains and encourage the children to sort the vehicles into the boxes when we tidy up			Observation recording children's comments when sorting vehicles	
Young children			• 'Shows interest in shape by sustained construction activity or by talking about shapes or arrangements'	Encourage children to talk about the shapes that they choose and build, model the names of shapes and positional language: take photos of children's constructions and encourage them to talk about them	Observations of discussion with child and annotated photos of child's constructions, recording the child's comments Case study of child 'J'	

EYFS, Early Years Foundation Stage.

differentiating mathematical activities in the case study to the indicators where you evidence how you adapt provision for individual children, such as 4.2 and 5.3.

You can use your journal to analyse an observation of a child exploring a mathematical concept to identify her stage of development and plan next steps and activities to support her. You can also reflect on the activities that best support children's mathematical development such as those based on their interests. Ellie, an Early Years Teacher trainee, used her journal to reflect on her conversation with Albie, age three, who wanted to add four candles to the playdough cake he had made for his Spiderman toy, saying 'My Biderman is four today'.

You may choose to write an assignment based on your observations of maths activities during your school placement. You could explore the continuum of mathematical development through the early years and into Key Stages 1 and 2, and provide examples of your own practice and identify how these strategies support a child's learning in school. This would then help you to evidence 3.1 and 3.3.

Document portfolio

You can include your session plans for mathematical activities in your document portfolio, especially if you highlight how you differentiate these activities and relate them to EYFS requirements.

You can include observations of a key child engaging in a maths activity with your reflections on this observation and your plans for their next steps and a focus activity to further support the child's development.

If you have mentored a colleague on strategies to promote children's mathematical understanding then your co-worker may be able to provide a witness testimony. This would need to emphasise your understanding of appropriate strategies to support children's mathematical development.

If you have delivered training or led a project to extend opportunities for mathematical learning then you may have minutes of a staff meeting or training handouts that can evidence your understanding of appropriate strategies to promote children's mathematical understanding.

You may have an order form that records the resources you requested to promote mathematical activities or emails between yourself and another professional that highlight how you plan to support the mathematical development of a child with special needs.

Observations

You can arrange to be observed engaging in a series of mathematical activities with babies, toddlers and pre-school children and you can share your plans for the activity with your observer to highlight your understanding of EYFS requirements and the strategies you use to differentiate this activity. During an observation you can demonstrate how you use daily routines to introduce mathematical learning.

Suggested reading

A note on debates in the teaching of mathematics

The teaching of mathematics gives rise to debate and controversy and some of the books in this section will introduce you to these issues.

These issues include the effects of passing on our own fears about mathematics to the children we teach, which you can read about in Haylock, and debates on the creativity of mathematical thinking, which you can read about in Briggs' *Creative Teaching: Mathematics in the Early Years and Primary Classroom*. The work of Donaldson and Hughes will introduce you to the importance of providing open-ended mathematical tasks and problem solving in situations that make 'human sense'.

You can read about the damaging belief that some people are good at maths and others just aren't, and the dangers of an overemphasis on providing the 'right' answer rather than involving children in mathematical problem-solving activities in Boaler's *The Elephant in the Classroom.* She also addresses the important issue of women's access to higher-level mathematics.

SUGGESTED READING

Boaler, J (2009) *The Elephant in the Classroom: Helping Children Learn and Love Maths.* London: Souvenir Press.

Briggs, M (2012) *Creative Teaching: Mathematics in the Early Years and Primary Classroom.* London: Routledge.

Donaldson, M (1978) *Children's Minds.* London: Fontana.

Hansen, A (2013) *Games, Ideas and Activities for Early Years Mathematics.* Harlow: Pearsons.

Haylock, D (2010) *Mathematics Explained for Primary Teachers.* London: SAGE.

Hughes, M (1986) *Children and Number: Difficulties in Learning Mathematics.* Oxford: Blackwell.

Pound, L and Lee, T (2010) *Teaching Mathematics Creatively* (Learning to Teach in the Primary School Series). London: Routledge.Skinner, C and Stevens, J (2013) *Foundations of Mathematics: An Active Approach to Number, Shape and Measures in the Early Years.* London: Bloomsbury.

Tucker, K (2014) *Mathematics Through Play in the Early Years.* London: SAGE.

Standard 4: Plan education and care taking account of the needs of all children

Introduction

This Standard asks you to evidence how you provide care, educational programmes and activities that are appropriate for children of all ages, stages of development and abilities. You must evidence how you plan a balanced and flexible educational programme, use a range of teaching approaches and lead group activities that promote individual children's interests, development and intellectual curiosity and constantly reflect on the effectiveness of your provision. You must demonstrate how you observe individual children and use these observations to plan a child's next steps.

You must evaluate the effectiveness of areas of your provision that relate to education and care and support the process of continuous improvement. You must demonstrate that your educational programme is balanced and flexible, meets the needs of the children and is stimulating enough to promote their love of learning.

As observation and planning are such core aspects of your work as practitioner, you should find few unfamiliar issues in this Standard, so in this chapter we will focus on what you are required to evidence and how you can do this.

Education and care

In Standard 4 you are asked to evidence how you plan both *education and care*. Some years ago there was an emphasis on bringing care and education together. It was considered that separating out education and care was a false division, as children learn from all their experiences, not just those that are seen as educational.

If you share songs with a child when you are changing his nappy, do you call this education or care? However, in Standard 4 you are specifically asked to evidence how you plan both *education and care*, so you must make sure that your evidence clearly addresses both of these.

Make sure that throughout your evidence for Standard 4 you provide examples of your practice that relate to both education and care. Make lists of all the activities you carry out that relate to education and those that relate to care.

You will then be able to identify where these overlap and use your lists to identify the activities and routines you support, such as circle times and group activities, and choose to evidence a cross-section of these.

Age requirements

If you are not involved in planning for individual children and groups of children on a daily or weekly basis, it may be difficult to evidence this Standard in enough detail. If you look at the statements for Standard 4, 4.1 and 4.4 you will see that you are required to plan and lead activities with *all children*, taking account of their age, stage of development, circumstances, interests and abilities.

This suggests that you must evidence your planning for individual children at different ages, stages of development and abilities. You may need to spend a regular period of time working with groups of children of different ages and abilities, so that you can provide enough detailed evidence of your practice.

If you are a practitioner, you will have plenty of evidence, but this may only relate to one age group. Consider taking on an age-related placement so that you can evidence how you plan and lead activities for babies, toddlers and pre-school children. If you read Chapter 5 on age range requirements, you will find some information to help you decide whether this is necessary.

Standard 4 and leadership

There is plenty of scope for demonstrating leadership in Standard 4. You could find out whether your colleagues feel they need support in planning and lead training. Or, mentor a new colleague or student as s/he may need help to understand your planning systems.

You could evaluate the effectiveness of your planning procedures and propose a revised or alternative approach or facilitate a discussion in a staff meeting on providing a balanced and flexible programme and highlight the particular needs of babies.

In 4.4 you are asked to evidence how you lead group activities. However, this does not provide evidence of your leadership role as required in Standard 8, as leading a group activity is considered personal practice.

Standard 4.1: Observe and assess children's development and learning, using this to plan next steps

Standard 4.1 is about your understanding of the planning cycle and how you use observation and assessment to plan a child's next steps. You must evidence your understanding of the importance of observation and how it informs your planning for an individual child. You must provide evidence of your observations and how you have used them to assess a child's learning and development and choose that child's next steps.

You need evidence that shows that you do not observe a child only once, and that observation and assessment are ongoing processes. Your profile books should demonstrate how you are continually observing children and revising their next steps. If you are doing this appropriately, the profile book will also show how the quality of your observation and assessment promotes the child's learning and development. You must also include examples of individual observations, assessments, next steps and planning for a series of children. If you can include examples relating to children of different ages, stages of development and abilities you will be able to use this evidence for other Standards as well, and evidence your experience with each age range.

The other Standards that overlap with 4.1 include:

- 1.2, where you *set goals that stretch and challenge children of all backgrounds, abilities and dispositions*;

- 2.1, in your evidence of being *accountable for children's attainment, progress and outcomes*;

- 3.1, where you need to demonstrate a *secure knowledge of early childhood development*;

- 4.2, where you plan activities that take into account the *stage of development* of a child and his or her interests;

- 5.2, where you *adapt education and care to support children at different stages of development*.

Observation methods

You must evidence your understanding of the role of observation and provide a series of examples of observations of children of different ages, using a range of observation methods.

You may have many short observations that you recorded on a sticky note during an activity that you later add to a child's profile book or bring with you to a planning meeting. You could also have a series of short narrative observations that you completed to help you review how well a new child was settling in.

If you wanted to find out more about a child's concentration and the activities he engages in, then you may have completed a time sampling observation. You could demonstrate how this observation helped you to identify a child's interests and that he spent more time engaging in physical play outdoors than at the activities on the tables and you can outline the implications for your planning.

Assess children's development and learning

In 4.1 you are asked to observe and assess children's learning and development. You must evidence how you use an observation to assess a child's development and make reference to the Early Years Foundation Stage (EYFS) outcomes and assessment methods.

You may be able to evidence this process through a case study or reflections in your journal about a specific child, and through your focus activity-planning sheets, entries in profile books and individualised education plans (IEPs). The reference to *assessment* means that you can also evidence 4.1 through your completed two-year-old checks. You may also have evidence for 4.1 in a completed (anonymised) CAF form that you have contributed to.

'Plan next steps'

You must evidence how you use your observations to assess children's development and learning and decide on their next steps. You must provide examples of this assessment process, and show how it has led you to decide on specific next steps that you can relate to EYFS outcomes. You may have these records of next steps in a child's profile book or IEP.

You must also use observations to identify children's interests, explain why this is important and show how this informs your planning. You may find that some of your evidence here overlaps with 4.2, which asks you to plan activities according to the ability and interests of each child.

Leadership and 4.1

You will be able to evidence your leadership role for Standard 8 in your evidence for 4.1; for example, by demonstrating how you have helped a colleague use different methods of observation and understand the planning cycle. You can also evidence how you evaluate the planning cycle in your setting and promote improvements or lead a staff development event on planning next steps.

However, you do need strong evidence of your own practice for 4.1, so if you are in a management role, you may need to consider spending time with a group of children so that you can build up your evidence.

Evidence for 4.1

To evidence 4.1 well you must provide plenty of examples of your observations of individual children and how you have used these to assess their learning and development against EYFS outcomes and any individual goals you have set for them, for example, in an IEP. Your evidence must draw clear links between your observations and the next steps you plan for a child.

Written assignments, case studies and your reflective journal

Written assignments, case studies and your reflective journal provide you with opportunities to reflect on your observations of a child in depth and demonstrate how you use observations to assess children's learning and development and plan their next steps.

Present a case study of your work with an individual child, possibly a child with special educational needs (SEN) and quote from an observation to highlight how you used this to identify any concerns and assess that child's development.

However, you can also use an assignment or case study to explore how you used observations to help you identify areas where provision could be improved. Reflect on how you have identified the need for a change in the environment and how your rationale for this change came from what you identified in your detailed, individual child observations.

For example, you may have observed children engaging in the sand tray to identify how they were learning through these activities and identify any problems with the area and then introduce a change to address these issues. You would observe the area before the change and then observe the same children enjoying the improved area after the change so as to evaluate its impact on the children's learning and development. You can use these 'before' and 'after' observations to evidence how you assessed children's development and provided resources to support them in their next steps.

Document portfolio

You can include:

- copies of your child observations in your document portfolio alongside your records of their next steps and planned activities;

- excerpts from a child's profile book to show how you continually observe, assess and plan and to demonstrate the positive impact your practice has on the child's progress over time. As you are asked to *assess children's development and learning* you can include anonymised copies of any IEPs you have contributed to, as well as any completed two-year checks;

- a completed EYFS Profile: be aware that this will evidence how you have observed and assessed a child, but may not highlight next steps;

- observations for children of a range of abilities, interests and ages, as this will help you to evidence other Standards, such as 4.2, where you need to *plan balanced and flexible activities and educational programmes that take into account the stage of development, circumstances and interests of children*. It will also help you to evidence your practice with each age range – babies, toddlers and pre-school children;

- if you have led any training on observation and assessment, then you can include records of this in your document portfolio.

Observations

When you arrange to be observed leading an activity with a group of children, share your planning notes with your mentor or tutor. These can outline how your previous observation and assessment of a child led you to plan this activity and provide examples of differentiation for several children within the group. Even if they choose not to take part in your activity on the day, the evidence is still valid.

You can show your mentor or tutor a profile book and planning records you have contributed to and describe how you used your observations to inform your planning and the next steps for a child.

You can also explain the ways in which your observations help you evaluate your provision as well as individual children's progress. You can also highlight any areas in the room where you introduced changes and explain how your observations of children's engagement in that area led you to make these changes.

SUGGESTED READING

Brodie, K (2013) *Observation, Assessment and Planning in the Early Years – Bringing it all Together.* Berkshire: Open University Press, McGraw Hill International.

Kamen, T (2013) *Observation and Assessment for the EYFS.* London: Hodder Education.

Palaiologou, I (2013) *Child Observation for the Early Years.* London: SAGE.

Pre-school Learning Alliance (2014) *Observation, Assessment and Planning in the Early Years.* London: Pre-school Learning Alliance Publications.

Standard 4.2: Plan balanced and flexible activities and educational programmes that take into account the stage of development, circumstances and interests of children

Standard 4.2 looks at how you plan activities and educational programmes that take into account children's individual needs. You must demonstrate that you plan both individual activities and educational programmes and that your planning is differentiated to take account of each child's stage of development, circumstances and interests.

Check that you understand the meaning of each phrase in this context and that your evidence addresses each area. We will now look at each phrase in more detail.

'Plan activities'

You are asked to plan both activities and educational programmes that take into account the individual needs of children. You can thus evidence your weekly, daily and individual activity plans, plans for the outdoor area and for outings and the decisions you make about how to promote communication and key person relationships during daily routines, such as snack and changing times.

You must provide planning documents that demonstrate how you differentiate activities, routines and other planned events for children of different ages and stages of development and with varied interests and circumstances. You can also evidence your planning through your observations and your contributions to individual child profile books, IEPs and differentiated weekly planning sheets for the baby, toddler and pre-school rooms.

If you are a manager or want to demonstrate your leadership role, you can use your journal or a written assignment to reflect on your involvement in the planning cycle and how you lead and support colleagues in their planning.

'Educational programmes'

Educational programmes is a phrase that is used in schools more than it is in the early years, so it is one that you may not be familiar with. In schools it is used to refer to the National Curriculum programmes of study and any additional programmes, such as Forest Schools or fire safety.

In the early years, this term tends to refer to the educational aims and the programmes offered, such as EYFS, and any additional programmes your setting follows, such as Letters and Sounds.

When you use this term to describe your provision as a whole, it can help you move away from seeing each day as a series of separate activities and routines, and consider how it is experienced by the children, as a whole. For example, a policy to promote key times has an impact on key relationships and communication throughout the day, at rest times, snack times and changing times.

You must identify what this phrase means in the context of your own setting and how it relates to your practice. You will have identified your role in planning individual activities in Standards 5 and 6; you must now identify all the ways in which you contribute to the educational programme as a whole.

One way to contribute to the educational programme is to ensure that your setting meets EYFS requirements regarding learning and development and contribute to an educational programme for a specific child, for example, through an IEP.

You can also evidence how you introduce an educational programme across your setting, perhaps by introducing regular outings, extending maths and literacy activities in the garden, or introducing Forest School or baby yoga sessions.

'Take into account the stage of development ... of children'

To *take into account the stage of development ... of children* you must evidence how you differentiated or adapted your planning to meet the needs of a specific child. If you include a weekly planning sheet in your document portfolio, you must consider, 'does this demonstrate how I differentiated or adapted this activity for a particular child and why I did this?'

The reference to a child's *stage of development* means that you need to make explicit links between what you have planned and the needs of a child at that stage of development. This may overlap with your evidence for 2.2, where you demonstrate your understanding of the developmental needs of babies, toddlers and young children through your actions, explaining why you plan for them in this way.

'Take into account ... the circumstances of children'

In Standard 4 you are required to take into account children's *circumstances* when you plan for them. This gives you an opportunity to demonstrate your understanding of how a child's development can be influenced by external factors.

You can evidence this in many ways. You may explain in your planning notes that you have set up a baby clinic role-play area and invited a mother to bring in her new baby because two children in your group were struggling to prepare for the birth of a new sibling.

You may have a child who has been bereaved or whose parents have recently separated and can evidence how you shared stories about loss and separation with them and made sure that they had regular key times with you throughout the day.

If you know a child lives in overcrowded accommodation with no access to the outdoors, you might evidence how you planned a series of outdoor activities and outings for them.

'Take into account ... the interests of children'

To *take into account ... the interests of children* when you plan for them, you must evidence how you use your daily observations and conversations with parents to find out about each child's interests and then demonstrate how you plan around these interests. For example, if a child is settling in, you can evidence how you ask the child's parents about his interests and then demonstrate how you plan activities based on these interests.

You could include in your evidence a brief observation of a child enjoying an activity of his choosing and a planning document that demonstrates how you used the observation to plan an activity for him. You can evidence your observations of a child's schemas and then how you provide resources to help him explore the schema further. You could also evidence how you involve children in planning and choosing activities.

Balanced and flexible activities

As you must evidence how you plan *balanced and flexible activities*, start by forming an overview of your provision as a whole and consider how the children themselves experience the routines and activities you provide throughout the course of a day.

Ensure that the children experience a balance of activities, indoors and outdoors, lively activities and quiet times, time to explore an activity at their own pace, group times and one-to-one key times and then check that the routines are appropriate for each age group.

There are questions that you can ask yourself to help you reflect on this.

- Is the selection of activities provided each day broad and balanced?

- Are our routines flexible enough to accommodate the needs of individual children?

- Do our routines allow for children to make choices, for example, to choose to have their snack when they are hungry?

- Do children always have access to literacy and maths activities, both indoors and outdoors?

- Is there a balance between indoors and outdoors activities?

- Can children choose when to spend time outside?

- Is there a balance between providing activities at set times and supporting individual routines, particularly in the baby room?

- Do the babies have adequate time outdoors? And regular times with their key person?

- Is there a balance between group times, such as snack time and circle time, and times when children can become absorbed in an activity of their choice?

- Do we make adjustments for individual children, for example, for a child who needs a rigid routine and to be prepared for changes, and a child who is tired or unwell and needs a quiet space?

Planning flexible activities

As well as ensuring your overall educational programme is balanced, you must ensure that the individual activities are flexible. For an activity to be flexible, it means that if you have planned one activity and children want to adapt the activity or are interested in something else, you adapt your plan.

An example of a flexible approach would be that if one morning it starts to snow, you would change your plans for the day and enjoy and explore the snow with the children. It also means that the resources you have chosen are rich enough that each child can use them in their own way. Think about how you can evidence this, perhaps through your evaluations of an activity or a mentor or peer observation.

You could evidence how you promote a flexible approach throughout your setting. You could lead a discussion in a staff meeting on the importance of a flexible approach to planning. One Early Years Teacher led a discussion on why we need to avoid becoming overly focused on goals and outcomes as this can encourage passive learning because children will focus on responding to our demands.

Planning flexible activities also refers to how you organise the day. If you provide free flow between inside and outside and activities that address each area of learning both outside and inside, then this is a flexible approach.

If you institute rolling snack, to provide children access to snacks at a time of their choosing and with an adult there to engage with them, then you are planning flexible activities.

If you are working in the baby room, provide a flexible approach that is based on each child's individual routine to provide continuity from home. If you do not have recent experience of working in a baby room this is an area where you may lack evidence. Chapter 5 on age range requirements will help you decide whether you need a baby room placement.

Evidence for 4.2

Your evidence for 4.2 can take many forms, but check that each piece of evidence clearly addresses at least one of the key phrases in 4.2. For example, a planning document that lacks information on why you planned this activity, in this way, for this particular child, will not provide evidence of planning *that take[s] into account the stage of development, circumstances and interests* of a child.

You are asked to plan both activities and educational programmes and show how you have taken into account the needs of individual children. Your evidence must demonstrate how you differentiated all aspects of your provision, activities and routines, for children at a variety of stages of development and with varied interests and circumstances.

You can evidence this when you provide examples of planning documents that demonstrate how you plan and differentiate activities for individual babies, toddlers and pre-school children. This could include weekly and daily planning sheets for babies, toddlers and pre-school children and your observations and next steps for a particular child. You could include these in your document portfolio or share them with your tutor or mentor.

If you are a manager or would like to evidence your leadership role you can reflect on how you lead and support colleagues in planning and develop your setting's planning processes. This will also help you evidence 4.4, where you are required to *reflect on the effectiveness of activities and educational programmes to support the continuous improvement of provision.* You will find that there is some overlap with your evidence for Standards 5 and 6. However, you must make sure that you understand the differences between these Standards and that your evidence reflects this.

Written assignments, case studies and journal entries

You can reflect on your role in developing planning systems, educational programmes and flexible routines, leading and supporting colleagues and planning for individual children in a written assignment, case study or journal entry as these will give you the scope you need to evidence your role in detail.

You could outline your setting's planning process and describe in detail how this takes account of children's individual needs. You could give examples of planning for babies, toddlers and pre-school children to demonstrate how you take account of the age and stage of development of a child. You could also evidence how you ensure that activities and routines are balanced and flexible, especially for babies.

CASE STUDY

Amy's journal

Journal entry May 7th

In my observations last week I noted that four of the pre-school boys, D, M, K and P, were frequently looking out of the window and asking if they could go outside. They were often noisy and could not settle to take part in our creative activities.

I decided to keep a tally of how much time the pre-school children spent outside and how much time these four boys spent engaged in activities inside versus outside.

Today I presented my findings in the staff meeting and we discussed how these four boys in particular seemed more able to focus on a structured activity if it was outside. We agreed we needed to do more research on the benefits of introducing free flow and extending access to the outdoors. In the meantime, I took on responsibility for planning a creative activity outside every day, starting with ones based on their interests in cars and transport.

Your document portfolio

You could include:

- a range of planning sheets;
- focus child activities;
- IEPs;
- entries in a profile book.

Make sure that these evidence how you plan for children of different ages, interests, circumstances and abilities. Ensure you don't include too many of these and that the documents you choose clearly show how you planned to meet the needs and interests of individual children.

You can also include any documents that record how you supported colleagues with their planning, such as a witness testimony or handouts from a staff training event. These will need to highlight why you addressed this aspect of planning and how you supported your colleagues.

Observations

You can arrange to be observed leading an activity of your choice, and you can provide a copy of your differentiated planning document for this activity. Make sure that it is clear why you planned and differentiated this activity for these children and during the activity you will need to demonstrate how this activity is flexible and relates to children's interests.

You can also explain to your mentor or tutor how you have adapted practices and the organisation of the room to ensure that routines and activities are balanced and flexible.

SUGGESTED READING

Barber, J and Paul-Smith, S (2012) *Early Years Observation and Planning in Practice: Your Guide to Best Practice and Use of Different Methods for Planning and Observation in the EYFS*. London: Practical Pre-school Books MA Education Ltd.

Brodie, K (2013) *Observation, Assessment and Planning in the Early Years – Bringing it all Together*. London: Open University Press, McGraw Hill Educational.

Standard 4.3: Promote a love of learning and stimulate children's intellectual curiosity in partnership with parents and/or carers

Standard 4.3 asks you to evidence how you *promote a love of learning and stimulate children's intellectual curiosity* in partnership with their parents. *Love of learning* and *intellectual curiosity* within your setting are interesting concepts and you will need to think about what these mean in practice. You may feel confident that as a practitioner you do promote children's love of learning and intellectual curiosity, but can you identify how your actions promote these? And how you promote these concepts with parents?

It may be helpful to look at each of the key phrases. *Promote* means that you must evidence the specific actions that you take. One Early Years Teacher involved parents in developing a science area and Forest School experiences demonstrated how to *promote* intellectual curiosity. His colleague, Maria, created a role-play area with costumes, props and early literacy activities based on children's favourite story book to *promote* their love of learning and shared this with their parents.

You must promote both *love of learning* and *intellectual curiosity*, so you will need to define each term and understand how they differ. Think about what each term means within the context of early years, the difference between *love of learning* and *intellectual curiosity* and what it is that you say or do that promotes and encourages parents to promote them.

Think about how you know whether your actions did have a positive impact on a child's *love of learning* and *intellectual curiosity*. Identify ways to measure and evaluate the impact of your actions on a particular child and reflect on how stimulating the setting is for the children in your group. Is the environment appropriately stimulating for the children in that room at that time and do you encourage parents to extend activities at home?

Think about how this relates to EYFS and particularly your role in promoting an enabling environment. You can also consider how this relates to the impact of the organisation and routines in your setting. Do you provide adequate opportunities for children to spend extended periods of time on one activity or project and revisit it the following day?

Other considerations you can explore are learning styles and schemas. Do you consider children's individual learning styles and schemas in your planning and discover these with parents? If this doesn't happen, how might it affect a child's motivation and love of learning?

Promoting 'love of learning' and 'intellectual curiosity'

Once you have identified what is meant by *love of learning* and *intellectual curiosity*, you can look at how the environment, resources, activities and interactions with practitioners can promote these. For example, an environment rich in print, with communication-friendly spaces and science activities is likely to promote a child's love of learning.

Activities planned and resources carefully chosen to support children at their particular stage of development and based on their interests, when combined with careful use of open questioning and engagement in sustained shared thinking, is likely to support their intellectual curiosity. In discussion with parents you can choose resources according to the children's interests, developmental needs and schemas and evidence the positive impact of planning according to these interests. You can also identify the positive attitudes and behaviours you can foster and share this with parents.

Identifying your impact on a child's 'love of learning' and 'intellectual curiosity'

To evidence that you promote *love of learning* and *intellectual curiosity*, you must think about how you can evidence the impact of your actions. You could evaluate children's levels of engagement when you plan for or support them in a task or activity, particularly if it is one of their own choosing, and the strategies for promoting engagement you share with parents.

Look back on peer observations of your practice and the observations you have made of a particular child to identify how you engaged with this child to promote her engagement, love of learning and intellectual curiosity. Then evaluate your impact on that child's levels of engagement and enthusiasm for learning and identify how you shared these strategies with parents.

Ask a colleague to observe you in your interactions with a particular child during an activity and in your discussion with their parent about this activity. Peer observations of engaging in sustained shared thinking with a child may also evidence how you promoted that child's intellectual curiosity.

Look back to your evidence for 2.4, where you evidenced how you engage in sustained shared thinking with a child. Identify what it was that you did and said that promoted the child's engagement and further exploration and think about how to share this with parents.

When you provided rich resources and asked open questions, such as 'what if … .?' were you promoting that child's natural intellectual curiosity? If you set up a garden area that involved planting and areas where children could search for mini-beasts, were you promoting *a love of learning*? Try to pinpoint what you did and said and the resources you provided and why. Then look back at your observations. How did the child respond to the resources you provided and the ways in which you helped to explore them? Can you share successful strategies with parents?

CASE STUDY

'in partnership with parents and/or carers'

Maria, an Early Years Teacher trainee, created a role-play area based on Daphne's favourite story book to promote her love of learning. She explained to Daphne's parents that she and Daphne had worked together to create simple costumes and props to use in the role-play area. She explained how these captured Daphne's interests and could be used to help her develop the skills and goals outlined in her IEP. She then spent time with Daphne's parents talking about how they could create similar activities at home to support their daughter's interests and development.

Evidence for 4.3
Written assignments, case studies and your reflective journal

You can use a written assignment, a case study or entry in your journal to record in detail the conversations you have had with children of different ages and analyse what it was you did and said to promote their love of learning and intellectual curiosity. Try to provide examples that relate to children of different ages.

CASE STUDY

Beverly's journal

Journal: April 29th

I am in my second week of my placement in a nursery class in my local primary school. Today I read through my observations from the first week and noticed that the children are particularly interested in the natural world, the mini-beasts in the garden and the fish and African snails in the communal area.

I also noticed that Clara, the nursery teacher, is really brilliant at involving the children in unusual creative activities, and particularly good at involving children with English as a second language. Today she let me help her introduce an ink drawing activity using old-fashioned quills. She had invited some parents to join in and they and the children were fascinated.

This gave me an idea, based on an article I had read in Nursery World. I suggested to Clara that I could ask the local farm if we could come in to observe the eggs they keep in an incubator and then come back each week to observe the chicks once they are born to see how they grow.

She said the farm was run by one of the parents, so why didn't I ask them if we could have an incubator in our hall, as they had organised this for another school. I'm really excited and have started thinking about involving the children in feeding the new chicks and observing them and drawing them as they develop.

Your document portfolio

Your observations of individual children can evidence how you promote both *love of learning* and *intellectual curiosity* if they record what it is that you did and said and you analyse how you engaged with the children to promote their interest and curiosity. You can also use your observations and planning records to evidence how you identify what a child is interested in and then plan an activity or provide resources to engage that child further.

You can observe an area of provision and evaluate how stimulating and engaging the children find the area and reflect on the quality of the interactions they have with adults. You can relate this to EYFS enabling environments and consider how you could develop the area further.

You may have records of conversations where you engaged in sustained shared thinking with a child to promote intellectual curiosity.

You could record any discussions you have with colleagues about how to enrich the environment and engage and stimulate the children.

You may have records of resources you ordered to support children's explorations, such as a wormery, and you can include these records in your portfolio alongside evidence of how you then used the resources.

However, you also need evidence of working in partnership with parents to promote these attributes. You can include relevent records of meetings with parents, entries in home link books and records of involving parents in projects such as making story sacks or developing a planting area.

Observations

When you arrange for your tutor or mentor to observe you engaging in an activity, explain how this will promote the intellectual curiosity of the children you will be working with. Think about the resources you use and how you can engage with each child to build on natural curiosity and love of learning.

257

If you have set up areas to foster children's interests, such as a science table, planting area or mini-beasts' garden, explain your rationale and describe how you will share this with parents.

Leadership

To evidence your leadership for 4.3 you can facilitate a discussion with your team or lead a review of resources and the environment.

You could lead a discussion on the attitudes, qualities and skills that adults need to foster, for example, through exploration, listening to children and promoting active learning and how to share this with parents.

SUGGESTED READING

Bayley, R, Featherstone, S and Ingham, K (2013) *Child-initiated Learning: Hundreds of Ideas for Independent Learning in the Early Years.* London: Bloomsbury Publishing.

Edwards, C, Gandini, L and Forman, G (eds) (2011) *The Hundred Languages of Children: The Reggio Emilia Experience in Transformation.* California: ABC-CLIO, LLC.

Effective Pre-School, Primary & Secondary Education (EPPSE) Available online at: **www.ioe.ac.uk/research/153.html** (accessed 22/10/2014).

Moylett, H (2013) *Active Learning: A Practical Guide To How Babies And Young Children Learn.* London: Practical Pre-school Books.

Moylett, H (2014) *Characteristics of Effective Early Learning: Helping Young Children Become Learners for Life.* Oxon: McGraw Hill Open University Press.

Scade, N (2014) *Outstanding Early Years Provision in Practice: How to Transform your Setting into an Exceptional Learning Environment.* London: Practical Pre-school Books.

Thornton, L and Brunton, P (2010) *Bringing the Reggio Approach to your Early Years Practice.* Oxon: Routledge.

Standard 4.4: Use a variety of teaching approaches to lead group activities appropriate to the age range and ability of children

In 4.1 you were asked to evidence how you *plan balanced and flexible activities and educational programmes that take into account the stage of development, circumstances and interests of children*. In 4.4, you are again asked to plan activities that take account of children's developmental needs, but now you also need to evidence your role leading the activities whilst using a variety of teaching approaches.

We will look at each key phrase in detail, but first you must evidence all the actions you engage in when you lead an activity. These include planning, identifying learning outcomes and key vocabulary, identifying the role the adult needs to take, choosing resources, identifying any health and safety issues, differentiation and strategies for managing behaviour, promoting social skill and engaging in sustained shared thinking. Then you need to identify the range of *teaching approaches* you are using and we will look at this in detail below.

'Group activities'

Group activities can include planned or focus group activities, such as messy play, mark making or cookery. It can also include any group times that you lead, such as circle time. To meet the criteria for 4.4 you will need to show this is an activity you planned for a group of children and that you led the activity and made sure that it was appropriate for the ages and abilities of the children.

You must think about what makes an activity appropriate for each age group; for example, what an appropriate group activity for babies would look like. Think about the benefits of learning through group activities as this can inform your actions during the activity.

'Lead group activities'

To evidence that you *lead group activities* you need to demonstrate why you chose the activity, why it was appropriate for the age range and abilities of the children involved and how you led it. You must describe the resources you chose and why, your actions during the activity and how you communicated with each child to support their development.

You can also evidence how you set up and introduced the activity, how it extends a previous activity or relates to children's interests, how you model turn taking and help children to share, how you listen to children and use open questions and engage in sustained shared thinking and how you encourage colleagues to support the children's learning during the activity. You can also record any brief observations you made during the activity and how you use these to plan a child's next steps and include these in your evidence.

Remember that leading an activity in this context does not provide evidence of your leadership role, but of your personal practice. However, if you are modelling the activity for a colleague or student, then this is evidence of leadership.

Leadership and group activities

If you are modelling an activity, then you can evidence how you communicated with your colleague before and during the activity and how you gave your co-worker feedback and support afterwards. This will provide evidence for 4.4 and also for 8.4.

'Appropriate to the age range and ability of the children'

In 4.4 you are asked to evidence how you plan group activities that are *appropriate to the age range and ability of children*. You must evidence how you have planned and led group activities for children of different ages, including babies, toddlers and young children, and how you adapt group activities for children with SEN. You can do this when you evidence how the activity relates to EYFS and individual children's next steps.

You can demonstrate how your activities are appropriate for children of different ages by including examples of planning for babies, toddlers and pre-school children. If, for example, you include plans for circle time for toddlers and pre-school children, then comparing these plans will demonstrate how you adapted circle time for each age group. If you work in a mixed age range, you can demonstrate how your plans are differentiated for the older and younger children in the group.

You could also ask a colleague to observe you leading an activity with two age groups, for example, mark-making activities with babies and pre-school children. These observations, when placed together, should demonstrate how you adapt activities for different ages.

As you are required to demonstrate how you *lead group activities appropriate to the age range … of children*, you do need to demonstrate how you plan for each age group. If you are in a management role or only work with one age group, you may need to think about whether you have enough evidence for 4.4. You may need to think about spending regular periods of time with each age group so that you can build up evidence of leading group activities for different ages and abilities. There is information on deciding whether you need an additional placement in Chapter 5 on age range requirements.

To evidence that activities are *appropriate*, demonstrate how each activity is developmentally appropriate and adapted for children's abilities and relates to their next steps. You also need to show that your activities are flexible enough to respond to unexpected, spontaneous moments of learning, for example, when a child uses the resources you provided in an unexpected way.

Use a variety of teaching approaches

In 4.4 you are asked to evidence how you use a range of teaching approaches to lead group activities. The use of the term *teaching approaches* can be off-putting, but in the context of early years it just refers to the ways in which you routinely support children's learning and development. Make sure that you evidence the full range of approaches or methods that you use.

These approaches can include the strategies you use to:

- encourage active learning and children's independent choices;
- provide access to all areas of learning outdoors as well as indoors;
- ensure that activities are differentiated and accessible for all children;
- create a rich and stimulating environment;
- plan a range of whole-group and small-group activities;
- provide resources that children can explore in their own way;
- use open questions to promote a child's thinking skills;

- provide communication-friendly spaces;
- extend children's thinking skills through engaging in sustained shared thinking;
- use circle time to support children's social skills;
- provide resources to support children's schemas and interests;
- use routine times, such as snack time and nappy-changing times, to focus on developing attachment relationships and communication skills.

Evidence for 4.4

The evidence you have for 4.2, on planning balanced and flexible activities, should help you find some of your evidence for 4.4. However, your evidence for 4.4 also needs to highlight your role in leading an activity as well as your planning. It also needs to highlight how you led differentiated activities for group of children of different ages and abilities.

Written assignments, case studies and your journal

Written assignments, case studies and your reflective journal provide you with an opportunity to describe how you led a group activity in detail. You can present your rationale, explain why the activity is appropriate for the developmental needs and abilities of the children, outline the resources you chose and why and highlight any health and safety considerations you identified. When you describe how you led a group activity, you can outline your actions at each stage, the teaching approach this demonstrates, how you supported each child and your interactions with individual children and colleagues.

CASE STUDY

Building a den to promote pre-school children's social skills

Amy, an Early Years Teacher trainee, used a written assignment to describe why and how she led a group activity to build a den to promote pre-school children's social skills, such as sharing and turn taking. She described how she modelled turn taking and saying 'please' and 'thank you'. When one child pushed another, she used it as an opportunity to talk about the Golden Rules they had chosen earlier that week, and asked them why one of the rules they had chosen was 'no pushing'.

Your document portfolio

You can include your differentiated plans for group activities in your document portfolio if you specify why you planned this activity and how it relates to the age range and abilities of the children involved. This evidence will be stronger if you can also evidence your understanding of the benefits of learning through group activities at different ages and how you choose activities that are developmentally appropriate for each age group.

However, your plans only provide part of your evidence for 4.4 as you have to demonstrate how you have led these activities and the teaching approaches that you used. You can ask a colleague or your mentor or tutor to observe you during an activity and you can include this in your document portfolio alongside your plans.

To evidence how the activity is 'appropriate' you can link your plans to your observations of the children and next steps you identified for them. You can combine this evidence with your evaluations of each activity, where you reflect on your role in the activity, what worked well, what you would do differently next time and what you learnt from the activity about each child.

Observations

You can arrange for your tutor or mentor to observe you using a range of teaching approaches when leading group activities with children of different ages (an activity with songs and instruments with babies and a messy-play activity with toddlers).

In your plans and while you are being observed, make sure that you demonstrate how you relate the activity to EYFS areas of development and each child's next steps, abilities and areas for development. You can also emphasise how you took account of diversity and equality issues and health and safety, chose your resources with care and interacted with the children to promote their learning and development. If you want to evidence your leadership, too, then you can arrange for a colleague to shadow you during the activity and you can model listening skills and open questions.

SUGGESTED READING

Bilton, H (2014) *Playing Outside: Activities, Ideas and Inspiration for the Early Years*. Oxon: Routledge.

Coulson, G and Cousins, L (2013) *Games, Ideas and Activities for Early Years Phonics* (Classroom Gems). London: Pearsons.

Peet, L (2013) *100 Ideas for Early Years Practitioners: Outstanding Practice* (100 Ideas for Teachers). London: Bloomsbury.

Sutherland, H (2014) *Gifted and Talented in the Early Years: Practical Activities for Children aged 3 to 6*. London: SAGE.

Standard 4.5: Reflect on the effectiveness of activities and educational programmes to support the continuous improvement of provision

Standard 4.5 provides you with an opportunity to reflect on provision throughout your setting and take an active role in supporting improvements. You are asked to review teaching activities and educational programmes (see 4.1 for a discussion of the meaning of *educational programmes*) and support your colleagues in the cycle of continuous improvement.

You must demonstrate that you know what effective practice looks like, that you reflect on the effectiveness of your provision, identify areas that need improvement and take steps to develop these areas. You must show that you have a commitment to a cycle of constant observation, review and improvement.

Research Kolb's learning cycle as an example of how you can assess your setting's constant cycle of reflection and continuous improvement (Kolb, 1984). This is a really useful method for you to use.

Reflection

In Standard 4.5 you are asked to *reflect on the effectiveness of teaching activities and educational programmes*. Most practitioners evaluate individual activities, but 4.5 asks you to take this one step further and reflect on your educational programmes as well. This means that you need to evaluate your provision as a whole – everything in it that a child experiences in a day, from how you greet children when they arrive, right through to the programmes you introduce, your routines, your activities, how you organise the room and how you manage key times.

This means that, as well as reflecting on individual activities, you will need to set aside time to reflect on how effective each area of your provision is. You could observe individual areas of provision, such as circle time or literacy activities in the garden. If you can observe how frequently children access this area, how they use the resources and the levels of their engagement, then you will have started to evaluate *effectiveness*.

Your reflective journal provides you with a place where you can record your observations, analyse them and gather your thoughts and you can use these entries as evidence. If you need any guidance on using a journal, see Chapter 4 (Assessment methods).

Leading reflective practice

To evidence leadership for 4.5 you can encourage your team to reflect on areas of provision and have conversations about what they feels works well and why, and which areas they feel need attention. You can record your conversations with your team in your journal or staff meeting minutes. You may also want to think about planning a system for regular observations and reviews of areas in your setting so as to involve all your team in the cycle of continuous improvement.

'Teaching activities and educational programmes'

The reference to *teaching activities and educational programmes* means that you need to reflect on the effectiveness of both individual activities and your provision as a whole. *Educational programmes* refers to the programmes you institute and follow to support children's learning and development, such as EYFS (2014) and any additional programmes you offer, such as Forest School or Every Child a Talker (ECAT).

Educational programmes also refers to your provision as a whole, which includes everything that a child experiences. This includes activities and areas of learning, but also routines, outings, access to the garden, snack and meal times, rest times and circle times, and times of transition between activities. This is because children learn from everything they experience, not just those activities we designate as 'educational', and also because Standard 4 asks you to look at both education and care.

Identifying the effectiveness of your provision

Standard 4 asks you to *reflect on the effectiveness of teaching activities and educational programmes*. Your first step could be to review your environment against EYFS (2014) requirements. You could observe the areas of learning, indoors and outdoors, and consider how effectively teaching activities and the environment promote the EYFS key principles, such as an enabling environment.

If your setting is involved in a quality improvement scheme and you can show how this involves you in reflecting on the effectiveness of your provision, then this will provide evidence for 4.5. If you were involved in the decision to implement a programme such as ECAT, then your rationale for introducing this may show that you had identified a need for development.

If you are involved in preparing the Self-Assessment Report (SAR) for Ofsted you will also have some evidence of identifying areas where provision is effective and areas with scope for improvement. You must highlight which contributions to the SAR you made.

You can also review your provision by asking the children themselves for their views on particular activities. One Early Years Teacher tried various methods to find out children's opinions. One strategy she tried was to ask the children during circle time to run over to the activity they had most enjoyed. She would then ask them which activities they would like to see out the following day.

Parents will also have opinions on the effectiveness of your provision and you can refer to their views when you evaluate your provision. You can ask for their opinions during an open day or through a suggestions box or parent questionnaire.

'Support the continuous improvement of provision'

In your observations you may have identified an area for improvement, for example, extending access to the garden for babies or introducing rolling snacks. You must find a way to record how you identified the need for this and what it is that you did to promote this development through your individual actions and your leadership role.

If you are involved in implementing schemes such as ECAT, ITERS and ECERS (see below), then this will provide evidence of how you support the continuous improvement of teaching activities and the environment. You must highlight what your actions were and the reasons for them and this can contribute to your evidence for 1.1.

You may also have evidence of supporting staff development in relation to a specific area of provision and this can help you evidence 4.5. You may have led a staff training event or supported a colleague one to one on implementing new planning structures or led the development of maths activities in the garden. This will provide evidence of how you *support the continuous improvement of provision* and it may also provide evidence of leading staff development for 8.4 and reflecting on and improving provision for 8.6.

CASE STUDY

ITERS and ECERS

*Julia, an Early Years Teacher trainee and deputy manager in a small community nursery, had identified several areas for development in the toddler and pre-school rooms while building up her evidence for 4.5. She attended training on the Infant/Toddler Environment Rating Scales (ITERS) and the Early Childhood Environment Rating Scales (ECERS) (*www. ecersuk.org*: ECERS-R and ITERS-R were developed by Thelma Harms, Richard Clifford and Debby Cryer at the University of North Carolina) as she felt that these might be the tools that her setting needed to help them develop.*

She explained to her manager and the staff team that the Early Childhood Environment Rating Scale – Revised (ECERS-R) and the Infant Toddler Environment Rating Scale – Revised (ITERS-R) are designed to help practitioners measure and evaluate the quality of their provision.

She explained that they include a range of statements, or 'indicators', to help them evaluate the quality of each area of provision and signpost areas for improvement and measure the impact of the improvements.

Julia explained that there are seven broad dimensions of quality and, even if they decided not to follow ITERS and ECERS, these seven dimensions could help them decide how to organise their evaluation of the setting.

Each member of the team decided to take on responsibility for observing one of the seven areas:

1. *space and furnishings;*

2. *personal care routines;*

3. *language and reasoning;*

4. *activities;*

(Continued)

(Continued)

5. *interaction;*

6. *programme structure;*

7. *provision for parents and staff.*

When the team shared their findings a month later, they decided to continue this process of review and observe the four additional areas introduced later by the Effective Provision of Pre-school Education (EPPE) Project (An extension to the ECERS-R (the ECERS-E) was designed by Professor Kathy Sylva, Professor Iram Siraj-Blatchford and Brenda Taggart as part of the EPPE Project):

1. *literacy;*

2. *mathematics;*

3. *science and environment;*

4. *diversity (including planning for children's individual needs, celebrating diversity, respecting other cultures and gender diversity).*

Julia found more helpful information on the website at **www.ecersuk.org** *and she used her reflective journal to record this whole process and analyse her own observations. She felt that ITERS and ECERS helped her evaluate and support improvements for 4.3 and helped her evidence 8.5, where she needed to* reflect on and evaluate the effectiveness of provision, and shape and support good practice.

Evidence for 4.5

You will need to observe individual teaching activities and your provision as a whole and use your reflective skills to analyse their effectiveness. You can use your journal or a written assignment to evidence this.

You then need to use these reflections, alongside evidence of your discussions with colleagues, parents and children, to help you decide where there are areas for development.

Finally, use these conclusions to help you plan and carry out the steps you need to take to improve provision and support colleagues in the continuous improvement of your provision. You can cross-reference this evidence to 8.6, which asks you to review and improve practice.

Written assignments, case studies and your reflective journal

You can use your journal entries, a case study or a written assignment to evidence in detail how you reflect on teaching activities and the educational programmes and take an active part in developing effective practice. For example, you may choose to write about a project to develop planting and science activities in the garden after you observed that children in the pre-school room were interested in mini-beasts and that the activities in the garden tended to focus on physical skills.

To evidence how you support a cycle of continuous improvement, you need to record:

- how you observed and reviewed teaching activities and areas of provision;
- identified an area or teaching approaches in need of development;
- the actions you took to improve this and how you supported your team;
- your evaluations of the changes you implemented;
- any further areas you identified as still needing improvement;
- how you planned to address these.

Your document portfolio

In your document portfolio you can include your observations and reflections on current practice, your suggestions for improvements and your involvement in the process of continuous improvement. You can also include reflections in your journal on the changes you promoted or minutes of a staff meeting where you led a discussion on areas for development.

CASE STUDY

Julia and the sand tray

Julia, a deputy manager and Early Years Teacher trainee, included a copy of an observation and staff meeting minutes in her document portfolio. She had completed a series of observations of the garden area and shared one of these with her colleagues in a staff meeting. In the observation she had identified that children were rarely using the outdoor sand tray.

She encouraged colleagues to take turns to observe the indoor and outdoor sand trays to compare the ways the children used them and see if they could identify the reasons for the lack of interest in the sand tray in the garden. She had wondered whether it might be because of where the tray was positioned or whether it was because the resources were not stimulating enough or that there was not enough adult input.

Julia added to her evidence of her role in this process by presenting her journal entries and minutes of the following staff meeting, where the team discussed their findings in her document portfolio.

Observations

You can arrange for your mentor or tutor to observe you leading an activity that relates to an improvement you introduced and you can briefly explain your role in promoting continuous improvement in your planning notes. For example, you may have introduced mark-making activities outside so you can plan to be observed leading a mark-making activity in the garden role-play area.

You could also point out any areas where you have suggested and led improvements, for example, by introducing rolling snacks or communication-friendly spaces and supported staff to develop their skills in these areas.

SUGGESTED READING

Canning, M and Canning, N (2013) *Implementing Quality Improvement & Change in the Early Years.* London: SAGE.

Harms, T, Clifford, R and Cryer, D (n.d.) *Early Childhood Environment Rating Scale – Revised (ECERS-R) and the Infant Toddler Environment Rating Scale – Revised (ITERS-R).* Available online at: **www.ecersuk.org** (accessed 22/10/2014).

Kolb, DA (1984) *Experiential Learning: Experience as the Source of Learning and Development.* New Jersey: Pearsons.

Siraj-Blatchford , I, Sylva, K, Taggart, B, Melhuish, E, Sammons, P and Elliot, K (2003) *The Effective Provision or Pre-school education (EPPE) Project (1997–2003).* London: Institute of Education. Available online at **www.ioe.ac.uk/research/153.html** (accessed 22/10/2014).

Standard 5: **Adapt education and care to respond to the strengths and needs of all children**

Introduction

In Standard 5 you will evidence your understanding of children's developmental needs and how you adapt your provision to support children whose learning and development are affected by a range of factors. You must demonstrate how you adapt both education and care to support the learning and development of children of different abilities and at different stages of development using a range of approaches.

Standard 5: the main topics

Standard 5 asks you to evidence how you adapt both education and care according to the needs and strengths of a child and demonstrate how you do this for all children. You need to evidence how you adapt your provision to build on children's strengths and support their needs, particularly when a child has a special educational need or disability.

The topics to address in your evidence for Standard 5 include:

- your awareness of the factors that can inhibit a child's learning and development and how you can address these: these factors could include loss, separation, changes in family circumstances, a chronic illness or disability or learning a new language;

- your awareness of child development: in particular, the intellectual, social and emotional development of babies and young children and how you adapt education and care to support them at different stages of development;

- your understanding of the communication needs of babies, toddlers and pre-school children and how you adapt education and care to support their communication needs at different stages of their development;

- your understanding of the needs of children with special educational needs and disabilities and how you use a range of strategies to engage and support them;

- your understanding of the ways in which transitions can affect a child and the strategies you use to support children through transitions at home and in your setting;

- that you recognise when a child is in need of additional support and you know how to access this support for them.

Standard 5: working with babies

Standard 5 is one of the Standards that require evidence of your work with babies. In 5.2 you must evidence that you know how to adapt education and care to support children at different stages of development and *demonstrate an awareness of the physical, emotional, social, intellectual development and communication needs of babies and children.*

This means that you need to evidence your work with toddlers, pre-school children and babies. If you are a manager, or you lack experience with both babies and children, you might wish to consider taking on an additional, age-related placement. You can find information on this in Chapter 5 on age range requirements.

Similarities and differences with Standard 4

You may notice similarities between Standards 5 and 4 as both Standards ask you to evidence how you adapt education and care and take account of the needs of all children. Both Standards also require you to evidence how you differentiate activities to meet the developmental needs of individual children. Your evidence for Standard 5, as for Standard 4, needs to demonstrate your understanding of child development and how you have supported children of different ages and with differing needs.

However, in Standard 4 you were asked to evidence how you *Plan balanced and flexible activities and educational programmes that take into account the stage of development, circumstances and interests of children* (4.2) whilst leading activities and maintaining a reflective overview of your provision as a whole. In Standard 5 you will start to identify how you meet the needs of individual children in depth.

Standard 5 is much more concerned with individual children and how you meet their needs. You are asked to evidence how you differentiate provision and evidence your understanding of the factors that can affect a child's development. You must demonstrate how you support all children through their developmental stages and transitions and find additional sources of support when necessary.

Child development: similarities and differences with 2.2

As you evidence your understanding of child development in Standard 5, you may notice similarities with Standard 2.2 and possibly 3.1 and 4.2 as well, and you may be able to cross-reference some of your evidence. However, in Standard 5 you must consider the impact that special educational needs, disabilities and transitions can have on a child and identify strategies to support them. You must include detailed evidence that relates to your work with specific children.

Many of your routine work documents, such as profile books and individual education plans (IEPs), will help you evidence this Standard.

Standard 5.1: Have a secure understanding of how a range of factors can inhibit children's learning and development and how best to address these

In your evidence for 5.1 you will explore everything you know about the factors that can inhibit a child's learning and development and what you can do to address these. These factors can include physical disabilities, family circumstances and emotional and social factors and you must demonstrate that you employ strategies to support a child in relation to a specific factor.

For example, you would understand that if a child lives in a small flat with no access to the outdoors it can have an impact on her physical development and you would evidence how you plan plenty of physical activities in the garden to support her.

If you have a child with hearing loss, you might evidence how you introduce soft fabrics and furnishings into the room to reduce noise levels, position the child near you during circle time and introduce Makaton signs.

Remember that you are asked to:

- identify a range of factors that can affect a child's learning and development;
- demonstrate a *secure understanding* of the impact these factors can have;
- describe the strategies you employ to address each factor.

Make sure that your evidence relates to a range of factors and clearly demonstrates your understanding of how each factor can inhibit learning and the strategies that you have used to help the child overcome these factors.

A 'secure understanding'

You must evidence that you have a *secure understanding* of how a wide range of factors can affect a child's ability to learn and develop. For example, if a child is in a wheelchair, you can demonstrate that you understand not only the impact of his disability, but also that his learning will be inhibited if he cannot independently reach activities on the floor or if the tables are the wrong height for the wheelchair, and that being in a wheelchair can have an impact on the development of that child's motor skills.

You must evidence that your understanding is *secure*, so think carefully about the depth of your understanding. You may need to extend your reading in certain areas, for example, in relation to the impact of bereavement if you have a key child who has recently lost a close family member.

You also need to think about how you can evidence this depth of understanding. Often a written assignment or case study allows you to explore the reasons for your actions in some detail. You can also evidence your understanding through entries in your reflective journal or through records of delivering training on this topic.

'A range of factors'

You must evidence your understanding of *how a range of factors can inhibit children's learning and development*. These factors may be physical, emotional, social or a result of a child's circumstances or disability. Identify a wide range of factors that have had an impact on the children in your care and think about your understanding of the impact these have had and how you can evidence this.

You can identify some of the emotional factors that can affect a child's learning and development, such as adjusting to the birth of a new sibling, parents' separation, bereavement or loss of a pet. You could explore the impact of social factors and family circumstances, such as parental substance misuse or depression, or moving home or country.

You could explore other factors, such as the impact of being a looked-after child, as many studies have shown that being a looked-after child can have a significant impact on learning and development (Maclean and Gunuion, 2003). You could reflect on the impact of belonging to a minority culture or non-traditional family or learning English as a second language.

You must evidence that you understand how these factors affect a child's learning and development before you go on to demonstrate how you support the child to overcome these difficulties.

Addressing the factors that can inhibit a child's learning and development

Once you have identified how a factor can inhibit a child's learning, you need to evidence how you acted to address this. Remember that you need to address the impact of each factor on the child's learning and development in some depth.

Evaluating your strategies

As you are asked to demonstrate *how best to address* the impact of each factor, you must evaluate the effectiveness of your strategies.

One way you can evidence this is to reflect on the impact of a disability, such as a visual impairment, and then identify the steps you have taken to reduce the impact of these factors. This might involve organising a quiet space for a child to rest in when overtired or ordering large-print books and resources from the RNIB (**www.rnib.org. uk/SHOP**). You would need to evidence how you sought advice from the child's specialist to help you reorganise the room and provide accessible resources.

If you are supporting a child in a wheelchair, you would need to make sure he will be able to access all areas of learning. You might have to think about how to adapt group activities such as ball games or parachute activities and order equipment that has been adapted for that child for the garden.

If you had considered the impact of a child moving to a new town, then you might evidence how you supported that child to manage this by setting aside times to share books or activities on changes and journeys, to talk about what had changed and give that child the vocabulary she needed to express her feelings.

One Early Years Teacher, David, was concerned about the impact of planned activities to celebrate Mothers' Day on his two key children. One child had recently lost his mother and the other has two fathers, but David had noticed that some staff avoided talking to her about both her fathers. He introduced a discussion in a staff meeting about the importance of recognising and supporting a child's family life. He spoke about the setting's equality policy, the importance of recognising the full range of attachment relationships a child has, and how to support a child after bereavement.

Cross-referencing your evidence with 5.3, 5.4 and 5.5

You may find that some of your evidence for 5.2 may also help you evidence 5.3, where you are asked to *Demonstrate a clear understanding of the needs of all children, including those with special educational needs and disabilities, and be able to use and evaluate distinctive approaches to engage and support them*.

You may be able to cross-reference some of your evidence to 5.4, where you will demonstrate how you *Support children through a range of transitions* and to 5.5, where you show how you *Know when a child is in need of additional support and how this can be accessed*.

CASE STUDY

The impact of trauma on thinking and learning

One Early Years Teacher, Leila, discovered that her key child, Charlotte, had experienced trauma as a result of witnessing a series of violent incidents at home and that these incidents had had an impact on Charlotte's mother's ability to be there for her daughter.

(Continued)

(Continued)

She decided to read up on the work of the Tavistock Trauma Team and the ways that trauma can interfere with a child's thinking and learning to support Charlotte and to extend her secure understanding of the impact of trauma to help her evidence 5.1 (Garland, 1998).

She began to understand that when a child is worried about what is happening at home or is in a constant state of hypervigilance or alarm as a result of a trauma, her mind will be too occupied to focus on play and learning.

Leila also read that if a child did not have secure attachment relationships before a trauma took place, then she may lack positive internal models of adults as supportive or a sense of the world as a safe place to help her manage this new trauma. She also wondered if the impact of Charlotte's mother's emotional unavailability following these incidents would affect her attachment relationship and have an impact on other areas of development as well as her learning.

Leila realised that this makes the role of the key person all the more important and that the nursery environment, with its routines and predictability, could provide a positive model of the world as a safe place for Charlotte to internalise. She decided that her first strategy would be to support Charlotte's mother in her relationship with Charlotte and focus on their key person relationship, so that Charlotte could experience adults who are predictable, supportive and responsive.

Leila used her journal to help her reflect on what she was learning through her reading. She also recorded the strategies she tried and her evaluations of these. She anonymised these journal entries and included them in her document portfolio as evidence for 5.1 to show how she identified and addressed a factor that inhibited Charlotte's learning and development.

Domestic violence

A month later, Charlotte and her mother moved into a refuge and Leila discovered that the violent incidents Charlotte had witnessed occurred between her parents and that her father had been arrested as a result of this domestic abuse.

Leila decided that she needed to read about domestic violence so that she could better understand the impact on Charlotte of living in a house where her mother was constantly afraid and emotionally unavailable and life was unpredictable and dangerous. She also wanted to think about the impact of Charlotte being uprooted from her home and living in a refuge full of other families, also in a state of trauma.

She found an article that outlined the impact of domestic violence on a child's learning and development (Tiret, 2012) and noted that it suggested that the impact varies according to the age of the child. The article suggested strategies for settings and emphasised the importance of promoting positive attachment relationships.

She discussed Charlotte's situation in a staff meeting and provided copies of excerpts from the article for her colleagues to help them understand and support Charlotte:

> *With regards to young children, domestic violence affects them differently at different developmental stages. As children grow and develop, each age presents new learning tasks. Witnessing or hearing of a parent being harmed by their partner can threaten a child's sense of security and interfere with normal healthy development ...*
>
> *Infants and toddlers are learning how to form secure attachments and are learning through play and exploration. When exposed to domestic violence, infants and toddlers learn that parents may be incapable of consistently responding to their needs, which interferes with the development of a strong infant–parent bond. Children become fearful of exploring their world, which may interfere with play and subsequent learning ...*
>
> *Young children can benefit from supportive caregivers and safe places like child care or a school setting. Caregivers and teachers can provide a nurturing environment where children can rely on predictable routines.*
>
> *(Tiret, 2012)*
>
> *Leila included her journal reflections, this handout and the minutes of the staff meeting in her document portfolio to help her evidence 5.1.*

Evidence for 5.1

You need to make sure that your evidence highlights:

- that you are aware of a range of factors that can inhibit a child's learning and development, such as health concerns, social and emotional factors and changes in circumstances;

- that you understand how these factors can affect a child;

- you have explored various strategies to help overcome these factors.

Try to include examples that relate to different factors, and demonstrate how you have supported children of different ages.

Written assignments, case studies and your journal

You can use a written assignment, a case study or your journal to explore the impact of a particular factor on one child's development and how you have supported that child. As you need to evidence how *a range of factors* can inhibit a child's ability to learn, you must provide a series of examples relating to different factors.

One Early Years Teacher trainee used a case study to describe how she reorganised the outdoor area and had equipment modified so that every activity would be accessible for a pre-school child with a physical disability. She was aware that this child's lack of confidence also had an impact on his ability to engage in activities, so she involved her team in planning a series of small group activities outdoors to develop his confidence and involved him in risk assessing his choice of activities.

Your document portfolio

Here are some suggestions to help you think through which documents to include. Remember to ensure that they clearly evidence your understanding and actions and add some explanatory notes if needed:

- entries from your journal;

- a case study;

- notes from a staff development session you delivered or minutes from a staff meeting where you discussed the needs of a particular child;

- copies of emails between yourself and an external professional where you discussed how best to support a child and entries in a child's profile book to evidence the strategies you used to support that child in his development.

Observations

Remember to choose an activity that enables you to demonstrate how you have adapted activities or provided resources to support a child who was affected by a particular factor.

Use your planning notes to highlight how an activity will support the needs of a particular child. For example, you may be supporting a key child who is distressed while her mother is staying in hospital for several weeks with a younger sibling. You can explain in your planning notes that you are delivering a cooking activity with your key child's grandmother so as to support their attachment relationship while her mother is away. You could use your plans to outline the importance of supporting this child's attachment relationships and the role of attachment in promoting healthy development and cross-reference this to 2.3.

SUGGESTED READING

Baker, L and Cunningham, A (2009) Inter-parental violence: the pre-schooler's perspective and the educator's role. *Early Childhood Education Journal,* 37: 199–207. Available online at: **www.semosafehouse.org/pdfs/Early_Childhood_Exposure_to_DV.pdf** (accessed 22/10/2014).

Barker, L, Jaffe, P, Ashbourne, L and Carter, J (2002) *Children Exposed to Domestic Violence: An Early Childhood Educator's Handbook to Increase Understanding and Improve Community Responses.* Available online at: **www.lfcc.on.ca/ece-us.pdf**.

Garland, C (1998) *Understanding Trauma: A Psychoanalytic Approach.* London: Karnac.

Tiret, HB (2012) *Learn How Domestic Violence Negatively Impacts Young Children Throughout Different Developmental and Age Periods.'* Available online at: **http://msue.anr.msu.edu/news/domestic_violence_impacts_children_differently_at_different_ages** (accessed 22/10/2014).

Standard 5.2: Demonstrate an awareness of the physical, emotional, social, intellectual development and communication needs of babies and children, and know how to adapt education and care to support children at different stages of development

Standard 5.2 asks you to evidence your understanding of children's development and how to adapt the education and care you provide for them at different stages of development.

You must evidence how you *adapt education and care to support children at different stages of development* and do this in relation to children and babies' *physical, emotional, social, intellectual development and communication needs.*

You must provide evidence of your awareness of the physical, emotional, social, intellectual development and communication needs of babies, toddlers and pre-school children and provide examples that relate to each age group.

As you are asked to evidence *an awareness*, you could evidence this through your practice, or through a discussion of your theoretical understanding, either in a written assignment or journal entry or through training notes you provide for colleagues.

Similarities and differences: 2.2, 3.1 and 4.1

There are similarities between 5.1 and 2.2, 3.1 and 4.1, as in all these you are required to demonstrate your understanding of the development of children from birth to five and evidence your understanding through your actions and reflection.

However, in 5.2 you need to evidence your understanding of child development in relation to each of these areas: physical, emotional, social and intellectual development and communication needs.

Another difference between 5.2 and 2.2, 3.1 and 4.1 is that in 5.1 you need to evidence how you adapt both education and care.

'Education and care'

Over the last 30 years the distinction between settings that provide care and those that provide education has gradually reduced, as has the belief that certain actions relate to care and others to education. It is now recognised that children learn from everything they experience so it is not appropriate to separate these concepts. However, in 5.2 you need to identify aspects of your practice that relate to *care* and others that relate to *education,* so that you can evidence how you adapt both education and care.

Age-related requirement

Standard 5.2 is one of the bullet points which explicitly requires you to evidence your practice with babies as well as young children. You need to demonstrate an awareness of the *physical, emotional, social, intellectual development and communication needs of babies and children* and know how to adapt this provision to support children at different stages of development.

As you are asked to demonstrate an *awareness*, you can evidence this through your theoretical knowledge rather than through your practice, but this evidence will be stronger if you can also provide examples of practice. You may need to consider taking on an additional placement to provide the evidence 5.2 requires. Chapter 5 on age range requirements will give you some more information on this.

'Communication needs of babies and children'

In 5.2 there is a specific requirement to demonstrate your awareness of the communication needs of babies and children and how to adapt your provision to support these. You must evidence the ways in which you support children's communication with each age group and this will overlap with some of your evidence for 2.5, which requires you to demonstrate how you listen to babies, toddlers and pre-school children.

Make sure that in your evidence you highlight your understanding of the communication *needs* of babies and children at each stage of development and how you use activities (*education*) and routines and key times (*care*) to support children's communication.

You must evidence how you adapt your approach to support children with speech delay or additional communication needs. For example, any evidence you have of supporting a child with speech delay, a stammer or selective mutism, or of following strategies suggested by a speech and language therapist can help you evidence this.

Read the Early Years Foundation Stage (2014) requirements regarding communication with children at different stages of development for guidance and refer to this in your evidence. Communication is one of the three prime areas in EYFS and relates to how children develop their *understanding* and *speaking* skills and *listening and attention*.

Adapt children's care

Now you need to look at the requirement to evidence how you adapt children's care. Look at how EYFS promotes children's care and how you meet these requirements to support children at different stages of development. You must evidence how you have adapted your provision to support the care needs of a child. You could evidence how you follow individual care routines for a child, follow your setting policy for giving medicines, create a quiet area in the toddler room so a child who has been ill can rest when necessary, ensure all staff are aware of children's allergies or describe how you adapt the environment for a child with a physical disability.

Table S5.1 Evidence checklist for 5.2

5.2	Demonstrate awareness of child development	Adapt education	Adapt care	Babies/toddlers/pre-school children	Evidence
Physical	Rationale for extending opportunities for physical activities	I lead on developing opportunities for physical activities indoors and outdoors for toddlers	Babies: follow home routines	Toddlers	Plans
Emotional	My rationale for introducing persona dolls with pre-school children	Introduce persona dolls in circle time	Introduce key person's responsibility for changing own key child	Pre-school children	My journal
				Babies and toddlers	Plans and evaluations of activities
Social			Use key times to promote interactions with babies	Babies	Staff meeting minutes and profile book
Intellectual		Planning according to Early Years Foundation Stage areas of learning outdoors as well as indoors		Pre-school	Planning documents and observations
Communication development	Rationale for introducing Every Child A Talker	Introduce communication-friendly spaces	Introduce Makaton signs for drink etc.	Toddlers	Staff meeting minutes: training on developing babies' communication skills

Evidence checklist for 5.2

As you need to evidence several aspects of your practice in 5.2, Table S5.1 can help you identify what you need to evidence, organise the evidence you have and identify any gaps in your practice that you need to address.

Evidence for 5.2

You must evidence your knowledge and understanding across all aspects of children's development and care at each stage of development, so keep track of what you evidence you have and where it is.

If you have designed a chart that tracks your evidence for each Standard across all the sources of evidence (journal, observations, document portfolio, etc.) you will find this particularly helpful for 5.2. There is information on how to create a system for tracking your evidence in the 'tracking evidence' section on the website.

You have to address many aspects of your practice in 5.2 and your evidence needs to be detailed enough to show the depth of your understanding. Although you must *demonstrate an awareness* rather than evidence practice, if you can provide detailed examples of your words and actions your evidence will be much stronger.

You can cross-reference much of your evidence for 5.2 as it will be relevant for other Standards, too; for example, Standard 4 where you are also asked to differentiate provision and 2.4 where you engage in sustained shared thinking to promote a child's intellectual development.

Written assignments, case studies and your reflective journal

You can evidence your understanding of the physical, emotional, social and intellectual development and communication needs of babies, toddlers and pre-school children in detail in a written assignment or case study where you focus on, for example, a series of activities you have introduced to promote children's development and you can relate this to EYFS requirements.

One Early Years Teacher, Cathy, used a case study to describe her understanding of the developmental needs of toddlers. She outlined how this awareness led her to extend opportunities for physical activities and introduce communication-friendly spaces in the garden and to start using Makaton signs to support the communication needs of two key children in particular.

As well as evidencing her awareness of toddlers' physical and communication needs through this case study, she also described how she promoted toddlers' intellectual development through activities within the den that the toddlers helped her plan and set up in the garden. She finally described how she had introduced rolling snack and snacks outdoors in the den and related this to adapting care routines for toddlers.

Document portfolio

Here are some suggestions to help you think about which documents to include:

- planning sheets;

- anonymised IEPs;

- completed Common Assessment Framework (CAF) forms;

- emails to wider professionals, such as speech and language therapists;

- training notes for staff development sessions you have led on child development, differentiation or adapting care routines.

Check that each piece of evidence you include clearly demonstrates your understanding of at least one area of child development (physical, emotional, social, intellectual development and communication needs) and relates to at least one age group. Consider whether the evidence as a whole addresses each area of development and the needs of each age group.

Observations

You can use the activity plans you share with your tutor or mentor to highlight how you have adapted the activity or care routine to support a child's physical, emotional, social, intellectual development and communication needs. Your plans could emphasise how you promote consistency between babies' routines at home and the setting, or how you created communication-friendly spaces to support a toddler with speech delay or will introduce persona dolls to support the social development of pre-school children.

When you are observed engaging with children in a group activity, you can demonstrate how you adapt the activity to support the physical, social, intellectual and social developmental or communication needs of a particular child and refer to this in your planning notes. You could, for example, arrange to be observed promoting communication during routines such as changing babies, or leading the introduction of rolling snack or using Makaton, Picture Exchange Communication System (PECS) cards or augmentative and alternative communication (AAC) with children with special educational needs.

When you decide what you would like an observation to focus on, read through 5.2 carefully and think about how you can use the observation to demonstrate several aspects of this indicator, such as how you adapt care routines for babies, toddlers and pre-school children.

SUGGESTED READING

Ajay, S and Cockerill, H (2014) *Mary Sheridan's From Birth to Five Years: Children's Developmental Progress.* Oxon: Routledge.

Berk, L (2012) *Child Development.* London: Pearsons.

Buckley, B (2012) *Children's Communication Skills: From Birth to Five Years*. London: Routledge.

Donaldson, M (1986) *Children's Minds*. London: Fontana.

Romski, MA and Sevcik, RA (2005) Augmentative communication and early intervention: myths and realities. *Infants and Young Children*, 18 (3): 174–185.

Smith, PK, Cowie, H and Blades, M (2011) *Understanding Children's Development*. New York: Wiley.

Standard 5.3: Demonstrate a clear understanding of the needs of all children, including those with special educational needs and disabilities, and be able to use and evaluate distinctive approaches to engage and support them

You may notice similarities between 5.3 and the rest of Standard 5 and aspects of Standard 4, as they all require evidence of your understanding of how all children develop and how you adapt your provision to meet children's individual needs. What makes 5.3 different is that it specifically mentions children with special needs and disabilities and asks you to use and evaluate programmes to support them.

You must evidence your understanding of a range of disabilities and special needs and how to support the children who experience these. This might include identifying a child with developmental or speech delay, autism, a hearing impairment or a chronic health condition.

You then must identify and evaluate *distinctive* approaches to support the child, both those suggested by other professionals, and those developed within your team. You must evidence how you work alongside other professionals such as the special educational needs co-ordinator (SENCO) or speech and language therapist and show how you follow and evaluate the strategies they suggest.

'Demonstrate a clear understanding of the needs of all children'

Four steps can help you identify and gather your evidence for 5.3.

Step 1: the needs of all children

Think about how you can demonstrate your understanding of the *needs of all children*.

You may find a suitable range of evidence in your observations, next steps and entries in profile books for children of different ages, needs and abilities. You may already have referenced this evidence to other Standards that ask you to plan for individual children, such as 4.1, 4.2 and 5.2.

If you have supported a colleague to understand the needs of a particular child or group of children, or led a discussion on a child's needs, then you may be able to evidence this. Your planning for particular age groups may also evidence your understanding of their developmental needs, for example, when you plan treasure baskets for babies and heuristic play for toddlers.

Step 2: demonstrate a clear understanding of the needs of ... children ... with special educational needs and disabilities

Check you have strong, detailed examples that demonstrate your understanding of the needs of children with special educational needs and disabilities. Your evidence must demonstrate an understanding of the needs of children with a range of disabilities and special educational needs.

For example, you may have one key child with speech delay and have previously worked with a child on the autism spectrum. You can examine your observations, next steps and planning for each child to see whether this clearly illustrates your understanding of their needs. You may need to use a case study to explore your understanding of the needs of one child in more depth.

Step 3: be able to use ... distinctive approaches to engage and support them

Identify the various approaches, or strategies, you have used to involve and support a child with special educational needs or a disability. You must evidence your use of more than one approach and describe each approach clearly enough so that the difference between the approaches you use (and the reason for the change in approach) is *distinct*.

Distinctive approaches can include the strategies you use to adapt activities and your provision overall for a particular child, such as using large-print books, left-handed scissors, visual timetables, activities that are physically accessible and Makaton. You can refer to any additional resources you provide to support a child with a disability or special needs, but this is more suitable evidence for 8.1. In 5.3 you need to demonstrate how you use these resources as part of an overall strategy to support a child.

Distinctive approaches also refers to the strategies you use to support a child that has been identified in an IEP or through consultation with an external professional, such as an area SENCO or speech and language therapist. You must evidence how you follow these strategies to support and engage a child and you may be able to do this through a peer observation, case study or reflections in your journal. If you explain the strategies suggested by another professional to your team so that they feel confident using them, you can cite this as evidence of leadership for 5.3 and 8.4.

Your descriptions of the approaches or strategies you use needs to demonstrate how this strategy helped engage a child and support him. For example, you could evidence a strategy to engage a child by talking to the parents of a child with autism about their child's current interests and provide activities that relate to this. You can also evidence how you use a strategy to engage a child by providing smaller group activities and breaking an activity down into manageable chunks.

You must evidence how you support the child through this strategy or approach. You may be able to evidence this in your planning notes if they are detailed enough to highlight the steps you use to support the child, for example, by sitting with him at meal and circle times or preparing him for moments of transition. You could also ask a colleague to observe you using a specific strategy to support a child, such as engaging with a child with a disability in activities in the ball pool or sensory room.

Identifying the approaches you use to support a child with special educational needs or a disability

You can use Table S5.2 to help you identify the approaches or strategies you use to engage and support a child with special educational needs or a disability and how you can evidence this. One example has been added to help you.

Table S5.2 Approaches to support a child with special educational needs or a disability

Child with special educational needs or disability	My strategies	How I engaged and supported a child	Strategies in child's individual education programme (IEP)	Strategies suggested by external professional	My evidence
Child J: Is seeing hospital specialist, possibility of attention-deficit hyperactivity disorder	Visual timetable Reward chart Break down instructions into smaller chunks	As key person I sit with him during meals and circle time Plan and spend one-to-one time with him engaging in maths activities in garden using his favourite cars and bikes	Small group activities Extend key times See his current next steps	Waiting for report from area SENCO	Observations Planning notes IEP Profile book Report from area SENCO Report from hospital specialist

SENCO, special educational needs co-ordinator.

Step 4: evaluate distinctive approaches

Evaluate the effectiveness of each *distinctive approach* or strategy that you have used. You may have this evidence in your routine evaluations of activities or in the notes you make after you have observed a child and these evaluations can add to your evidence for 5.3.

Make sure that your evaluations relate to the effectiveness of the approach you tried, the impact on the child and what you have learnt from this. Make sure that you reflect on each approach in enough detail and depth. You may find that a case study provides you with the scope you need to explore the impact of each approach in depth.

Identify the frameworks that inform your practice

If you are to evidence how you follow appropriate approaches to supporting children with special educational needs or disabilities, then you need to make some reference to the frameworks that inform your practice. You need to identify which frameworks relate to your practice with children with special needs and disabilities and show how they inform your practice.

These frameworks include EYFS (2014), your setting's special educational needs policy, the revised SEND Code of Practice 0 to 25 years (Department for Education and Department of Health, 2014), the Special Educational Needs and Disability Act (2001) and the Every Child Matters agenda (Department for Education and Skills, 2003a) which promotes positive outcomes for all children.

Evidence for 5.3

As you are asked to evidence your understanding of the needs of all children, you must evidence your work with a range of children of varying ages, some with special educational needs and disabilities and others without additional needs. You need to identify how you have engaged and supported these children, describe the different approaches you used and evaluate their effectiveness. This can include strategies you and your colleagues developed and those suggested by other professionals.

Written assignments, case studies and your reflective journal

You can use a detailed assignment or case study to describe and reflect on an approach you used with a particular child in detail. This will give you the scope you need to evidence how you identified the child's needs, tried a range of strategies to engage with and support him, and then reflect on the effectiveness of each approach.

A detailed case study will also help you to evidence other Standards which ask you to demonstrate your understanding of child development and how to differentiate provision, such as 1.2, 2.2, 3.1, 4.1 and 5.2.

You can use your reflective journal to record your thoughts as you experiment with different strategies as this will enable you to review and compare strategies.

Document portfolio

You could include:

- copies of planning documents;
- observations;
- IEPs;
- completed CAF forms;
- copies of email communication with other professionals and records of meetings where you have discussed strategies to support an individual child.

If you have led a discussion with your team on using strategies to support a child with special educational needs or a disability, than you can include a copy of the minutes of this meeting.

If you have documentary evidence of buying equipment and adapting the environment to support a child with a disability, then you can cross-reference this evidence to 8.1 as well.

Observations

When you arrange to be observed engaging in an activity with a group of children, you can record in your planning how you will engage and support a particular child and share this with your tutor or mentor. You must demonstrate the strategies or approaches that you have identified in your planning notes, or provide a rationale for your change of approach.

You can show your mentor or tutor any ways in which the environment reflects changes you have introduced to support a particular child. This might include a visual timetable, new tables that are the right size for a child's wheelchair, resources that have been adapted or large-print books. You must explain how these resources are part of an approach you use and describe how they help you to engage and support a particular child.

CASE STUDY

British Sign Language (BSL) for Kids

Adele is the key person for a child with hearing loss and another child with speech delay. A colleague told her that BSL provides a range of sets of PECS cards for young children and these might be useful and help her to support her two key children.

She found that she could order the BSL for Kids range of PECS cards over the internet and chose an Early Years Activities Picture Exchange Communication Keyring (AAC/ASD) Visual Aid Resource from **www.amazon.co.uk.**

She also found a BSL for Kids page on Facebook and used this to find out what other resources were available and order a set of cards on going for a hearing test (www.facebook. com/pages/BSL-For-Kids/323218077695423).

She decided that once the resources she ordered had arrived, she would share them with her colleagues in a staff meeting and discuss with them how they could best use them. She felt that together they would be able to identify some strategies they could introduce to support her two key children.

SUGGESTED READING

Dukes, C and Smith, M (2009) *Recognising and Planning for Special Needs in the Early Years* (Hands on Guides). London: SAGE.

Roffey, S and Parry, J (2013) *Special Needs in the Early Years: Supporting Collaboration, Communication and Co-ordination.* London: Routledge.

Tassoni, P (2003) *Supporting Special Needs: Understanding Inclusion in the Early Years* (Professional Development). Oxon: Heinemann.

Wall, K (2012) *Special Needs and Early Years: A Practitioner Guide.* London: SAGE.

Standard 5.4: Support children through a range of transitions

If we take a child's physical pain seriously, then we must also do the same for their emotional pain.

(Margot Sutherland, 2006; in Gould, 2012)

Standard 5.4 is about the ways in which you support children to help them manage the transitions in their lives. The key to evidencing this indicator well is to identify how you support children through *a range of transitions* and transitions that are both within your setting and in a child's home life.

You must identify how a transition can affect children and the strategies you will use to support them. You can explore why transitions affect children and why and how practitioners can support them through these times.

Transitions in your setting

You will be able to identify several transitions that children experience when they attend your setting. The initial transition is when they start attending and you can evidence your role in the settling-in process. You can identify all the ways in which you make this transition easier for children, for example, by carrying out a home visit and getting to know their interests.

When children move between rooms in your setting, this is also a transition and some children may need more support at this time. If you organise visits to their new room and to spend time with their new key person, then you can evidence this for 5.4. Other transitions within the setting include when a child stops having a rest time or starts to stay for afternoons. You may have evidence of supporting children through these transitions, possibly in their profile book or in the records of your conversations with their parents.

There are also times of transition between activities and the routines of the day that some children can find difficult, such as tidying up and preparing for lunch or moving from free-flow activities to sitting still during circle time. You may use a visual time-table to help a particular child prepare for changes in the daily routine and you can evidence this for 5.4.

Children also experience transitions when staff members leave, or even when they are just absent for a few days, especially if this was their key person. You may be involved in identifying ways to reduce staff turnover and have regular bank staff that the children can get to know, or set up systems where children have an alternative attachment figure if their key person is away. You may also identify the impact on children of having a different person drop them off and collect them at the end of the day and have developed a way to support them through this.

If you are working with pre-school children, then you will probably be involved in preparing them for the transition to school. You may be able to evidence how you help them develop the skills and independence they will need for school, find books on starting school to share and encourage discussions about what their new school might be like.

You might be able to evidence how you visit the local school with a group of children and encourage them to take photos of key areas that they can then use to make a book about their new school. Timothy, an Early Years Teacher trainee in a nursery class attached to a primary school, regularly invited the reception class children and their teacher to visit the nursery for story time. The reception teacher would read stories and spend time with the children who would be joining her class. She would then invite Timothy and the new children to visit the reception class at play time so that they could get used to the large playground. Timothy reflected on this process in his journal to help him evidence 5.4.

The EYFS Profile and any other transition records that you have written and share with a child's school are also evidence of supporting this transition. You can also evidence the conversations you have had with parents where you encourage them to help prepare their child for the move to school.

You may find additional evidence of supporting children to manage transitions within your setting in your settling-in records, 'all about me' forms, observations and entries in profile books or in the minutes of a staff meeting where you planned strategies to support a child.

Transitions in a child's home life

There are many transitions outside the setting that can affect children and part of your role as key person is to support them to manage these. These transitions can include moving home or town or, for some children, moving country. Other children have to adjust to having a new person live with them, such as a parent's new partner or an elderly grandparent.

Other transitions include bereavement, the arrival of a new sibling, parents' separation or a change of childminder. A change in a child's health can involve a series of transitions, especially if this involves a long stay in hospital and if you support a child with an illness or disability then you may also be able to cross-reference this to 5.3. Children with special educational needs or a disability may find some transitions particularly difficult and you may have identified strategies to support them in their IEP.

A change in the time a child spends with a parent, especially if one parent moves out of the family home, is a transition a child is very likely to need support with. If a parent enters into a relationship with a new partner, this is also a transition the child will need to adjust to.

You may be able to use your observations and records of discussions with colleagues to evidence how you identified that a child was experiencing a transition and needed extra support. You will then need to evidence the strategies you use to help a child manage a transition and you may have evidence of this in your observations, planning notes or records of a discussion with a child's parents.

You may find evidence in your journal that looks at how, for example, you introduced books and activities to help a child with the arrival of a new sibling or a recent bereavement. You may also have planning notes that record how you have used persona dolls during circle time to help children explore and manage their emotions.

Evidence for 5.4

You must evidence how you identified the impact of a range of transitions on specific children and how you support children to manage these transitions, both within your setting and at home. Your evidence must be detailed and show how you understood the impact of the transition on the child, worked with the child's parents or carers to help them support their child, supported the parents themselves, promoted the key person relationship and used strategies and resources to engage with the child.

Your evidence can relate to how you settle new children in your setting and into a new room, and how you prepare them for starting school. However, you need evidence of supporting children through a range of transitions, outside the setting as well as within it, so you can evidence how you support children through changes in their home life or in their own health and abilities.

Written assignments, case studies and your reflective journal

The decisions you make when you decide how to support a child through a transition are based on your understanding of child development and the needs of the individual child. A written assignment or short case study will give you the scope you need to evidence your knowledge and understanding and the rationale for your actions.

For example, this would give you the scope to highlight your understanding of the impact of starting nursery and how this relates to your understanding of attachment theory and then describe and reflect on your actions at each stage in the process of helping a child to settle. You may find that you prefer to use your reflective journal to do this as it could allow you to explore the strategies you use in greater depth.

You could also use a case study to evidence how you have supported a child and family over a period of time, for example, by helping a family that is new to the area to contact local services and resources.

Often the most important strategy during a time of transition is to support the child's key attachment relationships. You can evidence this in detail in a case study or assignment where you can record and reflect on your actions and conversations with parents or carers. You would be able to describe how you provided them with support in their relationship with their child, particularly if one parent has moved away. You could also record how you focus on promoting the child's key person attachment by planning extended key times.

Document portfolio

Here are some suggestions to help you select documents to include:

- work documents that evidence how you support a child through a transition;

- records of carrying out a home visit and following your setting's settling-in policy and completing an 'all about me' form;

- the settling-in policy itself if you were involved in revising it;

- a witness statement from a parent or records of the resources you ordered to support a child, such as books on bereavement or starting school;

- records of learning some key phrases in a child's home language and plans for activities based on the child's interests to help that child settle in;

- observations of supporting a child to move to a new room or transfer records that you share with a child's new school.

Observations

Here are some suggestions:

- Be observed helping a new child settle in or carrying out an activity that helps a child manage a transition, for example, taking a toddler to visit the pre-school room.

- Be observed supporting a child to manage changes in the daily routines by using a visual timetable to help that child move between activities, such as clearing up before lunch or coming in from the garden.

- Be observed using new resources you introduced to support a child through a transition. This might include a box where children can bring in something from home and keep it safe, or a photo display of the child and their family.

- Be observed leading circle time where you share a book on having a new sibling or use puppets or persona dolls to help children talk about their experiences or feelings.

- Be observed working with a group of children on an activity that will support them to manage a transition, such as making a photo book to help them prepare for school or one about their new home or new baby.

CASE STUDY

Using role-play area to support transitions

Jeremy, an Early Years Teacher trainee, arranged for a colleague to observe him involving the children in setting up a role-play area. He had identified that his key child, Paris, was distressed when his father was repeatedly flying abroad because of his job. Jeremy had observed a colleague plan a baby clinic role-play area to support a group of children who were still adjusting to the birth of a younger sibling.

He wondered if this was an approach that could help him support Paris so he involved Paris in setting up an airport role-play area in the garden. He hoped that this would pro-vide opportunities for Paris to talk about his feelings and together they could explore issues around distance and separation and Paris could remind himself that flights leave and then they return, as will his father.

CASE STUDY

Using photo books

Audrey, an Early Years Teacher trainee, took her key children to visit their new school and take photos of key areas such as the main entrance and playground. She asked her mentor to observe her in the activity where she helped the children to make their own book on starting school.

Her colleague, David, another Early Years Teacher trainee, was working with his three-year-old key child, Carl. He asked his mentor to observe him making a photo book with Carl, whose older sister and her new baby had moved in with him and his mother. Carl found it hard to share his mother and adapt to living with new people. David hoped that this book might facilitate discussions about this change and help Carl adjust to these new relationships.

SUGGESTED
READING

Allingham, S (2012) *Transitions in the Early Years: 4 (Early Childhood Essentials)*. London: MA Educational.

Bayley, R, Featherstone, S and Hardy, M (2003) *Smooth Transitions: Ensuring Continuity from the Foundation Stage* (Early Years Library). London: Bloomsbury.

Dunlop, W and Fabian, H (2006) *Informing Transitions in the Early Years: Research, Policy and Practice*. Berkshire: Open University Press, McGraw Hill.

Fisher, J (2010) *Moving on to Key Stage 1*. Berkshire: Open University Press, McGraw Hill International.

Gould, T (2012) *Transition in the Early Years: From Principles to Practice*. London: Featherstone Education.

O'Connor, A (2012) *Understanding Transitions in the Early Years: Supporting Change through Attachment and Resilience*. London: Routledge.

Trodd, L (2013) *Transitions in the Early Years: Working with Children and Families*. London: SAGE.

Standard 5.5: Know when a child is in need of additional support and how this can be accessed, working in partnership with parents and/or carers and other professionals

Standard 5.5 asks you to identify when a child is in need of additional support and how you can access this support. This will usually involve making a referral to an external service and you must demonstrate that you know how to make this referral and work in partnership with this external professional and the child's parents or carers.

You must demonstrate the ways in which you identify when a child needs support, what that support could be, and when this involves more than your setting can provide, who you will make a referral to and how you do this. You must evidence how you maintain regular contact between yourself, the child's parents and/or carers and the other professional.

'Additional support'

Because 5.5 asks you to work *in partnership with parents and/or carers and other professionals*, the term *additional support* in this context refers to any support a child needs that is beyond what you can provide within your setting. It can refer to the support provided by a wide range of professionals, such as those who provide medical support; support for a child with a special need or disability support for a child's emotional and behavioural needs; or protecting the child from harm.

'Know when a child is in need of additional support'

You must focus on how you identify a child's need for additional support and what form that support should take. For example, you can demonstrate how your regular observations and your discussions with parents helped you to identify a child's needs and record conversations you have with colleagues or your SENCO to help you identify how best to support this child.

You must evidence the strategies you use and the steps you take in this process of identifying a need for additional support and demonstrate how you do this in conjunction with a child's parents or carers. For example, you may have identified a child's additional needs through triangulated observations or through completing the two-year-old check. You may have shared your observations of a child with challenging behaviour with colleagues, implemented strategies and found over time that these were not proving adequate so sought additional support from the educational psychologist.

You may have noticed a physical change in a child, such as hearing loss, and spoken to the child's parents and advised them to follow this up with their GP. You may have identified that a child had a special educational need and worked through the stages of the Code of Practice with your SENCO, but eventually decided the child needed additional support so made a referral.

Another way in which you can identify a child's additional needs is through completing a CAF form. If you are considering completing a CAF for a child, you may have identified that a child has additional needs, but find that only when you complete the form itself do you know which particular referral is needed.

Access additional support

You must demonstrate that you *know when a child is in need of additional support and how this can be accessed*. You need to know who it would be best to refer a child to and how to make this referral.

There are a wide range of professionals that you can refer a child to, and in 5.5 you need to demonstrate that you have this breadth of understanding. You must be aware of the roles and expertise of the different professionals that are available so as to know who it is most appropriate to consult in each situation.

These professionals may include your area SENCO, a health visitor, an educational psychologist, play therapist or physiotherapist. You must demonstrate that you identify when a child needs support and who is the most appropriate person to refer to and that you know how to access this support.

For example, you may identify a child's need for additional emotional support if she is struggling after the death of a sibling. If a situation involves domestic violence you may make a referral to social services and through them contact a local refuge.

You might make a referral to an educational psychologist if you need additional help to support a child with challenging behaviour or make a referral for speech and language therapy for a child with speech delay. If you are concerned about a child with special educational needs, you might contact your area SENCO.

There are also different ways in which to make a referral and you need to be familiar with the systems you have to follow. Your setting will have procedures that you must follow and you need to make sure that you and your colleagues know these and have an up-to-date list of contacts. However, if you work in a children's centre, you may have internal procedures to follow when making a referral to the services within your centre and you need to be familiar with these, too.

'Working in partnership with parents and/or carers and other professionals'

You must demonstrate how you work with parents/carers and other professionals when you support a child with additional needs. You must understand why this partnership is important and evidence all the ways in which you foster ongoing communication with both parents and the professionals.

You may have evidence of your daily conversations with a parent about her child's progress or records of meetings you have arranged to discuss a concern. You may have a series of emails or letters between yourself and another professional that show how you have worked together to support this child. You may also be able to demonstrate that you invited a professional to visit your setting to demonstrate the strategies or care routines you need to follow or that you arranged for the professional to send you a report.

Access support

Working through Table S5.3 will help you recognise the occasions where you have identified that a child needs additional support, how you recognised this need, who you referred them to and the ways in which you worked in partnership with the child's parents/carers and external professionals.

Use the top line in the table to identify all the professionals that you can refer a child to and the ways in which you can maintain contact with both them and the child's parents. The left-hand columns record the instances where you recognised that a child needed additional support and how you made this decision. The final column records where you have relevant evidence, for example, in a completed CAF form for child 'P'. Some examples have been added to help you.

Similarities and differences: 5.3, 5.4 and 5.5

In 5.3 you may have provided some evidence of working with other professionals to support a child with a special educational need or disability. In 5.5, however, you need to evidence the step before this, where you make the decision to involve an external professional. For 5.5 you need to evidence when you noticed a child needed support, how you knew this and who you referred the child to.

You can also think about how 5.5 relates to 5.4, which looks at how you support a child to manage a transition. For example, you may have evidence of referring a child for play therapy when that child found a transition very difficult, such as after a bereavement or other loss.

Table S5.3 Identifying sources of support

Child with 'additional needs':

e.g.
- emotional
- behavioural
- health
- disability
- family circumstances

How you identified the child's needs

e.g. observation
CAF
Parents
Two-year-old check

Sources of support and examples of working in partnership

	Partner-ship with parents/carers	Area SENCO	Health visitor	GP/ hospital consult-ant	SLT/ physio-therapist	Educational psychologist	Other	Evidence
Child 'A' Observed 'A' during activities and circle time and noticed didn't respond to my comments to him during group times, but did one to one. Completed two-year-old check which raised concerns	Discussion about 'A's listening skills at home, whether he hears better in a quiet environment			Suggested parent take child to GP and ask about hearing test; we gave her a letter outlining what we've observed and copy of two-year-old check			Hearing specialist: asked if she could share her results with us and who we could speak to about strategies to support 'A'	Observations Two-year-old check Records of conversations with parents Copy of my letter to GP Copy of hearing specialist's report with strategies we follow
Child 'P' Observations of 'P' finding group times difficult and very upset when left by Dad at nursery in morning	Meeting with Mum, who explained Dad has moved out and 'P' very upset and won't sleep: suggested strategies					Suggested parents visit our drop-in sessions with educational psychologist to discuss concerns and help 'P' manage parents' separation		Records of parent meeting Strategies from educational psychologist Next steps for 'P'

CAF, Common Assessment Framework; SENCO, special educational needs co-ordinator; GP, general practitioner; SLT, speech and language therapist.

Similarities and differences: working with other professionals

In 5.5 you are asked to demonstrate how you work in partnership with other professionals and a child's parents or carers to support a child with additional needs. You may have noticed that Standard 8 also asks you to evidence your partnerships with other professionals, but there are some key differences between the requirements in Standard 8 and 5.5.

In 8.3 you are asked to *Take a lead in establishing a culture of co-operative working between colleagues, parents and/or carers and other professionals*. You must demonstrate how you encourage other colleagues to form these partnerships with parents and other professionals, as you yourself have done in your evidence for 5.5.

In 8.7 you are asked to demonstrate that you *understand the importance of and contribute to multi-agency team working*. Here you must evidence your knowledge and understanding of what a multi-agency partnership is and why these partnerships are so important.

Evidence for 5.5

For 5.5 you must demonstrate:

- how you identify a child's additional need;
- when and how you decide the child needs external support;
- how you access this support.

You then need to evidence how you work in partnership with other professionals and the child's parents/carers.

Written assignments, case studies and your reflective journal

- You can present a case study or written assignments to describe how you identified that a child was in need of support and referred that child to other relevant services. You need to evidence how you are able to recognise a range of children's needs, such as social, emotional, behavioural or medical needs, as well as special educational needs and disabilities.

- You can also use your journal to explore who you need to refer a child to and how you need to do this and reflect on your communication with the professional and parent or carer.

Document portfolio

You could include:

- copies of emails between yourself and your area SENCO or local services;
- a completed referral form;
- a shared report or a completed CAF form.

Remember, all these documents need to be anonymised so that the children and setting cannot be identified.

Observations

Here are some suggestions:

- Be observed during a meeting between a parent and yourself regarding a potential referral for her child or a meeting or phone call between yourself and another professional (remember, you need the parent's informed consent for this).

- Be observed leading a staff training session on how to identify a child's additional needs and make an appropriate referral.

- Show your mentor or tutor the contact details of relevant services that you have used, a completed referral form, a two-year-old check where you identified a concern and any relevant notes in a child's profile books or other records.

SUGGESTED
READING

Gasper, M (2012) *Multi-agency Working in the Early Years: Challenges and Opportunities.* London: SAGE.

Siraj-Blatchford, I, Clarke, K and Needham, M (2007) *The Team Around the Child: Multi-agency Working in the Early Years.* London: IOE Press.

Walker, G (2008) *Working Together for Children: A Critical Introduction to Multi-Agency Working.* London: Continuum International.

Standard 6: **Make accurate and productive use of assessment**

Introduction

Standard 6 provides you with an opportunity to demonstrate your understanding of Early Years Foundation Stage (EYFS, 2014) assessment requirements and your role in leading and sharing formative and summative assessments with parents, children and other professionals.

You must demonstrate the ways in which you follow all EYFS assessment requirements and how these assessments enable you to plan appropriate goals for individual children. These assessments need to be ongoing and formative, for example, when you observe a child before deciding on his next steps, and summative, such as the end-of-stage EYFS Profile (EYFSP) and the two-year-old progress check.

Formative and summative assessment

The purpose of formative assessment is to monitor a child's learning and development and provide ongoing feedback that identifies strengths and areas where a child may need extra support. Using an observation to identify a child's next steps is an example of formative assessment.

The purpose of summative assessment is to evaluate a child's learning and development at a set point in time against a standard or benchmark: the two-year-old progress check, EYFSP and SATS tests at the end of Key Stages 1 and 2 are examples of formative assessments.

'Accurate and productive use of assessment'

As you are asked to make *accurate* and *productive* use of assessment in Standard 6, you need to evidence both how you ensure your assessments are accurate, for example, by observing a child on more than one occasion, and that you use the assessments effectively, for example, by using the two-year-old check to identify appropriate goals for a child and/or areas where progress is less than expected.

Annex 1 of the Teachers' Standards (Early Years)

Annex 1 of the *Teachers' Standards (Early Years) 2013* provides you with a comprehensive overview of the EYFS assessment requirements that you need to evidence for

Standard 6. This includes the two-year-old progress check, the EYFSP and ongoing (formative) assessment through regular observations.

Standard 6: key topics

There are three key topics that you must address in Standard 6:

1. leading assessment within the framework of EYFS;

2. engaging with parents and other professionals in the ongoing assessment and provision for a child;

3. sharing feedback with parents and children to help children progress towards their goals.

Your evidence for Standard 6

You must evidence examples of formative and summative assessment and highlight your understanding of the EYFS assessment framework. If you have completed a two-year-old progress check or EYFSP and use these to support a child's development, then this can demonstrate your knowledge of the EYFS assessment framework and demonstrate how you make *accurate and productive use of assessment*. You can evidence how you share these assessments with children, parents and other professionals to promote the child's learning and development.

You can provide evidence of regularly sharing feedback with parents through your entries in their child's profile book, home link book or records of the daily feedback you share. A completed individual education plan (IEP) or Common Assessment Framework (CAF) will also provide evidence of the ways in which you work with parents and other professionals to identify goals for children and help them work towards these.

Sharing feedback with children

Think carefully about how you can evidence the ways in which you regularly share feedback with children. Tim, an Early Years Teacher trainee, spends time once a fortnight looking over children's profile book with them and asking the children what they feel they have achieved and what they would like to be able to do next.

Standard 6: leadership opportunities

Standard 6 provides you with plenty of opportunities for you to demonstrate your leadership role as you are asked to *understand and lead assessment*. You may have colleagues or students who lack confidence in planning differentiated activities or who need support with the two-year-old progress check. If you provide one-to-one support or a lead a staff training session to develop practice in relation to assessment, then you will have good evidence of leadership for Standard 6 that you can also cross-reference to 8.4. However, if you include any training notes, you need to make sure that you annotate these to make it clear how the materials relate to a particular aspect of Standard 6.

Similarities and differences: Standards 4, 5 and 6

One of the best ways to get to know the Standards is to recognise how they relate to each other and find patterns between them. Standards 4, 5 and 6 are closely related to each other as each Standard looks at differentiation, but from a different viewpoint.

Standard 4 looks at how you plan for individual children whilst reviewing your provision as a whole. Standard 5 looks at how you plan for individual children within the context of their individual needs, circumstances, special educational needs (SEN) and disabilities. Standard 6 also looks at differentiation, but through the framework of EYFS assessment requirements.

Standard 6.1: Understand and lead assessment within the framework of the EYFS framework, including statutory assessment requirements (see Annex 1)

Standard 6.1 relates to your understanding of the EYFS assessment requirements. You must demonstrate your own practice and understanding of the requirements and how you lead the process of assessment within your setting. This includes both ongoing, routine, daily formative assessments and summative assessments, such as the progress check at age two, the EYFSP and any other reports you produce for parents or other professionals or a child's new school.

You must evidence your understanding of the EYFS framework as well as the statutory assessment requirements, so you must highlight the relationship between of the statutory requirements and EYFS requirements in general. One way to evidence this understanding of assessment requirements and the EYFS framework as a whole is to link your observations and 'next steps' to EYFS areas of learning and the EYFS outcomes.

You must evidence how you share your daily assessments with parents and how you involve parents when completing an IEP or CAF as this is an assessment requirement. You must demonstrate how you share the two-year-old progress check with parents too, as this is also a requirement.

You will probably have plenty of evidence of using a range of assessment methods, such as daily observations and assessments. However, if you are not familiar with certain requirements, such as the EYFSP, find out more about this, perhaps by shadowing a colleague.

There are various sources of evidence that you can consider for 6.1. You can demonstrate your understanding and practice through reflections in your journal or a case study, entries in a profile book, an IEP or a CAF form. You can demonstrate how you lead practice through the minutes of a staff meeting or any guidance you provide for colleagues.

However, it is important that you make sure that your evidence relates to both EYFS requirements as a whole, such as the EYFS outcomes, and the statutory assessment requirements, such as the EYFSP.

If you are working in a management role, your evidence of understanding and leading assessment may be quite different from that of a practitioner. Make sure that the evidence you do have clearly demonstrates your understanding of all EYFS requirements and how you support colleagues to manage these, even if you do not complete the assessments yourself.

Guidance in Annex 1

Annex 1 outlines all the EYFS assessment requirements that you need to understand and evidence for 6.1. It reminds you to provide evidence of completing the progress check at age two and/or the assessment at the end of EYFS, the EYFSP. It also provides detailed guidance on how to complete these assessments and how to use them.

For example, EYFSP profiles need to be completed for all children, including those with SEN or disabilities, and Annex 1 suggests making reasonable adjustments to the process and seeking specialist assistance when necessary. There is detailed information for reception teachers on sharing the profile report with the year 1 teacher and parents and on the additional short commentary on children's skills and abilities that needs to be completed in relation to the three characteristics of effective learning.

The guidance in Annex 1 on the progress check at age two reminds practitioners to provide parents with a short written summary of their child's development in the prime areas and identify strengths and areas where progress is 'less than expected'. There is information on forming a targeted plan and informing other practitioners if the concerns are significant or an SEN or disability is identified.

There is useful information on how to share the report with parents and encourage them to share it with other professionals, such as the health visitor, and the need for the report to be completed in time to inform the Healthy Child Programme health and development review at age two.

Section 2.1 in Annex 1 reminds you that you also need to evidence your ongoing, formative assessments to help you *recognise children's progress, understand their needs, and to plan activities and support.* It suggests that you need to observe children's interests and learning styles and use your observations to inform your planning and to identify any learning and development needs which you can share with parents and any relevant professionals.

To evidence 6.1 you must read Annex 1 and follow the detailed guidance carefully so that you provide evidence of completing the checks at age two and/or the EYFSP and evidence your ongoing assessments within the EYFS framework, such as profile books and IEPs, which will overlap with your evidence for 6.2.

'Lead assessment'

Standard 6.1 asks you to evidence how you *lead assessment* and you must think about how you can evidence this within the context of your role. For example, if yours is a management role, then you may have evidence of providing information on EYFS assessment requirements and setting up appropriate assessment systems in your setting. This will also help you evidence how you *understand* assessment requirements. However, you need to make sure that you can evidence your support for ongoing formative as well as summative assessment methods.

If you are a practitioner, you may have plenty of evidence of your daily formative assessments and how you share these with parents. However, you also need to think about how you can evidence how you *understand and lead assessment*. You may be able to evidence this through supporting a colleague to understand the daily assessment requirements and sharing ongoing assessments with parents. You may be able to lead a staff development session on EYFS assessment requirements or invite a colleague to shadow you while you complete a two-year-old progress check.

Similarities and differences with other Standards

You must evidence how you understand and lead assessment *within the framework of EYFS*, and *including statutory assessment requirements*. Some of your evidence for other Standards may help you evidence 6.1, such as 3.3, where you demonstrate your understanding of EYFS, and 5.3, where you demonstrate how you adapt provision for individual children.

What makes 6.1 different from other similar Standards is that you need to provide strong evidence of following the EYFS statutory assessment requirements. You must explicitly relate the assessments you include as evidence to the EYFS assessment requirements. You have excellent guidance on these requirements in Annex 1, which you can find at the end of the *Teachers' Standards (Early Years)* document (Gov.uk, 2013d).

Evidence for 6.1

You must make sure that all your evidence of assessment for 6.1 clearly and explicitly relates to both the EYFS framework and the EYFS statutory assessment requirements. Highlight your understanding of the framework and requirements, so as to demonstrate that you *understand and lead assessment within the framework of the EYFS framework*. Annex 1 will help you identify the areas you need to evidence for 6.1.

Written assignments, case studies and your reflective journal

Written assignments and case studies provide you with an opportunity to evidence the depth of your understanding of both the EYFS framework and statutory assessment requirements and how you lead assessment, possibly in relation to an individual child. You can provide very detailed evidence of assessment if you present a case study about a child with SEN or a disability where you can describe the process of assessment step by step, for example, moving from daily observations and the two-year-old progress check through to an IEP or CAF form.

You can also use an assignment, case study or journal entry to describe in detail how you have led and supported colleagues in relation to EYFS and the assessment requirements and this will also evidence your own understanding. You may have evidence of leading a training session, making a presentation in a staff meeting, mentoring a colleague or encouraging that person to shadow you, for example, when you complete an IEP.

Document portfolio

In your document portfolio you can include:

- examples of a completed progress check at age two and an EYFSP that you have completed;

- annotated examples of your ongoing assessment of individual children to show how you follow EYFS assessment requirements and relate these to the EYFS outcomes and areas of learning;

- records of observations, assessments and next steps and planning documents that relate to these;

- completed and anonymised IEPs and CAF forms if you highlight your own contributions.

Remember to evidence how you *understand and lead assessment*, so make sure that any documents you include highlight your understanding and leadership actions. Your documents also need to evidence how you share your assessments with parents and other professionals, where appropriate, as this is a requirement of EYFS.

If you have produced any information for parents or practitioners on the EYFS statutory assessment requirements, then you can include these in your portfolio as they will demonstrate your understanding and leadership.

Observations

You can arrange to be observed:

- supporting a colleague in completing a two-year-old progress check, an IEP or an EYFSP;

- sharing information with a parent or other professional (this is an EYFS requirement);

- modelling the daily process of ongoing assessment for a colleague or student (during the observation itself and in your additional notes you can highlight your understanding of the EYFS framework and assessment requirements).

You can share your key children's profile books with your mentor or tutor to show how you have assessed each child within the EYFS framework. If you have completed an IEP or CAF, progress checks at age two or an EYFSP, then you can share these, too.

Bradbury, A (2013) *Understanding Early Years Inequality: Policy, Assessment and Young Children's Identities.* Oxon: Routledge.

Hutchin, V (2012) *Assessing and Supporting Young Children's Learning: for the Early Years Foundation Stage Profile.* London: Hodder Education.

Kamen, T (2013) *Observation and Assessment for the EYFS.* London: Hodder Education.

Standard 6.2: Engage effectively with parents and/or carers and other professionals in the on-going assessment and provision for each child

Standard 6.2 asks you to evidence how you engage with parents and with other professionals and work together to assess and plan provision for a child. You can evidence your regular communication with parents where you share feedback and plan appropriate provision for their child, which you have evidenced for 6.1. You must evidence how you work with the parents of a child who has special needs or a disability and engage with the other professionals who support this child. You must demonstrate how you work together over time to assess the child's needs so that you can continually adjust your provision for that child.

Your evidence must demonstrate how you identify a concern, share it with parents and involve other professionals when necessary. You can evidence how you identified a concern through completing a two-year-old progress check, or assessing a child against the areas of development appropriate for that child's age or stage of development and summarise your progress through the stages of the SEN Code of Practice (Department for Education and Department of Health, 2014).

A parent or other professional may have identified a concern and you must evidence how you found a way to share information with the other professional. This could involve occasions where a GP identified a child's hearing loss, a health visitor was concerned about a child not reaching developmental milestones or a parent was concerned that a child is not experimenting with sounds at the age when her siblings were doing this.

'Other professionals'

Be aware that when the Standards refer to *other professionals,* this means professionals who work externally to your setting. For example, you could evidence your work with the area SEN co-ordinator (SENCO), but not the SENCO based in your setting. Also, the term *other professionals* only refers to professionals whose role is to support a child in a particular area of development, such as a physiotherapist or health visitor. It does not include the other professionals you could invite into your setting to promote children's understanding of the wider community, such as a dentist, fire fighters or the police.

Think about the range of professionals you engage with, such as health visitors, area SENCOs, GPs, and speech and language therapists, and consider how you can evidence the ways in which you share information with them. These can include the occasions where you engage with parents and/or other professionals, such as at IEP or CAF meetings and meetings to discuss any concerns raised in the two-year-old progress check or the EYFSP.

As it is usually parents who take their children to sessions with external professionals, such as for speech therapy or investigations at the hospital, think about how you can share information with the other professional and provide evidence of this.

'Engage effectively' with parents and other professionals

You must evidence how you *engage effectively* with parents and other professionals. Record all the ways you do this, and use this list to help you identify how you can evidence that this communication is regular and effective.

This evidence can include records of meetings, emails where information is shared, a completed CAF form, written records of ongoing communication with a health care professional, letters from the hospital or shared reports and programmes to support the child's development.

As 6.2 asks you to evidence that you *engage effectively* with parents and wider professionals, you must evidence the stages of your involvement in detail so that you can reflect on whether this was, in fact, effective. If can identify what the signs of effective engagement are, then you can review your evidence and ensure that you highlight what made your engagement effective.

'On-going assessment and provision for each child'

In 6.2 you are asked to use your engagement with parents and other professionals to support the *on-going assessment and provision for each child.* You must evidence the purpose of this engagement and make sure that you demonstrate how it supports your planning and provision for the child.

If you have worked alongside the area SENCO to develop an IEP for the child and have shared this with colleagues who work with the child, then this is appropriate evidence for 6.2. If a parent meets with a professional, such as a physiotherapist or speech therapist, you must evidence how you communicate with them to share their report and recommended goals and strategies with you and that you put the recommendations into practice.

Similarities and differences: 'working with other professionals' in 5.5, 6.2, 8.3 and 8.6

Standard 6.2 is one of four indicators that ask you to evidence your work with wider professionals to support a child's learning and development. This emphasis on the importance of professionals working together has become a governmental priority as a result of the inquiries into the deaths of Victoria Climbié and Baby P (Laming, 2003, 2009) that identified that agencies failed to work together. Procedures were set in place to ensure that in the future professionals would work together and share information and this is reflected in this emphasis on working with other professionals within the Standards.

You must evidence how you *engage effectively with parents and/or carers and other professionals in the on-going assessment and provision for each child*. Some of your evidence may be cross-referenced to 5.5, where you demonstrate how you *know when a child is in need of additional support and how this can be accessed, working in partnership with parents and/or carers and other professionals*.

There are two other indicators that relate to working with other professionals and these are 8.3 and 8.6. There are significant differences between these and 6.2, as in 8.3 you are asked to demonstrate how you ensure that your colleagues work effectively with parents and other professionals and in 8.6 you need to evidence that you understand and contribute to multi-agency team working.

Similarities and differences: working with parents in 2.7, 4.3, 6.2, 6.3, 5.5 and 8.3

Standard 6.2 is one of a group of indicators that ask you to evidence your work with parents. The first indicator is 2.7, where you are asked to understand the important influence of parents/carers and engage with them to support their child's development. Standard 6.2 also looks at how you engage with parents to support their child's development, but its focus is narrower as it looks at how you work with parents and other professionals to assess and plan provision for a child and the specific procedures you follow when supporting a child with additional needs.

In 2.7 you will have evidenced your ongoing communication with parents, sharing feedback and information on the development of their child, formally and informally, through reports, parents' evenings and daily conversations at the end of the day. You can cross-reference this evidence to 6.2, but in 6.2 your evidence needs to relate to your work with parents and other professionals to support a child with SEN or a disability.

There are similarities between 2.7 and 6.2 and another indicator, 5.5, where you are asked to demonstrate how you work with parents and other professionals when a child is in need of additional support. You may find that this can overlap with your evidence for 6.3, where you share feedback with parents to help children *progress towards their goals*.

Standard 4.3 relates to working with parents, but within a different context as you are asked to work in partnership with parents to *Promote a love of learning and stimulate children's intellectual curiosity*. Your evidence of working in partnership with parents for 8.3 may overlap with your evidence for 6.2, as in 8.3 you need to evidence how you foster *a culture of co-operative working between colleagues, parents and/or carers and other professionals*.

Evidence for 6.2

Your evidence for 6.2 needs to address several areas of practice, and these include:

- that you *engage effectively* with parents and the other professionals who support a child: you need to identify the parents and professionals you have worked with and demonstrate how or why this engagement was effective;

- how you keep in regular contact with other professionals so as to share information and act on their recommendations for the child;

- your role in the process of ongoing assessment and provision for the child, for example, using a report from another professional to plan goals for a child;

- your ongoing communication with the parents to discuss, decide on and revise appropriate goals for their child.

Evidence checklist for 6.2

Table S6.1 will help you collate and evaluate your evidence for 6.2. Use it to record examples of your practice and identify where you have any gaps. When you have a list of appropriate examples, think about where you can find the evidence, identify what you can do to address your gaps and evaluate the effectiveness of the communication you are evidencing.

One example has been added to Table S6.1 to give you some ideas.

Written assignments, case studies and your reflective journal

In a written assignment or case study you can present a detailed analysis of your work with a child with SEN or a disability and evidence your work with the child's parents and the wider professionals involved with the child. You can reflect on your

Table S6.1 Evidence checklist for 6.2

Examples of engaging with parents	Examples of engaging with wider professionals	Evidence of engagement with parents and other professionals	Evidence of engaging in ongoing assessment and provision	Evidence that engagement was 'effective'
Meetings with parents of 'A' to support them and share strategies after GP identified child 'A's hearing loss: three formal meetings, regular informal conversations at end of day and use of home link book	Contact with GP and SLT via email and phone call and invitation to SLT to visit setting and address the team to share strategies	Letter from GP, emails to and from SLT and notes made from phone call Minutes of meetings with parents, entries in home link book	Report from SLT suggesting strategies Minutes of staff meeting where SLT shared these strategies with colleagues Minutes of meeting with parents to discuss strategies Strategies added to profile book and planning sheets	Contact with GP and SLT resulted in changes to goals set for 'A' and to environment to reduce background noise. Introduction of some Makaton signs Profile book has evidence of A's increasing progress

GP, general practitioner; SLT, speech and language therapist.

engagement with the parents and professionals in detail and highlight your role in the ongoing assessment and provision for the child within your setting.

You may also be able to describe how you made adjustments to daily routines and care routines for the child or adapted the environment to support the child, for example, by introducing soft furnishings to reduce noise levels to support a child with hearing loss.

Document portfolio

In your document portfolio you could include:

- emails and/or letters between you and other professionals or parents;
- entries in profile book and home link books;
- a completed CAF form;
- reports from other professionals that you place alongside an IEP that you developed in response to the report.

Remember, in each document you need to highlight your contribution and documents need to be carefully anonymised.

Observations

You could arrange to be observed with parents to discuss their child's progress and revise their goals, with reference to their IEP and the report from a professional (ensure that the parent understands what will be involved in the observation and agrees to this).

Show your mentor or tutor records of your communication with parents and other professionals and evidence of your ongoing assessment and appropriate provision for the child. This could involve showing them copies of the report from a professional and the IEP that you devised, based on the suggestions from the report.

SUGGESTED READING

Gasper, M (2012) *Multi-agency Working in the Early Years: Challenges and Opportunities*. London: SAGE.

Roffey, S and Parry, J (2001) *Special Needs in the Early Years: Collaboration, Communication and Coordination*. London: David Fulton.

Siraj-Blatchford, I, Clarke, K and Needham, M (2007) *The Team Around the Child: Multi-agency Working in the Early Years*. London: IOE.

Tassoni, P (2003) *Supporting Special Needs: Understanding Inclusion in the Early Years*. Oxford: Heinemann.

Ward, U (2013) *Working with Parents in the Early Years*. London: SAGE.

Standard 6.3: Give regular feedback to children and parents and/or carers to help children progress towards their goals

Introduction

Standard 6.3 is about the quality, regularity and purpose of the feedback that you share with children and their parents/carers. You must demonstrate that you share feedback regularly and evidence how the process of sharing feedback actually helps a child to progress.

The wording in 6.3 gives you several pointers that can help you understand what to evidence. The feedback you give must be *regular*, so you need to evidence that this is an ongoing process and why this is important. Your feedback must help children *progress*, therefore you need to think about how your feedback helps children move towards their goals and what it is that makes your feedback effective.

You must give feedback to *children and parents and/or carers*, so think about how you share feedback with parents and other carers, where appropriate, and the methods you use to share feedback with the children themselves.

You have to use feedback to help children progress *towards their goals*. So your feedback needs to be specific enough to relate to the goals that have been identified for a child. You need to demonstrate that you keep these goals in mind when you are working with a child. If you can't remember a child's individual goals you cannot help him to work towards them effectively or give specific enough feedback and praise.

Sharing feedback with children

Throughout EYFS there is an emphasis on children as active partners in their own learning and this is relevant in 6.3, as children can be encouraged to identify their own goals, evaluate their progress themselves and make decisions as to their next steps. Your role in this is to help children identify what they have achieved and what they want to achieve next, and you can do this through the positive feedback you provide.

Think about the quality of your feedback when you share feedback with children and how you encourage them to evaluate their progress for themselves. You might find it helpful to identify the qualities of effective feedback and then evaluate the quality of your own feedback so that you can evidence how your feedback does help children *progress towards their goals.*

Consider how your praise and detailed feedback help children move towards their goals and encourage them to set their own goals. Identify ways to involve children in giving feedback on their own progress and, on some occasions, on activities within the setting.

There are many ways in which you can involve children in evaluating their own progress. For example, you can look together at photos from when they were younger and at entries in their profile book and ask them about what they can do now that they couldn't do then. You can also involve children in evaluating the day's activities. Although this involves evaluating activities rather than their own progress, this helps children to develop these skills. Some practitioners give children stickers with happy and sad faces and ask them to stick them on to the activities they most liked and didn't like.

Giving praise

To strengthen your evidence for 6.3, demonstrate how you give praise and understand what makes praise effective. General praise has been shown to be less effective than specific praise (Burke and Herron, 1996) because it does not give children enough information to help them understand what they have done well and why.

Compare these two statements and consider which will best help children identify their next steps:

> *You are such a good boy today!*

> *I love the way that you shared the blue bike with Peter today. When you had finished your turn, you took the bike over to him and said, 'your turn!' Do you remember how hard it was for you to share the bike last week? And this week you shared it with Peter!*

Sharing feedback with parents and/or carers

You must evidence how you share regular feedback with parents and/or carers to help children to progress towards their goals. You need to share these goals with the child's parents/carers, and, if possible, make decisions about goals and next steps with them. You may have evidence of this process if you have worked with parents to develop an IEP for their child.

Demonstrate that sharing feedback is a two-way process, that you set up systems whereby parents can share their observations of their child's progress with you, whether through daily conversations, joint entries in profile books or a home link book.

You may have evidence of sharing feedback on a daily basis, such as at the end of each day, or of more formal systems, such as termly reports or parents' evenings, as well as the two-year-old progress check and EYFSP which need to be shared with parents.

Evidence for 6.3

Evidence for 6.3 needs to be detailed. You need to record an almost verbatim account of a conversation with a child or parent where you have given feedback. If your account is not detailed, it will not be possible to judge whether your feedback was specific and appropriate and promoted the child's progress, as in the second example in the section on giving praise, above.

You must identify what makes your feedback effective so as to evidence how this feedback helped a child progress towards her goals. If you can identify what the qualities of effective feedback are, you will be able to highlight these qualities in your evidence. You may find it helpful to use your reflective journal to help you evaluate the quality of your feedback and record examples as they occur. You can then add these reflections to your document portfolio or quote from them in a written assignment or case study.

Remember, feedback needs to be regular, so you need to provide examples of giving feedback on more than one occasion. You also need evidence of giving praise that is specific and relates to the goals for that child. Your evidence must demonstrate your role in involving the child as an active partner in this process, helping children to identify where they have made progress and where they want to progress to.

Written assignments, case studies and your reflective journal

You can use a written assignment or case study to describe feedback you gave that was regular, specific, related to the child's goals and of high quality. You can provide several examples to make sure that you have enough good evidence, and if you can, provide examples relating to children of different ages. If you have chosen to write a case study about an individual child, this will provide opportunities for you to record the feedback you gave and demonstrate how you used feedback to promote that child's development.

Document portfolio

In your document portfolio you can include:

- examples of conversations with children that you have transcribed or that have been recorded in a peer observation and highlight where there is evidence of you giving praise and feedback;

- minutes of staff meetings;

- handouts from training sessions where you led staff development on giving positive feedback, as long as you clearly relate this to 6.3;

- records of sharing feedback with parents, such as records of conversations with parents, excerpts from home link books and an IEP or completed CAF form. Remember to check that these include very clear evidence of your role in sharing feedback.

Amy and Louie

Amy, an Early Years Teacher trainee, asked her mentor, Marjorie, to observe her with her key child, Louie (three years), when she shared feedback on Louie's progress with his father on the one morning each week when he drops Louie off and later in the day when she had arranged to spend time with Louie looking through some photos of him that Amy had taken during an outing to a nature reserve.

Marjorie was able to record that:

> *Louie pointed to himself in a photo, standing by the duck pond, and Amy said, 'yes, you were looking at the ducks. Do you remember what you did next?' Louie nodded and said 'bread'. Amy agreed, 'yes, you remembered that ducks like to eat bread and you were able to find some bread in the rucksack. Then you broke it up into tiny pieces to give to the ducks. You said that the ducks were only tiny so needed tiny pieces of bread.'*

> *Amy then followed Louie's lead in discussing what he wanted to do on the next outing to the nature reserve. He wanted to feed the fish, but did not know what they would like to eat. Amy encouraged him to find some books in the book corner to help them find out what fish like to eat.*

Observations

When the assessor observes you in an activity with a group of children, you can remind yourself to give feedback that is positive, regular, specific and helps children progress towards their goals. Demonstrate how you differentiate the feedback that you give according to the child's age and stage of development and how you involve children in reviewing their own progress.

You could arrange to be observed sharing feedback with a child's parents (make sure they have given informed consent, meaning that they have consented and fully understand what this would involve). You can show your mentor or tutor the profile books or photos you share with children to encourage them to identify their own progress. You can also explain any systems you introduced, such as smiley stickers, to involve children in giving feedback.

Burke, R and Herron, R (1996) *Common Sense Parenting*. Nebraska: Boys Town Press. Available online at: www.boystownpress.org (accessed 22/10/2014).

Martin, DL (1977) Your praise can smother learning. *Learning*, 5(6): 43–51.

Meyer, W (1979) Informational value of evaluative behavior: influences of social reinforcement on achievement. *Journal of Educational Psychology*, 71(2): 259–268.

Moylett, H (2014) *Characteristics of Effective Early Learning: Helping Young Children Become Learners for Life.* Berkshire: McGraw-Hill Education, Open University Press.

Tapp, A and Lively, DL (2009) Think twice before you speak: using effective praise in the early childhood and university setting Saginaw Valley State University. *Research in Higher Education Journal,* 3: May. Available online at: **www.aabri.com/manuscripts/08128.pdf** (accessed 22/10/2014).

Whalley, M (2007) *Involving Parents in their Children's Learning.* London: Paul Chapman.

Standard 7: **Safeguard and promote the welfare of children, and provide a safe learning environment**

Introduction

Standard 7 is about how you keep children safe. It asks you to demonstrate your understanding of health and safety and safeguarding requirements and how you promote children's welfare. You will evidence your understanding of legal requirements, guidance, policies and procedures and show how this informs your practice in relation to health and safety, safeguarding and promoting children's welfare.

There are two points to bear in mind:

1. You need to evidence your knowledge and understanding of legal requirements, guidance, policies and procedures and then demonstrate how each of these informs your practice.

2. You need to be very clear about the difference between health and safety and safeguarding and understand what is meant by *promoting the welfare of children*.

Understanding key terms

The key to meeting Standard 7 is to understand each key term and plan your evidence for each in turn. As a general rule, health and safety protects children from objects and the environment, and safeguarding protects children from people. As an example, health and safety practices can include risk assessing the environment, whereas safeguarding includes safer recruitment practices.

Promoting the welfare of the child refers to practitioners' overall responsibilities for children's safety and welfare and can include health promotion activities, healthy-eating programmes, encouraging children to manage risks and following the Every Child Matters agenda and the Early Years Foundation Stage (EYFS) Safeguarding and Welfare Requirements. As it relates to protecting children from harm, there is some overlap with your evidence for safeguarding.

For guidance on how each term is used, see the National Children's Bureau factsheet *Children's Welfare and Safeguarding in the Early Years Foundation Stage* (NCB, 2010).

Similarities and differences: 7.1, 7.2 and 7.3

There are three indicators for Standard 7. The first, 7.1, asks you to evidence your understanding of legal requirements and guidance regarding health and safety, safeguarding and promoting the welfare of the child. In 7.2 you are asked to evidence your practice in relation to health and safety and in 7.3, to evidence your knowledge and practice in relation to safeguarding (Figure S7.1 highlights those areas of overlap).

So, although health and safeguarding are placed together in 7.1, they are then separated out in 7.2 and 7.3 and it is really important that you are aware of this when you reference your evidence. If you have a clear understanding of the difference between the two concepts, this should not be difficult.

Organising your evidence for Standard 7

You might find it helpful to separate out your evidence for Standard 7, so that you collate and reference your evidence in relation to health and safety requirements and practice for 7.1 and 7.2 and then separately collate and reference evidence relating to legal requirements, procedures, policy, guidance and practice for safeguarding for 7.1 and 7.3. Your evidence of promoting children's welfare needs to be referenced to 7.1, but some evidence may overlap with 7.2 and 7.3.

Promoting children's welfare

In the opening statement for Standard 7 and again in 7.1 you are asked to actively *promote the welfare of children*. Any evidence you have of following the EYFS (2014) Section 3: The Safeguarding and Welfare Requirements, promoting healthy eating and life choices and involving children in risk-assessing activities will help you evidence this.

If you look closely at the opening statement for Standard 7, you will see that you are asked to *promote the welfare of children and provide a safe learning environment*. This means that you need to consider all the ways in which you are guided by EYFS (2012) to promote children's welfare and not just the EYFS Safeguarding and Welfare Requirements (Gov.uk, 2014b).

Leadership opportunities and your evidence

You must evidence your understanding of legal requirements, policy and procedure so you need to make sure that you evidence your knowledge and understanding and the implications for practice.

Demonstrate this knowledge through your leadership actions and, if these involve training or supporting colleagues, then you can cross-reference this evidence to 8.4.

For example, if you keep up to date on changing health and safety requirements and share this with colleagues, producing handouts or delivering training on food hygiene legislation or Manual Handling Operations Regulations (1992), you are demonstrating

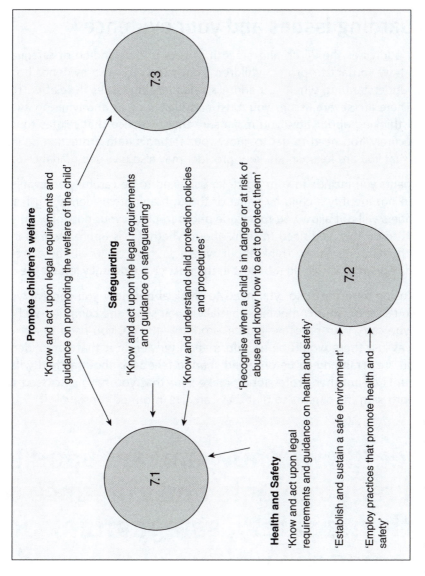

Promote children's welfare

'Know and act upon legal requirements and guidance on promoting the welfare of the child'

Safeguarding

'Know and act upon the legal requirements and guidance on safeguarding'

'Know and understand child protection policies and procedures'

'Recognise when a child is in danger or at risk of abuse and know how to act to protect them'

Health and Safety

'Know and act upon legal requirements and guidance on health and safety'

'Establish and sustain a safe environment'

'Employ practices that promote health and safety'

Figure S7.1 Overlapping areas in Standard 7

your understanding of health and safety requirements for 7.1 and evidence of leadership for 8.4.

If you deliver training on safeguarding legislation and procedures or revise your setting's safeguarding policy this can provide evidence of leadership for 8.4 and of your knowledge and understanding for 7.1 and 7.3.

Safeguarding issues and your evidence

Standard 7 addresses the depth and breadth of your understanding of safeguarding issues and how you act to protect children from harm. You can evidence how you apply this understanding when you address safeguarding issues in relation to your evidence. There are several issues you must consider, such as anonymising all documents and thinking about how you make sure that evidence that relates to a child is stored securely. You need to get to know your setting's data protection policy and make sure that you are following it. Your provider may also give you guidance on this.

Any documents you include in your portfolio will need to be carefully anonymised so that you do not identify a child by name or through any other identifying features. Many providers will not allow you to include photographs in your portfolio, but if you are allowed to do this, you need to think about whether it is appropriate to include photos with children's faces. Think about where your portfolio will be stored and what could happen to it – could it be lost in the post or accidentally left on the bus?

If you are using an e-portfolio, you need to think about how you can encrypt the evidence you save on your computer, especially if you share the computer with other people. If you carry your reflective journal around with you, you need to make sure that if it was lost there would be no information written in it that could identify a child. If you are arranging to be observed sharing feedback about a child with that child's parents or another professional, make sure that you have discussed this in enough depth with the parents so that they can give informed consent.

Standard 7.1: Know and act upon the legal requirements and guidance on health and safety, safeguarding and promoting the welfare of the child

Introduction

In 7.1 you must evidence how you protect children from harm by knowing and following legal requirements and guidance in three areas – health and safety, safeguarding and promoting children's welfare.

You must describe your knowledge of the legal requirements and guidance and demonstrate how they impact on your practice in each of the three areas. You will need a good understanding of the difference between these three areas and to identify any overlaps (Figure S7.1).

Key terms and evidence

Table S7.1 will help you identify and organise your evidence for 7.1.

Use it to list:

- your understanding of each term;
- relevant legislation and guidance;
- your practice and leadership actions;
- where you have evidence of your knowledge or actions.

Some examples have been added to help you.

Table S7.1 *Identifying knowledge and practice*

Standard 7	Knowledge, practice and leadership actions	Evidence
Health and safety	**Health and safety is:** how I protect children from the environment	
	Legislation and guidance:	My handouts for staff on food hygiene
	Food hygiene legislation, the Early Years Foundation Stage Safeguarding and Welfare Requirements	
	I have a food hygiene certificate	My risk assessment form
	My actions:	
	I designed a risk assessment form for the garden	
	I cascaded training I attended on health and safety	Mentor observation: delivering training
Safeguarding	**Safeguarding is:**	
	Legislation and guidance:	
	Our setting's safeguarding policy	Our revised safeguarding policy
	Our local authority's guidance and procedures	
	Training on signs and symptoms of abuse	Reflective journal: signs and symptoms of abuse and example of identifying my concerns
	My actions:	
	I helped revise our setting's safeguarding policy	
	I reported my concerns about a child	
Promoting the welfare of the child	**Promoting the welfare of children is:**	Completed (anonymised) Common Assessment Framework form
	Legislation and guidance:	
	Every Child Matters (ECM) outcomes	
	My actions:	Assignment that discusses promoting ECM outcomes
	I introduced healthy snacks and weekly cooking sessions and spoke to parents about healthy eating	Mentor observation and plans for cooking sessions

'Know and act'

Standard 7.1 is complex and you need to pay close attention to the wording. The phrase *know and act* lets you know that you need to evidence both your knowledge and your actions. One way to do this is to demonstrate the relationship between your knowledge and actions. You can do this when you explain why you follow certain procedures, for example, that you keep cleaning products in a locked cupboard as you adhere to COSSH (2002) regulations.

'Legislation and guidance'

You must demonstrate your knowledge of both *legal requirements* and *guidance* so you must understand the difference between the two. *Guidance* may be statutory or non-statutory and *legal requirements* include both legislation, such as the Health and Safety at Work Act (1974), and statutory guidance which is legally binding, such as *Safeguarding Children and Safer Recruitment in Education* (Department for Education, 2006).

Here is a summary of some of the key terms you need to be familiar with for Standard 7.

- Legislation: an Act that has been passed in Parliament, such as the Health and Safety at Work Act (1974).

- Policy: this includes setting policies, such as your safeguarding policy, and documents that outline Government policy, such as the 2011 policy statement *Supporting Families in the Foundation Years* (Department for Education, 2011b).

- Statutory frameworks: these detailed frameworks outline procedures practitioners must follow and are underpinned by legislation, such as the Common Assessment Framework and EYFS (2014) statutory framework.

- Statutory guidance: Government guidance can be statutory or non-statutory. Statutory guidance has legal force and settings and local authorities must follow this guidance unless they can show they are doing something as good or better. One example is *Working Together to Safeguard Children* (Department for Education, 2013b).

- Non-statutory guidance: this includes recommendations on good practice that have no legal force, so settings can choose whether or not to apply them. However, there can be an expectation that a setting will follow the guidance. *Early Years Outcomes: A Non-statutory Guide for Practitioners and Inspectors to Help Inform Understanding of Child Development Through the Early Years* (Department of Health, 2013c) is an example of non-statutory guidance that Ofsted expects providers to follow.

The **www.gov.uk/government/collections/early-learning-and-childcare-guidance-for-early-years-providers** website provides examples of statutory and non-statutory guidance and frameworks that you can refer to in your evidence.

Identifying legal requirements and guidance

In 7.1 you need to identify legal requirements and guidance relating to health and safety, safeguarding and promoting children's welfare so it may be helpful to identify your knowledge and understanding of each area in turn.

One key document you need to refer to is EYFS (2014), section three on Safeguarding and Welfare Requirements, as this relates to all three areas. You could, for example, refer to the section on suitable people to explain the rationale for the procedures you follow in relation to safeguarding. You could then describe how you carry out the requirements of 'safety and suitability of premises, environment and equipment' to promote health and safety practices and refer to the sections on 'food and drink' and 'managing behaviour' as a rationale for your actions to promote children's welfare.

You will find some overlaps between each area. For example, it is clear that following correct procedures when reporting an accident is a health and safety issue. However, when you record what a parent tells you about an accident a child had at home, you may also be following safeguarding procedures.

You must evidence your wider knowledge of the national legislation and guidance you comply with. In relation to health and safety you could show how you adhere to food hygiene regulations (**www.food.gov.uk/enforcement/regulation**), the Health and Safety at Work Act (1974), Manual Handling Regulations (1992), Control of Substances Hazardous to Health (COSHH) (Amendment) Regulations (2004), fire safety in the workplace regulations (**www.gov.uk/workplace-fire-safety-your-responsibilities**) and portable appliance testing (PAT) requirements (**www.pat-testing.co.uk/legal**). Every Child Matters Outcomes (Department for Education and Skills, 2003a) also relate to keeping children healthy and safe.

To evidence your understanding of safeguarding legislation you could reflect on the implications for practice in the Children Act (2004), The Childcare Act (2006), *Working Together to Safeguard Children* (2013) and the role of the Disclosure and Barring Service (DBS). You must demonstrate an excellent working knowledge of your setting's policy and procedures and local arrangements regarding safeguarding and this will also help you evidence 7.3.

Local authorities publish relevant guidance and you need to find out what local guidance is available. For example, the Welsh Government has published comprehensive guidance on preventing child sexual exploitation and the roles and responsibilities of professional organisations such as Local Safeguarding Children Boards, and education services and voluntary groups.

You must consider legislation and guidance that relate to promoting children's welfare, such as local initiatives or healthy-living programmes and the Every Child Matters Outcomes. The section on planning your evidence for 7.2, below, will help you identify additional examples.

Promoting children's welfare

In recent years a range of policy documents and legislation has been introduced to promote children's welfare and some of these are listed below.

You can use your journal to reflect on their implications for practice. This will help you evidence how you *know and act upon the legal requirements and guidance on … promoting the welfare of the child* for 7.1.

- *Improving the Quality and Range of Education and Childcare from Birth to 5 Years* (Department for Education et al., 2013)

- *More Great Childcare* (Department for Education, 2013a)

- *Foundations for Quality* (Department for Education, 2012b)

- *Early Intervention: The Next Steps* (Allen, 2011)

- EYFS (Department for Education and Skills, 2007a; Department for Education, 2014)

- *Common Assessment Framework* (Department for Education and Skills, 2007b)

- *The Children's Plan: Building Brighter Futures* (Department for Children, Schools and Families, 2007)

- The Childcare Act 2006

- Children Act 2004

- Every Child Matters (Department for Education and Skills, 2003a)

- *The Victoria Climbié Inquiry* (Laming, 2003)

- The SEN Code of Practice (Department for Education and Skills, 2001; Department for Education and for Health, 2014)

Evidence for 7.1

You must evidence your knowledge of legal requirements and guidance and how you apply this knowledge. Think about how you can best evidence this and, perhaps, consider whether one piece of evidence can cover both aspects.

Written assignments and your reflective diary

The advantage of using a written assignment or journal entry is that you can make explicit links between your knowledge and actions and describe both in detail.

For example, you could use a short written assignment or reflection to describe a safeguarding incident where you acted to protect a child from harm (for 7.3) and refer to the legislation and procedures you followed (for 7.1).

Document portfolio

You can evidence both your knowledge and actions in your portfolio by including work products if you highlight the legal requirements and guidance you were adhering to.

- You could include a risk assessment form or a health and safety policy you devised if you identify the requirements you were following.

- You can use your planning notes to outline the health and safety procedures you follow when preparing an activity such as cooking and highlight the food hygiene regulation you were following.

- If you are describing snack time you could evidence how you promote the 'stay healthy' outcome for Every Child Matters or local healthy-eating initiatives.

- You can also evidence your knowledge of legislation and statutory and non-statutory guidance in detail if you have produced handouts or information leaflets for colleagues that refer to specific requirements, such as Manual Handling Regulations (2002) or evacuation procedures.

Observations

Your tutor or mentor will observe your practice and will be able to evidence any references you make to legislation and guidance in your activities or planning notes for the session.

The activity plans can highlight all the health and safety procedures you follow and explain why you do this. Evidence of following health and safety procedures is evidence for 7.2, but if you describe how legislation informs your practice, then it also provides evidence for 7.1. For example, you can describe how you provide disposable gloves and aprons in accordance with the Health and Safety at Work Act 1974 or your plan ratios for an outing in line with EYFS requirements.

You could be observed:

- leading a fire drill;

- completing a risk assessment.

(Use your planning notes to identify the requirements for these actions.)

You could:

- provide evidence of promoting Every Child Matters outcomes when you are observed introducing healthy ingredients in a cooking activity or taking part in a local healthy eating initiative, or when you provide information for parents on promoting children's well-being;

- arrange to be observed delivering training to a colleague or student on safeguarding or health and safety legal requirements and guidance and the implications of these for practice.

ONLINE RESOURCES

Every Child Matters Outcomes: **http://webarchive.nationalarchives.gov. uk/20100406141748/dcsf.gov.uk/everychildmatters**

Framework for the Regulation of Provision on the Early Years Register: **www.ofsted.gov.uk/ resources/framework-for-regulation-of-provision-early-years-register**

Health and Safety Legislation: **www.atl.org.uk/health-and-safety/legal-framework/health-safety-legislation.asp**

Health and Safety Legislation for the Early Years: **www.devon.gov.uk/index/cyps/early_years_and_childcare/zero14plus/docbank/healthsafety.htm**

Health and Safety Practice in Early Years Settings: **http://resources.collins.co.uk/free/BTECNationalCPLDF.pdf**

Safe Early Years Environments: **www.pre-school.org.uk/document/225**

Standard 7.2: Establish and sustain a safe environment and employ practices that promote children's health and safety

Introduction

In Standard 7.2 you must evidence your practice in relation to health and safety. This includes all the routine health and safety practices you follow every day as well as any new practices you introduce. You must ensure that the environment is safe, for children and adults, and you engage in practices that promote children's health and safety.

'Establish and sustain'

You must *establish and sustain a safe environment*. You must evidence how you *established* or instituted practices to promote a safe environment, such as introducing risk assessments for outings. You must also evidence how you *sustain* a safe environment, for example, by ensuring that all practitioners understand how to fill out the new risk assessment form and use it regularly. Another example might be that you *establish* a safe environment when you create a list of children with allergies, and you *sustain* it when you regularly check that this list is kept up to date.

'Employ practices': identifying your evidence

Identify what it is that you do when you *employ practices that promote children's health and safety*. Make a list of all the practices you engage in to promote health and safety and then use this list to help you plan your evidence for 7.2. This might include routine activities such as completing risk assessments, checking allergy lists and wearing gloves when changing nappies.

If you are a manager, the practices you employ to promote children's health and safety may differ. These could include having responsibility for fire drills, organising PAT testing and ensuring adequate staffing to adhere to ratios.

You can then divide this list into areas you can evidence in written assignments or your reflective journal, work products to evidence in your portfolio and routine practices your mentor or tutor can observe you carrying out.

Planning your evidence for 7.2

Table S7.2 will help you to identify and organise your evidence for 7.2. Identify examples of your practice that relate to establishing and sustaining safe practices and identify where you may have evidence of this.

Table S7.2 *Evidence for 7.2*

Establish safe practices	Evidence	Sustain safe practices	Evidence
Introduce shoe covers in baby room	Letter to parents in portfolio	Use gloves and aprons when changing nappies	Mentor observation
Introduce risk assessments for outings	Portfolio	Ensuring that visitors sign in	Mentor observation
Train staff in using new risk assessment forms	Mentor observation	Make sure agency staff are aware of the lists and photos of children with allergies	Mentor observation

Comparing 7.1 and 7.2

In 7.1 you were asked to *act upon the legal requirements and guidance on health and safety,* so it can be helpful to reflect on the difference between this and what is required in 7.2, where you evidence how you *establish ... a safe environment.*

You may find an overlap between your health and safety evidence for 7.1 and 7.2, but you may need to emphasise certain aspects of the evidence differently for each indicator. For example, in your evidence for 7.1 you will explain that you are carrying out a risk assessment as you follow the EYFS Safeguarding and Welfare Requirements (2014). However, for 7.2 you could describe how you introduced risk assessments for outings to *establish ... a safe environment.*

Comparing 7.1 and 7.3

You need to make sure that your evidence for 7.2 relates only to health and safety and not safeguarding. You need to identify which piece of evidence relates to health and safety and which to safeguarding and it is not always obvious.

For example, activities to protect a child from harm by another person, such as ensuring DBS checks are carried out, relate to safeguarding. However, having a visitors' signing-in book can relate to both safeguarding and health and safety, depending on the context. It relates to safeguarding when you are monitoring who has access to the setting, but health and safety when you use it to check the building is evacuated during a fire or fire drill.

Evidence for 7.2

Organising your evidence

You must evidence both how you set up new practices and systems to promote health and safety and how you follow routine health and safety procedures as set out in your health and safety policy and the EYFS Safeguarding and Welfare Requirements (2014).

As health and safety is such a priority in early years, you will have plenty of evidence for 7.2, so you need to decide which evidence to include and where and you will have started to do this in the section on planning your evidence, above.

Written assignments and your journal

Written assignments and journal entries enable you to evidence changes you have introduced and present your rationale and this can include any changes to health and safety practices you have introduced.

- You could use assignment to describe changes you introduced in the environment in your evidence for Standard 8 and you can include a reference to any health and safety procedures you introduced.

- You could use a written assignment, journal entry or a document in your portfolio to describe how you developed a garden area for babies and include a rationale for the health and safety practices you introduced.

- You could reflect on how you introduced a new risk assessment form and delivered training on health and safety issues outdoors to evidence how you *establish ... safe practices*. You could then describe how you encourage staff to complete the risk assessment form every morning to evidence how you *sustain* safe practices.

- You could use your written assignments, journal entries and planning documents to record any health and safety procedures you follow when you engage in an activity, such as cooking or an outing.

Document portfolio

You can include a significant amount of evidence of establishing and sustaining a safe environment in documents in your portfolio, but you need to make sure that you don't repeat evidence or include too much on 7.2 at the expense of other Standards.

You could include:

- completed medicine forms;
- accident report forms;
- lists of children with allergies;
- completed fire drill forms.

Do not include any blank pro formas, even if you designed them yourself. Forms only count as evidence if you can show that you have completed or contributed to them, so make sure each form you include has your signature on it.

Observations

When your tutor or mentor observes your practice s/he will have plenty of opportunities to observe how you follow and establish health and safety procedures. Again, you need to organise your evidence and make sure that you are observed following a wide range of health and safety procedures. Plan each observation so that you present a good cross-section of your practice, and don't over-evidence one area at the expense of another.

You don't need to be observed carrying out a risk assessment more than once, but you do want to show how you ensure that visitors sign in when they arrive, that safety gates are closed, that you adhere to ratios, store chemicals in a locked cupboard and follow food hygiene regulations. You can also demonstrate any new systems you introduced, such as risk assessments for the baby garden area.

When you are observed engaging in an activity with children, your plans for the session can highlight the health and safety procedures you will follow and why. For example, if you are leading a cooking activity you may write about how you checked whether any children had allergies. You can also focus on health and safety during the activity, for example, supporting children to engage in their own risk assessment for a new activity or monitoring them carefully when they use a knife.

Green, S and Hughes, C (2008) *Protection, Safety and Welfare for the Early Years.* Dulwich: Step Forward Publishing.

Parker, L (2012) *The Early Years Health and Safety Handbook.* Oxon: Routledge.

Parker, L (2013) *How to do a Health and Safety Audit.* (Health and Safety for Early Years Settings) Chiswick: David Fulton.

Standard 7.3: Know and understand child protection policies and procedures, recognise when a child is in danger or at risk of abuse, and know how to act to protect them

Introduction

In 7.3 you must evidence your knowledge and understanding and your practice in relation to safeguarding, addressing each of three requirements, that you:

1. know and understand child protection policies and procedures;

2. recognise when a child is in danger or at risk of abuse;

3. know how to act to protect them.

In 7.1 you will evidence your knowledge of legislation and guidance relating to safeguarding and in 7.3 you will evidence your knowledge and understanding of child protection policies and procedures.

Safeguarding and child protection

In 7.1 the Standards refer to *safeguarding* and in 7.3 to *child protection*. Be aware of the difference between these terms as this will have an impact on the evidence you choose for each indicator.

Child protection is the term traditionally used to describe the actions you take to protect a child from possible abuse or exploitation.

Safeguarding includes child protection, but has a wider meaning. It refers to everything you do to protect children from harm and actively promote their welfare and relates to the Every Child Matters agenda. You must address this broader meaning in your evidence for 7.1, but focus solely on child protection for 7.3.

For further information on safeguarding and child protection see **www.education. gov.uk**, **www.safeguardingchildren.co.uk/** and **http://en.wikipedia.org/wiki/Child_ safeguarding**.

Child protection policies and procedures: your evidence

You must evidence your knowledge of the child protection policies and procedures in your setting and there are several ways in which you can do this, by:

- reflecting on policy and procedure in your journal;
- reviewing your setting's policy;
- recording your knowledge and understanding in a written assignment on safeguarding;
- demonstrating that the actions you took when you identified a safeguarding concern were in accordance with your setting's policy and procedures;
- work documents recording how you followed setting safeguarding procedures, such as anonymised reports;
- handouts and other records from delivering training for colleagues on safeguarding policy and procedures.

Identifying a concern

You must evidence a time when you recognised that a child was *in danger or at risk of abuse* and acted (or knew how to act) to protect that child. You must identify a specific situation where you had a safeguarding concern and followed the correct reporting and recording procedures. If you are a manager or safeguarding officer, your responsibilities will extend further and you can evidence this.

If you feel you do not have this experience, remember that all you are asked to do is identify a concern and report it appropriately. It doesn't matter whether you later discover the cause of your concern did not relate to safeguarding.

For example, if you recorded that a child regularly arrived on Monday morning in the same, unwashed clothes she had worn on Friday, then this is appropriate evidence of identifying a concern. You may later discover this was not a child protection issue, perhaps that the child's mother has been unwell throughout her pregnancy. This would still provide good evidence for 7.3 as long as you noted your concern and acted appropriately.

Another example might be that you reported your concern that a child whose parents have separated has become reluctant to leave on the Fridays when he stays with his father. You might later find out that this was because the child was unhappy that his father had a new girlfriend. What 7.3 asks you to do is identify your concern and follow it up according to policy and procedures, so this example would provide good evidence for 7.3, even though on investigation this turned out not to be a safeguarding situation. You can evidence any situation where you suspect that a child is at risk of abuse. This includes emotional abuse and neglect, as well as physical or sexual abuse.

Know how to act to protect a child

You must demonstrate an incident from your own practice where you acted to protect a child who you identified might be at risk. You may be able to evidence a range of situations, for example, where a child made a disclosure and you responded appropriately or a case where you suspected neglect and reported your concerns. You must show that you know how to respond appropriately and record and report your concerns according to your setting's policy and procedures.

If you do not have any evidence of identifying and acting on a concern, then 7.3 gives you the option of providing hypothetical evidence. You must demonstrate that you *know how to act to protect* a child in a range of hypothetical situations.

Evidence for 7.3

Your evidence for 7.3 needs to address each of these three key areas:

1. your knowledge and understanding of child protection policies and procedures;

2. an example of a situation where you identified a child may be at risk;

3. a description of how you acted to protect that child from harm.

You will find you can use a range of sources of evidence for 7.3 and here are some suggestions.

Safeguarding and your evidence

You need to ensure that the evidence you submit for your Early Years Teacher Status is appropriately stored and anonymised. Follow guidance from your provider and your setting's data protection policy, especially if you are storing your evidence on a computer that you share with your colleagues or family. Anonymise your evidence so that no individual children can be identified, for example, in a completed Common Assessment Framework form or individual education plan. You might also want to make an informed decision about using photographs, if your provider permits you to include these, and seek parents' permission for sharing materials about their child when appropriate.

Written assignments and your reflective journal

A short written assignment or journal entry would enable you to outline your knowledge and understanding of safeguarding policy and procedures, how you identified that a child may be at risk and how you acted to protect them.

If you lead training on safeguarding this will evidence your knowledge and understanding and you can use an assignment or journal entry to describe and reflect on this.

Document portfolio

You can include a range of evidence in your document portfolio (any evidence relating to a specific child must be anonymised). You can include:

- records of concerns you have identified and notes from meetings and case conferences;

- leaflets you have created for parents and colleagues on safeguarding procedures (especially if they include case studies that demonstrate your understanding of how to act to protect a child);

- records of promoting safer recruiting procedures can be included, if your role in promoting these is clear;

- a review of your setting's safeguarding policy suggesting any necessary changes (you can highlight the changes you introduced and why this will provide evidence of your knowledge and understanding);

- evidence of training you delivered on safeguarding (include information on legislation and guidance, so you can cross-reference this to 7.1).

Observations

If you lead training or mentor a colleague on safeguarding or review the safeguarding policy then you can arrange to be observed doing this to highlight your knowledge and understanding of policy and procedure.

Leadership opportunities

If you are not familiar with all aspects in your setting's safeguarding policy and procedures, then it is very likely that your colleagues are not either, so 7.3 can provide you with an opportunity to demonstrate leadership.

You may be able to identify gaps in your colleagues' understanding and lead a training session or support them individually to address these gaps. You could focus on recognising signs and symptoms of abuse, different types of abuse or how to respond to a disclosure and record and report your concerns.

You might feel you need to lead a training session on the impact of domestic violence and why this is now categorised as child abuse following on from a discussion of a situation your key child is experiencing.

CASE STUDY

Leading a professional discussion

Maria has been asked to lead a half-hour staff continuing professional development session on safeguarding, but is unsure what to focus on in such a short session.

She decided to use the time to promote a professional discussion by asking her team to explore four questions. She would then use her journal to reflect on the experience and to evidence her understanding and practice for 7.3.

The four questions she chose to ask were:

1. *Can you tell me about the legal requirements and guidance relating to safeguarding? What procedures does our policy promote?*

2. *Can you outline the procedures you will follow if you suspect a child is at risk of harm? If a child makes a disclosure?*

3. *Can you outline the actions you will take if a parent makes an allegation against a member of staff? How can you protect yourself against allegations of abuse?*

4. *What makes a child more vulnerable to abuse?*

Online resources

Safeguarding policy documents are available through the www.gov.uk website at **www.gov.uk/government/collections/safeguarding-children** and include:

- *Improving Safeguarding for Looked-after Children: Changes to the Care Planning, Placement and Case Review (England) Regulations* (2014)

- *Working Together to Safeguard Children* (2013)

- *Safeguarding Children and Safer Recruitment* (2013)

- *Working Together to Safeguard Children: Equality Analysis* (2013)

- *Forced Marriage* (2014)

- *Safeguarding Children Statistics: The Availability and Comparability of Data in the UK* (2011)

- *Safeguarding Disabled Children: Practice Guidance* (2009)

Information on the disclosure and barring service can be found at: **www.gov.uk/ government/organisations/disclosure-and-barring-service.**

SUGGESTED READING

Katz, A (2012) *Cyberbullying and E-safety: What Educators and Other Professionals Need to Know*. London: Jessica Kingsley.

Lindon, J (2012) *Safeguarding and Child Protection: 0–8 Years* (4th edn): *Linking Theory and Practice*. Oxon: Hodder.

Powell, J, Uppal, EL (2012) *Safeguarding Babies and Young Children: A Guide for Early Years Professionals*. Maidenhead: OUP McGraw Hill Educations.

Pre-school Learning Alliance (2013) *Safeguarding Children* (2nd edn). London: Pre-school Learning Alliance.

Pre-school Learning Alliance (2013) *Safeguarding through Effective Supervision*. London: Pre-school Learning Alliance.

Reid, J Burton, S (eds) (2014) *Safeguarding and Protecting Children in the Early Years*. Oxon: Routledge.

Rushford, C (2012) *Safeguarding and Child Protection in the Early Years* (Early Childhood Essentials). Herne Hill: MA Education.

Standard 8: Fulfil wider professional responsibilities

Introduction

Standard 8 addresses your role in leading practice within your setting. There is a strong emphasis on your role in supporting practitioners and this relates to the introduction of Early Years Professionals as 'agents of change'. There is an expectation that as an Early Years Teacher or Early Years Professional you will model and implement effective practice and support the professional development of your team.

The positive impact that you have on your setting is referred to in the Standards as your 'leadership' or 'leadership and support' role. It is in Standard 8 that you evidence this leadership role and your wider responsibilities in relation to several key areas. You will demonstrate that you are a reflective practitioner who evaluates the effectiveness of your provision, promotes equality of opportunity and supports the work of multi-agency teams. You will demonstrate your support for your colleagues' professional development by delivering training, reviewing policies and practice, mentoring and supporting colleagues and modelling good practice.

You must demonstrate your leadership role in relation to the specific areas outlined in indicators 8.1 to 8.7. Pay close attention to the wording in each indicator for guidance. In summary:

- In 8.1 you must promote equality of opportunity and anti-discriminatory practice.

- In 8.2 you must make a positive contribution to the wider life and ethos of the setting. This can include evidence of any changes you introduce to practice and procedures or to the environment.

- In 8.3 you must support colleagues to develop their partnerships with parents and external professionals to support a child with special needs or a disability.

- In 8.4 you must model and implement effective practice and support your colleagues in developing their practice, for example, through mentoring and modelling good practice.

- In 8.5 you must take responsibility for leading practice through supporting the professional development of your colleagues and yourself. You must identify training needs within your team and either provide the required training yourself or arrange for colleagues to attend external training.

- In 8.6 you must reflect on the effectiveness of your provision and use these reflections to inform your practice when you introduce any changes and shape and support good practice.

- In 8.7 you must demonstrate your understanding of the importance of, and how you contribute to, multi-agency team working.

Your leadership role: strengthening your evidence

Your evidence of your leadership actions and the positive contributions you make to your setting will be strengthened if you demonstrate a range of leadership methods to support your colleagues in their practice. These leadership methods can include modelling good practice, providing opportunities for a new colleague to shadow you, one-to-one coaching sessions, mentoring a student and leading professional discussions and training sessions.

You can demonstrate that you adapt your leadership style according to the needs of the situation. For example, your approach may be more authoritative in relation to a health and safety issue, but you adopt a more facilitative leadership style when encouraging a colleague to take on a new area of responsibility. You can find information on leadership styles and methods in Chapter 10, on understanding 'personal practice' and 'leadership'.

Cross-referencing your evidence

If you support a colleague in her practice in relation to a specific area, such as preparing a child to manage a transition, this will help you to evidence Standard 8 (and 8.4 in particular). However, you may also find that the support you offer helps you to evidence your knowledge and understanding for one of the other Standards, such as 5.4, which looks at supporting children through transitions.

When you find that your leadership actions demonstrate your understanding of an area within another Standard, then you can cross-reference your evidence to this Standard as well as Standard 8. For example, if you identified that your team needed further safeguarding training and led a staff training event on safeguarding legislation, policy and procedures, then you can cross-reference your evidence to 7.1 and 7.3 as well as 8.4 and 8.5.

Leadership in the early years

You may find it helpful to develop your understanding of leadership styles and methods and issues relating to leadership in the early years. There are several texts that can help you explore these issues.

O'Sullivan, J (2010) *Leadership Skills in the Early Years: Making a Difference.* London: Continuum.

Robins, A and Callan, S (2014) *Managing Early Years Settings: Supporting and Leading Teams.* London: SAGE.

Rodd, J (2005) *Leadership in Early Childhood: The Pathway to Professionalism.* Berkshire: OUP McGraw Hill-Education.

Saunders, L, Iram Siraj-Blatchford, I and Laura Manni, L (2007) *Effective Leadership in the Early Years Sector: The ELEYS study (Issues in Practice).* London: Institute of Education.

Standard 8.1: Promote equality of opportunity and anti-discriminatory practice

In Standard 8.1 you will demonstrate how you promote equality of opportunity and anti-discriminatory practice within your setting. These are two distinct areas of practice and you will evidence the strategies you use to promote both equality of opportunity and anti-discriminatory practice and review and implement good practices across your setting. You must demonstrate an understanding of both terms, appreciating that equality of opportunity and anti-discriminatory practice relate to all areas of practice, from recruitment through to children's access to learning opportunities.

You must understand what each term means and how they differ and recognise the implications for practice in the early years. As you are asked to *promote* good practice, you will need to demonstrate positive actions and strategies and highlight how these promote equality of opportunity and anti-discriminatory practice.

This chapter will help you to understand the meaning of each term and their implications for practice.

The principles of equality of opportunity and anti-discriminatory practice can be applied across all areas of practice in your setting and you need to show your understanding of the importance of addressing these issues across your provision so that the strategies are comprehensive and effective and avoid appearing tokenistic.

For example:

- You can demonstrate how you actively challenge incidents of discrimination, racism and bullying and use your understanding of anti-discriminatory practice to review setting policies and recruitment and employment practices.

- You can evidence the strategies you employ to address issues of equality of opportunity in relation to inclusion, gender, sexual orientation, age, ethnicity, religion and socio-economic status.

- You can highlight the strategies you use to create an environment that supports and respects children, families and staff and evidence the strategies you have in place to support, for example, local traveller families and looked-after children.

Leadership opportunities for 8.1

If you find it difficult to understand the difference between the terms *equality of opportunity* and *anti-discriminatory practice* and how you can apply these to your practice, then it is likely that your colleagues find this difficult, too. You could use this opportunity to lead staff development on understanding equality and diversity and encourage colleagues to reflect on their practice.

Once you have clarified your understanding of the terms *equality of opportunity* and *anti-discriminatory practice* you will be able to evaluate how well various aspects of practice provide equality of opportunity and anti-discriminatory practice. When you identify an area where there is scope for improvement, you can evidence the strategies you introduce to address this and promote good practice.

You must evidence the range of issues that you address to *promote* both equality of opportunity and anti-discriminatory practice. So, identify what good practice looks like, and show that you are taking a proactive role in moving your setting forwards. You can do this, for example, by evaluating and updating equality policies and procedures.

Cross-referencing your evidence for 8.1

If you reflect on practice in your setting and take steps to shape and support good practice, you can cross-reference your evidence for 8.1 to 8.6. If you identify that staff need additional training on equality of opportunity and anti-discriminatory practice and provide this training yourself, you can cross-reference your evidence for 8.1 to 8.4 and 8.5. If you introduce changes in practice that make a positive contribution to the life and ethos of your setting, you can cross-reference this evidence to 8.2.

Understanding equality of opportunity and anti-discriminatory practice

Standard 8.1 asks you to evidence how you promote equality of opportunity and anti-discriminatory practice. First you must check your understanding of the meaning and scope of both terms and how they relate to the early years. The following part of this chapter will support you in this.

'Equality of opportunity' and diversity – definitions and principles

To provide strong evidence for 8.1 you must appreciate the meaning of the term *equality of opportunity* and identify all the ways in which you can apply this principle to your practice. You can read the definitions and principles of equality of opportunity below and compare these to the definitions in your equality or inclusion policy.

Consider how to apply these definitions and principles, and evaluate whether your practice does consider the needs of, and provide equality of opportunity for, all children and families.

Compare the definitions of 'equality of opportunity' to the definitions of 'diversity'. Diversity is closely related to equality of opportunity so it can be helpful to appreciate how these terms relate to each other.

> *Equal opportunity is a stipulation that all people should be treated similarly, unhampered by artificial barriers or prejudices or preferences*

> **(http://en.wikipedia.org/wiki/Equal_opportunity,** quoting Paul de Vries)

Equality in the UK

Equality in the UK is about fostering and promoting the right to be different, to be free from discrimination, and to have choice and dignity and to be valued as an individual, with a right to their own beliefs and values.

Diversity

The word diverse means 'varied and different' so 'diversity' is about more than equality. It is about valuing variety and individual differences and creating a culture, environment and practices which respect and value differences for the benefit of society, organisations and individuals.

***Equality of opportunity** is the absence or removal of barriers to economic, social and political participation on the grounds of difference – for example, due to a person's gender, race or disability. It is an organisational process and culture that stems from an explicit commitment to the inclusion of all social groups, and valuing diversity.*

***Diversity** refers to the full range of individual values, attitudes, cultural perspectives, beliefs, ethnic background, sexual orientation, skills, knowledge and life experience in any given group of people.*

Taking diversity seriously means recognising that:

- *individuals have a right to their own personal value system and no one has a right to impose their value system on others*

- *the organisation must make clear what its value system is, define what is unacceptable and champion behaviour that supports its values*

> **(www.learning-work.co.uk/docs/5354_E&D2_4_7.pdf)**

What is equality and diversity?

Although sometimes used interchangeably, the terms 'equality' and 'diversity' are not the same.

***Equality** is about 'creating a fairer society, where everyone can participate and has the opportunity to fulfil their potential' (DoH, 2004) … For example … Women* *make up almost 75% of the NHS workforce but are concentrated in the lower-paid occupational areas … (DH, 2005). People from black and minority ethnic groups comprise 39.1% of hospital medical staff yet they comprise only 22.1% of all hospital medical consultants (DH, 2005) … An equalities approach understands that who we are, based on social categories such as gender, race, disability, age, social class, sexuality and religion – will impact on our life experiences.*

***Diversity** literally means difference. When it is used as a contrast or addition to equality, it is about recognising individual as well as group differences, treating people as individuals, and placing positive value on diversity in the community and in the workforce.*

Historically, employers and services have ignored certain differences such as background, personality and work style. However … one way in which organisations have responded to the issue of diversity in recent years has been the development of flexibility in working practices and services. For example, an employer may allow an employee to work a flexible working pattern to accommodate child care arrangements, or a GP practice may offer surgeries at the weekends to accommodate those who work full time during the week.

(www.faculty.londondeanery.ac.uk/e-learning/diversity-equal-opportunities-and-human-rights/what-is-equality-and-diversity)

Ask yourself the following questions and discuss them with your team:

- How do you define *equality of opportunity*?

- How do the definitions above compare to the definition of *equality of opportunity* in your equality or inclusion policy?

- Can you identify the relationship between *equality of opportunity* and 'diversity'?

- How does your setting put these principles into practice?

- What actions and strategies help you put these principles into practice?

- Can you identify any gaps in your current practice? How can you address these gaps? What actions and strategies could you introduce to address these gaps in practice?

- Can you identify your setting's value system? How does this value system promote equality of opportunity and recognise diversity? Can you identify actions you can introduce to promote this positive value system?

Your reflections on these questions will help you to evidence 8.1 and 8.6. If you discuss these questions with your team then this can contribute to your evidence for 8.1 and 8.4. If you introduce changes that make a positive contribution to the ethos of the setting, then you can cross-reference this evidence to 8.2.

Equality of opportunity in the early years

Here is an excerpt from an equality of opportunity policy for an early years class within a primary school.

Equality of opportunity requires that everyone has an equal chance to develop themselves to their full potential and be safe and free from harm. The Early Years Foundation Stage (2014) states that 'children should be treated fairly regardless of race, religion or abilities'.

Consequently, equality of opportunity implies that:

- *equality of access exists for all*

- *social inclusion exists for all*

- *life choices are widened, not restricted*

- *talents are fostered, not suppressed*

- *no one experiences disadvantage or discrimination*

- *stereotypes are challenged*

- *all forms of bullying and harassment are condemned and challenged*

- *change is managed for the benefit of all*

- *individual and community needs are responded to in a sympathetic and imaginative manner*

- *individuals and groups are allocated appropriate levels of support to ensure that their potential is fulfilled*

- *the principle of equity applies*

(Durham High School for Girls, 2013)

Use this statement, highlighting the implications of equality of opportunity for practice, to help you to:

- identify and evaluate your setting's policy and practice in relation to equality of opportunity;

- identify Early Years Foundation Stage (EYFS) requirements in relation to equality of opportunity;

- promote awareness of equality of opportunity within your team: you can facilitate a discussion on the points listed in the policy above and explore strategies to put each principle into practice.

Any notes you make when you reflect on and evaluate your practice can be used as evidence for 8.1 and 8.6. Any minutes or notes made during the meeting that highlight your contribution to a team discussion can be included as evidence for 8.1, 8.4 and 8.5.

Equality of opportunity and inclusion

A Government publication for practitioners and managers states that:

Meeting the individual needs of all children lies at the heart of the early years foundation stage (EYFS). Every child deserves the best possible start in life, and support to fulfil their potential. A child's experience in the early years has a major effect on their future life chances.

All early years providers must have and implement an effective policy for ensuring equality of opportunities and for supporting children with learning difficulties and disabilities. Practitioners should concentrate on each child's individual learning, development and care needs to make sure that the children and families with whom they work are fully included.

Providing an inclusive setting that promotes equality of opportunity does not mean that all children should be treated the same, but that the unique skills and abilities of each child should be recognised and developed.

(Gov.uk, 2009)

Ask yourself and discuss with your team:

- How does your setting's inclusion policy promote equality of opportunity?

- How does your setting's practice recognise and develop the *unique skills and abilities of each child*?

- Does your setting provide positive images of children with learning difficulties and disabilities?

Your actions and reflections on these questions can support your evidence for 8.1, 8.2, 8.4 and 8.6.

CASE STUDY

Understanding anti-discriminatory practice

Bobby, an Early Years Teacher trainee, decided that he needed to understand 'anti-discriminatory practice' in more depth. He read two definitions of anti-discriminatory practice and reflected on some questions that he had found while researching this issue (www.silkysteps.com/forum/showthread.php?t=6769) and shared them with his team to encourage them to think about anti-discriminatory practice in the setting.

> *Anti-discriminatory practice is practice designed to tackle discrimination, and describes the actions taken to prevent or curb any form discrimination against individuals, races and communities.*

> *Anti-discriminatory practice in the Early Years can be defined as an approach to working with families that promotes:*

>> - *diversity and the valuing of all difference*

>> - *self-esteem and positive group identity*

>> - *fulfilment of individual potential.*

(Working with Children in Barnet, 2014; **www.barnet.gov.uk/ WorkingWithChildrenInBarnet/info/30097/ diversity_and_anti-discriminatory_practice**)

After reading the case study above, consider:

- What does anti-discriminatory practice means to each of you personally (**www. silkysteps.com/forum/showthread.php?t=6769**)? You may, for example, have strong views on an issue, but hold these back when in a professional situation.

- 'Is there something you would like to change to make our setting more inclusive?' 'How would you make these changes?'

- Can you think of any experiences or provision that you have come across that you found helpful and that are anti-discriminatory? For example, parent and toddler car-parking spaces at the supermarket. Ask yourself, 'why were they put there?'

- Why do we have low-level tables, chairs, washing and hand-drying facilities in our setting and how is this anti-discriminatory?

- Bringing in food or other items to celebrate a special occasion helps to raise everyone's knowledge of the event, its history and the reason for celebration. Why is this anti-discriminatory?

Promoting anti-discriminatory practice

The excerpt below is from Working with Children in Barnet (2014), which provides guidance for practitioners on anti-discriminatory practice and highlights three main features.

Read the excerpts from the document below and consider the following questions:

- What are the main features of anti-discriminatory practice?

- How do these relate to practice in my own setting?

- What are any areas for improvement?

- Can I share the three features of anti-discriminatory practice with my team to facilitate an evaluation of existing practice?

> Anti-discriminatory practice can be defined as an approach to working with families that promotes:
>
> - diversity and the valuing of all difference
>
> - self-esteem and positive group identity
>
> - fulfilment of individual potential.
>
> Everyone has internalised layers of expectation based on personal upbringing and experiences that operate on a conscious and subconscious level. A key worker acknowledging the extent of the baggage that they may bring to an environment is a vital first step along the road to anti-discriminatory practice.
>
> **Putting it into practice**
>
> In terms of addressing discriminatory practice one of the functions of a key worker should be to 'work with and encourage families to address threatening, offensive

and prejudiced behaviour including domestic abuse, bullying, overtly racist, sexist or homophobic behaviour'.

It is important to note that:

- *The aim of anti-discriminatory practice is not to generate discomfort, conflict or negativity, although these feelings may be encountered along the way.*

- *Treating families the same is not the same thing as treating them equally. To treat equally it is important to recognise that society does not provide a level playing field; a variety of factors may have to be taken into account. It is important not to expect to find easy or right answers to everything.*

While some knowledge can be desirable and useful, it is counter-productive if it leads to assumptions, for example, that families from a particular culture or religion will have an identical interpretation or application of those ideas. This is a process which involves getting to know people on a personal and professional basis and avoiding pre-judgement and fixed expectations. This approach will often demand creative and individual solutions.

Appreciation of diversity encourages:

- *the exploration and valuing of differences.*

- *a readiness to develop mutual understanding that goes beyond tolerance to a broader appreciation of the varied nature of human life.*

- *acknowledgment that there is often curiosity and sometimes fear of difference that has to be surmounted through information, knowledge and a willingness to gain new understanding.*

What does anti-discriminatory practice look like in your setting (www.pre-school. org.uk/providers/inclusion)?

Use your reflections on the excerpt above to identify key features of anti-discriminatory practice and actions that promote anti-discriminatory practice. You might find it helpful to try and visualise what anti-discriminatory practice would look like in your setting.

Record your ideas in Table S8.1 as this will help you identify your evidence for 8.1. Bobby, the Early Years Teacher we met earlier in this chapter, has added some of his ideas to help you start.

Understanding equality and diversity legislation

Your setting has to comply with a range of equality and diversity legislation that promotes equality and reduces discrimination and that addresses age, sex, sexuality, disability, race or religion.

Table S8.1 *What does anti-discriminatory practice look like?*

Diversity and the valuing of all differences	Plan events to celebrate differences in identities, cultures, religions and abilities.
	Discuss how we can use these celebrations and our routine interactions with families to show that we value differences.
	Resources review: to check that they reflect differences, e.g. positive images of children and adults with disabilities
Self-esteem and positive group identity	Plan a team meeting:
	– to raise awareness of the impact of discrimination and social inequalities on children and families
	– to identify how we can show children that we value and respect their background
	– to evaluate our policies, practices and procedures to check that they do not discriminate, even unintentionally
	– to talk about how we can use activities and key times to promote children's self-esteem.
	Use circle time activities to promote a sense of belonging.
	Directly address any threatening or discriminatory behaviour
Fulfilment of individual potential	As key person I can emphasise that I value the individuality of children and families.
	I can support parents in reaching their potential, e.g. through introducing them to the adult education classes in our centre.
	I can celebrate children's achievements and share them with their parents

This legislation includes:

- Disability Discrimination Act 2005;

- Special Educational Needs and Disability Act 2001 and 2014;

- Race Relations (Amendment) Act 2000;

- Convention on the Rights of the Child (United Nations, 1989);

- Human Rights Act 1998, The Sex Discrimination Act 1975 (as amended);

- Employment Equality (Sexual Orientation) Regulations 2003;

- Equality Act 2010.

You need to ask yourself:

- How familiar are you and your team with equality legislation?

- How do your setting's policies and procedures comply with the legislation?

- How do you support your team to develop their understanding of equality legislation?

Legislation is designed to protect people from discrimination, but on its own it cannot change people's attitudes:

- What can you do to challenge discriminatory attitudes?

- How prepared are your team to challenge incidents of prejudice or discrimination?

STANDARD 8

Your responsibilities under the Equality Act 2010

The Equality Act 2010 has implications for practitioners and managers in the early years and you may find it very helpful to look at the requirements and 'protected characteristics' outlined in the Act. The 'protected characteristics' include age, disability, gender reassignment, marriage and civil partnership, pregnancy and maternity, race, religion and belief, sex and sexual orientation.

If you are a practitioner or manager you may find yourself in a situation where you need to provide information for parents or staff on their rights against discrimination on the grounds of the protected characteristics in the Equality Act. You can find information for parents on their rights under the act at **www.equalityhuman rights.com/publication/equality-act-2010-summary-guidance-services-public-functions-and-associations**.

If you are a manager you will need to understand your setting's responsibilities under the Equality Act 2010 and can find guidance in *Equality Act 2010: Summary Guidance on Services, Public Functions and Associations*.

The Preschool Learning Alliance (2011) also provides information and guidance on your responsibilities under the Act in *Guide to the Equality Act and Good Practice*. This looks at the provision of services for children and families and employment practices.

If you research your responsibilities under the Equality Act 2010 and share this information with colleagues and parents, perhaps by producing a leaflet, then this can help you to evidence 8.1.

Evaluating your setting's equality policy

You can use what you have learned so far in this chapter to help you evaluate your setting's equality and inclusion policies. You can find additional information in your local authority's guidance on equality in the early years and look online for further support and guidance, for example, by reading Suffolk County Council's *Guidance for Promoting Equalities in Early Years and Childcare* (**www.suffolk.gov. uk/assets/suffolk.gov.uk/Education%20and%20Careers/Children%20and%20 Young%20People/Early%20Years%20and%20Childcare/2012-02-02%20EYC%20 Guidance%20For%20Promoting%20Equality.pdf**).

Make sure that your policy includes definitions, principles and responsibilities, and examples of good practice that are appropriate for your setting.

The Suffolk Guidance suggests that:

> All childcare settings should have an equality policy in place to ensure their setting communicates effectively to the many different families within their local area. This policy should outline how you consider equality in every aspect of your childcare business in order to avoid discrimination. It should show your Aims, details of the Equalities Act legislation and what Methods you use to ensure equality.

An equalities policy needs to include:

- *Your statement of intent*

- *Your aim*

- *The legal framework for the policy: including details of the Equalities Act*

- *The methods you use to ensure equality:*

  Admissions

  Employment

  Training

  General issues including equality action plan.

Equality and inclusion

You must ensure that you and your team understand the relationship between inclusion and equality and implement strategies that promote them both. You may find it helpful to extend your reading on equality and inclusion, for example, by looking at the literature on promoting equality, diversity and inclusion from the Pre-school Learning Alliance (**www.pre-school.org.uk/providers/inclusion.**)

If you plan to lead a training event on equality and inclusion, you can think about drawing your colleagues' attention to the rights of children and adults to be treated equally, and check that they are all familiar with recent reforms to special educational needs provision. You must raise awareness of the relationship between inclusion and equality, and emphasise that special educational needs provision, including Early Years Action and Action Plus (**www.gov.uk/children-with-special-educational-needs/types-of-support**) and the Early Support programme (**www.gov.uk/help-for-disabled-child/early-support-programme**) form part of your approach to promoting equality.

Children's rights, equality and inclusion

Central to all equality and inclusive practices are children's rights and the Pre-school Learning Alliance's discussion of United Nations Convention on the Rights of the Child can provide a focus for a discussion on equality and inclusion in the early years (**www.pre-school.org.uk/providers/inclusion**).

The United Nations Convention on the Rights of the Child is an international human rights treaty which was adopted by the United Nations in 1989. The Convention outlines the basic human rights to which children aged up to 18 everywhere are entitled: the right to survival; the right to the development of their full physical and mental potential; the right to protection from influences that are harmful to their development; and the right to participation in family, cultural and social life. The Convention protects these rights by setting minimum standards that government must meet in providing health care, education, and legal and social services to children in their countries, although the Convention has not yet been enshrined into UK law.

A right to be included

By using the principle that inclusion is a right for all children, early years settings can make sure that every child:

- *has an equal chance to learn and develop*

- *participates equally in activities*

- *is given the opportunity to communicate in their preferred format*

- *has their individual needs known and met*

- *feels safe and know they belong*

- *is valued as a unique individual and*

- *feels strong and confident about their identity.*

Early years settings should ensure that a child's right to be included is at the heart of their practice by fully implementing the Early Years Foundation Stage framework and guidance.

For more information about equality and inclusion you can visit the Equality and Human Rights Commission website at **www.equalityhumanrights.com.** If you share this information with colleagues or reflect on what you have learnt with your colleagues, then this will help you to evidence 8.1.

CASE STUDY

Gender equality

Wendy attended a training day on equality and diversity. On her return she decided to share what she had learnt with her team so that they could develop practice in relation to gender equality and to help her evidence her practice and leadership for 8.1, 8.4 and 8.5.

She explained to the team that the training had made her think about equality and gender issues that she had not previously considered, especially whether girls and boys in the setting access all areas of learning equally.

Her team were interested in what Wendy had to say and decided to observe an area of learning each for a week to see what they could discover about gender roles and learning.

A week later the team brought their observations to the staff meeting to share. When they compared their findings they found they all agreed on the following points:

- *More boys than girls accessed the construction materials, bikes, climbing frames and football area.*

- *More girls than boys spent time in the home corner and book corner and engaging in literacy activities.*

Wendy facilitated a discussion where the team tried to identify some strategies they could adopt to address these inequalities. Each member of the team then took on one area of responsibility.

Margaret decided that she would look at images of girls and boys and men and women across the setting. She looked at images in books, posters and puzzles and identified that they needed to order resources that have more positive images of girls and boys, and of adults in non-traditional roles. Margaret then invited Robert's mother, Fran, who was a builder, to involve the children in designing and building a sand area outdoors as part of a project on building. She also invited Fraser's father, who was a male nurse, to spend some time in the setting and support play in the hospital role-play area.

Margaret created photo books of both activities so that the children would have non-traditional images of gender roles that they could relate to.

Annie decided that she would look at how the team were deployed during activities and whether this had an impact on how girls and boys accessed the activity. She set up a rota to ensure that a female member of staff was always available in the construction and football areas and around the bikes. She completed a series of observations and recorded how girls' access to these areas increased when a female member of staff was present.

Annie also observed differences in the ways girls and boys accessed construction materials. Girls tended to incorporate small-world play, so Annie suggested that small-world resources should be stored alongside the construction area.

Annie's other concern was that boys were not accessing the home corner and literacy activities. She arranged that the male member of staff, Patrick, would take on responsibility for sharing stories with the boys and asked him if he would like to review the books and literacy activities. Patrick suggested placing books about subjects the boys identified with on display and in the home corner.

Patrick also asked fathers to bring in resources from home to add to the home corner and Fraser's father brought in some car magazines and shaving foam. Patrick then began to plan a project to encourage fathers to share stories with their sons.

Heather chose to address parents' gender stereotypes as this was an issue she was facing with her key child, Ritu. Ritu's father had said that he did not want her to climb or ride bikes as these activities were not appropriate for a girl. Heather decided to create a display on how children learn through physical activities and led an open-evening discussion on learning through physical play.

Heather also created a bilingual leaflet on learning through physical play and the requirements of EYFS which she planned to share with Ritu's father. She also used this opportunity to speak to parents about children wearing appropriate clothing, as she was concerned that some girls were wearing traditional outfits and slip-on sandals that limited their ability to climb safely.

(Continued)

347

CASE STUDY *continued*

Patrick explained to the team that he felt there was a need to develop literacy activities outside to encourage boys' participation. After observing boys' interest in transport, he involved them in setting up a bus station outside, writing timetables and bus tickets together. He also provided buckets of lightly coloured water and large paint brushes that the boys could use to paint the railings and their names on the ground.

Linda asked to take on responsibility for monitoring access to the popular outdoor activities, including the bikes, football and climbing frames. She was very interested in girls' football as she coached a local girls' team. She introduced a turn-taking system using large egg timers and weekly girls'-only football sessions so that children did not need to fight for their turn. She found that all the quieter children, boys and girls, benefitted from this system.

The team decided that they would like to share what they had learnt with the play group who shared their premises. They wrote up their actions and strategies as a case study and created a checklist that the playgroup could use to evaluate their provision.

Questions in the checklist included:

- *Do you have positive, non-traditional images, for example, of girls as doctors or working in construction?*
- *Do you invite parents who work in non-traditional roles to visit the setting, such as a father who is a nurse or hairdresser?*
- *How do you how engage male members of staff to support boys' literacy?*
- *How do you resource the home corner so that it is attractive for boys?*
- *How do you monitor and support girls' access to construction, science and physical activities?*

Wendy kept records of her reflections in her journal, observations from before and after the changes, minutes of the meetings she led and the case study and questionnaire for the playgroup. This all provided evidence of her personal practice and leadership for 8.1.

CASE STUDY

Celebrating diversity

Margaret, the Early Years teacher trainee who we met in the previous case study, decided that she wanted to explore the relationship between equality and diversity to help her identify new strategies she could use to celebrate children's culture, language and backgrounds. She used her reflections on this to help her to evidence 8.1.

Margaret's journal

I can ask the parents of my key children to let me know some important words in their child's home language. I asked Ritu'd and Stephanie's parents to come in and share traditional stories and songs with the group during circle time and they seemed quite interested. Polly's and Caro's parents brought in resources from home for the role-play area and talked to me about the festivals and customs they celebrate at home.

I am reading our policy on equality and diversity and it has reminded me of several other strategies I can try out to promote equality and celebrate the diversity in a child's life.

- I can carry out a resources audit to check whether the resources in the toddler and pre-school rooms reflect the diversity of the children in our setting and provide some positive images.

- I can look out for dual-language books, books that reflect different family types and non-traditional gender roles and with positive images of children with disabilities. This is especially important for Polly and Caro. I can also look at the range of scripts and languages used in the print round the room.

- I can check whether the setting provides positive images of children and adults with disabilities and how accessible the resources and furniture are.

- I can look at our training needs and identify how well prepared staff feel they are when dealing with children with physical disabilities and learning disabilities.

- I can think about how well we support children in non-traditional families: in the resources audit I can check whether images in books, posters and puzzles reflect the reality of children's lives. For example, do we have any books that can reflect Robert's experiences living with his Mum and her girlfriend?

- I can lead training to support staff in developing sensitivity when working with non-traditional families, such as Roma families, families with same-sex parents, grandparents who are carers and looked-after children: I need to ensure that staff are aware that the environment needs to reflect these families positively.

- I can look at how we manage events like Fathers' Day and Mothers' Day so as not to exclude children who may not have a father or mother, or who have an alternative significant attachment figure. For example, I could ask Jasmine if she wants to make a card for her aunt, Jackie.

- We can extend our celebrations of children's culture and festivals and link them to other areas of learning. I can plan a project on lights, to combine science activities using torches and a shadow theatre with our celebration of Hanukkah and Diwali, both festivals of light, and our visit to see the Christmas lights in the town.

A resources audit

You can carry out a resources audit to review the resources you have and identify any gaps. You may note that you only have white dolls in the role-play area or have no skin-tone paints and crayons available for children to use when they draw pictures of themselves and their families.

You might also realise that you have three new Polish children in your room, but the dual-language books are only in English and Turkish. You may have a child who has a disability due to start in your room and realise you need resources with positive images of children with disabilities. You can use these to promote the child's self-esteem and provide opportunities for the other children to ask questions about disabilities before the child starts.

CASE STUDY

Reviewing setting policies and procedure

Margaret's colleague, Josie, was also completing her Early Years Teacher Status and wanted to evidence 8.1 through reviewing her setting's policies and procedures.

She decided to review:

- *Recruitment processes: to see whether the staff team reflect the backgrounds of the children. She decided that if they didn't, they will need to think about how and where they advertise their vacancies and look at the unintended consequences of current practice.*

- *Parents' access to setting policies: what access to policies do parents have if they do not read English or have literacy problems? She asked her colleagues how they ensure that parents who do not speak English can discuss their child's progress with their key person.*

- *She asked colleagues how confident they felt to deal with incidents of bullying, abuse or discrimination. If a child or parent made a racist remark, did they know how to deal with this?*

- *She applied for Free Deaf and Interpreter Awareness and shares what she learns with her team (free training for non-profit-making organisations, voluntary groups and charities in London: **www.communityid.co.uk/big-lottery/free-training**).*

CASE STUDY

Raising awareness training of prejudice-based bullying

Bobby, an Early Years Teacher trainee in a nursery class in a primary school, decided to address bullying and discrimination in his evidence for 8.1. He was aware that a discussion about his key child, Felix, who has two fathers, led to some homophobic comments from certain colleagues. He was concerned that these comments could have a negative impact on Felix and his fathers and on his colleague, Nadine, who, he had noticed, no longer spoke about her partner Cherry since this incident.

In the following whole-school staff meeting he presented the findings of the charity Stonewall on homophobic bullying in schools, explaining that homophobic bullying is frequently unchallenged and has a damaging impact on children. The School Report (Stonewall, 2012), he explained, shows that more than half (55 per cent) of gay young people experience homophobic bullying and almost all (99 per cent) hear the phrases 'that's so gay' or 'you're so gay' in school.

He spoke about a second report, called *The Teachers' Report* (Stonewall, 2009), which found that young people who don't conform to gender stereotypes and those with gay friends or family are often targeted. Bobby explained that he feared this could happen to Felix, particularly as he progresses through the school. Bobby explained that anyone can be targeted, purely because they are different, and if the school has a gay member of staff or parent, a vulnerable teenage parent or a girl who is a 'tomboy', then they need to be aware of these issues.

Bobby asked his team:

- How well do you know the family circumstances of your children, parents and colleagues?

- If you don't, is this because they don't feel confident sharing this with you?

Bobby explained that, although sometimes it is not appropriate to know everything about a family, we need to think about how staff, children and parents might feel if they believe that the important people in their lives are not accepted by the school.

He asked his team:

- What can you do to ensure that parents, children and colleagues feel confident sharing information about their family circumstances with you?

- What will be the benefits of developing honest, respectful relationships, especially with parents?

He provided a handout that outlined Ofsted's 2012 inspection framework (**www.ofsted. gov.uk/resources/framework-for-regulation-of-provision-early-years-register**) which specifically asks schools what they are doing to combat homophobic language and bullying. He mentioned that, according to Stonewall, 'schools that create a positive environment and celebrate diversity report significantly lower rates or homophobic language and bullying' and that 'nine in ten teachers report that they've never received training on how to prevent and respond to homophobic bullying' (**www.stonewall.org.uk/at_school/education_for_all/secondary_schools/homophobic_bullying/**).

In his rationale for the session Bobby explained that staff need 'the courage to tackle the issue and deal with bullies confidently. Make sure they understand the aspect and background of bullying, can identify signs of bullying and know what strategies to use to address it' (Smith, 2013).

His final comments to his team were that it can be easy to assume that all forms of bullying, including homophobic and disability-related bullying, occur higher up in the school, but these issues have arisen with Felix and this shows that the nursery, too, needs to be aware of these issues and address prejudice-based bullying. He shared his hope that if the team has a clear policy on how to deal with these incidents, then their response will be considered, well thought out and effective.

Tackling bullying and discrimination

Bobby followed up his comments in the staff meeting in the previous case study by arranging a meeting where staff could discuss as a group how to deal with incidents of bullying and discrimination.

He designed a set of five scenarios for the team to discuss. He hoped that this would help the team to identify strategies they could use if they were confronted with an incident of bullying or discrimination. He encouraged colleagues to talk about how well prepared they felt they were to challenge inappropriate comments and what they could do as a team to build up their confidence in this area.

The five scenarios were:

1. *A small group of parents come to you to say they have heard that the new child in the nursery is HIV-positive: they say that they will remove their children from the nursery if this child stays.*

2. *A parent volunteer with a disability is helping a child put on his coat. The child says, 'I don't want Amy's mum to touch me with her funny arm!'*

3. *A member of staff is aware that her key child is being brought up by her mother and her mother's partner, Tessa. She says she can no longer be this child's key person as her religion views gay relationships as a sin.*

4. *A parent volunteer notices a child has fallen over. She goes up to the child and says, 'come on now, it's time to get up – boys don't cry!'*

5. *Two pre-school children from a traveller family are due to start in the nursery. You are aware that some parents are threatening to protest outside the travellers' site. You are concerned this could escalate and that this threat of violence could affect the children. How can you deal with this situation and is this a safeguarding issue?*

Bobby asked his colleague, Nadine, to take detailed minutes of the meeting so that he could use these to evidence how he promotes anti-discriminatory practice for 8.1 and his leadership role for 8.4 and 8.5.

Nadine felt that the team ethos had improved after these discussions and wrote a witness testimony for Bobby, outlining how his intervention had made 'a positive contribution to the wider life and ethos of the setting' and this helped him to evidence to 8.2 as well as 8.1.

Children's books

If you carry out a resources audit you may find that the books that you have do not accurately reflect the experiences of the children in your group. Here is a list of some of the many books you could order to provide positive images of different families to celebrate the diversity of children's lives and promote children's self-esteem.

- *The Great Big Book of Families* by Mary Hoffman and Ros Asquith
- *The Family Book* by Todd Parr
- *Mom and Mum Are Getting Married* by Ken Setterington
- *The Boy Who Cried Fabulous* by Leslea Newman
- *Priscilla and the Pink Planet* by Nathaniel Hobbie
- *Dogs Don't Do Ballet* by Anna Kemp and Sara Ogilvie
- *The Paper Bag Princess* by Robert Munsch
- *Oliver Button is a Sissy* by Tomie dePaola
- *It's Okay to be Different* by Todd Parr
- *The Sissy Duckling* by Harvey Fierstein
- *Uncle Bobby's Wedding* by Sarah S. Brannen

Evidence for 8.1

Standard 8.1 is a complex indicator to evidence as you need to demonstrate how you apply the principles of *equality of opportunity* and *anti-discriminatory practice* across policy and practice and in a range of areas. You need a good understanding of the relationships between equality of opportunity, anti-discriminatory practice, diversity and inclusion and to demonstrate the various ways in which this understanding informs all areas of your practice.

There are many ways that you can evidence your understanding of equality and anti-discriminatory practice. Check that your evidence demonstrates that you apply these principles across your practice. Plans for celebrating religious festivals or holding an international evening do provide evidence for 8.1, but on their own this would not evidence adequate depth and breadth of practice.

You can focus in detail on one area in your evidence, as long as you identify some of the other areas and considerations. For example, you may:

- decide to evidence your understanding of the legislation, frameworks and policies that promote equality of opportunity and anti-discriminatory practice and review your setting's policies and practice in relation to inclusion and gender;
- focus in detail on strategies to promote inclusion, but reflect on your understanding of the importance of celebrating the rich cultural heritage that children and their families bring to your setting;
- review your staffing and recruitment policies;
- address issues of gender stereotyping on children's access to areas of learning;
- focus on raising staff awareness of diversity and equality and then encourage the team to carry out a resources audit.

353

You will be able to cross-reference some of your evidence for 8.1 to other indicators in Standard 8 and several other Standards. For example, if you promote colleagues' awareness of equality and diversity you will have an impact on the ethos of the setting (8.2), demonstrate that you reflect on practice (8.6), identify training needs (8.5) and model effective practice (8.4). You will also evidence your understanding of the important influence of parents and the importance of working in partnership (2.7) and the strategies you can follow to support a child with special needs (5.3).

Written assignments, case studies and your reflective journal

As you are asked to *promote* equality of opportunities and anti-discriminatory practice, you can evidence 8.1 through your descriptions of your actions and the rationale that you present. You could:

- write about how you reviewed the equality policy or led a staff training event on understanding the needs of looked-after children;

- present a case study that evidences your support for a child with special needs and your understanding of principles and practice in relation to inclusion, which will help you to evidence 8.1 as well as 5.3;

- present a case study on a project you led to tackle the negative impact of, for example, gender stereotypes on children's access to areas of learning and how this is reinforced by the gender stereotyping and 'colour coding' of children's toys;

- use a case study to review the strategies you use to support a child who is HIV-positive and challenge any discriminatory attitudes among colleagues or parents.

Document portfolio

You can use a range of work products and documents to evidence 8.1. These could include:

- training notes from a session you led on equality and inclusion or a review of your recruitment and equality policies that you led;

- a resources audit and order form for new resources;

- plans for activities to celebrate festivals;

- revised menus that demonstrate how you consult with parents on their child's dietary requirements;

- activity plans that evidence how you involve parents in sharing stories and songs in their home language.

You need to make sure that each piece of evidence clearly shows what you did and why, and how this promotes equality. You may have parent newsletters that demonstrate how you involve families in celebrating festivals or encourage fathers to share books with their children and explain that policies are available in a range of languages.

Observations

You could arrange to be observed:

- leading a resources audit on equality and inclusion;

- mentoring a student on equality and inclusion;

- leading an activity where children have access to skin-tone paints and paper and look at each other's skin tones and appreciate that no two people's skin tones are exactly the same;

- sharing stories that encourage children to feel positive about differences and that reflect and celebrate the reality of their lives;

- arranging for a parent to involve children in cooking a traditional dish or encourage a child to teach the group how to count to ten in his home language;

- introducing new Makaton signs to the group so that all the children can communicate with a child with special needs;

- meeting with parents when you review their child's individual education plans and look at strategies to promote their child's inclusion and self-esteem (ensure that they have given their informed consent).

SUGGESTED READING

Baldock, P (2014) Understanding Cultural Diversity in the Early Years. London: SAGE.

Brown, B (2008) *Equality in Action – A Way Forward with Persona Doll*. Stoke-on-Trent: Trentham Books.

Cignam, J (2014) *Supporting Boys' Writing In The Early Years: Becoming A Writer In Leaps and Bounds*. London: David Fulton.

Cowne, E (2003) *Developing Inclusive Practice: The SENCO's Role in Managing Change*. London: David Fulton.

Dickins, M (2002) All being equal. *Nursery World*, 2 January. Available online at: **www.nurseryworld. co.uk/nursery-world/news/1087316/equal** (accessed 22/10/2014).

Farrell, M (2003) *The Special Education Handbook*. London: David Fulton.

Henry, A (1996) Literacy, black self-representation and cultural practice in an elementary classroom: implications for teaching children of Afro-Caribbean heritage. *International Journal of Qualitative Studies in Education*, 9 (2): 119–134.

Hills, G (2013) *The Equality Act for Educational Professionals: A Simple Guide to Disability Inclusion in Schools*. London: Routledge.

Holland, P (2003) We Don't Play with Guns Here: War, Weapon and Superhero Play in the Early Years (Debating Play). Berkshire: OUP Mc-Graw Hill Education.

Issa, T and Hatt, A (2003) *Language, Culture and Identity in the Early Years*. London: Bloomsbury.

Kapasi, H and Lane, J (2008) Approaching race equality training in the early years. Race Equality Teaching. Summer.

Lane, J (2006) *Right from the Start – A Commissioned Study of Antiracism, Learning and the Early Years*. Focus Institute on Rights and Social Transformation (FIRST). Available online at: **www.publications. parliament.uk/pa/cm200910/cmselect/cmchilsch/130/130we24.htm**.

Lane, J and Ouseley, H (2006) We've got to start somewhere: what role can early years services and settings play in helping society to be more at ease with itself? *Race Equality Teaching* (spring).

Nutbrown, C and Clough, P (2006) *Inclusion in the Early Years.* London: SAGE.

Ranjhun, AF (2002) *Implementing the Code of Practice for Children with SEN.* London: David Fulton.

Roffey, S (1999) *Special Needs in the Early Years.* London: David Fulton.

Siraj-Blatchford, I and Clarke, P (2000) *Supporting Identity, Diversity and Language in the Early Years.* Buckingham: Open University Press.

Smidt, S (ed.) (1998) *The Early Years: A Reader.* London: Routledge.

Spencer, C and Schnelling, K (2003) *Handbook for Pre-School SEN Provision: The Code of Practice in Relation to the Early Years.* London: David Fulton

Wall, K (2003) *Special Needs and Early Years: A Practitioner's Guide.* London: SAGE.

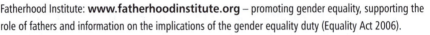

WEB RESOURCES

Fatherhood Institute: **www.fatherhoodinstitute.org** – promoting gender equality, supporting the role of fathers and information on the implications of the gender equality duty (Equality Act 2006).

Inclusive Technology: **www.inclusive.co.uk/early_learning/index.shtml** – resources, communication aids, articles, web sites and contacts

Lane, J (2008) Race Equality Teaching. Available online at: **www.childrenwebmag.com/articles/ rights-quality/race-equality-teaching** (accessed 29/10/2014).- Makaton: **www.makaton.org/**.Royal National Institute for the Blind: **rnib.org.uk** – fact sheets, resources, sources of information and support.

Royal National Institute for the Deaf: **www.rnid.org/** – information, resources, publications, technology, Disability Discrimination Act, fact sheets, reading, technology.

Scope: **www.scope.org.uk/support** – for information about young children with cerebral palsy.

Standard 8.2: Make a positive contribution to the wider life and ethos of the setting

Standard 8.2 asks you to evidence the positive contribution you make to the wider life and the ethos in your setting. Your contribution to *the wider life* includes anything that you introduce that is in addition to or adds to practice in your setting, such as regular outings or Forest School activities. Your contribution to the ethos of the setting includes any actions that raise awareness of and contribute to the values and beliefs that underpin their practice, such as promoting equality and diversity.

Standard 8.2 is an opportunity to evidence the ways in which you use your personal qualities and skills to extend practice in your setting. You can evidence how you share your skills, interests and hobbies with colleagues and children to introduce new activities, such as dance, carpentry or art using found materials. You can also evidence how you encourage colleagues to think about the beliefs and values that underpin their practice and that may be in their mission statement or policies and identify innovative strategies to promote these through their practice.

'Wider life'

To evidence 8.2 well, you must appreciate what is meant by *wider life* and *ethos* within the context of the early years and your own setting and identify how you make a positive contribution to both of these. The term *wider life* is commonly used in relation to schools, where it can describe the additional activities teachers provide for children, such as out-of-classroom activities that benefit the school as a whole. These could include after-school sessions such as running a music club or organising sports events.

You must establish what *wider life* means in the context of your role and your setting. It could be that you speak an additional language and have created a set of bilingual children's books, or you have worked with a group of parents to create a set of story sacks they can take home and share with their children. For example, Valery, an Early Years Teacher trainee who had been a dance teacher, introduced regular dance sessions for toddlers and talked to staff and parents about the benefits of dance for children's physical and creative development.

'Ethos'

Ethos can be defined as the set of values that an organisation holds, and that are underpinned by certain behaviours. It is a term used in the early years and you will be able to find a reference to your setting's ethos within its policies and mission statement. For an ethos to be effective, however, it needs to be explicit and understood and influence practice.

You must be familiar enough with the stated ethos of your setting to identify how it informs your practice and whether there are areas that need to be addressed. If you can encourage your colleagues to reflect on how their ethos informs their practice, then you have appropriate evidence of making a positive contribution to the ethos of the setting for 8.2.

Each setting will have their own ethos statement, tailored to reflect their values and beliefs. Sometimes the ethos is a statement of principle, and in other cases it describes how the principles are put into practice. For example, in Wendy's setting the ethos states that children learn through play and it is through stimulating play-based experiences that children develop and learn at their highest level. The ethos also emphasises the importance of the key person relationship and of providing training for all staff.

The ethos for Bobby's nursery class within a primary school emphasises that the nursery follows the standards and principles set out in EYFS, to ensure that the children are kept healthy and safe, are able to learn and develop and are suitably prepared for learning in school. The ethos also emphasises the importance of quality and consistency, that learning opportunities are planned around a child's interests and needs, there are regular opportunities for assessment and the nursery promotes equality of opportunity and anti-discriminatory practice and practitioners work in partnership with parents.

To evidence the positive impact you have had you will need to take three steps.

1. Find out about your setting's stated ethos.

2. Review the ethos and identify any areas for development, either in the ethos itself, or in how well it informs practice.

3. Consider how you can make a positive contribution to this ethos and review the impact of any changes you have introduced.

All changes in a setting have an impact on the ethos, either directly or indirectly, so you need to review your actions and find out what impact they had on the ethos, the culture and values of your setting. For example if you introduced Every Child a Talker (ECAT), this will have a positive impact on how adults and children value children's communication and will enhance your setting's ethos in this area.

You also need to think about your own personal set of values and how these relate to the ethos and inform your practice. For example, Josie's younger sister spent time in the care system so she has a particularly strong awareness of the needs of looked-after children. She led a series of discussions to raise colleagues' awareness of these issues and invited a social worker to speak about how practitioners can support their key children's foster carers.

You must be aware of the factors that can have an unintended impact on how effectively the ethos is implemented. Practitioners will need to identify any dissonance between the ethos of their setting and the personal beliefs they hold. For example, if a practitioner believes that her role in the baby room is to provide high-quality care and a secure attachment relationship and that education comes later, this could have a significant impact on the quality of the activities she provides for babies.

You may also want to consider the impact of the expectations parents hold and their understanding of the setting's stated ethos. They may also be able to share their impressions of whether your ethos really does inform practice. You may believe that your actions promote an ethos that values partnerships with parents, but a parent who does not speak English and is not provided with an interpreter may not feel that partnerships with parents are valued at all.

You may also find that the ethos some parents expect from your setting is not the same as what is stated in your mission statement or policies. Margaret discovered in a meeting with Ritu's father that he strongly believed that some activities are appropriate for girls and others are not, so she had to explain to him that this contradicted the ethos expressed in the setting's equality policy. Although you are to evidence your own contribution to the ethos, an ethos needs to be explicit to be effective and those responsible for putting an ethos into practice need some awareness of the impact of their own motivations, beliefs and values. So, it can be helpful to consider the impact of the intended and unintended effects of the beliefs and values held by you, your colleagues and your parents on the ethos before you decide what actions you need to take.

'Make a positive contribution'

Make a positive contribution refers to everything you introduce that adds to the practice in your setting. This can include introducing new events and activities such as a summer fair or international evening, baby yoga classes, sports days or a project to develop the toddler garden area. It can also refer to your role in supporting colleagues so that they feel able to introduce new activities or events themselves.

Many of your actions will *make a positive contribution* both to the *ethos* and the *wider life* of your setting. For example, if you invite parents with knowledge of gardening and carpentry in to help build a garden area for the babies, this makes a positive contribution to the *wider life* of the setting. It can also lead to greater parental involvement in the setting, so through your actions you will also have expanded the ethos of partnership to include encouraging parents to share their skills.

Making a positive contribution can also refer to the ways in which you promote effective practice, introduce changes and lead and support your team. You can describe the changes you introduce in a written assignment or your reflective journal where you can identify any positive changes to the environment and *wider life* of the setting and evaluate their impact on the ethos. You can also evidence your leadership actions, by, for example, mentoring a new member of staff or leading a training day, if they result in a *contribution to the wider life of the setting* or promote a positive ethos.

Your evidence must highlight what your positive contribution was and assess its impact on the wider life of your setting, its stated ethos and the ethos of those within it – parents, children and staff.

Cross-referencing your evidence for 8.2

Your evidence for 8.2 may overlap with your evidence for other Standards where you evidence any positive contribution you make to the wider life and ethos of your setting. For example, if you have introduced Forest School activities then this is evidence of promoting a stimulating environment and you can cross-reference this to 1.1.

If you have raised awareness of equality and diversity issues, then you can cross-reference this evidence to 8.1. If you *reflect on and evaluate the effectiveness of provision, and shape and support good practice*, then you can cross-reference this evidence to 8.6.

Identify your setting's ethos and make a positive contribution

You may find that your setting has an ethos that is outlined in one document, such as a mission statement. However, you may need to read through all your setting's policies to piece together the various aspects of this ethos.

However the ethos is expressed, think about the strategies you can use or have used to make a positive contribution to this ethos. There may be a need to raise colleagues' awareness of certain features in the ethos or to identify an area of practice that the ethos fails to address. The following tips can help you identify where a positive contribution is most needed and how you can evidence this.

- Review the areas of practice addressed in your setting's ethos and identify any gaps, such as an emphasis on listening to children. Identify any actions you can take to make a positive contribution in this area.

- Identify any gaps in practitioners' understanding of the ethos and how it informs their practice: you can lead a staff discussion to address any gaps in understanding and evaluate how effectively current practice reflects the ethos.

- Identify any contradictions between features of your setting's ethos and the unconscious or unstated ethos, values and beliefs that inform practice: for example, there may be an ethos that promotes partnerships with parents, but a belief that costs must be reduced where possible. So, if the staff rotas do not allow for key persons to spend time at the start and end of the day with parents, then practice does not reflect the ethos.

- Discuss with your team any situations where current practice reflects unexpressed or unstated beliefs rather than the stated ethos; for example, some staff may believe that 'it is not good for children to go outside when the weather is cold'.

- Lead a staff training session on the values and beliefs practitioners think the ethos should express.

- Find out what parents and children believe that the ethos is, and what they believe it should be (these may not be the same).

- Review the effectiveness of your contribution to the ethos and its impact on practice, for example, through parent interviews.

Make a positive contribution to the wider life of your setting

Once you have identified what is meant by the phrase, *wider life of the setting* you can start to identify what it is that you do to contribute to this. You may already have identified a range of activities or events that you introduced that you consider have made a positive contribution to the wider life of your setting. However, if you feel that you need to extend your practice in this area, this activity will help you identify some strategies to help you evidence 8.2.

Look at your personal skills, interests and hobbies and think about how you could adapt these to introduce new activities in your setting. For example, if you are a keen gardener, you could use your skills to develop an area for vegetables in the toddlers' garden. If you are also the key person of a child with a visual impairment you might plant sweet-smelling flowers and herbs to demarcate the areas. If, for example, you love yoga, you might set up baby yoga sessions as part of your focus on promoting partnerships with parents.

If you can identify a new area where you can make a positive contribution you can evidence this for 8.2. You will need to share your rationale with your team and work together to develop strategies to introduce this change. You need evidence that the contribution you made was *positive*, so you must evaluate the impact of this change, for example, by carrying out observations before and after the change, or using a staff/parent questionnaire.

CASE STUDY

Rachel's contribution

Rachel decided that she would evidence her role in introducing IT sessions for children and parents for 8.2. Rachel, an Early Years Teacher trainee, is a teacher in a nursery class attached to a small primary school and she had noticed that the ICT facilities in the school were far more advanced and plentiful than those available in the nursery. She knew she could use her contacts from her previous role as ICT specialist to source some new resources and some ICT support.

She felt she had three tasks ahead of her. The first was to raise the awareness in the school about the importance of ICT in the early years and highlight the importance of providing opportunities for parents to develop their skills and support their children in their learning. The second activity was to raise funds and identify parents who could help decorate the unused storage room and turn it into a comfortable ICT suite. The third task would be to install the computers and train colleagues in the programs that the children could use and set up weekly training for parents in basic computing skills.

Rachel introduced what became known as 'the Friday bake-off', which involved the children in baking cakes and selling them to parents and children in the playground at the end of every Friday afternoon. Rachel was allowed to use the profits to pay for materials to decorate the empty room and invited Androulla, a parent who ran her own painting and decorating company, to bring her team in over the weekend to paint the room for them.

Rachel then led a series of individual ICT training sessions with her team after school for a week to introduce her colleagues to the programs that the children could use. She gave a short presentation in the whole-school staff meetings on the importance of providing opportunities for parents to develop skills for employment, and cited Every Child Matters.

She presented her team's evaluations of the training and their observations of how children were using the ICT resources to the head teacher. The head teacher was impressed and agreed to provide cover one morning a week for a term, so that Rachel could deliver the first ten-week introductory ICT course for parents herself.

Rachel asked her colleagues, the children and parents to evaluate the new ICT activities and shared the feedback with her team. Together, they used these comments to help them to identify the positive impact of the changes and look at what they had added to the ethos of the school. For example, parents felt the school supported their own development as well as the development of their children.

Evidence for 8.2

Written assignments, case studies and your reflective journal

An assignment or case study gives you scope to present the rationale for your actions and the steps you have taken and to evaluate the impact of the changes.

You can also use an assignment or case study to describe in detail any changes you have introduced across the setting, such as if you introduced ECAT. You can describe your *positive contribution* and demonstrate how this adds to the wider life of your setting and has a positive impact on the ethos. For example, if you introduced children's involvement in planning across the setting, it will have an impact on the ethos as well as the wider life of the setting, as staff, parents and children will recognise that children are active partners in their own learning.

You can also use an assignment to review the ways that you involve children and parents in evaluating your contribution and the impact of the setting's ethos on its practice and procedures. You can, for example, use a case study to examine how the setting's ethos promotes inclusion and the steps you have taken to ensure that this ethos is carried out in practice to support the self-esteem of your key child with a disability.

You can use your journal to reflect on your understanding of how the ethos informs your practice and relates to your professional values and beliefs and how you encourage your colleagues to reflect on their values and beliefs.

Document portfolio

You could include:

- a review of or contribution to your setting's ethos and policy documents (it must highlight the positive contributions that you made);
- rationale and plans for new activities or events you have introduced that contribute to the wider life of your setting;
- records of your discussions with parents around the setting's ethos and its impact;
- a witness statement from a parent explaining how changes you introduced had a positive impact on the parent and child.

Witness testimonies from colleagues can also help you evidence 8.2 if they highlight, for example, how you supported a colleague to introduce a new event or activity or to review the setting's ethos.

Observations

You could arrange to be observed:

- leading an activity that demonstrates the positive contribution you have made;
- taking part in a project you have introduced that has a positive impact on the wider life of the setting, such as a baby drop-in session or toy library;

- leading a session of a 'Men Behaving Dadly' group you established to encourage fathers to play and share stories with their children on a Saturday morning.

Cross-referencing your evidence for 8.2

As the changes you introduce for 8.2 will have a positive impact across your setting, you will be able to cross-reference your evidence for 8.2 to a range of other Standards. For example, if your actions created a stimulating environment, then you can cross-reference this evidence to 1.1. If you promoted an ethos of anti-discriminatory practice and encourage colleagues to discuss how this ethos could influence their practice, then you can cross-reference this evidence to 8.1.

SUGGESTED READING

Bryce-Clegg, A and Jennie Lindon, J (2012) *Planning for the Early Years: Gardening and Growing.* London: Practical Pre-School Books.

Chalmers, D (2013) *Drama Activities for the Early Years - Promoting Learning Across the Foundation Stage Curriculum.* Bedfordshire: Brilliant Publications.

Constable, K (2014) *Bringing the Forest School Approach to your Early Years Practice.* Oxon: David Fulton.

Kingdon, Z and Gourd, J (2013) *Early Years Policy: The Impact on Practice.* London: Routledge.

Miller, L, Cable, C and Drury, R (eds) (2012) *Extending Professional Practice in the Early Years.* London: OUP and SAGE.

Sargent, M (2014) *The Project Approach in Early Years Provision.* London: Practical Pre-School Books.

Thornton, L and Brunton, P (2014) *Bringing the Reggio Approach to your Early Years Practice.* Oxon: David Fulton.

Tomlinson, P (2013). *Early Years Policy and Practice: A Critical Alliance* (Critical Approaches to the Early Years). Northwich: Critical Publishing.

Standard 8.3 Take a lead in establishing a culture of co-operative working between colleagues, parents and/or carers and other professionals

Standard 8.3 addresses your role in supporting partnerships between parents, colleagues and the other professionals who support a child. You will promote an understanding of the importance of co-operative working and emphasise that, when supporting a child with a special need or disability, all those involved in a child's care need to work together closely, to ensure continuity, to share strategies to promote the child's learning and development and to ensure the child's safety.

As 8.3 is part of Standard 8, you need to demonstrate your leadership. You must *take a lead in establishing* a culture of co-operative working between practitioners, parents and the other professionals who support their child. You must evidence how you introduce, or *establish*, new practices that promote a culture of co-operative working and lead your team by supporting their relationships with parents and professionals so that they can best support a child and keep that child safe.

Standard 8.3 is one of several Standards where you evidence your role within a multi-agency or multi-disciplinary team so you may be able to cross-reference your evidence for 8.3 to these other indicators, 5.5, 6.2 and 8.7. Be aware that in 8.3 you need to demonstrate how you *take a lead* and promote co-operative working. You may be able to relate your evidence for 8.3 to the other Standards where you evidence your support for a child, such as 6.2.

'Other professionals'

The first point you need to consider when you plan your evidence for 8.3 is what is meant by *other professionals*. This is not a reference to the professionals who work in your local community who you may invite in to support children's understanding of the world, such as fire fighters, the police or your local dentist. These are the *professionals* who support children's health, welfare, learning and development and who work outside your setting (unless you are in a children's centre).

These professionals will support the health, welfare, learning or development of a specific child and the child's parents and key person need to work closely with them so that they can share the strategies or health care routines the professional has recommended. For example, you may have supported a colleague to work alongside the area special educational needs co-ordinator (SENCO) to support a child with special needs.

You may find that you need to support the partnerships between parents, colleagues and a range of other professionals. These professionals could include a speech and language therapist, physiotherapist, hospital consultant or a family's social worker, GP or health visitor. You may also need to facilitate a culture of co-operative working between a colleague and the professionals who work alongside them to contribute to a Common Assessment Framework (CAF) or who attend a Team Around the Child (TAC) meeting. You may also find that if a child has a particular medical condition or disability, then experts in this field may be able to support parents and practitioners, and your role will be to facilitate a culture of co-operative working.

'A culture of co-operative working'

In 8.3 you must demonstrate that you take a lead role in *establishing* a culture of co-operative working between practitioners, external professionals and the parents of the child they support. You must ensure that practitioners, parents and external professionals all understand the importance of these partnerships and that your setting has systems in place to ensure that this three-way communication takes place.

Your colleagues and parents and the professionals outside your setting must know what these systems are and feel that they are appropriate and fit for purpose. Check that colleagues and parents feel confident enough to contact professionals who may be unfamiliar to them, and feel able to ask them to share information and expertise for the benefit of the child.

There are several situations where your colleagues may find themselves needing to work co-operatively with parents and professionals. They may have proceeded through the stages of SEN support and now need to request the support of an external professional. Although it may be the SENCO who makes a referral at this point, the child's key person and parents need to understand what is happening, who the referral is being made to and why, and this is where you can provide some support and guidance. In another situation, you might respond to a colleague's concern about a child's health by encouraging him to think about how he can speak to the child's parents about this and recommend that he take the child to see the health visitor or GP or go straight to hospital.

If a child has an ongoing health concern or disability, such as a hearing loss, then you can encourage the child's key person to explain to the parents that the setting needs to be kept informed of the child's health requirements so that they know how to support the child safely. Your role can be to remind your colleague that he may need to ask the parents to give their permission for the professionals to share a report with the setting or to request permission for the key person to contact the professional directly, to ensure that the best possible care is provided.

Other situations may arise where you can support the communication between a colleague, other professionals and parents. These include situations when a request is made for an assessment for a statement, when working together to complete a CAF, or when there is a safeguarding concern.

Practical strategies

There are various ways in which you can demonstrate your role in promoting a culture of co-operative working. Some of these strategies are simple and practical, and others involve raising colleagues' awareness and providing information and guidance. You must first review current practice and consult with your team to find out where they most need your support.

One of the most important strategies is to ensure that colleagues understand why co-operative working is important. Talk to colleagues about why, when and how they might need to develop co-operative working practices with other professionals and parents and what the professional boundaries and issues of confidentiality are. Your colleagues may need to discuss what their responsibilities are and build up their confidence so that they feel comfortable enough to contact and work closely with unfamiliar, external professionals.

You may find that colleagues want to learn more about the precise roles and responsibilities of the external professionals and what the boundaries of their roles are; for example, the differences between a physiotherapist and an occupational therapist.

365

Other colleagues may appreciate some guidance on the support that can be offered within the setting for a child with special needs or a disability and when it is appropriate to refer a child for additional support.

There are some very practical strategies you can evidence to demonstrate how you promote a culture of co-operative working.

- You could make sure that the names and contact details of other professionals are updated and easily available.

- You could produce a simple guide to your setting's referral process.

- You could provide training on the referral system and statementing process and how to maintain contact with external professionals who do not visit the setting.

- You could ensure that secure systems are set up for sharing emails and reports with external professionals and that all colleagues are confident using these systems.

- You could invite an external professional to come and meet your team and talk about her role and share strategies that can support the learning and development of all children. For example, you could invite a speech and language therapist to talk about the strategies she recommends to support the language and communication of all children. She may also be able to provide guidance on introducing Makaton signs and reducing sound levels in the room to support a child with hearing loss.

- You could ask a health visitor to talk about the ways in which she supports families and the range of issues she can address and when it might be appropriate for a practitioner to contact her with a concern.

Your setting may already have good systems in place to promote effective communication between parents and practitioners, but there may be a need for you to introduce systems to support communication between parents and professionals, and practitioners and professionals. You could encourage practitioners to talk to parents about asking a professional to share a report with the setting or provide guidance for practitioners, if, for example, certain health procedures need to be followed.

You can make sure that colleagues feel confident explaining to parents why this three-way communication is important, whilst appreciating that this is a time when parents may feel very sensitive. Parents may worry about the setting knowing about their child's condition for a variety of reasons. They may, for example, worry about their child being 'labelled', or that practitioners will lower their expectations once they know their child has a diagnosis.

The importance of 'co-operative working': keeping children safe from harm

Standard 8.3 emphasises the importance of co-operative relationships between parents, colleagues and external professionals because these relationships support children to fulfil their potential and, even more importantly, can protect a child from harm.

For these two reasons you must ensure that there is continuity between the strategies used to support a child with a disability or special need at home and in your setting. You must make sure that recommendations and strategies suggested by other professionals are thoroughly understood by parents and practitioners alike. A lack of understanding would at the very least reduce the effectiveness of a strategy to support a child's learning and development, but in the case of a medical issue, it could have serious consequences for a child's health. You must raise colleagues' understanding of the ways in which the strategies a professional suggests can protect a child from harm.

You will find this emphasis on working in partnership with parents and professionals in three other indicators, 5.5, 6.2 and 8.7. The reason why these partnerships have such prominence within the Standards relates to the issues raised in the aftermath of the death of Victoria Climbié, when it was recognised that the failure of the agencies involved to share information had contributed to her death.

You may find that you can evidence 8.3 in relation to child protection. For example, have you supported partnerships between colleagues and other professionals during a safeguarding case? Do your colleagues appreciate the importance of multi-agency working in a safeguarding situation? Can you ensure that they have access to regularly updated lists of who to contact in a child protection emergency?

Standard 8.3 can be a difficult statement to evidence, but for the reasons highlighted above it is an important one as if every Early Years Teacher can raise their colleagues' awareness of the importance of multi-agency working to protect children from harm, then this will have an impact on how well children are protected. You might wish to share these reasons with colleagues to help them appreciate quite how significant this culture of co-operation and communication can be.

Standards 5.5, 6.2, 8.3 and 8.7: similarities and differences

Standard 8.3 is one of four indicators that promote effective partnerships between practitioners, parents and wider professionals. You will find similarities between 8.3 and both 5.5 and 6.2. In 5.5 you are asked to *know when a child is in need of additional support and how this can be accessed, working in partnership with parents and/or carers and other professionals*. In 6.2 you are asked to *engage effectively with parents and/or carers and other professionals in the on-going assessment and provision for each child*.

In all three indicators the *professionals* mentioned are those who you consult to promote a child's learning, development, health or welfare, such as a health visitor or your area SENCO. However, the key difference between 5.5 and 6.2 and 8.3 is that the first two indicators focus on your own engagement with parents and the professionals who support their child, but in 8.2 you must evidence your leadership role and your role in establishing a culture of co-operative working between your colleagues, parents and other professionals.

Standards 5.5 and 6.2 ask you to evidence your personal practice and this can be difficult if currently none of your key children have contact with other professionals.

However, you have a wider brief in 8.3, when you evidence your leadership role and the strategies you introduce to promote *a culture of co-operative working*.

If you find it difficult to take on leadership responsibilities in your setting, perhaps because you are not a manager, it might be helpful to think about the range of leadership styles you can use and find an approach you feel comfortable with. There is more information on this in Chapter 10, on understanding 'personal practice' and 'leadership'.

The final indicator that relates to your work with other professionals is 8.7. Here you must demonstrate that you understand and contribute to multi-agency team working. If you support you colleagues in their work with other professionals in a safeguarding situation, or TAC meeting or when completing a CAF form for 8.3, then you may be able to cross-reference this evidence to 8.7 as well, to demonstrate your leadership role and your knowledge and understanding. However, 8.7 is similar to 5.5 and 6.2, as you are primarily asked to evidence your personal practice.

Evidence for 8.3

You must evidence how you take a lead in creating a co-operative culture between practitioners, parents and other professionals in your evidence for 8.3. There are many ways in which you can evidence this and because of the confidentiality issues involved you will need to decide which ways feel more appropriate for you than others. For example, you might feel that it is more appropriate to ask a colleague for a witness testimony than be observed preparing that co-worker for a meeting with parents and professionals.

You will need to review your evidence carefully and decide whether it does adequately meet the requirements for 8.3 or if it is more appropriate for the other indicators where you evidence your partnerships with parents and other professionals, 5.5, 6.2 and 8.7. Remember that these three indicators relate to your personal practice and in 8.3 you need to evidence how you *take a lead*.

Identifying your evidence for 8.3

In 8.3 you will need to evidence how you establish a culture of co-operative working. These questions can help you identify evidence that can demonstrate this and evaluate how well each piece of evidence meets the specific requirements of 8.3:

* What does a *culture of co-operative working* look like?

* Does my team demonstrate and understand the importance of this approach?

* If not, what can I do to foster this understanding and establish this culture?

* If some aspects of this co-operative culture are in place in my team, are there areas for further development that I can address?

* What practical strategies can I use to address any areas for development?

* What leadership actions feel appropriate and comfortable in this situation?

- What actions have I already carried out and how can I evidence them? For example, how did I *establish* a culture of co-operative working?

- How have I developed links between my team and external professionals?

- What have I done to support parents in their relationships with other professionals?

- How have I encouraged colleagues to help parents feel secure enough to share information from other professionals with the setting?

Written assignments, case studies and your reflective journal

The advantage of an extended piece of writing is that you can present your rationale and describe the steps you took to establish this culture of co-operation in detail and evaluate their impact. Remember to check that you have anonymised all references to children, parents and the setting itself.

You may already have written a case study to evidence your support for a child with special needs. If you demonstrated that you supported your colleagues in their relationships with parents and other professionals, then you can cross-reference this evidence to 8.3. You can then evaluate the effectiveness of your role in promoting a culture of co-operative working. You can also use your journal to evaluate any strategies you use to establish and sustain a culture of co-operative working.

Document portfolio

When selecting documents to help you evidence 8.3, remember that all documents must be anonymised and that they must clearly demonstrate your actions in relation to 8.3. If the document does not clearly evidence your actions or the reasons for your actions, then you can add an explanatory note.

You could include:

- a list you created for colleagues with the contact details of the professionals working within your local authority;

- a guide you created for colleagues that outlines the stages of Early Years Action and Early Years Action Plus and that highlights when, how and why they should contact an external professional;

- minutes or observations from training you delivered on the referral process or how to make contact with a professional who already works with a child in your setting;

- a leaflet you have produced for parents outlining the roles of the professionals who support children's health and development and highlighting the importance of sharing information from them with their child's key person;

- witness testimonies from parents, colleagues or other professionals (as long as they clearly address the criteria of 8.3);

- a witness testimony from a colleague about how you invited *other professionals* to visit your setting to develop relationships with the team;

- a record of how you supported a colleague in her work with the area SENCO;

- a witness testimony from a parent that addresses 5.5 and 6.2 as well as aspects of 8.3;

- meeting records from a TAC or CAF meeting you attended demonstrating how you promoted co-operation between parents, practitioners and other professionals.

Be aware that a completed CAF form can provide evidence that you have worked with other professionals for 6.2, but may not provide evidence of your role in taking a lead and developing a culture of co-operation, though this may be evidenced in the minutes of the meeting.

Again, records of emails between yourself and others may only evidence your practice rather than your leadership, unless they highlight your support for the relationship between colleagues, parents and professionals. An email where you invite a professional to visit and meet the team, however, could evidence 8.3. These must all be anonymised.

Observations

You could arrange to be observed:

- being shadowed by a colleague in a meeting with an external professional and using your co-worker's observations of the meeting as evidence;

- helping a colleague prepare for a meeting with a parent and/or other professional. You could demonstrate how you support your colleague in their understanding of the referral system, to develop confidence in talking to parents about the wider support that is available for their child, and to appreciate how difficult this conversation may be for the parents;

- leading a staff development event on working with other professionals, perhaps sharing materials you have produced on the roles, responsibilities and contact details of the professionals who work in your area;

- facilitating a meeting between a colleague and another professional and being observed supporting their partnership.

SUGGESTED READING

Gasper, M (2009) *Multi-agency Working in the Early Years: Challenges and Opportunities.* London: SAGE.

Roffey, S and Parry, J (2001) *Special Needs in the Early Years: Collaboration, Communication and Coordination.* London: David Fulton.

Siraj-Blatchford, I, Clarke, K and Needham, M. (2007) *The Team Around the Child: Multi-agency Working in the Early Years.* London: IOE.

Tassoni, P (2003) *Supporting Special Needs: Understanding Inclusion in the Early Years.* Oxford: Heinemann.

Ward, U (2013) *Working with Parents in the Early Years.* London: SAGE.

Standard 8.4: Model and implement effective education and care, and support and lead other practitioners including Early Years Educators

In Standard 8.4 you will evidence your positive impact on the quality of practice within your setting. You will evidence how you lead and support your team and demonstrate your own good practice through modelling and implementing *effective education and care*. You need to pay close attention to the wording in 8.4, as you must evidence both your personal practice and leadership, and demonstrate how you *model* and *implement effective education* and *effective care* and *support and lead other practitioners including Early Years Educators*.

It is in 8.4 that you will demonstrate that as an Early Years Teacher you understand what effective education and care look like and can implement strategies to support and improve practice in your setting. As the indicator states, the strategies you will evidence need to include implementing good practices, mentoring colleagues, modelling good practice and leading and supporting colleagues through, for example, training events and professional discussions.

Once you have identified the key areas you need to evidence in 8.4, you can look at each in more detail. If you pay close enough attention to the wording in each phrase it will help you to appreciate how and in what depth you need to evidence this indicator.

'Education and care'

The first phrase we will look at is *education and care*. You are asked to *model and implement* good practice in relation to both *education and care*. As mentioned in previous chapters, it has been recognised that children learns from all their experiences in the setting, not just those we designate as *education*. It can be hard to separate education and care as, for example, you can introduce learning experiences during care routines, such as counting the animals on the frieze while children wash their hands before lunch.

However, in 8.4 you need to differentiate between education and care so you can provide examples of modelling and implementing effective *care* and of modelling and implementing effective *education*.

'Implement effective education and care'

You must *implement* effective education and care. *Implement* refers to any new practices that you introduce. For example, if you introduce a flexible approach to rest times then that is evidence of implementing effective care. If you introduce story sacks then that is an example of implementing effective education.

Implement can also refer to any practices you carry out because you understand that these are necessary to promote *effective education and care*. For example, you would *implement* EYFS requirements.

What is essential for 8.4 is that you demonstrate your understanding of why you implement these practices and how they contribute to *effective education and care*.

'Model and implement'

In 8.4 you are asked to *model and implement effective education and care*, so once you have identified some examples of promoting *effective education* and *effective ... care*, you can review the strategies you used in each example and recognise where you modelled and where you implemented good practice. Once you have identified a couple of good examples of modelling and implementing effective practice in relation to both education and to care, then you can think about how you can evidence this.

One example that evidences implementing *effective education and care* and modelling good practice is rolling snack. If you introduce rolling snack, the process of establishing this is evidence of *implement*. If you then demonstrate good practice during a rolling snack session to colleagues, you have evidence of *modelling*. You can use rolling snack to demonstrate both *education* and *care* too. For example, if you introduce healthy snacks this evidences *implement effective ... care* and if you model turn taking, positive behaviour management strategies and sharing songs and rhymes with children during snack time then you are demonstrating *model ... effective education* as well.

'Model' and 'support'

You will find it easier to evidence 8.4 if you understand the difference between *model* and *support*. *Model* refers to any situations where you demonstrate your practice for a colleague to observe and learn from. For modelling to be effective and relevant, you need to model good practice in an area where a colleague needs, or has asked for, support, such as behaviour management.

Supporting colleagues is a wider concept. You *support* a colleague if you engage in one-to-one conversations and mentoring sessions or ask coaching questions, such as 'what if ... ?' You also *support* a colleague when you provide opportunities for him to shadow you or you carry out a peer observation which you then discuss with your colleague to help him develop his practice. For the support you provide to be most effective and motivating, again you need to address an area where your colleague has identified that he needs support and if you support him in a way that is non-threatening and non-judgemental.

You can model good practice for a colleague to support his practice in a specific area. If you engage in conversations to support a practitioner while you are modelling the activity, then this is evidence of both supporting a colleague and modelling good practice. So, one piece of evidence, if it is good, can evidence both *model* and *support*. For example, you can model how to communicate with parents if a member of staff finds this difficult. If you then discuss the conversation you modelled and look at strategies to help the practitioner to develop these skills for himself, then this count as both modelling and support.

'Support and lead other practitioners'

There are many ways that you can demonstrate how you *support and lead other practitioners* and you will find that there is some overlap between these two terms. However, you do need to identify the differences between the two terms so that you can identify what it is that you do when you *support* and when you *lead* your team. One difference you might note is that you *support* a colleague, but you *lead* a team.

CASE STUDY

Annie thinks about supporting and leading

Annie, an Early Years Teacher trainee, reflected in her journal that she believed that:

> *I 'support' a colleague when I answer a question, provide guidance when someone asks me for it and when I help them manage a situation they are finding difficult. I support a student when I answer their queries or help them understand a task in their portfolio. 'Support' is something I give a colleague on a one-to-one basis, it is the gentle guidance given only when needed or asked for.*
>
> *When I 'lead other practitioners' I am being more proactive, rather than reactive. I lead others when I introduce a new practice or say to colleagues that this is the appropriate way to carry out their practice. I lead colleagues when I talk about new requirements, such as EYFS (2014) or provide a rationale for any changes I believe we need to introduce. However, I want to find a leadership style that is facilitative, rather than authoritative or authoritarian and that empowers colleagues to take on leadership responsibilities themselves.*

The section in Chapter 10, on understanding 'personal practice' and 'leadership', on leadership styles can help you identify appropriate leadership methods and styles. This chapter also looks at how to take on leadership responsibilities if this is not part of your current role.

You *lead* other practitioners when you lead a training event, and this can include anything from a ten-minute session in a staff meeting to a whole day of INSET training. Leading practitioners involves raising colleagues' awareness of good practice and new developments, encouraging colleagues to engage in professional discussions and become reflective practitioners. It also involves introducing and demonstrating new practices such as introducing literacy activities in the garden and presenting the rationale for any changes in practice.

You also *lead other practitioners* when you encourage and empower colleagues to share their own expertise and feel confident enough to take on responsibility for developing an area of practice that interests them, such as a photography project. You lead other practitioners when you encourage them to identify the reasons for their actions and be able to share their professionalism with others, for example, to support and mentor a student. You also lead practitioners when you support them to review your setting policies, or arrange for them to visit another setting and encourage them to share with their colleagues what they have learnt during the visit.

The most important issue to be aware of when you are both leading and supporting others is to check that the support you are offering is the support that they need, and not just the support you feel confident providing. You also need to look at using leadership strategies that are empowering and raise colleagues' confidence, self-esteem and belief in their own professionalism.

Although 8.4 does not explicitly ask you to evidence your work with each age range, your evidence will be much stronger if you provide examples of leadership and support in relation to each of the three age ranges.

Leadership styles

Leadership can be demonstrated along a continuum of leadership styles from authoritative to facilitative. You need to think about what would be an appropriate leadership style for you in this context and one that you feel confident with. You can review the continuum of leadership styles and reflect on which styles are appropriate for your role, and for each particular task. Different situations call for different approaches and your skill will enable you to choose the most appropriate approach in each situation. You will find information on Tannenbaum and Schmidt's leadership continuum (**www.managementstudyguide.com/continuum-leadership-behaviour. htm**) in the Chapter 10, on understanding 'personal practice' and 'leadership'.

It can be difficult to demonstrate leadership if you are not a manager and this is not part of your work role or when you are on placement. In these situations reading about leadership styles can help you find a suitable approach, and one that you feel comfortable with. There is more information on overcoming your personal barriers to taking on a leadership role in Chapter 10, on understanding 'personal practice' and 'leadership'.

Think about how you can demonstrate a range of leadership methods. If you reflect on the situations where you have demonstrated leadership, you may find that you rely on only one or two methods. These are probably the ones you feel most confident with. You need to make sure that across your evidence you demonstrate a range of leadership methods. These can include one-to-one support, modelling good practice, providing opportunities for shadowing, posing questions such as 'what if … ?', setting up mentoring opportunities, introducing changes and leading team training events. You can use the information on the range of leadership methods in Chapter 10, on understanding 'personal practice' and 'leadership', to help you can consider which leadership interventions would be appropriate and relevant in each situation.

It is important that you only evidence examples of leadership that have value for the children and colleagues in your setting, so take time to find out what is needed. You may find that observations of the provision, peer observations and exploration in your reflective journal can help you to decide where you need to focus.

There is one other aspect of leadership you can consider. Good leaders make themselves redundant as they support their colleagues to become the next leaders. Your role as leader is to model and support as necessary, but also to delegate and encourage others to develop their skills and responsibilities. One strategy you may find helpful is to find out what a practitioner has a passion for and help that person develop her expertise and take on responsibility for modelling good practice in this area.

'Early Years Educators'

You are specifically asked to evidence the leadership and support you offer Early Years Educators. The Government has introduced this new level 3 qualification alongside Early Years Teacher Status and the intention is that as Early Years Teacher you will support the new Early Years Educators.

If you are not working with an Early Years Educator, you will need to think about how you can evidence this aspect of 8.4. Perhaps you have close links with another setting which does employ an Early Years Educator and you can support that person with a particular activity or project? You may belong to an early years network that an Early Years Educator attends and you can demonstrate some support through your contributions to the group.

Rationale for change

Change can be difficult to adjust to and when you *implement* good practice, you may find that you need to introduce changes that colleagues may find difficult. If you plan to introduce any change in practice you need to present a clear rationale that highlights why this change is necessary. If, for example, you completed time-sampling observations in the garden and found that girls were not accessing the climbing equipment as frequently as boys, then you have evidence that you can share with your team that demonstrates why this is an area where changes need to be made.

You may find it helpful to read about managing change to think about why colleagues may find change difficult and think about how you can support them through a period of uncertainty.

Cross-referencing your evidence

You will find your evidence for 8.4 overlaps with any examples of leadership that you demonstrated in your evidence for other Standards. For example, if you deliver training in safeguarding you will evidence 8.4 as you will be leading other practitioners, but you will also be evidencing Standards 7.1 and 7.3 on safeguarding, because of the content area of the training.

Similarly, there will be some overlap of evidence in areas where you have implemented or modelled good practice. For example, if you implemented new planning practices in the toddler room you can cross-reference this evidence against both the Standards relating to planning, such as 4.1 and 4.2 as well as 8.4, as you will demonstrate how you implement effective practice.

Evidence for 8.4

In your evidence you must provide examples of modelling education and care and of implementing effective practices in relation to both education and care. You must provide examples of supporting practitioners one to one and of leading your team, possibly through staff development events. Include examples of leading and supporting colleagues who work with babies, toddlers and pre-school children, and a colleague who is an Early Years Educator.

Written assignments, case studies and your reflective journal

You can use a written assignment to:

- describe how you helped colleagues develop their practice in line with EYFS (2014) requirements;

- demonstrate how you support colleagues in their work with a specific age range and highlight what effective education and care look like with this age group;

- describe a range of interventions that promote effective education and care. For example, if you introduced maths activities in the garden you can describe the activities and resources you introduced and to guidance you provided through discussions, handouts or even a reminders poster on the wall;

- outline any changes you have implemented to care routines and explain any changes you introduced to the environment to support care routines.

You can also evidence how you support and model effective education and care for a child with special needs in an assignment or case study. You can use your journal to analyse examples of providing support, to examine how effective your support was and what your next steps might be. You can also use a journal entry to explore the links between EYFS and effective education and care.

Document portfolio

There may be several documents that you can include in your portfolio to evidence 8.4, such as:

- a witness testimony from a member of staff whom you mentored to evidence how you have supported that person;

- a peer observation recording you modelling an activity for a new member of the team;

- evaluation forms from staff who attended a development event that you led;

- handouts and other information you have written for staff (you need to say how you supported colleagues to understand these).

You need to review your portfolio evidence and check you have a good balance of evidence that addresses how you promote both education and care and have a balance between evidence of leading groups and supporting practitioners one to one. You also need to check that you have evidence of implementing effective practice yourself, for example, through your actions to introduce story sacks or rolling snack.

Observations

You can arrange to be observed working with a group of children and modelling this activity for a student or member of staff. This means that you will need to choose an activity that is both relevant for the individual children in your group and that the member of staff needs support with. You need to make it clear in your planning notes how you will be modelling practice and why this practitioner needed your support in this way. During the observation itself you will need to make it very clear how you are modelling practice and how you are supporting the practitioner, for example by asking prompt questions or modelling open questions. You will find that it will strengthen your evidence if you are observed modelling good practice with babies, toddlers and pre-school children.

You can also arrange to be observed mentoring a student or new member of staff, for example, when you support that person to understand planning requirements. You may wish to choose the sessions carefully, so that you are observed supporting a student or practitioner to identify what makes education and care effective.

You may find that the support you provide can help you to evidence another indicator. For example, if you are observed supporting a colleague in understanding attachment, and discuss attachment and settling routines, then this will evidence 8.4 and 2.3.

SUGGESTED READING

Allen, S and Whalley, M (2011) *Leading Practice in Early Years Settings* (Achieving EYPS Series). London: Learning Matters.

Drury, R, Campbell, R and Miller, L (2013) *Looking at Early Years Education and Care.* Oxon: Routledge.

McDowall Clark, R and Murray, J (2012) *Reconceptualizing Leadership in the Early Years.* Berkshire: McGraw Hill-Education.

Miller, L, Cable, C and Drury, R (eds) (2012) *Extending Professional Practice in the Early Years.* London: OUP and SAGE.

Miller, L, Cable, C and Devereux, J (2013) *Developing Early Years Practice* (Foundation Degree Texts Series) Oxon: David Fulton.

O'Sullivan, J (2010) *Leadership Skills in the Early Years: Making a Difference.* London: Continuum.

Price, D and Ota, C (2014) *Leading and Supporting Early Years Teams: A Practical Guide.* London: David Fulton.

Robins, A (2014) *Mentoring in the Early Years.* London: Paul Chapman.

Robins, A and Callan, S (2014) *Managing Early Years Settings: Supporting and Leading Teams.* London: SAGE.

Rodd, J (2005) *Leadership in Early Childhood: The Pathway to Professionalism.* Berkshire: OUP McGraw Hill-Education.

Saunders, L, Siraj-Blatchford, I and Manni, L (2007) *Effective Leadership in the Early Years Sector: The ELEYS study* (Issues in Practice). London: Institute of Education.

Standard 8.5: Take responsibility for leading practice through appropriate professional development for self and colleagues

Standard 8.5 provides you with an opportunity to demonstrate how you support the professional development needs of yourself and your colleagues. You will evidence how you identify practitioners' needs for professional development and address these needs by providing mentoring and support, access to training or by delivering training yourself.

You will be able to evidence how you take time to find out from colleagues what their professional development needs are, so that you can provide opportunities that are personalised and, therefore, effective.

Standard 8.5 provides a chance for you to demonstrate that, when you organise or lead a training event or mentor or support a colleague, you have taken the time to make sure that the support on offer will address your colleague's needs.

'Take responsibility for leading practice'

Look carefully at the key terms in 8.5 to appreciate the breadth of evidence required. You are asked to *take responsibility* for *leading practice* through *appropriate professional development*. You need to evidence your leadership role and demonstrate how you work with colleagues to identify their professional development needs and, especially if you are a manager, identify colleagues' professional development needs yourself.

Take responsibility for providing *appropriate professional development* opportunities that can address the needs you have identified, either by providing support or training yourself, or by directing colleagues to available, external training opportunities.

Remember that you are asked to *take responsibility for leading practice*. This means that your support for the professional development of yourself and others must lead practice forwards. You will demonstrate *leading practice* when you can evidence that the support or training you provide has had a positive impact on practice.

Cross-referencing your evidence for 8.4 and 8.5

As you must evidence how you lead practice, there will be some overlap between 8.5 and your evidence for 8.4, where you are asked to *model and implement effective education and care and lead other practitioners*.

If you wish to cross-reference some of your evidence of supporting a colleague or modelling good practice to 8.5 as well as 8.4, then you will need to demonstrate that you are addressing an identified professional development need. This is because 8.4 looks at the strategies you use to support and lead other practitioners and 8.5 looks at both how you identify and support the professional development required to move practice forwards.

'Appropriate professional development'

You are asked to lead practice *through appropriate professional development*. Professional development, in this context, can include a wide range of strategies. You could evidence how you organise a place for a colleague on a training day, agree to fund a place for a colleague on an early childhood studies degree programme, set up a system to promote peer mentoring or organise exchange visits to other settings.

You could also provide reading materials, model good practice, support colleagues in managing change and provide one-to-one coaching or mentoring support. What you need to remember, however, is that in 8.5 you need to demonstrate how this addresses a professional development need and that you are leading practice. This is why your evidence of the more general mentoring and coaching support you offer will provide stronger evidence for 8.4 than 8.5.

'For ... colleagues'

You must evidence that you provide appropriate professional development *for self and colleagues*, so in your evidence you need examples of identifying and supporting the professional development needs of your colleagues and of reflecting on your own training needs. We will look at identifying your own professional development needs later in this chapter.

If you are not a manager and supporting colleagues' professional development is not one of your routine responsibilities, you need to find a leadership method that will feel comfortable for you and your colleagues. You need to gain the trust of your team and identify some strategies that feel appropriate before you can start to identify and address colleagues' professional development needs.

If you develop a practice of listening carefully and exploring issues with your colleagues, they will feel more comfortable having these conversations with you and you will have some ideas about where they may need support.

You need to remember that your colleagues may not feel comfortable sharing with you any gaps in their knowledge or practice and you will have to show that you are trustworthy. Respectful, trusting relationships need to be built up over time, and you need to make this a priority if you want your role as an Early Years Teacher to be truly effective.

Chapter 10, on understanding 'personal practice' and 'leadership', will suggest some strategies you may find non-threatening and effective, especially once your team learn through experience that your approach will be supportive, empowering and non-judgemental. At this point you might find a more informal approach helpful, such as sharing points from an article you found interesting or modelling a new activity you read about in *Nursery World*.

Once you have developed your confidence, think about other methods to support professional development, such as delivering training or promoting a professional discussion during a staff meeting. For example, during a staff meeting you can present information and provide written materials that colleagues can take away with them to address an area where they felt they needed additional support. You can also evidence 8.5 when you model good practice yourself or invite a colleague to model good practice to address a professional development need.

'For self'

You must evidence that you take responsibility for your own professional development and demonstrate how this helps you to *take responsibility for leading practice*. Use your journal to reflect on your professional development needs and the steps you will take to address these. Share these reflections with your manager when completing your annual appraisal and then include your appraisal in your document portfolio.

Once you have identified a particular professional development need, you can consider a range of strategies to address this; for example, you do not have to identify a need to attend additional training, if that is not appropriate. You could, instead, identify a need to extend your reading in a particular area, for example, to support your understanding for one of the Standards.

In fact, any gaps in your knowledge or practice that you identify and address to help you achieve your Early Years Teacher Status can help you to evidence 8.5. This includes any additional reading that helps you to evidence a Standard, such as 3.4, or the research you plan to carry out during your school placement, for example, to help you evidence 3.1 and 3.3. You might find that your journal is very helpful here, as you can use it to record the stages in this process and highlight how what you are learning has a positive impact on how you lead practice.

You can use your reflective journal to reflect on a range of professional development opportunities, such as:

- a training event you chose to attend and how this impacts on your practice;

- visits to other settings to observe good practice;

- your further reading and the impact of this on your practice;

- what you have learnt while shadowing a colleague or learning a new skill;

- what you have learnt during a short placement, such as your school-based placement or a placement in a baby room;

- training materials you developed for colleagues so as to cascade your learning.

Remember that including a training certificate does not provide evidence of professional development as it only evidences that you attended a training event. However, you can evidence your professional development when you describe what you have learnt and reflect on how this informs your practice.

Manager's role

If you are a manager, you will have more opportunities to evidence 8.5. You can, for example, evidence your role in leading appraisals. You can evidence how you use each appraisal to explore with each practitioner what they feel their most pressing training needs are and demonstrate how you arrange for these needs to be met. However, appraisals only occur at fixed intervals, and training needs may arise at any time.

If, for example, a colleague becomes key person to a child with autism or a medical condition, she will need training on how best to support that child as soon as possible. You will need to evidence how you support your co-worker and provide access to appropriate professional development opportunities.

If you are a setting manager you may also have access to external training events that you can recommend, particularly those run by your local authority. If you can demonstrate that you identified appropriate training needs and arranged for colleagues to attend a relevant training event, then this provides some evidence for 8.5. You may have emails or documents that demonstrate that you identified a training need and booked a colleague a place on an external training course. If you have identified training needs in your self-evaluation form (SEF) then you can include this, too, to help you evidence 8.5.

Remember that in 8.5 you need evidence of *leading practice through appropriate professional development*. Arranging for a colleague to attend training or shadow a colleague is not enough; you need to demonstrate how this led to an improvement in practice.

CASE STUDY

Identifying training needs

Louise, an Early Years Teacher trainee, identified a need for safeguarding training in her team. She was aware that if training is to be relevant and appropriate and have a positive impact on practice, it needs to address the areas where colleagues need support, so Louise decided to deliver a safeguarding quiz in a staff meeting. She discovered from the answers to the quiz that colleagues were confident identifying signs and symptoms, but were less sure about reporting procedures. Louise decided that the training she would deliver would focus on this.

Identifying professional development needs in your team

There are many strategies you can use to identify professional development needs. Often you can find out what colleagues' needs are just through your daily conversations or discussions during team meetings.

In 8.5 you must lead practice, so you must make sure that the professional development you promote is relevant enough to have a positive impact on practice. For example, a colleague may ask for help with observations. Rather than provide guidance on every aspect of observation, you need to find out exactly which aspects your co-worker finds difficult. It may be that he struggles to understand which observation method is best in which situation, or that he finds it hard to use an observation to identify 'next steps'. You might even find out that his concern is his poor spelling and that he needs support with managing his dyslexia.

A quiz in a team meeting can be an effective strategy to gain an overview of the professional development needs of your team, but for it to be effective you need to create an atmosphere which is non-threatening and non-judgemental. If you have been developing an ethos of reflective practice in your setting, then colleagues are also less likely to feel undermined by revealing gaps in their understanding or practice. It is up to you to create an environment where practitioners feel safe enough to acknowledge that they have something to learn.

If you are leading a change in practice and support colleagues in adapting to the change, perhaps by helping them to develop the new skills they need, then this can provide some evidence for 8.5.

CASE STUDY

Reflective practice

Lesley, an Early Years Teacher trainee, felt that it was important to promote reflective practice in her setting. She believed that if reflective practice was embedded within the team, then identifying training needs would become a natural part of this process.

*She discovered that the Pre-school Learning Alliance has a Quality Improvement scheme called Reflecting on Quality (**www.pre-school.org.uk/providers/quality-improvement/679/reflecting-on-quality**). Settings are awarded this kite mark if they can demonstrate that all practitioners in their setting are involved in a continuous process of reflection and self-evaluation.*

She decided that for her own professional development she needed to find out more about this Quality Improvement scheme and think about whether she could promote some of the principles of this scheme within her own setting. She thought that if she could reflect on this in her journal she would evidence how she was 'leading practice through appropriate professional development for self and colleagues' for 8.5.

'Professional development': additional strategies

We have looked at how you can take responsibility for colleagues' professional development through leading discussions and providing guidance and training. However, there are other strategies you can consider. You may find that some of these strategies will overlap with your evidence for 8.4, where you demonstrate how you support colleagues and model good practice.

You can evidence that you lead practice through appropriate professional development when you introduce a change in practice or develop the environment, for example, by introducing ECAT through cascading the training you received. Your presentation of the rationale for a change can promote professional development. For example, you can share your observations of how children are under-using an area of provision or provide an article for colleagues to read that looks at ways of improving practice. If you involve colleagues in this process of making informed decisions before introducing a change, then this promotes professional development.

You promote professional development when you support colleagues in preparing for the demands of a change in practice, either by providing space to explore how the prospect of change can be unsettling, or by looking at their need for additional training.

You also promote professional development when you engage in informal conversations with colleagues, such as when you encourage them to evaluate provision or ask 'what if … ?' questions. You can evidence this through witness testimonies from colleagues or by recording and reflecting on these informal conversations in your journal.

Evaluating the impact of 'professional development'

Training on its own does not change practice, so you need to provide opportunities for colleagues – and yourself – to reflect on what they have learnt and identify how this can have a positive impact on their practice.

You may not be able to allocate time for this, so you need to consider ways that you can embed what has been learnt so that it does, in fact, have an impact on practice. You can do this through revisiting a topic or reviewing the impact of a training session with a colleague or in a staff meeting a few weeks after it was first discussed.

Another way to embed learning is to ask a colleague who has attended training to cascade her learning. If she does not feel comfortable leading a training session, she can informally highlight the most useful points she learnt and how it impacts on her practice. You can then pick up on key points raised and explore them further through discussion or providing information and resources.

You must create opportunities for colleagues and yourself to evaluate training events, so that you can identify what worked well and what still needs to be addressed. You can create simple evaluation forms, or, at the end of the session, ask colleagues to describe or write on a sticky note one thing they will take away with them from the session. You can then use these points to create a summary sheet to recap the main points of the session. Any records of this process of evaluation can be included as evidence for 8.5 and some evidence may overlap with 8.4.

Evidence for 8.5

Your evidence for 8.5 needs to demonstrate how you take responsibility for leading practice and supporting the professional development of yourself and your colleagues. You can do this by evidencing how you identify and address professional development needs, through providing support, guidance and training, modelling good practice, providing access to external training opportunities or by arranging for an expert to visit your setting to share expertise.

For your evidence to be strong, you must demonstrate that you identified specific development needs and that the support you facilitate addresses these needs. You must avoid making the assumption that all colleagues need general training in a subject, such as observation. If you provide training that addresses areas where colleagues are confident rather than focus on their gaps, then they will have less interest in the process and possibly feel that they have not been listened to.

To strengthen your evidence for 8.5 further, you can review the evidence you have and check that you include examples of supporting the professional development of more than one colleague and of using a range of strategies. Think about how you identify your own professional development needs and find a way to make this process explicit. If this process is something that occurs only in your head, you need to find a way to record and evidence it, perhaps in your reflective journal or a written assignment.

If you feel you need to widen your experience to evidence 8.5, you can look at your SEF, check whether any areas of professional development still need to be addressed and take responsibility for addressing one of these areas.

Written assignments, case studies and your reflective journal

If you use a written assignment or case study to describe a change you have introduced or how you have promoted practice in a particular area, then this may help you to evidence 8.5. You would be able to outline your role in the process of identifying professional development needs and in ensuring that these are met. For example, if you described how you provided training for colleagues to help them plan and carry out heuristic play activities for toddlers indoors and outdoors, then you can evidence why this change was needed and how you help colleagues develop the appropriate skills.

You can use a case study, assignment or a series of journal entries to describe the various strategies you employed to *take responsibility for leading practice through appropriate professional development*. This might involve:

- providing team training yourself;
- providing one-to-one support for a particular colleague;

- arranging visits to other settings;
- employing an external trainer.

All these actions can provide evidence for 8.5, but what will make your evidence stronger will be the level of detail and reflection you provide. General statements, such as 'I led a staff training session on the new planning system', do not convey enough detail, either about what you did or why you did it.

Document portfolio

You may have a series of documents that you can include in your portfolio to evidence 8.5:

- If you are a manager you can include anonymised appraisal forms or records of training needs identified in your SEF and other documents.

- You can include emails or application forms that evidence how you arranged for practitioners to attend training as long as these clearly demonstrate your role in this process.

- You can provide evidence of supporting a practitioner's individual professional development through your planning notes or any materials you prepare for that person, or an evaluation or witness testimony she completes for you.

- If you delivered a training event, you can include a record of the reasons why this training was needed, a description of your actions and any handouts or other materials you provided.

You also need to evidence how you identify and address your own training needs. You can evidence your reflections on your professional development needs through your own entries on your appraisal form alongside entries in your reflective journal. You can include records of arrangements for and attendance at a training event, but you need to remember that all a certificate of attendance demonstrates is that you attended. If you reflect on what you learnt and how you will apply this to your practice, then your evidence is much stronger.

You may identify a need to develop your reading in a particular area for your Early Years Teacher Status, such as your understanding of babies' development or learning in school. You can evidence this process in your reflective journal, but also through sharing this knowledge with your colleagues, for example, in a handout or poster.

Observations

When you are observed leading an activity with children or in a meeting with a colleague, you can evidence how you support a colleague's professional development. You can do this by modelling a skill or activity for a colleague, or by leading a mentoring session. You need to make sure that your plans for the session highlight your role in identifying and supporting this colleague's professional development.

You can also evidence your own professional development when you are observed by a mentor or tutor. For example, you can highlight in your plans for the session the background reading and research you carried out or the training you attended to prepare you for this. For example, you may have attended training on Makaton and arrange to be observed leading circle time where you introduce a Makaton sign.

SUGGESTED READING

Allen, S and Whalley, M (2011) *Leading Practice in Early Years Settings* (Achieving EYPS Series). London: Learning Matters.

Miller, L, Cable, C and Drury, R (eds) (2012) *Extending Professional Practice in the Early Years*. London: OUP and SAGE.

Miller, L, Cable, C and Devereux, J (2013) *Developing Early Years Practice*. Oxon: David Fulton.

Price, D and Ota, C (2014) *Leading and Supporting Early Years Teams: A Practical Guide*. London: David Fulton.

Reardon, D (2012) *Achieving Early Years Professional Status*. London: SAGE.

Reed, M and Canning, N (2009) *Reflective Practice in the Early Years*. London: SAGE.

Robins, A (2014) *Mentoring in the Early Years*. London: Paul Chapman.

Robins, A and Callan, S (2014) *Managing Early Years Settings: Supporting and Leading Teams*. London: SAGE.

Rodd, J (2005) *Leadership in Early Childhood: The Pathway to Professionalism*. Berkshire: OUP McGraw Hill-Education.

Standard 8.6: Reflect on and evaluate the effectiveness of provision, and shape and support good practice

Standard 8.6 gives you an opportunity to demonstrate how you reflect on and evaluate the effectiveness of your provision so that you can shape and support good practice. You will use this process of reflection and evaluation to identify where provision needs to be improved or practice supported, and this is the essence of your role as Early Years Teacher. You are a *catalyst for change*, but not change for its own sake. (*Catalyst for change* was the phrase used to describe the role of the Early Years Professional: although this term is not used in the same way to describe the role of an Early Years Teacher, it still is a helpful concept that describes an important aspect of your role.) You will only introduce a change, or *shape … good practice* when the process of reflection and evaluation has led you to conclude that this will promote *good practice*.

There are several phrases in 8.6 that you need to be aware of. You need to evidence that you *reflect on and evaluate the effectiveness of provision*. This means that you need to both reflect on and evaluate a range of aspects of your provision, and if possible, provision across your setting. You will need to decide on the methods you can use to reflect on and evaluate your provision and how you can use this process to support improvements in practice.

Rae reflects on the effectiveness of provision

Rae, an Early Years Teacher trainee, was concerned that the water tray in the garden was rarely used. Over one week, Rae observed how frequently children accessed the water tray and analysed the quality of children's engagement while they were there and how staff supported children's learning. Rae shared her observations and reflections with the team the following week. She was aware that she could see where improvements could be made, but felt it might be more effective to suggest that as a team they decide on a strategy to improve practice in this area.

Rae was then able to support Dominique, a new member of staff who had studied boat building, to lead a project on boats. The children could design and make miniature boats that they could then test in the outdoor water tray.

As 8.6 is part of Standard 8, you must demonstrate your leadership role in a manner that feels appropriate for you. You must show that you use your reflections and evaluation to help you decide when, where and how you need to *shape and support good practice*. You will find that this may overlap with your evidence for 8.4, where you *implement effective education and care ... and lead other practitioners* and 8.5, where you *take responsibility for leading practice*. However, in 8.4 you are asked to evidence how you support your colleagues, but in 8.6 you need to evidence how you support colleagues so as to shape provision.

'Reflect on ... the effectiveness of provision'

The role of the Early Years Teacher is that of a reflective practitioner who leads and supports colleagues to improve provision. Therefore, one of the key qualities you need to demonstrate is your ability to reflect on your provision and use your reflections to inform your practice and the practice of your colleagues.

You must demonstrate how you engage in an ongoing process of continuous reflection, through the cycle of action, reflection and review. Think about how you can fully evidence this process, for example, through observations and entries in your journal. As Standard 8 asks for evidence of leadership, you can also evidence how you involve colleagues in this process of reflection and evaluation.

You will need to use your reflections and evaluations to *shape and support good practice*, so you need to be able to draw conclusions that you can apply to practice, and be in a position where you can influence practice and support colleagues. If you are not a manager and this is not part of your role in the setting, think about leadership strategies that feel appropriate. Chapter 10, on understanding 'personal practice' and 'leadership', has some suggestions you may find helpful.

You may find it helpful to read about developing reflective practice in the early years and there are some helpful texts in the 'Suggested reading' section of this chapter. You might find it particularly helpful to read about Kolb's learning cycle (Kolb, 1984;

www.ldu.leeds.ac.uk/ldu/sddu_multimedia/kolb/static_version.php), which looks at the stages of concrete experience, reflective observation, abstract conceptualisation and active experimentation.

If your setting takes part in a Quality Improvement scheme, such as the Pre-school Learning Alliance's *Reflecting on Quality* (**www.pre-school.org.uk/providers/quality-improvement/679/reflecting-on-quality**), then there may already be structures in place to support a setting-wide process of continuous reflection and improvement.

As you must evidence how you reflect and evaluate provision, think about how you can combine the need for an objective assessment of current practice with the benefits of more subjective, personal reflections, where you rely on your professional understanding to interpret what you observe. You may decide that in some situations you need to rely on your professional judgement rather than an objective evaluation.

Cross-referencing evidence of reflective practice

In each of the previous chapters you have been encouraged to reflect on your practice in your journal and use this to evidence your practice for a particular Standard. If you have reflected on and evaluated the effectiveness of your provision in these entries, then you can use this to evidence 8.6 as well.

For example, in your evidence for 1.1 you may have used your journal to reflect (8.6) on whether a particular area of provision was *safe and stimulating* (1.1) and then looked at how you could *shape and support good practice* (8.6) to ensure that *children feel confident and are able to develop and learn* (1.1).

If you need more information on how to use your reflective journal, you can find guidance in Chapter 4, Assessment methods.

'Reflect on and evaluate ... provision'

As you are asked to reflect on and *evaluate* provision, you must think about the areas of provision that you will review and the methods you can use to evaluate your reflections. For example, if you have completed observations that look at girls' access to the construction area, then you can analyse these to identify how you can *shape and support good practice* to encourage girls' participation.

There are several methods you can use to evaluate your reflections. A particularly effective method is triangulation, where you compare a range of perspectives. You could arrange triangulated observations, where you and your colleagues observe an area of provision and these several viewpoints are compared to form a fuller picture.

A parent questionnaire also provides you with an alternative viewpoint to compare to your own. You can organise a questionnaire that asks for parents' opinions on the area of provision you are reviewing so that this will provide information that you can reflect on and review with your team.

If you have completed time-sampling or tracking observations, you will have some information that you can share with your team and can ask them to share their interpretations of your data. If you have completed a narrative observation, you can share this with your team and consider the implications of the observation together. If you feel you need a more objective approach, you can request that another colleague observes the same area of provision so that you don't make decisions based on one single observation.

Another way to evaluate provision is to ask colleagues to share their reflections and opinions and use these differing points of view to form a three-dimensional understanding of the issues. You could also ask colleagues to identify the strengths and weaknesses of the existing system, possibly anonymously on sticky notes, and discuss these in a team meeting. You could then lead a SWOT analysis, to examine strengths, weaknesses, opportunities and threats.

An event may lead to a decision to reflect on an area of provision. For example, an incident in one area may prompt you to reflect on and evaluate safety issues. Or, you may have completed observations of a child with English as a second language settling in and wondered whether this process might be improved if colleagues were familiar with some key words in a new child's home language?

If you are involved in contributing to the SEF, this is another opportunity for you to reflect on and shape good practice. If you are involved in introducing a project that addresses an area of practice, such as ECAT or Forest or Beach Schools, then this can also help you to evidence 8.6. You can evidence your role in identifying the need for development in this area, and then highlight how you *shape and support good practice* through the project.

What is important is that you evidence the process of evaluating practice and, if you wish to strengthen your evidence, review a range of areas in your setting, not just those that are most obvious. For example, you may evaluate the settling-in routine for children with English as a second language, but not consider the impact of other equality issues, such as whether your resources appropriately reflect the backgrounds of the children.

Your role is to reflect on provision and identify steps to improve provision and it will be helpful, at this point, to think about where you will find your evidence. You may find evidence of reflective practice in entries in your journal, and evidence of evaluating provision in the minutes of a staff meeting, a completed SEF form or Quality Improvement documentation, as well as in your observations.

What is 'good practice'?

Standard 8.6 asks you to do more than reflect on practice – you have to use your reflections to help you *shape and support good practice*. So, before you start to evidence how you promote good practice, you need to make sure that both you and your colleagues have a very clear understanding of what good practice is.

You may have a reasonably good idea of what good practice looks like in accordance with EYFS requirements, but if you have a child join your setting who has a medical condition you are unfamiliar with, do you know what good practice would look like for that child? You may feel that you and your team are confident supporting pre-school children's communication skills, but if the pre-school and toddler rooms join together, how confident are you all in meeting the toddlers' needs – and the needs of the pre-school children in this new context?

'Shape and support good practice'

In 8.4 you evidence how you support and lead practitioners to implement effective education and care. In 8.6 there is some overlap with 8.4, but the emphasis is slightly different. Here, you must demonstrate how you use reflection and evaluation to shape and support good practice. This requires an understanding of what constitutes good practice (which we have looked at in the previous paragraph), and the ability both to support and shape this. You must understand how to review current provision, identify strategies to address any areas for improvement and support staff to develop their practice.

Actions that evidence how you *shape and support good practice* can include reviewing policies, sharing research findings, modelling good practice, leading training, introducing professional discussions and providing case studies for your team to explore. You must demonstrate your own reflective practice and support colleagues to become reflective practitioners themselves.

If you have worked with a local authority advisor to develop your provision, you can include evidence from your discussions and records of planned actions. You will need to highlight your own evaluations of the next steps that you identified. If the advisor raised any issues and you acted on her suggestions, then your evidence only meets the second half of 8.6.

You might find it helpful to look at the role of policies in shaping practice. If you can be involved in the annual review of your setting's key policies, then this may help you to evidence how you *shape and support good practice*. If you highlight why you suggested certain changes, then this will provide evidence of reflection and evaluation.

Remember that several Standards ask you to evidence your practice within each age range, babies, toddlers and pre-school children. It will help you to meet this requirement if you reflect on and shape and support practice with each age group. If you carry out an age-related placement, 8.6 can be one of the indicators you plan to evidence through your work on this placement.

If you have a leadership or management role in your setting, then shaping provision may be one part of your general responsibilities. If this is not a part of your role, then you must consider what approaches would be appropriate and feel comfortable for you. Chapter 10, on understanding 'personal practice' and 'leadership', has some guidance on this.

You need to remember that 8.6 differs from 8.4 as your starting point is the developmental needs of the setting, rather than of individual practitioners.

A helpful starting point can be to identify all the ways in which you have and can shape provision. This might include an occasion when you have encouraged a professional discussion in a team meeting, or introduced rolling snack. You might also have a plan to introduce mark-making activities in the garden to support boys' literacy development.

Once you have identified these examples of your practice you can think about the process of reflection that led you to identify these areas as a priority and think about how you can evidence your role in shaping and supporting good practice. Use Table S8.2 to help you in this. Rae, an Early Years Teacher trainee, has shared some examples of her practice to help you start.

Table S8.2 *'Shape and support good practice'*

My reflections and evaluations	My actions to 'shape and support good practice'	My evidence
In my journal I identified a need for all practitioners to engage in reflective practice. We need a framework to help us to continuously review and improve practice In my observations on my toddler room placement I noticed that due to high noise levels at times it was difficult to support toddlers' communication skills.	I discussed this with my manager and we are looking at different ways to organise this I carried out some research on Every Child A Talker (ECAT) (**www.foundationyears. org.uk/files/2011/10/ecat_guidance_ for_practitioners_31.pdf**) and 'communication-friendly places' to see if we could introduce them in the toddler room. I will present my findings at a staff meeting next week	My journal Minutes of meeting with my manager My reflections on my observations My observations My notes on ECAT Minutes of staff meeting Case study about promoting toddlers' communication skills

Shaping provision: promoting a collaborative approach

For changes you introduce to become successfully embedded, you need to involve your team. If you promote a collaborative, co-operative approach, all colleagues will understand the rationale for change and have a sense of ownership in the process. This will also help you to make the most of the expertise within your group. You may have identified a need for development in one area, but your colleagues may be able to suggest a more effective strategy to address this as they have more direct experience or relevant expertise.

You need to present your evaluation and rationale for change and promote a culture of collaborative working and the sharing of expertise to identify the best way forwards. If you try to impose a change on your setting without colleagues' support, then it is unlikely to succeed. The exception to this is a safeguarding or health and safety issue that needs to be addressed immediately.

Collaborative leadership strategies include listening to colleagues, creating an environment of trust so that colleagues feel safe to make suggestions, finding out about areas of expertise and interest and delegating tasks to the person who feels passionate about this.

You can also go further and ask, 'what do you think are our problem areas and what do you think we can do about this?' Each approach is appropriate in certain circumstances, and you will need to decide which to use and when. You need to be careful, however, that if you use the third approach you still have evidence of your own role in reflecting on and evaluating practice for 8.6.

Reviewing your changes

As you are engaging in the reflection and evaluation in 8.6, you need to make sure that you provide clear evidence of evaluating your own actions. You must reflect on provision and support good practice, therefore you need to show that changes you introduced have improved provision and do promote *good practice*.

You can review the effectiveness of the changes you introduce through parent questionnaires, professional discussions with colleagues, triangulated 'before and after' observations and observations of individual children engaging in this area before and after you introduced a change.

If you are unsure about how to evaluate your changes, you may find it helpful to read more about the reflective cycle and you will find some helpful texts recommended in the section on 'Suggested reading'.

When you evaluate your change, you will probably see that not everything will have worked out as you had hoped and you have some additional small changes or improvements to introduce. You are not expected to evidence a change where everything turns out perfectly, but you do need to demonstrate that you review your change and plan to address any areas where practice still needs to improve. It is important that you remember to evidence all these stages in the process.

Action research

If you have any evidence of identifying an area for development and leading action research in this area, then this will help you to evidence 8.6. If you wish to learn about carrying out action research in early years settings, there are helpful texts recommended in the section on 'Suggested reading'.

CASE STUDY

Rae's action research

Rae decided she wanted to carry out action research in her setting. She had observed that Ellie, a two-year-old girl who had just started in the toddler room, settled more easily when her older brother, Louie, was allowed to visit from the pre-school room. Rae observed Louie introducing Ellie to the tea set in the home corner where they spent an hour pouring out cups of tea for each other.

This process of observation and reflection led Rae to think about carrying out some action research on the benefits of encouraging contact between siblings who are based in different rooms, at certain points during the nursery day. She spoke to her manager about designing a piece of research to look at children's experiences at rest, snack and story times both with and without their sibling/s present. The theory she wished to test was that children may feel more secure at these times with their siblings present, as this was more likely to mirror their experiences at home.

Evidence for 8.6

Written assignments, case studies and your reflective journal

Your reflective journal is a crucial tool for evidencing the process of reflection and evaluation for 8.6, so if you are at all unsure as to how to use it, you need to read the texts recommended under 'Suggested reading' and the Chapter 4, Assessment methods.

You may find that a written assignment or case study will help you to evidence how you *shape and support good practice*. You can describe how you introduced a change in practice and present the rationale for this change and the work you have done to support colleagues' practice in this area.

You need to make sure that your evidence is detailed and you explicitly record each stage in the process of reflection and evaluation. You can include brief quotes from your journal if this will evidence the direction and depth of this process. If you carried out any research into good practice in a specific area or provision, then you can describe this and consider the implications for practice.

You can also use an assignment or case study to record how you evaluated any evidence you collated, for example, through observations or a parent questionnaire, as well as the conclusions you reached. You can describe how you use these evaluations to inform your plans and how you presented this to your team. You need evidence of supporting colleagues to understand the rationale for change and to develop any additional skills they will need. You can describe any team meetings you led on this topic, training you provided and any one-to-one support you provided for colleagues.

You may have modelled new practice for colleagues and provided opportunities for them to shadow you and you can use an assignment or case study to describe these interventions in detail and evidence the impact this had on practice. You can then describe how you evaluated the effectiveness of these changes, perhaps through your observations of interactions with individual children before and after the change, and you can include brief quotes from these observations. If you identified additional small changes required or extension activity you planned to add, then you can describe what you still need to do.

Document portfolio

There are several documents that you can include in your portfolio to help you to evidence 8.6. These can include:

- minutes of a staff meeting;

- completed parent questionnaires;

- a witness testimony or training notes from a meeting where you suggested a change in practice;

- evidence of your involvement in revising a policy;

- your SEF if you highlight your role in the process of reflection, evaluation and *shaping and supporting good practice*.

If you have worked alongside a local authority advisor to develop your provision, then you can include records of your work together, as long as it is clear what your contributions were.

In addition:

- If you are the setting manager, your Ofsted report may include some comments that evidence what you have done to shape provision and you can evidence any actions you initiated to address Ofsted action points.

- If you are involved in a Quality Improvement scheme, any ways in which you have contributed to the evaluation of current practice and promoted good practice can be included as evidence.

- If you have completed a placement, you need to make sure that you have several documents to evidence any changes you introduced and your process of reflection, evaluation and support for colleagues. You can also include a detailed witness testimony and any other documents that evidence the changes you introduced while on this placement.

Observations

You can arrange to be observed carrying out a new routine or an activity you introduced as a result of your evaluation of practice. If, for example, you introduced rolling snack and the use of snack times to promote interactions between children and practitioners, then you can arrange to be observed leading rolling snack. In your plan for the session you can highlight the changes you introduced and how this supports good practice.

You may have introduced changes and shaped and supported practice with children in each age group – babies, toddlers and pre-school children. You can arrange to be observed working with each age group, carrying out an activity in an area where you have made a positive impact. You can highlight in your plans for the session how you identified a need for this change, perhaps using a quote from your journal or quoting from the findings of the parent questionnaire. If, however, you completed a short placement with one age group and were not able to be observed during this time, you need to make sure that you record plenty of evidence of your role in shaping and supporting good practice in your document portfolio, your journal and an assignment or case study.

You may be able to demonstrate how the changes you introduced had an impact on the fabric of the room, its organisation, planning systems, routines or activities. You need to think about how you can evidence these changes during an observation, either by making reference to them in your planning notes or by arranging to be observed mentoring a colleague in the new system. You can emphasise during the mentoring session the benefits of this change in practice, for example, that more observations are carried out at key times now that rotas have been adjusted to increase key times and practitioners have received the training on observation.

SUGGESTED READING

Brock, A (2014) *The Early Years Reflective Practice Handbook.* London: Routledge.

Hallet, E (2013) *The Reflective Early Years Practitioner.* London: SAGE.

Kolb, DA (1983) *Experiential Learning: Experience as the Source of Learning and Development.* London: Prentice Hall.

Lindon, J (2012) *Reflective Practice and Early Years Professionalism Linking Theory and Practice.* London: Hodder.

Mukherji, P and Albon, D (2010) *Research Methods in Early Childhood.* London: SAGE.

Paige-Smith, A and Craft, A. (2011) *Developing Reflective Practice in the Early Years.* Berkshire: OUP McGraw-Hill Education.

Reed, M and Canning, N (eds) (2010) *Reflective Practice in the Early Years.* London: SAGE.

Thornton, L and Brunton, P (2010) *Bringing the Reggio Approach to your Early Years Practice* (Bringing ... to Your Early Years Practice). Oxon: David Fulton.

Standard 8.7: Understand the importance of and contribute to multi-agency team working

In Standard 8.7 you will evidence that you understand why multi-agency working is so important and demonstrate how you have contributed to a multi-agency team. This indicator requires clear evidence of your understanding of the importance of a multi-agency approach and your practice in contributing to one of these teams, so you need to make sure that you provide good evidence of both your understanding and your practice. This indicator is one of four that look at your work with other professionals, so you will need to appreciate why this indicator is different from the other three, and the implications of this for your evidence.

To evidence 8.7 well, you must understand what is meant by *multi-agency team working* and appreciate the difference between this and the reference to *other professionals* in 5.5, 6.2 and 8.3, as this will have implications for your evidence. You must carefully compare this indicator to 5.5, 6.2 and 8.3, so that you can make sure that the evidence you provide for each is appropriate.

Because you will have looked at your role in working with other professionals in detail in 5.5, 6.2 and 8.3, in this section we will focus on understanding the term *multi-agency team working*, look at how this indicator differs from 5.5, 6.2 and 8.3 and consider how you can evidence 8.7. If you need more information on working with other professionals, you can look again at the sections for 5.5, 6.2 and 8.3.

Understand the importance of multi-agency team working

In Standard 8.3 you were reminded that one reason for the importance of fostering a culture of co-operation between practitioners, parents and external professionals was that sharing expertise and information can ensure a child is safe and that supports children to reach their potential. Reference was made to the Laming (2003) Inquiry into the death of Victoria Climbié where it was felt that the failure of agencies to work together contributed to her death. You need to be particularly aware of the importance of multi-agency team working in any situation where a safeguarding concern has been raised.

You need to identify the multi-agency teams that you have contributed to and the case study below will help you to identify what a multi-agency team is. For example, you might be able to evidence how you worked in a multi-agency team and contributed to a TAC meeting or CAF, or worked with a range of other professionals to support a child with a medical condition, disability or special need.

CASE STUDY

Multi-agency team working

Beth, an Early Years Teacher trainee, used her journal to reflect on her experience in a multi-agency team supporting her twin key children. She described how she attended CAF and TAC meetings and shared her observations, information from the two-year-old progress check and from her conversation with the twin's parents. She then described how she worked particularly closely with two other professionals, David, the twins' doctor and Max, the family's social worker.

If you are concerned that you may not have enough appropriate evidence for 8.7, look back at your evidence for 5.5, 6.2 and 8.3 to see if you have any relevant evidence you can adapt for 8.7. If you still do not have relevant evidence, there are strategies you can use to address this gap in your practice. For example, you could arrange to shadow a professional who is part of a multi-agency team, and interview her about her work. In this case, you would need to write a case study to demonstrate that you would know what you would do if you were working in a multi-agency team in a range of hypothetical situations.

What is a 'multi-agency team' working?

In Table S8.3, you will find a series of definitions that relate to partnerships, interdisciplinary, multi-disciplinary, multi-agency and intersectoral team working. Read through these definitions and think about how each term relates to your work with other professionals. If you can identify the differences between these terms, it can help you clarify your understanding of what is meant by 'multi-agency team working'.

These definitions come from the work of Albon and Mukherji (2008: 140–141) who draw on Naidoo and Wills' (2009) exploration of the terminology used to describe the relationships involved in working together in health promotion.

You can relate the definitions to your own experience and practice in your setting or children's centre, and think about how you can evidence your role in any of these teams. You can also find your own definition of each of these terms, if you find these more appropriate for the context of your work in the early years.

Table S8.3 Definitions of partnership, interdisciplinary, multi-disciplinary, multi-agency and intersectoral team working

	Definition from Naidoo and Wills (2009)	Alternative definition	Evidence
Partnership	Sharing of power and joint action between agencies at local and national levels		
Inter- or multi-disciplinary working	This includes the joint working of people with different roles within the same organisation or across sectors. The term can be used less narrowly in the early years		
Service agreements and contracts	These are set out to clarify the mutual responsibilities each partner has in relation to improving health		
Multi-agency	This refers to organisations who belong to the same sector such as health, education or social services. Naidoo and Wills consider that this refers to groups from the statutory providers of public services working together		
Intersectoral	This differs from multi-agency working as more than one sector can be involved, such as the public sector, private sector and voluntary groups. The World Health Organization (WHO Report, 1997, in Naidoo and Wills, 2009) uses the term *intersectoral collaboration* to describe the process where different partners work together to improve health. These partners can include health authorities, businesses, voluntary bodies, government and individuals		

Why is multi-agency team working important?

In your evidence for 8.7 you will need to demonstrate that you *understand the importance of and contribute to multi-agency team working*. So, to evidence 8.7 well, you need to identify all the reasons why this approach is important. Table S8.4 can help you record your thoughts and organise your evidence for 8.7. Beth, the Early Years Teacher trainee, has added her thoughts to help you start.

Table S8.4 Why multi-agency team working is important

The reasons why multi-agency team working is important	My evidence
1. When I work closely with the twin's medical team, they can provide advice and guidance to ensure that I am aware of their medical needs and can keep the twins safe and healthy in the setting and give them the correct medication	My journal Minutes of meetings Emails from David
2. Sharing information and working in a multi-agency team is crucial whenever a safeguarding concern is raised	Handouts from safeguarding training I delivered for my team
3.	
4.	
5.	
6.	
7.	
8.	
9.	
10.	

Cross-referencing Standards 5.5, 6.2, 8.3 and 8.7

In Standard 8.3 we looked at the similarities and differences between the indicators that ask you to evidence your work with *other professionals*. In 8.7 you need a clear understanding of the differences between these three indicators and 8.7. Table S8.5 will help you identify these similarities and differences and the implications for your evidence. Beth, the Early Years Teacher trainee, has added her thoughts to Table S8.5 to help you start.

Table S8.5 Standards 5.5, 6.2, 8.3 and 8.7 – similarities and differences

	5.5	6.2	8.3	8.7
Similarities	'other professionals' Evidence personal practice	'other professionals' Evidence personal practice	'other professionals'	Evidence personal practice
Differences			Evidence leadership	'multi-agency team working'
My actions				
My evidence				

Evidence for 8.7

Written assignments, case studies and your reflective journal

Your evidence for 8.7 needs to address your understanding of the importance of multi-agency team working and demonstrate how you have contributed to a multi-agency team and you can address both of these areas in a written assignment or case study or through a series of entries in your journal. You can describe your understanding of the precise meaning of the term *multi-agency team working* and explain why this is so important, particularly in relation to safeguarding issues and keeping a child safe and healthy.

You can then describe your contributions to a multi-agency team in detail and highlight the benefits of this approach, making sure that all your evidence is carefully anonymised, so as not to identify the child or the setting. If you do not have enough evidence of contributing to a multi-agency team, then you can describe how you shadowed a colleague who does. You can also outline how you would respond in a range of hypothetical situations if you were part of a multi-agency team.

Document portfolio

You may have evidence of your contributions to a multi-agency team that you can include in your document portfolio. Some documents may clearly demonstrate your contribution to the team or the meeting, for example, the minutes of a TAC meeting, or CAF form. Other documents may not highlight your role so clearly, so you will need to add a note to the document to explain your role and highlight your actions and contributions.

You may have documents that evidence your understanding of the importance of multi-agency team working, such as handouts or notes from any training you have delivered, on safeguarding, for example, or on the roles of other professionals. If you have taken part in a multi-agency team or shadowed a colleague who does, you may have a colleague who can provide a witness testimony for you.

You may have a series of letters, reports and emails that record your contributions to a multi-agency team and you can include these as long as they are carefully anonymised.

Observations

You may not feel that it is appropriate to be observed taking part in a multi-agency team meeting due to issues of confidentiality. However, you can arrange to be observed delivering training or mentoring a colleague in the importance of multi-agency team working, perhaps in relation to completing a CAF form or a safeguarding concern.

SUGGESTED READING

Albon, A and Mukherji, P (2008) *Food and Health in Early Childhood: A Holistic Approach.* London: SAGE.

Anning, A, Cottrell, DM, Frost, N and Green, J (2010) *Developing Multiprofessional Teamwork for Integrated Children's Services.* Berkshire: OUP Mc Graw Hill-Education.

Cheminais, R (2009). *Effective Multi-Agency Partnerships: Putting Every Child Matters into Practice.* London: SAGE.

Gasper, M (2009) *Multi-agency Working in the Early Years: Challenges and Opportunities.* London: SAGE.

Naidoo, J and Wills, J (2009) *Foundations for Health Promotion* (Public Health and Health Promotion). Oxford: Elsevier.

Siraj-Blatchford, I, Clarke, K and Needham, M (2007) *The Team Around the Child: Multi-agency Working in the Early Years.* Staffordshire: Trentham.

Trodd, L and Chivers, L (2011) *Interprofessional Working In Practice: Learning And Working Together for Children and Families.* Berkshire: OUP Mc Graw Hill-Education.

References

Ainsworth, MDS and Bell, SM (1970) Attachment, exploration, and separation: Illustrated by the behaviour of one-year-olds in a strange situation. *Child Development*, 41: 49–67.

Ainsworth, MDS, Blehar, MC, Waters, E and Wall, S (1978) *Patterns of Attachment: A Psychological Study of the Strange Situation.* Hillsdale, NJ: Erlbaum.

Albon, A and Mukherji, P (2008) *Food and Health in Early Childhood: A Holistic Approach.* London: SAGE.

Allen, G (2011) *Early Intervention: The Next Steps.* London: Cabinet Office.

Allen, TD and Poteet, ML (1999) Developing effective mentoring relationships: Strategies from the mentor's viewpoint. *The Career Development Quarterly*, 48: 59–73.

Bennis, W and Nanus, B (1985) *Leaders: Strategies for Taking Charge.* New York: Harper & Row.

Bertram, T and Pascal, C (2002) What counts in early learning. In: ON Saracho and B Spodek (eds) *Contemporary Perspectives in Early Childhood Curriculum.* Greenwich, CT: Information Age, pp. 241–256.

Bond, B, Johnson, J, Patmore, M, Weiss, N and Barker, G (2013) *Passing the Professional Skills Tests for Trainee Teachers and Getting into ITT.* London: Learning Matters.

Bowlby, J (1969) *Attachment and Loss: Volume 1, Attachment.* New York: Basic Books.

Brock, A and Rankin, C (2008) *Communication, Language and Literacy from Birth to Five.* London: SAGE.

Brodie, K (2009) *Sustained Sharing Thinking.* Available online at: **www.kathybrodie.com/viewpoint/sustained-shared-thinking-important/** (accessed 20/10/2014).

Bronfenbrenner, U (1979) *The Ecology of Human Development: Experiments by Nature and Design.* Harvard: Harvard University Press.

Bruce, T (1991) *Time to Play in Early Childhood.* London: Hodder Arnold.

Burke, R. and Herron, R. (1996) *Common Sense Parenting.* Nebraska: Boys Town Press.

Children's Workforce Development Council (2009) *Why Employ an Early Years Professional?* Available online at: **http://webarchive.nationalarchives.gov.uk/20091118212822/http://cwdcouncil.org.uk/eyps/why-employ-an-eyp** (accessed 21/10/2014).

Control of Substances Hazardous to Health (COSHH) (Amendment) Regulations (2004) Available online at: **www.opsi.gov.uk/si/si2004/20043386.htm** (accessed 13/11/2014)

Cove, M (2006) Sounds familiar: the history of phonics teaching. In: M Lewis and S Ellis (eds) *Phonics: Practice, Research and Policy.* London: SAGE, chapter 9.

Da Ros-Voseles, D and Fowler-Haughey, S (2007) *Why Children's Dispositions Should Matter to All Teachers.* Available online at: **www.naeyc.org/files/yc/file/200709/DaRos-Voseles.pdf** (accessed 28/10/2014).

Department for Children, Schools and Families (2007) *The Children's Plan: Building Brighter Futures.* Available online at: **www.gov.uk/government/publications/the-childrens-plan** (accessed 13/11/2014).

Department for Children, Schools and Families (2008) *Statutory Framework for the Early Years Foundation Stage.* Nottingham: DCSF Publications.

Department for Children, Schools and Families (2010) *Challenging Practice to Further Improve Learning, Playing and Interacting in the Early Years Foundation Stage.* Nottingham: DCSF Publications.

Department for Education (2009) *Next Steps for Early Learning and Childcare.* Available online at: **http://webarchive. nationalarchives.gov.uk/20130401151715/www.education.gov.uk/publications/standard/_arc_SOP/Page9/DCSF-00173-2009** (accessed 20/10/2014).

Department for Education (2006) *Safeguarding Children and Safer Recruitment in Education.* London: Department for Education.

Department for Education (2011a) *Early Years Evidence Pack.* Available online at: **www.gov.uk/government/uploads/system/uploads/attachment_data/file/180884/DFE-00274-2011.pdf** (accessed 20/10/2014).

Department for Education (2011b) *Supporting Families in the Foundation Years.* Available online at: **www.gov.uk/government/publications/the-childrens-plan** (accessed 13/11/2014).

Department for Education (2012a) *Statutory Framework for the Early Years Foundation Stage.* Runcorn: Department for Education. **www.education.gov.uk/publications/standard/AllPublications?Page1/DFE-00023-2012** (accessed 13/11/2014)

Department for Education (2012b) *Nutbrown Review: Foundations for Quality: The Independent Review of Early Education and Childcare Qualifications: Final Report.* Runcorn: Department for Education.

Department for Education (2013a) *More Great Childcare: Raising Quality and Giving Parents More Choice.* Available online at: **www.gov.uk/government/publications/more-great-childcare-raising-quality-and-giving-parents-more-choice** (accessed 21/10/2014).

Department for Education (2013b) *Working Together to Safeguard Children.* Available online at: **www.gov.uk/government/publications/working-together-to-safeguard-children** (accessed 13/11/2014).

Department for Education (2013c) *Early Years Outcomes: A Non-statutory Guide for Practitioners and Inspectors to Help Inform Understanding of Child Development Through the Early Years.* Available online at: **www.gov.uk/government/uploads/system/uploads/attachment_data/file/237249/Early_Years_Outcomes.pdf** (accessed 13/11/2014).

Department for Education (2014) *Become an Early Years Teacher.* Available online at: **www.education.gov.uk/get-into-teaching/subjects-age-groups/early-years** (accessed 21/10/2014).

Department for Education (2014) *Statutory Framework for the Early Years Foundation Stage: Setting the Standards for Learning, Development and Care for Children from Birth to Five.* DfE Reference: DFE-00337-2014. Runcorn: Department of Education. Available online at **https://www.gov.uk/government/uploads/system/uploads/attachment data/file/335504/EYFS framework from 1 september 2014 with clarification note.pdf** (accessed 13/11/2014).

Department for Education and Skills (DfES) (2001) *Special Educational Needs Code of Practice.* DfES/581/2001. London: DfES.

Department for Education and Skills (DfES) (2003a) *Every Child Matters: Change for Children.* Norwich: The Stationery Office.

Department for Education and Skills (DfES) (2003b) *Birth to Three Matters.* Nottingham: DfES.

Department for Education and Skills (DfES) (2007a) *The Early Years Foundation Stage.* Nottingham: DfES Publications.

Department for Education and Skills (2007b) The Common Assessment Framework for Children and Young People: Practitioners' Guide. DFES-0337-2006. Available online at: **webarchive.nationalarchives.gov.uk/20130401151715/**

http://www.education.gov.uk/publications/standard/publicationDetail/Page1/DFES-0337-2006 (accessed 13/11/2014).

Department for Education, HM Treasury, The Rt Hon Nicky Morgan MP and Parliamentary Under Secretary of State for Education and Childcare (2013) *Improving the Quality and Range of Education and Childcare from Birth to 5 Years.* Available online at: **www.gov.uk/government/policies/improving-the-quality-and-range-of-education-and-child-care-from-birth-to-5-years** (accessed 13/11/2014).

Department of Health (2014) *Special Educational Needs and Disability Code of Practice: 0 to 25 years.* DFE-00205-2013. Available online at: **www.gov.uk/government/publications/send-code-of-practice-0-to-25** (accessed 13/11/2014).

Donaldson, M (1978) *Children's Minds.* London: Fontana Press.

Donaldson, M (1992) *Human Minds: An Exploration.* London: Penguin Press.

Dunn, J (1993) *Young Children's Close Relationships: Beyond Attachment.* London: SAGE.

Dunn, J (2004) *Children's Friendships: The Beginnings of Intimacy.* Oxford: Blackwell.

Durham High School for Girls (2013) *Policy for Equal Opportunities in the Early Years.* Available online at: **www.dhsfg.org.uk/docs/information/policies/early-years/equal-opportunities-in-the-early-years.pdf** (accessed 29/10/2014).

Early Education (2012) *Development Matters in the Early Years Foundation Stage (EYFS).* Available online at: **www.pacey.org.uk/pdf/Development-Matters-in-the-Early-Years-Foundation-Stage.pdf** (accessed 27/10/2014).

Fisher, R (2005) Thinking skills. In: J Arthur, T Grainger and D Wray D (eds) *Learning to Teach in Primary School.* Falmer: Routledge.

Franken, MW (1983) Sex role expectations in children's vocational aspirations and perceptions of occupations. *Psychology of Women Quarterly*, 8: 59–68.

Freud, A and Burlingham, D (1942a) *War and Children.* New York: International Universities Press.

Freud, A and Burlingham, D (1942b) *Young Children in Wartime: A Year's Work in a Residential Home.* Madison, CT: International Universities Press.

Freud, A and Burlingham, D (1944) *Infants without Families.* New York: International Universities Press.

Freud, A and Dann, S (1951) An experiment in group upbringing. *Psychoanalytic Study of the Child* 6: 127–168. Reprinted in Freud, A (1969) *Indications for Child Analysis, and Other Papers, 1945–1956.* London: Hogarth Press, pp. 163–229.

Garland, C (1998) *Understanding Trauma: A Psychoanalytic Approach.* London, Karnac.

Geddes, H (2006) *Attachment in the Classroom: The Links Between Children's Early Experience, Emotional Well-being and Performance.* London: Worth.

Gerhardt, S (2004) *Why Love Matters: How Affection Shapes a Baby's Brain.* London: Routledge.

Goldschmied, E and Jackson, S (2005) *People Under Three: Young Children in Day Care.* London: Routledge.

Goleman, D (1995) *Emotional Intelligence and Social Intelligence: The New Science of Human Relationships.* New York: Bantam Books.

Gould, T (2012) *Transition in the Early Years: From Principles to Practice.* London: Featherstone Educational.

Gov.uk (2009) *Inclusion Development Programme: Supporting Children on the Autism Spectrum – Guidance for Practitioners in the Early Years Foundation Stage.* Available online at: **www.gov.uk/government/publications/**

inclusion-development-programme-supporting-children-on-the-autism-spectrum-guidance-for-practitioners-in-the-early-years-foundation-stage (accessed 29/10/2014).

Gov.uk (2010) *Reading at an Early Age: The Key to Success.* Available online at: **www.gov.uk/government/news/reading-at-an-early-age-the-key-to-success** (accessed 27/10/2014).

Gov.uk (2011) *The Early Years Foundation Stage (Tickell Review): Report on the Evidence.* Available online at: **www.gov.uk/government/publications/the-early-years-foundation-stage-review-report-on-the-evidence** (accessed 20/10/2014).

Gov.uk (2013a) *Improving the Quality and Range of Education and Childcare from Birth to 5 Years.* Available online at: **www.gov.uk/government/policies/improving-the-quality-and-range-of-education-and-childcare-from-birth-to-5-years/supporting-pages/early-years-teachers** (accessed 21/10/2014).

Gov.uk (2013b) *Early Years Outcome.* Available online at: **www.gov.uk/government/publications/early-years-outcomes** (accessed 20/10/2014).

Gov.uk (2013c) *National Curriculum.* Available online at: **www.gov.uk/government/collections/national-curriculum** (accessed 27/10/2014).

Gov.uk (2013d) *Early Years Teachers' Standards.* Available online at: **www.gov.uk/government/publications/early-years-teachers-standards** (accessed 29/10//2014).

Gov.uk (2013e) *Outcomes for Children Looked After by Local Authorities.* Available online at: **www.gov.uk/government/statistics/outcomes-for-children-looked-after-by-las-in-england** (accessed 31/10/2014).

Gov.uk (2014a) *Early Years Initial Teacher Training: A Guide for Providers.* Available online at: **www.gov.uk/early-years-initial-teacher-training-a-guide-for-providers** (accessed 21/10/2014).

Gov.uk (2014b) *Early Years Foundation Stage Framework. Statutory Guidance for the Early Years Foundation Stage.* Available online at: **www.gov.uk/government/publications/early-years-foundation-stage-framework--2** (accessed 17/11/2014).

Health and Safety at Work Act (1974) Available online at: **www.hse.gov.uk/legislation/hswa.htm** (accessed 13/11/2014).

HM Treasury, Department for Education and Skills, DWP and DTI (2004) *Choice for Parents, the Best Start for Children: A Ten Year Strategy for Childcare.* Available online at: **http://webarchive.nationalarchives.gov.uk/20130401151715/www.education.gov.uk/publications/eOrderingDownload/HMT-991151.pdf** (accessed 21/10/2014).

Institute of Education, University of London (n.d.) *National Priority Briefing Paper: Teaching Early Reading Using Systematic Synthetic Phonics (SSP).* Available online at: **www.ioe.ac.uk/study/documents/Study_Teacher_Training/Phonics_BriefingPaperv1.pdf** (accessed 27/10/2014).

Jarvis, P, George, J and Holland, W (2013) *Early Years Professional's Complete Companion.* Harlow: Pearsons.

Kolb, DA (1984) *Experiential Learning: Experience as the Source of Learning and Development.* New Jersey: Pearsons.

Kram, KE (1988) *Mentoring at Work: Developmental Relationships in Organizational Life.* Glenview, IL: Scott Foresman.

Laming, Lord (2003) *The Victoria Climbié Inquiry.* London: The Stationery Office.

Laming, Lord (2009) *The Protection of Children in England: A Progress Report. The Lord Laming Review.* Nottingham: Department for Children, Schools and Families.

Learning-Theories.com (2014) *Semiotics (de Saussure, Barthes, Bakhtin).* Available online at: **www.learning-theories.com/experiential-learning-kolb** (accessed 20/10/2014).

Leicestershire County Council (2011) *Including all Children in Early Years Settings: A Guide to Implementing the Special Needs Code of Practice.* Available online at: **www.leics.gov.uk/updated_providers_handbook_jan2009v3.pdf** (accessed 31/10/2014).

Maclean, K and Gunuion, M (2003) Learning with care: the education of children looked after away from home by local authorities in Scotland. *Adoption and Fostering,* 27(2):20–31.

Manning-Morton, J and Thorp, M (2003) *Key Times for Play: The First Three Years.* Maidenhead: Open University Press.

Manual Handling Operations Regulations (1992) Available online at: **www.hse.gov.uk/msd/pushpull/regulations.htm** (accessed 13/11/2014).

Mathers, S, Ranns, H, Karemaker, A, Moody, A, Sylva, K, Graham, J and Siraj-Blatchford, I (2011) *Evaluation of the Graduate Leader Fund: Final Report.* DFE-RB144. London: Department for Education.

Naidoo, J and Wills, J (2009) *Foundations for Health Promotion* (Public Health and Health Promotion). Oxford: Elsevier.

National College for Teaching and Leadership (2014) *Allocations Methodology: Early Years Initial Teacher Training Academic Year 2015 to 2016.* Available online at: **www.gov.uk/government/uploads/system/uploads/attach ment_data/file/328686/early-years-allocations-methodology-itt-2015-to-2016.pdf** (accessed 21/10/2014).

NCB (2010) *Children's Welfare and Safeguarding in the Early Years Foundation Stage.* Available online at: **www.ncb. org.uk/media/58905/factsheet_4_finaltemplate_ready_safeguarding.pdf** (accessed 29/10/2014).

Oxfordshire County Council, Children's Centres and Sure Start (2010) *Guidance for Identifying and Supporting Young Children with Special Educational Needs for Early Years Settings, Schools & Support Services.* Available online at: **http:// schools.oxfordshire.gov.uk/cms/sites/schools/files/folders/folders/documents/SEN/guidance/EY_SEN_guidance_ leaflet.pdf** (accessed 20/10/2014).

Paton, G (2013) Start school at seven, say experts. *The Daily Telegraph,* 12 September.

Preschool Learning Alliance (2011) *Guide to the Equality Act and Good Practice.* Available online at: **https://shop.pre-school.org.uk/A134/guide-to-the-equality-act-and-good-practice** (accessed 17/11/2014).

Robins, A (2006) *Mentoring in the Early Years.* SAGE: London.

Rutter, M (1981) *Maternal Deprivation Reassessed* (2nd edn). Harmondsworth: Penguin.

Sammons, P, Sylva, K, Melhuish, E, Siraj-Blatchford, I, Taggart, B, Barreau, S and Grabbe, Y (2008) *Influences on Children's Development and Progress in Key Stage 2: Social/Behavioural Outcomes in Year 5.* Available online at: **http:// webarchive.nationalarchives.gov.uk/20130401151715/www.education.gov.uk/publications/eOrderingDown-load/DCSF-RR007.pdf** (accessed 31/10/2014).

Sargent, M (2011) *Using Projects to Promote Sustained Shared Thinking.* London: Practical Pre-School Books.

Schaffer, HR and Emerson, PE (1964) The development of social attachments in infancy. *Monographs of the Society for Research in Child Development,* 29 (3), serial number 94.

Siraj-Blatchford, I (2009) Conceptualising progression in the pedagogy of play and sustained shared thinking in early childhood education: a Vygotskian perspective. *Educational and Child Psychology,* 26 (2) June.

Siraj-Blatchford, I, Sylva, K, Muttock, S et al. (2002) *Researching Effective Pedagogy in the Early Years* (*REPEY*). Available online at: **www.ioe.ac.uk/REPEY_research_report.pdf** (accessed 12/11/2014).

Siraj-Blatchford, I, Sylva K, Melhuish, E et al. (2004) *EPPE: Final Report.* London: DfES and Institute of Education, University of London.

Smith, E (2013) *Preventing Prejudice-Based Bullying: Boost Staff Confidence to Tackle Unacceptable Behaviour and Language.* Plymouth: Optimus Education.

Stonewall (2009) *The Teachers' Report. Teachers' Perspective on Homophobic Bullying in Britain's Primary and Secondary Schools.* Available online at: **www.stonewall.org.uk/at_school/education_for_all/quick_links/educa tion_resources/4003.asp** (accessed 29/10/2014).

Stonewall (2012) *The School Report. The Experiences of Gay Young People in Britain's Schools.* Available online at: **www.stonewall.org.uk/at_school/education_for_all/quick_links/education_resources/7956.asp** (accessed 29/10/2014).

The Guardian Teacher Network (2012) *Early Years Professionals Deserve More Recognition.* Available online at: **www. theguardian.com/teacher-network/2012/sep/18/early-years-professionals-deserve-more-recognition** (accessed 21/10/2014).

Thornton, S (2008) *Understanding Human Development.* Basingstoke: Palgrave Macmillan.

Tiret, HB (2012) Learn how domestic violence negatively impacts young children throughout different developmental and age periods. Available online at: **http://msue.anr.msu.edu/news/domestic_violence_impacts_children_differ- ently_at_different_ages** (accessed 29/10/2014).

Truss, L (2003) *Eats, Shoots and Leaves: The Zero Tolerance Approach to Punctuation.* London: Profile Books.

Westcott, K (2012) *Five Things About Phonics.* Available online at: **www.bbc.co.uk/news/magazine-18493436** (accessed 27/10/2014).

Wood, D and Middleton, D (1975) A study of assisted problem-solving. *British Journal of Psychology*, 66(2): 181–191.

Working with Children in Barnet (2014) *Diversity and Anti-discriminatory Practice.* Available online at: **www.bar- net.gov.uk/WorkingWithChildrenInBarnet/info/30097/diversity_and_anti-discriminatory_practice** (accessed 29/10/2014).

Zachary, LJ and Fischler, LA (2009) *The Mentee's Guide: Making Mentoring Work for You.* Hoboken, NJ: John Wiley.

Index